Russia in Motion

STUDIES OF WORLD MIGRATIONS

Donna R. Gabaccia and
Leslie Page Moch, editors

*A list of books in the series appears
at the end of the book.*

Russia in Motion

Cultures of Human Mobility since 1850

Edited by
JOHN RANDOLPH AND
EUGENE M. AVRUTIN

UNIVERSITY OF ILLINOIS PRESS
Urbana, Chicago, and Springfield

Library of Congress Cataloging-in-Publication Data
Russia in motion : cultures of human mobility since 1850 /
edited by John Randolph and Eugene M. Avrutin.
    p. cm. — (Studies of world migrations)
Includes bibliographical references and index.
ISBN 978-0-252-03703-0 (hardcover : alkaline paper)
    1. Migration, Internal—Russia—History.
    2. Migration, Internal—Soviet Union—History.
    3. Migration, Internal—Russia (Federation)
    4. Migration, Internal—Government policy—Russia.
    5. Migration, Internal—Government policy—Soviet Union.
    6. Domicile—Russia—History.
    7. Domicile—Soviet Union—History.
    8. Domicile—Russia (Federation)
    I. Randolph, John, editor.
  II. Avrutin, Eugene M., editor.
III. Series: Studies of world migrations.
HB2067.R868   2012
304.80947—dc23   2011045146

Contents

Acknowledgments

The editors would like to thank the Russian, East European, and Eurasian Center (REEEC), the Department of History, the Center for Advanced Studies, the Hewlett Foundation, the Program in Jewish Culture and Society, and the College of Liberal Arts and Sciences at the University of Illinois at Urbana-Champaign for their steadfast support of this project. Nor could it have been completed without the assistance and expertise provided by REEEC's outstanding staff, and in particular Melissa Agee, Katrina Ross Chester, and Theresa Schafroth. We would like to express our gratitude to them here. Last, we wish to recognize John W. Slocum and his colleagues at the Initiative on Global Migration and Human Mobility of the John D. and Catherine T. MacArthur Foundation, whose generosity has supported this project from its inception, and who provided financial assistance for the production of this book.

Shortly before we went to press, we were saddened to hear of the death of Anatolyi Remnev, our deeply respected colleague and a contributor to this volume. An international authority on the history of imperial governance in the Russian Far East, Professor Remnev taught at Omsk State University for more than twenty-five years. His generosity and insight will be sorely missed by scholars all over the world.

[blank page viii]

Introduction

JOHN RANDOLPH AND
EUGENE M. AVRUTIN

The past quarter-century has seen many attempts to recall and interpret the meaning of human mobility and the political, social, and cultural importance of physical movement through space. Partly, no doubt, this has to do with our own sense of living in a world in flux, a new era in which nothing holds still for long and where states that seemed permanent appear to vanish overnight. It should also be said that scholars of premodern and "big" history have demolished stereotypes about the sedentary character of the preindustrial world. While the speed and capacity of industrial transport remain truly astonishing, early modern people spent much of their time and energy getting around, not least because staying in place was a luxury few could attain. For as long as we know, as Leslie Page Moch and others have observed, "moving up," or more simply surviving, has required "moving out."[1] Last, but perhaps most important, recent scholarly interest in mobility is driven by a desire to explore the practical, technological, and spatial sides of human history and to remember subjects made invisible by sedentary histories and the political myths built from them. "Culture, we are told, no longer sits in places," writes the geographer Tim Cresswell, "but is hybrid, dynamic—more about routes than roots."[2] More attuned than ever to the power of movement in our own lives, scholars are redoubling their efforts to understand its role in the politics, society, and culture of the past. The study of human mobility is becoming less a topic in its own right and more a prism for reexamining the whole of human life.

As the historian Gijs Mom and colleagues observe in a recent review of the field, this broadening, interdisciplinary interest in catching life "in motion" is forging new connections between the traditional scholarly fields that study human movement. Until quite recently the history of human movement was often treated as a subdiscipline whose role was to serve as a structural context for, or special case within, the main focus of study: the supposedly settled life of nations. "Transport history," written as infrastructure history, described the limits (of speed, destination, and capacity) within which human economies and polities may be thought to have developed. In this role, it occupied a respected but small and specialized niche in scholarship, as a kind of economic history.[3] Migration studies, meanwhile, became a vast discipline unto itself, committed variously to conceptualizing the "laws" behind mass movements and to understanding the ways in which states and societies are changed by them. With a scholarly pedigree extending deep into the nineteenth century, this tradition strenuously contested nationalist claims that human history is first and foremost an internal development, rooted in the evolution of sedentary communities. Yet as scholars in and outside this tradition have increasingly noted, one ironic side-effect of this field's growth was to artificially separate the "waves" of migration (as distinct objects of study) from the more constant flow of human movement, and thus indirectly segregate the figure of "the migrant" from humanity at large.[4] Dimensions of human mobility that do not fall under the rubric of "transport" or "migration" history—the constant practical motions on which politics, society, and culture all depend—have long remained on the periphery of scholarship, in part for lack of willingness to focus on the defining role of movement in human life.

Where might the Russian Empire and its successor states fit in histories of a moving world? How do our understandings of their modern political, social, and cultural history change when we foreground the role played by human mobility within them? Since their rapid, imperial expansion in the seventeenth century, Russian politics, society, and culture have exerted a profound influence on movement throughout Eurasia. The circulation of people, information, and things across Russian space during this period transformed populations, restructured collective and individual identities, and created enduring legacies that still govern how people move through much of the world.[5] If at times Russian Eurasia might seem to have been an autonomous sphere within the great migration systems connecting humanity—routing some populations around and keeping other populations within its own internal orbits—periods of revolutionary strife in the early twentieth century saw the sudden eruption of post-Russian populations into world movement networks. Likewise, the tumultuous era since 1991 raises fascinating questions about continuity and change in the governance, practice, and cultural importance of human movement in the post-Soviet world. The purpose of this volume is to turn to a large era of Russian experience—defined by industrial transport, mass mobilization, and resettlement—to explore how some of its crucial themes may be interpreted anew through closer attention to how all this movement was made and what it meant.

Unfortunately, there are, as yet, no survey histories of Russia's role in human mobility. Writing one will require scholars to attempt to integrate several fields, combining histories of transport and migration with political, social, and cultural concerns. In this volume, we hope to provide useful models for such inquiries—various means of integrating movement back into the mainstream of history—and to demonstrate how greater attention to mobility can help scholars deepen their understanding of the past. Specifically, we have chosen to focus on three themes: the role of human movement in Russian governance; the processes by which the social "horizons" orienting movement were made within Imperial Russian, Soviet, and now post-Soviet space; and the political and cultural power of different modes of movement, historically and today. In what follows, each of these themes will be addressed by a series of essays, chronologically arranged.

Historical and Conceptual Context

As specialists know, the first chronicles to conceive of a land called Rus' imagined it as a crossroads of the world, defined by mighty river routes and trading networks that ran east, west, north, and south. As late as the early eighteenth century, the Swedish prisoner-turned–travel writer Phillip Johann Strahlenberg said of Russia, "This great Empire is so situated, that it not only can have good relations with itself, but also *Communication* by land and sea with all four parts of the globe."[6] Strahlenberg and his contemporaries were dimly aware of what the "Eurasianist" and new Imperial schools of Russian historical writing have since underscored: that these lines of communication" were also the sinews of the great Mongol empire that preceded Russian power. And indeed it was by taking over these earlier exchanges (of people, wealth, and information) that Moscow's rulers were able to conquer the vast continents of Siberia and the steppe so rapidly, accounting for most of Russia's astonishing geographical growth.[7] If, as its apologists liked to repeat with relish, the Russian Empire held sway over one-seventh of the earth's landmass, it was not least due to extraordinary efforts to create cultures of movement and exchange that could link it together.[8] All the while, demographic development, migratory movement, and colonization—on foot, cart, and horse—complicated these attempts to create an orderly imperial space and powered its expansion from below.[9]

Against such a backdrop, it is perhaps unsurprising that the road—and the idea of open-ended travel across boundless spaces, by sleighbelled sledge or fiery troika—emerged as one of modern Russian culture's most powerful cultural symbols by the early nineteenth century: a vision, indeed, of Russia itself.[10] Yet it also should be said that the first thing one learns about roads in Russian history is that they were bad; that before the advent of industrial transport, the obstacles to movement were so great that it took fantastic exertions to create even minimal motion; that this relative immobility exacerbated and was itself deepened by preindustrial Russia's sparse population, demanding climate and continental isolation from the great, oceanic mobility systems that had linked other parts of the world since the thirteenth century.[11] Perhaps understandably, under these conditions, social historians of Russia have traditionally given relatively little attention to the nitty-gritty question of how people, things, and information circulated around this enormous imperial space. Instead they have preferred to speak of the sharp, infrastructural "limits of the possible" posed by these difficulties.[12]

Paradoxically, then, spatial expansion—and the struggle to consolidate this political, social, and cultural domain—is widely acknowledged to be a central problem of modern Russian history; and yet the processes of movement and circulation that defined and sustained this realm have generally been cast as cruel context rather than as main story.[13] Perhaps the greatest attention, in this early period, has been focused on the means by which imperial authorities attempted to order and control human mobility across their expanding Russia: first, through the bondage of peasants to the land (serfdom) in the seventeenth century, and then through the introduction of passport controls governing internal movement in the eighteenth.[14] Many scholars see this continuing interest in controlling movement as a distinctive feature of modern Russian polity. Yet two diametrically opposed opinions dominate interpretation of this phenomenon, and with it the relationship between Russian expansion, human mobility, and social and political development. Some see the Russian Empire as a great demobilizer of nations, an order that sought to defend itself by constraining its peoples to defined roles and geographical ranges (including, most famously, individual villages for serfs and the "Pale of Settlement" for most Jews). This resulted in tight limits on movement across international borders, which (in this view) exacerbated Russia's relative isolation from a rapidly globalizing world.[15] For others, however, the rise of the Russian Empire is best told as a story of intentional and unintentional mobilization, of a land where imperial and social ambitions combined to propel populations back and forth along Eurasia's northern edge through voluntary and involuntary movement, transforming the politics, society, and culture of countless people. This tendency would find a culmination in the Soviet order—premised on mass shifts of population—which some have called a "mobilizational state."[16]

Born from the seventeenth century, these debates certainly did not end with the period that is the focus of our volume. But beginning in the early nineteenth century, three dramatic shifts combined to create new pressures and possibilities for human movement across Russian space—pressures and possibilities that greatly complicated the governance of human movement and accelerated and intensified its political, social, and cultural impact. Together, these trends justify regarding the period from 1850 to the present as a distinct era in human mobility. First, Russia's population exploded, due to internal growth and due to its consolidating power over populated lands absorbed in the eighteenth and nineteenth centuries (Ukraine, Poland, the Baltics, Finland, Bessarabia, and Transcaucasia, as well as parts of Central Asia). These new imperial populations not only added their weight to the development of Russian transport and migration systems, they also brought with them internal and transnational cultures of movement that held the potential to integrate Russia and the world in new ways. (An excellent example of this are the transnational networks of the Muslim hajj, which ran through the Black Sea area and are analyzed in this volume by Eileen Kane).

Second, Russia's industrial development and concomitant adoption of industrial forms of transport (the steamboat and the railroad in the nineteenth century, the automobile and the airplane in the twentieth) provided new speeds and above all new capacities for the regular movement of large populations. This created possibilities for large-scale mass movements that had not previously existed, even as it made vast feats of transportation more accessible to individuals. Third and last, industrialization and continued territorial expansion created the conditions for the emergence of three great new pathways for politics, society, and culture alike: (1) between the imperial borderlands and the metropoles of Moscow and St. Petersburg; (2) between the countryside and Russia's rapidly developing cities; and (3) between European Russia's densely populated lands and the vast subcontinents of Siberia and the steppe. The emancipation of Russia's serfs in 1861—alongside the other Great Reforms of the 1860s—loosened some of the harsher administrative restrictions on individual movement as well, although the result was less a liberal era of free migration than an era in which the government sought to channel and direct mass migration[17] (sometimes with unexpected results, as Faith Hillis's and Anatolyi Remnev's essays in this collection show).

Perhaps unsurprisingly, the vast majority of scholarly works to study human movement in Russian life have focused on this modern period, and specifically on the ways mass movements shaped the dramatic political evolution (across this space) from monarchical Russia, to Soviet socialism, and now to the post-Soviet world. Most historians of the nineteenth century have focused primarily on questions of urbanization and (more recently) colonization. The signal problems of this literature are, first, how patterns of peasant migration to the cities affected the urban landscape (and working-class culture) of the prerevolutionary period; and second, how the mass resettlement of European populations (sometimes state-ordered, sometimes poverty- or opportunity-driven) to Siberia and the steppe were changing the political, cultural, and environmental shape of Russia at the end of the nineteenth century.[18]

As historians shift their gaze to the twentieth century, and the revolutionary and Soviet experience, the focus changes from themes of migration and colonization to themes of mass mobilization and social transformation. Scholars have studied the instrumental use of mass movement to create political power and achieve revolutionary goals during the violent era from roughly 1905 to 1953.[19] Within the postwar and (eventually) post-Soviet periods, this focus on mass mobilization and instrumental mobility is replaced by a return to questions of migration, integration, and consolidation. Here the key issues include the role played by movement in the successes and ultimate failures of the Soviet system, and the degree to which long-term legacies have shaped patterns of movement and migration since the USSR's demise. (This is a period, as Elena Tyuryukanova notes in her essay, that began with an unprecedented liberalization of the migration controls governing the former Soviet Union, and yet has seen the patterns of human movement established in the twentieth century prove surprisingly resilient in "post-Soviet" space.) The roles of movement in nationalism (and anti-immigrant sentiment) within Russia and the new post-Soviet states are also a major area of research.[20]

Just as the focal point of research on human movement has shifted over time, basic understandings of what movement means often shift by scholarly field. "Mobility" has meant different things in different disciplines. For earth scientists, as Vincent Kaufman points out, it has meant "movement in a geographical space"; for transportation studies, "traffic flows"; while sociology has often seen mobility metaphorically as a descriptor not only of physical movement but of a "change of social position or role."[21] In its most basic sense, "mobility" connotes the ability of an entity to move or be moved through space, and draws our attention to the structures that makes such movement possible. Although this proliferation of potential meanings makes for an unruly field of analysis, it also points to one of the most basic advantages of studying how things move (or are moved). As Gijs Mom notes in a recent survey of the field, foregrounding questions of mobility helps illuminate how human agency, technology, culture, and space are interrelated and constitute one another.[22] In short, one advantage to paying attention to what happens "on the move" is that it can help us appreciate the intersection of many political, social, and cultural forces within the past and analyze their interplay without asserting the absolute supremacy of one over the other. (Benjamin Schenk's analysis of the social impacts of railroad construction makes this point eloquently, in our collection.)[23]

To give this volume thematic coherence across time, we have chosen to focus on three major themes: the governance, horizons, and modes of human mobility in modern Russian life. To conclude this introduction, let us consider each of these themes and the questions they provoke in more detail.

Governance, Horizons, and Modes of Mobility

Part I considers the challenges and tensions of governing human mobility in the industrial age. At the heart of this phenomenon lay shifts in the techniques used to identify and order the physical location of Russian populations. Partly in response to increased human motion, and partly for other political reasons, this was an age when each and every person was to be made knowable to the state through censuses and identity papers. In both Imperial Russia and Soviet settings, the preoccupation with techniques of governance based on the power of numerical representation emerged in the context of an effort to manage diversity, refashion populations, and govern the boundaries of an empire that increased in size from around 430,000 square kilometers in 1470 to around 22,430,000 square kilometers at the end of the nineteenth century.[24] Since the reign of Peter the Great, imperial law forbade subjects from traveling outside their permanent places of residence without an internal passport.[25] As in many other times and places, Russian administrators linked the regulation of geographic mobility to internal security, economic prosperity, and state revenue.[26]

In the second half of the nineteenth century, the relaxation and simplification of mobility regulations and the unprecedented construction of railways, roads, and large-scale industries created extraordinary opportunities for all people in the empire to travel not only to the empire's economically and culturally vibrant cities but also to the resource-rich territories of western Siberia and the far north.[27] In Russia, as in so many other places across the globe, the simplification of travel restrictions did not mean that bureaucratic regimes abandoned knowledge-based technologies—passports, travel permits, census records, and birth certificates—to manage population movements. On the contrary, paper documents proved invaluable for delineating right of movement and entrance, as well as facilitating the expulsion of unwanted social groups.[28]

The Soviet passport and registration system, which was initiated in 1932 to control internal migration to large cities, retained much of the hierarchical differentiation of the tsarist passport system. But as recent archival research has shown (including Gijs Kessler's essay in this volume), Soviet passport laws quickly acquired new functions. Over the course of the 1930s and beyond, passport laws provided the Soviet state with a powerful tool to secure territorial borders, fight crime, identify and cleanse "socially harmful elements," and remake populations. Masses of people—from criminals, ex-convicts, and itinerants to orphan children, disloyal national minorities, and various other suspect groups—were routinely targeted in sweeps of cities, border zones, and rail lines.[29]

In this way, governance *of* mobility created the tools to attempt governance *through* mobility: the intentional circulation and resettlement of populations for political ends.

Despite their voluminous regulations on mobility, the tsarist, Soviet, and post-Soviet states all had difficulties managing human movement. Even in the days of high Stalinism, documentary records could be easily manipulated, new public identities reinvented, and administrators and police officers bribed for the right price.[30] Whatever their ultimate ambitions, imperial Russian and Soviet regimes recognized the importance of the right to travel within and even (as was the case with Muslim and Russian Orthodox pilgrimages in the pre-revolutionary era) beyond the geographic borders of the polities, though both regimes placed tight controls on emigration.[31] In the pre-revolutionary era, for example, the state's refusal to legalize emigration—and thereby help supervise and profit from a program that would insure the orderliness of the movement, as was the case with the hajj—did not thwart nearly four million Poles, Germans, and Jews from leaving the empire. On the contrary, imperial borders remained highly porous and border controls notoriously lax. And while emigration became a big and profitable enterprise, involving steamship companies, travel agents, and border-control guards, the journey was fraught with danger and unpredictability.[32]

As this brief survey suggests, the desire to control human movement across Russian space and to utilize such movement controls as a means to accomplish broader political imperatives marks one of the continuities across recent Russian history, uniting the Imperial, Soviet, and post-Soviet periods. At the same time, this complex interplay between governance *of* and governance *through* mobility controls raises a series of important questions for historians, which our essays individually and collectively address. First, what were the actual political effects—as opposed to the planned ambitions—of these interventions into human movement? The question is not simply how well could Russian governments actually control the physical mobility of populations, but whether state institutions could successfully predict, govern, or manage their consequences. Chief among these effects (intentional or otherwise) would be the way in which new patterns of movement (and new techniques of movement control) spawned new political forces, communities, and forms of civic agency or citizenship. (Matthew Light's essay in this collection provides an example of this, as he traces the ways in which shifts in mobility governance since 1991 have altered the role of Moscow and its police force in governing civil rights in Russia and fostered, in effect, a special form of citizenship for the capital.) Another set of questions has to do with how industrial forms of movement created new political ideals and languages, in effect alternate visions of what Russia's political community could be. Chia Yin Hsu provides a case study of this phenomenon, as she considers the "global city" (and global Russia) envisaged at Harbin—on the Chinese border—by Russia's famous minister of finance, Sergei Witte, in the early twentieth century.

Of course, the problem of imagining the geography of movement in Russia, and the scope for action it allowed, was not unique to statesmen. The second part of our book examines the problem of movement "horizons"—the creation and perception of the realm open to human movement—and examines how these perceptions of space have influenced human action and notions of community in modern Russian history. How did people choose among the options available to them, in a world where state institutions aspired to control and shape movement processes but inevitably did so fitfully and incompletely? Where once historical demographers and scholars of migration were likely to conceptualize the history of human movement in rational terms, as a confluence of "push" and "pull" factors, recent scholarship on human mobility has focused on the social, technological, and conceptual contexts that shaped human decisions about when, why, and how to move.[33] Calling for more agent-oriented perspectives on migration, Dirk Hoerder writes, "The study of migration and acculturation has to incorporate the different forms of mobility. Returning travelers, pilgrims, and soldiers provide information on destinations for migrants. Experience in voyaging facilitates migratory moves."[34]

Such a focus on how individuals and groups perceived the destinations and routes available to them—the myriad *terrae cognitae* scholars and other outsiders often know little about—has three distinct advantages for historians.[35] First, it helps us reconstruct the range of choices available to people with much greater insight than a simple map or transport scheme. As Hoerder observes, it is not "'objective' data on these factors but their reflection in the minds of migrants that explains decisions to move."[36] Second, such knowledge helps us contextualize and interpret what historical demographers call "motility": "the way a person or group appropriates and makes use of the field of possibilities of movement" that exist for them in a given place or time.[37] Placed against the world then known and the practices of movement then in existence, the symbolic and political valences of movement can become clearer, and the "speed" of a society can be seen as not simply depending on its modernizing development.

Last, and perhaps most importantly in the context of Russian, Soviet, and post-Soviet history, study of human-movement horizons can help evaluate and rethink an ancient theme in history: the role of space itself in Russia's political, social, and cultural development. As was noted earlier, the expansion and maintenance of a Russian sphere of influence remains one of the central themes of modern history. In addition, scholars have devoted a great deal of thought to how Russia's vast geographical spaces have shaped the ideals and self-images of its peoples. While opinions about how geography has affected Russia's destiny have varied greatly over time—and have recently been the subject of several incisive studies—the problem of the perception of space as revealed in processes of migration, colonization, and everyday movement is only beginning to come into focus.[38] The essays of this section reinvestigate the classic question of space and its relationship to modern Russian history by examining how changing mental maps and itineraries were made and how they, in turn, influence issues of identity, motility, and political and social action.

Actual movement through space, of course, depends not only on the route traveled but also on the means by which it is traveled. The last part of our book examines modes of movement, and more specifically how different technologies of movement have been related to different kinds of social and political power. Although migration-oriented studies of human movement have, on occasion, lost sight of the means of transportation, these directly shape the physical and cultural meaning of mobility. To take but one rather ghastly example from Soviet history: Scholars have long known that deportation by train was one of the central mechanisms of Stalinist political terror, whether as practiced on kulak-farmers during collectivization or on occupied peoples during World War II. But as studies of these "special settlement" programs have shown, much of their appalling mortality (up to one third of deported peoples simply died on the road) had to do less with active extermination measures than with an equally culpable and terribly murderous contempt for transport methods. Like blithe geographers, those who ordered these mass conveyances indicated points A and B on a map but otherwise paid little attention to the "techniques by which these orders could be fulfilled," stranding thousands to die in unheated, hungry, fetid wagons.[39]

This contrasts sharply, as Diane Koenker's essay in this collection shows, with the elaborate and simultaneous planning that Soviet institutions bestowed on the development of Soviet tourism. These plans and projects were intimately concerned with how modes of travel might shape the Soviet character and distinguish good Soviet subjects from the rest of the world. As Gijs Mom notes in a recent essay, scholars would do well to take a closer interest in mobility as "a techno-cultural act or performance," one in which the means by which one moves about space says almost as much as (or more than) one's physical destination.[40] In her contribution to this collection, Sarah Phillips demonstrates, for example, that the ability of wheelchair activists to accomplish spectacular feats of mobility—such as a journey from St. Petersburg to Vladivostok—became an important tool in asserting the civic worth of disabled individuals in post-Soviet Ukraine. In the final analysis, modes of mobility are not simply logistical tools for exercising agency in society. They also shape the character of that agency, imparting to it their own qualities of movement through space. At the same time, they shape broader expectations about how people can participate in society at large.[41]

Having laid out our collection's central themes, we might now attempt to either summarize or analyze the contributions to follow, or risk some final, synthetic narrative about the history of Russia in motion—some latest version of what a textbook might say. But as it happens, we have no need to do the former and doubt whether it is the place of this volume to do the latter. On the one hand, we are fortunate that each of the sections to follow has its own preface, which offers additional context and commentary on the essays and considers the broader meaning of the questions they raise. On the other hand, our ambition here is not to create a new overview but rather to encourage new pathways for exploration. "Horses are men's wings," a nineteenth-century Russian proverb states, underscoring the ways in which movement makes possible so much of human life. "They'll carry water; they'll carry the military commander."[42] We hope that the questions we raise—as well as the specific, partial findings of each of the essays that follow—will help a broad range of scholars perceive the benefit of trying to catch Russia in motion, and the possible interpretive prisms through which they may attempt to do so.

Notes

1. Leslie Page Moch, *Moving Europeans: Migration in Western Europe Since 1650,* 2d ed. (Bloomington: Indiana University Press, 2003); Carla Hesse and Peter Sahlins, "Introduction," *French Historical Studies* 29.3 (Summer 2006): 347–57, esp. 356.

2. Tim Cresswell, *On the Move: Mobility in the Modern Western World* (New York: Routledge, 2006), 1. See also Stephen Greenblatt, "Cultural Mobility: An Introduction," in *Cultural Mobility: A Manifesto,* by Stephen Greenblatt et al. (Cambridge: Cambridge University Press, 2010), 1–23.

3. For useful histories of the development of transport history, see Gijs Mom, Gordon Pirie, and Laurent Tissot, "Towards a Paradigm Shift? A Decade of Transport and Mobility History," in *Mobility in History: The State of the Art in the History of Transport, Traffic, and Mobility,* ed. Gijs Mom, Gordon Pirie and Laurent Tissot (Neuchatel: Editions Alphil, 2009), 13–40; Gijs Mom, "What Kind of Transport History Did We Get?" *Journal of Transport History* 24.2 (2003): 121–38; Vincent Kaufmann, "Mobility: Trajectory of a Concept in the Social Sciences," in *Mobility in History: The State of the Art in the History of Transport, Traffic, and Mobility* (Neuchatel: Editions Alphil, 2009), 41–60.

4. On migration-studies paradigms and the growth in interest in agent-centered studies, see Dirk Hoerder, *Cultures in Contact: World Migrations in the Second Millennium* (Durham, N.C.: Duke University Press, 2002), 8–21.

5. The most fundamental empirical studies of Russian historical demography and migratory geography are the many works authored and edited by V. M. Kabuzan, including but not limited to *Narodonaselenie Rossii v XVIII–pervoi polovine XIX v. (Po materialam revizii)* (Moscow: Institut Istorii Akademii nauk SSSR, 1963); *Narody Rossii v pervoi polovine XIX v.* (Moscow: Nauka, 1992); *Russkie v mire: Dinamika chislennosti*

i rasseleniia (St. Petersburg: BLITS, 1995); *Emigratsiia i reemigratsiia v Rossii v XVIII–nachale XX veka* (Moscow: Nauka, 1998). On the early modern period, see also Richard Hellie, "Migration in Early Modern Russia, 1480s–1780s," in *Coerced and Free Migration: Global Perspectives,* ed. David Eltis (Stanford, Calif.: Stanford University Press, 2002), 292–323. For a longer-term perspective on peasant movement in Russian life, see David Moon, "Peasant Migration and the Settlement of Russia's Frontiers, 1550–1897," *Historical Journal* 40.4 (December 1997): 859–93.

6. Simon Franklin and Jonathan Shepard, *The Emergence of Rus, 750–1200* (London: Longman, 1996); Phillip Johann von Strahlenberg, *Historie der Reisen in Russland, Sibirien, und der Grossen Tartarey* (Leipzig: Kiesewetter, 1730), 176–77.

7. Stephen Kotkin, "Mongol Commonwealth? Exchange and Governance across the Post-Mongol Space," *Kritika: Explorations in Russian and Eurasian History* 8.3 (2007): 487–532. On the "gathering of the lands of the Golden Horde" as an integral part of Russian empire-making, see Andreas Kappeler, *The Russian Empire: A Multi-Ethnic History* (Harlow, U.K.: Longman, 2001). For a still broader perspective on the successive relationship of empires (not least through systems of exchange), see Jane Burbank and Frederick Cooper, *Empires in World History: Power and the Politics of Difference* (Princeton, N.J.: Princeton University Press, 2010).

8. For additional rumination on this theme, see Dominic Lieven, *Empire: The Russian Empire and Its Rivals* (New Haven, Conn.: Yale University Press, 2002), 201–6.

9. On demography and migration, see n.5 above. For examples of the complex relationship between migration and imperial development in the early modern period, see Michael Khodarkovsky, *Russia's Steppe Frontier, 1500–1800: The Making of a Colonial Empire* (Bloomington: Indiana University Press, 2002); V. I. Kolesnik, *Poslednee velikoe kochev'e: Perekhod kalmykov iz Tsentral'noi Azii v Vostochnuiu Evropu i obratno v XVII i XVIII vekakh* (Moscow: "Vostochnaia Literatura" RAN, 2003).

10. On this process, see John W. Randolph, "The Singing Coachman; or, The Road and Russia's Ethnographic Invention in Early Modern Times," *Journal of Early Modern History* 11.1–2 (February 2007): 33–61.

11. In English-language scholarship, discussions of the medieval "world system" generally place Russia off the map. See Hoerder, *Cultures in Contact,* 29; Janet L Abu-Lughod, *Before European Hegemony: The World System A.D. 1250–1350* (New York: Oxford University Press, 1989).

12. It is interesting to note, in this respect, that the most fundamental social history of Russia to be published recently—Boris Mironov's magisterial two-volume synthesis—has not a single chapter dedicated to transport. See B. N. Mironov, *Sotsial'naia istoriia Rossii perioda imperii—XVIII–nachalo XX v. : Genezis lichnosti, demokraticheskoi sem'i, grazhdanskogo obshchestva i pravovogo gosudarstva,* 2 vols., 3d ed. (St. Petersburg: D. Bulanin, 2003).

13. An important exception to this rule is Roland Cvetkovski, *Modernisierung durch Beschleunigung: Raum und Mobilität im Zarenreich* (Frankfurt am Main: Campus, 2006). The most important inroads into early modern mobility have been studies of Russian colonization and imperialism, in particular Russia's contacts with nomadic peoples of the steppe. See Khodarkovsky, *Russia's Steppe Frontier*; and Kolesnik, *Poslednee velikoe*

kocheve; as well as Michael Khodarkovsky, *Where Two Worlds Met: The Russian State and the Kalmyk Nomads, 1600–1771* (Ithaca, N.Y.: Cornell University Press, 1992); Carol Belkin Stevens, *Soldiers on the Steppe: Army Reform and Social Change in Early Modern Russia* (DeKalb: Northern Illinois University Press, 1995).

14. For a discussion of this literature, see our section on governance below.

15. This view, centered on the imposition of serfdom in the seventeenth century, has entered influential textbooks on movement in the modern world. See Moch, *Moving Europeans*; Dirk Hoerder, *Cultures in Contact*. See also Richard Hellie, *Enserfment and Military Change in Muscovy* (Chicago: University of Chicago Press, 1971); and Hellie, "Migration in Early Modern Russia."

16. See Rebecca Manley, *To the Tashkent Station: Evacuation and Survival in the Soviet Union at War* (Ithaca, N.Y.: Cornell University Press, 2009), 63. On mobilization as a technique of imperial politics, see Kotkin, "Mongol Commonwealth?"; Benjamin Nathans, *Beyond the Pale: The Jewish Encounter with Late Imperial Russia* (Berkeley: University of California Press, 2002); as well as many other recent works on nationality and colonization in the late Russian Empire.

17. On directed migration in particular, see Donald W. Treadgold, *The Great Siberian Migration: Government and Peasant in Resettlement from Emancipation to the First World War* (Princeton, N.J.: Princeton University Press, 1957); Willard Sunderland, "Peasants on the Move: State Peasant Resettlement in Imperial Russia, 1805–1830s," *Russian Review* 52.4 (1993): 472–85; Peter Holquist, "'In Accord with State Interests and the People's Wishes': The Technocratic Ideology of Imperial Russia's Resettlement Administration," *Slavic Review* 69.1 (2010): 151–79.

18. Although the literature is vast, some touchstones are Boris Mironov, *Sotsial'naia istoriia*, vol. 1, 19–76; Barbara A. Anderson, *Internal Migration during Modernization in Late Nineteenth-Century Russia* (Princeton, N.J.: Princeton University Press, 1980); Robert Johnson, *Peasant and Proletarian: The Working Class of Moscow in the Late Nineteenth Century* (New Brunswick, N.J.: Rutgers University Press, 1979); James H. Bater, "Transience, Residential Persistence, and Mobility in Moscow and St. Petersburg, 1900–1914," *Slavic Review* 39.2 (June 1980): 239–54; James H. Bater, *St. Petersburg: Industrialization and Change,* Studies in Urban History 4 (Montreal: McGill-Queen's University Press, 1976); Barbara Alpern Engel, *Between the Fields and the City* (Cambridge: Cambridge University Press, 1996); Willard Sunderland, *Taming the Wild Field: Colonization and Empire on the Russian Steppe* (Ithaca, N.Y.: Cornell University Press, 2004); Nicholas Breyfogle, Abby Schrader, and Willard Sunderland, eds., *Peopling the Russian Periphery: Borderland Colonization in Eurasian History* (London: Routledge, 2007); Jane Burbank, Mark von Hagen, and Anatolyi Remnev, eds., *Russian Empire: Space, People, Power, 1700–1930* (Bloomington: Indiana University Press, 2007); A. V. Remnev, *Rossiia dal'nego vostoka: Imperskaia geografiia vlasti XIX - nachala XX vekov* (Omsk: Izdanie OmGU, 2004). See also the discussion of Russian migration in Hoerder, *Cultures in Contact,* 306–30.

19. Touchstones of this literature are Sheila Fitzpatrick, *The Russian Revolution,* 3d ed. (New York: Oxford University Press, 2008); Peter Gatrell, *A Whole Empire Walking: Refugees in Russia during World War I* (Bloomington: Indiana University Press, 1999);

Stephen Kotkin, *Magnetic Mountain: Stalinism as a Civilization* (Berkeley: University of California Press, 1997); Lynne Viola, *The Unknown Gulag: The Lost World of Stalin's Special Settlements* (Oxford: Oxford University Press, 2007); Viktor Berdinskikh, *Spetsposelentsy: Politicheskaia ssylka narodov Sovetskoi Rossii* (Moscow: Novoe Literaturnoe Obozrenie, 2005); Norman M. Naimark, *The Russians in Germany: A History of the Soviet Zone of Occupation, 1945–1949* (Cambridge, Mass: Belknap Press of Harvard University Press, 1995). See also Cynthia Buckley, "The Myth of Managed Migration: Migration Control and Market in the Soviet Period," *Slavic Review* 54.4 (Winter 1995): 896–916; and Mary Buckley, *Mobilizing Soviet Peasants: Heroines and Heroes of Stalin's Fields* (Lanham, Md.: Rowman and Littlefield, 2006).

20. Among recent works, see Anne Gorsuch and Diane Koenker, eds., *Turizm: The Russian and East European Tourist under Capitalism and Socialism* (Ithaca, N.Y.: Cornell University Press, 2006); Cynthia Buckley and Blair A. Ruble, eds., *Migration, Homeland, and Belonging in Eurasia* (Baltimore: Johns Hopkins University Press, 2008); George J. Demko, *Population under Duress: The Geodemography of Post-Soviet Russia* (Boulder, Colo.: Westview Press, 1999); V. I. Mukhomel', *Migratsionnaia Politika Rossii: Postsovetskie Konteksty* (Moscow: Dipol'-T, 2005); L. M. Drobizheva, *Ethnic Conflict in the Post-Soviet World: Case Studies and Analysis* (Armonk, N.Y.: M. E. Sharpe, 1998); Robert John Kaiser, *The Geography of Nationalism in Russia and the USSR* (Princeton, N.J: Princeton University Press, 1994).

21. Kaufmann, "Mobility," 41.

22. Mom, Pirie, and Tissot, "Towards a Paradigm Shift?" 30.

23. See Tim Cresswell's discussion of the experiential dimensions of mobility in Cresswell, *On the Move,* 3. See also Tony Ballantyne and Antoinette Burton, "Introduction: The Politics of Intimacy in an Age of Empire," in *Moving Subjects: Gender, Mobility, and Intimacy in an Age of Global Empire* (Urbana: University of Illinois Press, 2009), 1–28.

24. Hellie, "Migration in Early Modern Russia."

25. On the internal passport system in tsarist Russia, see V. G. Chernukha, *Pasport v Rossii, 1719–1917* (St. Petersburg: Liki Rossii, 2007); Jeffrey Burds, *Peasant Dreams and Market Politics: Labor Migration and the Russian Village, 1861–1905* (Pittsburgh: University of Pittsburgh Press, 1998), 56–61; David Moon, "Peasant Migration, the Abolition of Serfdom, and the Internal Passport System in the Russian Empire, ca. 1800–1914," in *Coerced and Free Migration: Global Perspectives,* ed. David Eltis (Stanford, Calif.: Stanford University Press, 2002), 324–57; Charles Steinwedel, "Making Social Groups, One Person at a Time: The Identification of Individuals by Estate, Religious Confession, and Ethnicity in Late Imperial Russia," in *Documenting Individual Identity: The Development of State Practices in the Modern World,* ed. Jane Caplan and John Torpey (Princeton, N.J.: Princeton University Press, 2001), 73–78; Mervyn Matthews, *The Passport Society: Controlling Movement in Russia and the USSR* (Boulder, Colo.: Westview Press, 1993); and Eugene M. Avrutin, *Jews and the Imperial State: Identification Politics in Tsarist Russia* (Ithaca, N.Y.: Cornell University Press, 2010), chap. 3.

26. For a global perspective, see Adam M. McKeown, *Melancholy Order: Asian Migration and the Globalization of Borders* (New York: Columbia University Press, 2008).

27. See B. V. Tikhonov, *Pereselenie v Rossii vo vtoroi polovine xix v.* (Moscow: Nauka,

1978); and Anderson, *Internal Migration*. On the relaxation of residence restrictions for Jews, see Nathans, *Beyond the Pale*; and Yvonne Kleinmann, *Neue Orte—neue Menschen: Jüdisches Leben in St. Petersburg und Moskau* (Göttingen: Vandenhoeck and Ruprecht, 2006).

28. On the importance and intensification of controls such as quarantines, medical examinations, racial profiling, and passport checks during the age of mass migrations, see, for example, Leo Lucassen, "A Many-Headed Monster: The Evolution of the Passport System in the Netherlands and Germany in the Long Nineteenth Century," in *Documenting Individual Identity: The Development of State Practices in the Modern World,* ed. Jane Caplan and John Torpey (Princeton, N.J.: Princeton University Press, 2001), 235–55; McKeown, *Melancholy Order,* 121–238; Andreas Fahrmeir, Olivier Faron, and Patrick Weil, eds., *Migration Control in the North Atlantic World: The Evolution of State Practices in Europe and the United States from the French Revolution to the Inter-War Period* (New York: Berghahn Books, 2003); and Aristide R. Zolberg, *A Nation by Design: Immigration Policy in the Fashioning of America* (Cambridge, Mass.: Harvard University Press, 2006).

29. On the Soviet passport and registration system, see, for example, Nathalie Moine, "Passeportisation, statistique des migrations et controle de l'identite," *Cahiers du monde russe* 38.4 (1997): 587–600; Gijs Kessler, "The Passport System and State Control over Population Flows in the Soviet Union, 1932–1940," *Cahiers du monde russe* 42.2–4 (2001): 477–503; and David R. Shearer, *Policing Stalin's Socialism: Repression and Social Order in the Soviet Union, 1924–1953* (New Haven, Conn.: Yale University Press, 2009), chap. 8.

30. On imposture in the Soviet period, see Sheila Fitzpatrick, *Tear Off the Masks! Identity and Imposture in Twentieth-Century Russia* (Princeton, N.J.: Princeton University Press, 2005), 265–300; and Golfo Alexopoulos, "Portrait of a Con Artist as a Soviet Man," *Slavic Review* 57.4 (1998): 774—90.

31. In contrast to Muslims who traveled long distances, most Russian Orthodox believers kept their devotional practices local, usually traveling to saintly shrines within the borders of their home province. On Russian Orthodox pilgrimage and local belief, see Robert H. Greene, *Bodies Like Bright Stars: Saints and Relics in Orthodox Russia* (DeKalb: Northern Illinois University Press, 2010), 42–46. On the hajj, see Eileen Kane's essay in this volume; and Daniel R. Brower, "Russian Roads to Mecca: Religious Tolerance and Muslim Pilgrimage in the Russian Empire," *Slavic Review* 55.3 (1996): 567–84.

32. For an insightful analysis of Russia's emigration policy, see Eric Lohr, "Population Policy and Emigration Policy in Imperial Russia," in *Migration, Homeland, and Belonging in Eurasia,* ed. Cynthia Buckley and Blair A. Ruble (Baltimore: Johns Hopkins University Press, 2008), 165–81. On Jewish emigration in a transnational perspective, see Rebecca Kobrin, "The 1905 Revolution Abroad: Mass Migration, Russian Jewish Liberalism, and American Jewry, 1903–1914," in *The Revolution of 1905 and Russia's Jews,* ed. Stefani Hoffman and Ezra Mendelsohn (Philadelphia: University of Pennsylvania Press, 2008), 227–44.

33. For an eloquent rumination on the theme of mental "horizons" in human movement, see Daniel Roche, *Humeurs vagabondes: De la circulation des hommes et d l'utilite des voyages* (Paris: Fayard, 2003).

34. Hoerder, *Cultures in Contact,* 15.

35. For a classic call to study the world as known, or "geosophy," see John K. Wright, "Terrae Incognitae: The Place of the Imagination in Geography," *Annals of the Association of American Geographers* 37.1 (March 1947): 1–15.

36. Hoerder, *Cultures in Contact,* 17.

37. For a discussion of motility, see Kaufmann, "Mobility," 58. As an example of this research, see Elena Tyuryukanova's essay in this collection.

38. See Mark Bassin, *Imperial Visions: Nationalist Imagination and Geographical Expansion in the Russian Far East, 1840–1865* (Cambridge: Cambridge University Press, 1999); Mark Bassin, Christopher Ely, and Melissa K. Stockdale, eds., *Space, Place, and Power in Modern Russia: Essays in the New Spatial History* (DeKalb: Northern Illinois University Press, 2010); Sunderland, *Taming the Wild Field*; Valerie A. Kivelson, *Cartographies of Tsardom: The Land and Its Meanings in Seventeenth-Century Russia* (Ithaca, N.Y.: Cornell University Press, 2006); Christopher Ely, *This Meager Nature: Landscape and National Identity in Imperial Russia* (DeKalb: Northern Illinois University Press, 2009).

39. See Berdinskikh, *Spetsposelentsy,* 18, 56; Viola, *Unknown Gulag.*

40. Mom, Pirie, and Tissot, "Towards a Paradigm Shift?" 29.

41. For a particularly striking study of the ways in which a means of movement can shape social expectations about what can be accomplished, see Ann Norton Greene, *Horses at Work: Harnessing Power in Industrial America,* (Cambridge, Mass.: Harvard University Press, 2008), 18, 17–22.

42. "Loshad' cheloveku kryl'ia. Vozit vodu, vozit i voevodu," from N. I. Sokolov, *Iamskaia gon'ba i pochta v russkoi literature* (St. Petersburg: Tipografiia Ministerstva Vnutrennikh Del, 1900), 2.

PART I

Governing Mobility

[blank page 18]

Preface

CHARLES STEINWEDEL

If colonization was a "basic fact" of Russian history, as Vasilii Kliuchevskii wrote just over a century ago, then the involvement of political authorities in the process of movement is certainly another basic fact.[1] The vastness of the Eurasian plain made regulation of migration seem essential to state officials. Left to their own devices, people could, and often did, simply disappear in the empire's great expanse. As a result, the state often sought to prevent migration, to hold the population in place so it could be taxed, so that it would, ideally, make Russia's land productive, and so that men could be conscripted. At other times, state officials encouraged population movement to particular areas for security reasons or to develop resources. Finally, state officials—at times resigned in the face of the population's desire to move—sought to divert people to where they most wanted them. The essays in this section, ranging from Kiev in the Russian Empire's western borderlands to Harbin in the Far East, from the nineteenth century to twenty-first, help us recall key moments in the governance of mobility in Russia and the political legacies of this continuous and contested process.

The administrative regulation of mobility has been attractive to regimes professing very different ideologies. Despite dramatic ruptures in Eurasian history and the fact that those claiming authority in Russia have done so in the name of a hereditary dynasty, of Marxist socialism, and of nationalism and capitalism, a certain repertoire of techniques for governing mobility remained available to successive regimes. Peter the Great introduced internal passports in 1719, only two years before he accepted the title "emperor" (*imperator*), and they remained in use until the end of the empire in 1917.[2] Bolshevik leaders initially rejected such regulation of mobility as a tsarist anachronism, only to forcefully reassert it as a way to gain the ability to shape the urban population in a manner conso-

.

nant with economic planning, industrialization, and collectivization. Passports and residence controls became distinctive features of Soviet life until the Soviet Union's end in 1991. The collapse of socialism in favor of a mix of authoritarianism, capitalism, and nationalism yielded regulation of mobility that, as Matthew Light argues, has shifted from focus on residence and employment to street-level passport checks and raids that are often perceived as more intrusive than what came before.

The essays in this section help us see these continuities in new ways, in part by shifting our focus onto new populations. The historical literature on mobility in Russian Eurasia has largely concerned the urban-rural nexus and the peasantry. This is understandable. Since the Russian Imperial and Soviet populations remained overwhelmingly rural well into the twentieth century, mobility from the countryside to the city was crucial to both states. Scholarly examination of urban-rural movement very much reflected the interests of the states in question. The imperial government set up a resettlement administration (*pereselencheskoe upravlenie*) and kept statistics on migrants, while social-democratic theorists were absorbed in understanding the implications of movement to the city for worker consciousness.[3] Soviet leaders wrestled with how to deal with bagmen carrying food from the countryside during the 1920s, and with the flow of people to the industrializing cities in the 1930s.

Yet despite its size, peasant migration was neither the sole target of mobility governance nor the only one to have powerful political consequences. Faith Hillis and Chia Yin Hsu recall more focused but extremely significant government interventions in migration—and their unexpected consequences. Hillis focuses on the movement into Kiev of upwardly mobile Jewish and Ukrainian commercial elites whom state officials hoped would diminish the power of Polish nobles after 1863. A combination of policies and incentives to encourage migration succeeded in displacing members of the Polish *szlachta*. By 1905, however, the city's new populations had come into often violent conflict as an anti-Semitic right began to dominate local politics and undermine autocratic authority in the city. Hsu analyzes Russia's efforts to build and to populate cities in the Far East in order to insert the Russian Empire into international patterns of commerce and to build a colonial empire on the order of Russia's European rivals. The creation of Harbin, Port Arthur, and Dal'nii marked Russia's entry into Far Eastern trade. At the same time, the empire's eastern initiative involved it in international politics, most notably a clash with Japan, that called into question Russia's power as a colonizer. Without a landowning nobility in the East, and with less fear of proletarianization of supposedly loyal peasants, the tsarist autocracy tolerated a less estate-bound society and a more fluid ethnic environment than in central Russia. Yet, at the same time, the mobilization along the Chinese Eastern Railroad helped produce a new, racial sense of threat: what Hsu calls the "yellow peril."

Gijs Kessler examines the more familiar subject of peasant migration to the cities and the origins of the passport system but emphasizes ad hoc responses to economic imperatives. Limitations on movement were meant to rid cities of "unreliable elements" as much as to limit peasant in-migration. With the notable exception of forced labor, he argues that the Soviet state never "shifted to a planned administrative allocation of labor resources." Suspicion of the peasantry and concern with the purity of urban populations, however, soon produced the seemingly limitless desire for control of movement that came to characterize the Soviet Union. Matthew Light depicts late Soviet and post-Soviet efforts to regulate mobility in all their complexity. The post-Soviet liberalization changed efforts to regulate movement greatly. International travel became an accepted fact. Movement into Moscow became increasingly subject to questions of money, as we would expect from a capitalist system, rather than to socialism's administrative regulation based primarily on housing and the workplace. The interests of Moscow's city government diverged more markedly from those of federal authorities than in the Soviet period, however. As the collapse of the Soviet Union diminished the utility of some tools in the mobility-governance repertoire, others took on new importance. Intense street-level checks for identity documents and raids on work sites became common features of post-Soviet Moscow, resulting in a heightened sense of intimidation of those seeking to move to Moscow and greater corruption in the process of controlling it. All four authors resist the temptation to see regulation of mobility as a system simply imposed from above. Instead, the states established frameworks and incentives that people on the move elaborated and constituted in their own ways, often leading to unintended consequences.

Even as these essays describe government interventions in human movement, they also highlight one of mobility governance's most explosive consequences: the production of ethnic, racial, and other differences. At first glance, the role of boundary crossing in the creation of such cultural constructions may seem counterintuitive. Nationalisms often focused on place and emphasized stasis. The homeland, according to this logic—be it the Italian peninsula, the French "hexagon," or the German "home town"—defines the nation. The importance of the act of leaving that area in defining a people is less frequently emphasized. By contrast, these essays show the importance of Jewish and Orthodox commercial elites moving into Kiev in the creation of anti-Semitic politics; the building of Harbin and Dal'nii as a key moment in the crystallization of European and Asian racial distinctions in the East; and mobility to Moscow as a crucial point of contestation with Chechens and other peoples from the Caucasus. Ann Laura Stoler has emphasized that imperial formations are best considered "supremely mobile polities of dislocation dependent not on stable populations so much as on highly moveable ones."[4] Any large state whose leaders assume that the polity consists of different peoples with various economic and social roles, be it a (Russian) Empire, a (Soviet) Union, or a (Russian) Federation, will feature movement, and that movement helps redefine the groups in question.

We can fit Russian, Soviet, and post-Soviet efforts to govern mobility into broader conceptual frameworks in part because the challenges these states faced are not so different from challenges faced by other states. For instance, many European states had internal restrictions on travel. The Habsburgs restricted Jewish settlement, too. But for the most part, other European states had relaxed or abandoned internal regimes of control by the mid-nineteenth century. Internal and even external passports had largely disappeared by the 1850s and 1860s.[5] With Jewish emancipation, the Habsburgs gave up restrictions on Jewish residence in the 1860s. The Russian governing elite had a very different relationship with Jewish elites than the Habsburgs did. Pursuing Jewish conversion more aggressively and lacking interest in Jewish emancipation, the Romanov dynasty remained anti-Semitic under the last two emperors.[6] As Faith Hillis shows, however, the relaxation of the rules circumscribing a Jewish "Pale of Settlement" had much the same results in Kiev as the thoroughgoing emancipation of the Jews in Habsburg lands. In the Russian case, interests in economic development and pushing out Polish influence overcame interests in restricting Jews. The movement of Jewish commercial elites into Kiev produced an anti-Semitic politics similar to that found in Habsburg cities, most notably Vienna.

Chia Yin Hsu's treatment of Russian expansion into the Far East shows it to be quite similar to that of other European colonialisms in Asia. Much like the Germans in Shantung Peninsula, the British in Shanghai, or the French in Indochina, Russians interested in building a presence in the East and enriching themselves through capitalist development built urban infrastructure that fostered a new racial divide that at times overcame existing class or ethnic divides. Here, as elsewhere, mobility worked to break down status hierarchies and social boundaries while replacing them with new ones. In many ways, the Russian case plays out a "tension of empire" characteristic of other European imperial enterprises but with its own particular accent. As Frederick Cooper and Ann Laura Stoler have argued, the tension between liberal metropoles and illiberal empires was endemic to European expansion in the late nineteenth century.[7] Relative to the empire's self-consciously illiberal ruling ideology, Harbin was more tolerant and liberal. Yet the forces urbanization released in the East gave rise to new insecurities about race and Russian power, resulting in a renewed emphasis on specifically peasant migration directed by the state's "resettlement administration."

As Kessler suggests, the Soviet history of migration is a remarkable one, combining an effort to keep foreigners out and to keep Soviet citizens in while governing the movement of millions of people to build socialist industry in the largest country in the world. It was quite a task. The making of Moscow from Russia's second city into a megacity of over ten million people was certainly central to this story, as Matthew Light's fascinating account of movement into and out of the city suggests. His insightful comparison of Moscow with South African cities as "illegal cities" does much to illuminate how the local authorities have navigated a massive, national change in ideology. I might stress a contrast that he mentions only briefly, however.

Light notes that Moscow is "not ringed with migrant shantytowns." This gives pause for reflection. Moscow is one of the few cities in Eurasia or even in the world that has become a megacity since the 1930s without becoming like Mumbai, Sao Paulo, or Cairo—places where explosive growth has led to the creation of large slums at the extreme margins of civic and economic life.[8] Yet the cost in freedom of movement and civil rights in Moscow has been high.

In the end, can states in Eurasia, or anywhere else, control migration? Perhaps the question is not whether migration can be controlled, but how various political regimes try to manage migration, how they fail, and the broader political consequences of these efforts. Human movement is incredibly difficult to control. The interests of state and population are often radically divergent. Various parts of the state often differ over the desirability of controlling migration. In Imperial Russia, for instance, governors on the empire's periphery often welcomed internal migration, while those in central regions rejected it and the loss of human power it entailed. Controlling human movement requires a combination of tremendous resources, a determination to prevent movement throughout the state, and modern techniques of identification, surveillance, and control. Given resources and will, movement across a particular space, such as an international border, perhaps can be "controlled." Doing so across the entire geography of a state, however, is much more difficult. Humans—residents of Eurasia among them—are a peripatetic lot. Nonetheless, states leave a considerable imprint on human mobility, and movement shapes the political world in which we live.

Notes

1. Vasilii O. Kliuchevskii, *Sochineniia v deviate tomakh,* vol. 1 (Moscow: Mysl, 1987), 50.

2. Charles Steinwedel, "Making Social Groups, One Person at a Time: The Identification of Individuals by Estate, Religious Confession, and Ethnicity in Late Imperial Russia," in *Documenting Individual Identity: The Development of State Practices in the Modern World,* ed. Jane Caplan and John Torpey (Princeton, N.J.: Princeton University Press, 2001), 74.

3. Willard Sunderland, "The Ministry of Asiatic Russia: The Colonial Office That Never Was but Might Have Been," *Slavic Review* 69.1 (Spring 2010): 120–50; Peter Holquist, "'In Accord with State Interests and the People's Wishes': The Technocratic Ideology

of Imperial Russia's Resettlement Administration," *Slavic Review* 69.1 (Spring 2010): 151–79.

4. Ann Laura Stoler, "On Degrees of Imperial Sovereignty," *Public Culture* 18.1 (2006): 137–38.

5. Andrea Geselle, "Domenica Saba Takes to the Road: Origins and Development of a Modern Passport System in Lombardy-Veneto," in *Documenting Individual Identity: The Development of State Practices in the Modern World,* ed. Jane Caplan and John Torpey (Princeton, N.J.: Princeton University Press, 2001), 217; Andreas Fahrmeir, "Governments and Forgers: Passports in Nineteenth-Century Europe," in *Documenting Individual Identity: The Development of State Practices in the Modern World,* ed. Jane Caplan and John Torpey (Princeton, N.J.: Princeton University Press, 2001), 233; Leo Lucassen, "A Many-Headed Monster: The Evolution of the Passport System in the Netherlands and Germany in the Long Nineteenth Century," in *Documenting Individual Identity: The Development of State Practices in the Modern World,* ed. Jane Caplan and John Torpey (Princeton, N.J.: Princeton University Press, 2001), 251.

6. Richard S. Wortman, *Scenarios of Power: Myth and Ceremony in Russian Monarchy,* vol. 2 (Princeton, N.J.: Princeton University Press, 2000), 399–400, 505–6.

7. Ann Laura Stoler and Frederick Cooper, "Between Metropole and Colony: Rethinking a Research Agenda," in *Tensions of Empire: Colonial Cultures in a Bourgeois World,* ed. Frederick Cooper and Ann Laura Stoler (Berkeley: University of California Press, 1997), 3–4.

8. Mike Davis, however, has drawn attention to the increase in squatters living on the margins of society and to the deterioration of urban life in Moscow after the collapse of the Soviet Union. Mike Davis, *Planet of Slums* (London: Verso, 2006), 166–67.

1

Human Mobility, Imperial Governance, and Political Conflict in Pre-Revolutionary Kiev

FAITH HILLIS

The rulers of imperial Russia did not only seek to *limit* spontaneous movement and migration; they also *used* human mobility as a tool of governance. State policies lured settlers to Siberia and the Far East, sent exiled criminals and dissidents to frozen wastelands, and used transnational religious pilgrimages to showcase Russian power and to undermine the empire's rivals. The state's role in human-mobility processes was especially pronounced in the empire's western borderlands, where in 1863 the Polish nobility (*szlachta*), which had been the dominant political and economic force in the region since the early modern period, rose up against the imperial state. Having implemented a series of measures to declassify Poles—aimed at forcing them off of their rural lands and out of their urban properties—imperial officials enticed upwardly mobile migrants to the borderlands' major cultural centers, where they hoped the newcomers would replace Polish elites as the leaders of industry and culture. This essay examines these processes from the vantage point of Kiev, a major center of the de-Polonization campaign and the administrative seat of the empire's southwestern borderlands. It also explores the unintended consequences of this governance strategy, considering how the clashing interests of the newcomers eventually generated new conflicts in urban society and shaped local political culture.

In the aftermath of the 1863 revolt, imperial officials relied on the tens of thousands of migrants who arrived in Kiev to reduce Polish social and economic influence in the city. As bureaucrats declassified *szlachta* clans who had invested heavily in the local sugar industry, they enticed Jewish capitalists who had proven their entrepreneurial mettle in nearby shtetls to relocate to Kiev by offering them exemptions to the empire's rules on Jewish settlement. A series of tax incentives also attracted Orthodox merchants—primarily ethnic Ukrainians (or as they were known at the time, Little Russians) from the provinces just to the east of Kiev. Once these migrants arrived in the city, officials expected them not only to promote economic growth but also to contribute to the unfolding anti-Polish ideological campaign, which sought to claim Kiev as a primordially Orthodox locale.

By the 1870s, the rapid influx of upwardly mobile Jewish and Little Russian elites had achieved the state's major goal: the de-Polonization of Kiev. Successful Jewish and Little Russian migrants joined the city's most exclusive private clubs, served together in the municipal duma, and moved into the posh districts that formerly had been *szlachta* strongholds. As the two groups competed for limited economic and political resources, however, they increasingly found themselves in conflict. The imperial state's continued involvement with the two migrant communities further complicated intergroup dynamics: even as officials grew more reliant on Jews' participation in the local economy, they patronized efforts to promote Little Russian consciousness in the city, which often portrayed Jewish commercial elites as "exploiters" of the region's simple folk. By the early twentieth century, the conflict between the two parties had assumed a dynamic of its own that the imperial authorities struggled to control. Little Russian activists played a key role in the organization of grassroots political movements—and street violence—that protested against the power of local Jewish commercial elites. In Kiev, at least, ideological incitement from above and popular antipathies from below were not the only factors that produced a violent and mass-oriented anti-Semitic movement.[1] Human mobility—and the conflicts it produced—profoundly shaped the ideologies of Kiev's elites and influenced political outcomes.

Human Mobility and Imperial Governance: Peopling a De-Polonizing City

In the wake of the 1863 revolt, Kiev bureaucrats launched an ambitious campaign to destroy Polish influence in the city. The de-Polonization drive had two major (and not necessarily complementary) aims: to minimize the role played by the *szlachta* in the city's booming economy, and to undermine Polish political and cultural influence by claiming Kiev as a primordially Orthodox locale. Harnessing mobility processes to help them achieve both goals, local bureaucrats lured Jewish and Little Russian migrants to the city through a mixture of official policies and improvised incentives. Jewish entrepreneurs who had achieved success in the Pale of Settlement, officials hoped, could invest in the city's growing industrial sector; devoutly Orthodox Little Russian merchants and upwardly mobile professionals and intellectuals could assist in the task of making Kiev a "truly Russian" city.

The migration of successful Jewish entrepreneurs to Kiev began in earnest just before the Polish revolt. In 1859, the governor-general of the Southwestern Provinces convinced the minister of finance to reverse the statute that had banned Jewish settlement in the city since the 1830s, noting that permitting "useful" Jews to settle in the city would encourage economic development.[2] The steady stream of Jewish migrants to Kiev in the first years of the 1860s became a flood in the aftermath of the Polish revolt. Eager to ensure that the estates and factories left vacant by exiled or ruined Polish families did not fall into disrepair, city officials established one of the empire's most liberal Jewish settlement regimes, allowing Jewish merchants of both the first and second guilds permanently to reside in the city.[3] In 1863, Kiev's governor-general even petitioned the imperial ministries to waive the blanket injunction against Jewish acquisition of immovable property outside of the Pale, asking St. Petersburg to allow him to reward the city's successful Jewish entrepreneurs with hereditary honored-citizen status and plots of land.[4]

Within a decade of the Polish revolt, Jewish newcomers had achieved stunning economic success in Kiev. In the early 1860s, Israel Brodskii, who operated a network of shops and refineries across the Pale, moved to the city with several of his brothers. Having purchased a sugar plant and a brewery shortly after their arrival, the brothers quickly established reputations as the "sugar kings" of the Russian Empire; they ultimately acquired thirteen sugar-beet refineries managed by six joint-stock companies in Kiev Province alone.[5] By the 1870s, the Gal'perin, Zaitsev, Liebermann, and Saks families had also established a place among Kiev's most successful sugar barons.[6] The Kogen brothers, Karaites who hailed from Crimea, founded a small tobacco shop after their arrival and soon acquired the city's two largest tobacco factories.[7] The modest steamboat company founded by D. S. Margolin in the 1860s had become the largest Dniepr shipping company within a decade.[8] Even Evzel Gintsburg, one of Russia's most famed financiers, established a presence in Kiev, opening a commercial bank—which also boasted branches in Paris and St. Petersburg—in the city.[9] The marriage of Evzel's son Horace to the daughter of a Jewish sugar entrepreneur further enriched the Gintsburgs and strengthened their ties to Kiev, bringing six southwestern sugar refineries into the family's portfolio.[10] By 1874, one hundred Jews had achieved first-guild merchant status in Kiev, compared to only fifteen Gentiles; Jewish immigrants owned one-sixth of the commercial and industrial property in Kiev region, including twenty-seven sugar factories, 564 viticulture establishments, and 148 beer factories.[11]

The local authorities, who had opened the city to Jewish merchants in the first place, accommodated and rewarded Jewish entrepreneurial elites at many junctures. In the 1870s, Kiev's governor-general convinced the ministries that Jews who maintained a respectable "lifestyle and occupation" should be permitted to acquire property anywhere in the city.[12] Overjoyed at this news, one member of the Brodskii family built a handsome home in the city center, across from the duma building, although the authorities refused his request to build a synagogue on the premises.[13] The Kogens, too, erected several estates in the city's most prestigious districts.[14] By 1879, 101 Kiev Jews had purchased homes within city limits, sixty-four of which were located in the city's ritziest neighborhoods.[15] Local authorities also permitted Jewish merchants of the first guild to obtain residence permits for their employees—from domestic servants and tutors to lawyers and accountants—a policy that stimulated further Jewish migration. In 1863, three thousand Jews were registered in Kiev; a decade later, that number had risen to thirteen thousand out of a total population of 116,000, meaning that legally registered Jews comprised a healthy 11 percent of the city's population, outstripping the number of Polish inhabitants.[16]

In short, the men who ruled the empire not only created policies that permitted a Jewish entrepreneurial elite to emerge in Kiev; they also celebrated the arrival of the community's most successful businessmen into high society. The Brodskiis and Gintsburgs served on high-ranking commissions on the "Jewish question" that offered them direct access to ministers and even the tsar; Margolin was appointed Kiev's local representative to the Department of Trade and Manufacturing.[17] The Gintsburgs, who welcomed ministers and even tsars to their table on more than a few occasions, were granted baronial titles and an enormous Crimean estate in the 1870s.[18] In the process, Kiev's leaders signaled strongly to non-Jewish high society that a spirit of accommodation and toleration should prevail within the urban *beau monde*. The chairmen of the Kiev Stock Exchange (whom imperial law required to be Christian) welcomed Jewish participation in subcommittees; four of the five members of the committee that oversaw the construction in the 1870s of a grand new building for the exchange, located adjacent to the governor-general's headquarters, were Jewish.[19] The exchange's leaders, in turn, expressed their regard for the group's Jewish members by moving its weekly meetings to Fridays to avoid the Jewish Sabbath.[20] Meanwhile, Jewish entrepreneurs became visible fixtures in the city's charitable associations and the municipal duma.[21]

If city officials created incentives to encourage Jewish entrepreneurs to invest in Kiev, they also used tax breaks to lure Orthodox merchants and entrepreneurs to the city. Although these efforts attracted a handful of entrepreneurs from the Great Russian interior, most of the city's Gentile entrepreneurial migrants were native sons of the southwest. Drawn by tales of the vast fortunes to be made in the sugar industry, a number of Left Bank Ukraine's most prominent gentry clans, including the Kharitonenkos, Khanenkos, and Tereshchenkos, established a permanent presence in the city. These ethnic Ukrainian migrants might have abandoned the gentility of provincial life, but they remained determined to preserve their cultural heritage.[22] The Kharitonenkos, Khanenkos, and Tereshchenkos proudly traced their ancestry to the Cossack generals of the sixteenth and seventeenth century and devoted substantial time and money to protecting the traditions and language of the region's simple folk. The de-Polonizing state heartily endorsed these tasks; recovering the "pure" Orthodox culture of Little Russians, after all, would diminish the influence of Polish-Catholic culture in the borderlands.

Together, Little Russian mercantile elites and the governor-general's office created historical commissions and archeological associations that presented Kiev as a "primordially Russian" city, emphasizing its status as the capital of Kievan Rus' ("The Mother of Russian Cities") and as the site of the East Slavs' conversion to Christianity ("The Cradle of Russian Orthodoxy"). The historical commissions demonstrated a special interest in the centuries that Kiev spent under the Polish-Lithuanian Commonwealth. Under that "foreign" system, they claimed, the region's Orthodox masses had been subjected to cruel political domination by the Polish-Catholic nobility and economic exploitation by the Jewish estate managers and bankers retained by the *szlachta*.[23] As they compiled histories, published archival documents, and funded archeological digs, the Little Russian historical activists created a new pantheon of regional heroes. In particular, they were drawn to the seventeenth-century Cossack general Bogdan Khmel'nitskii, who led his regular armies as well as bands of peasants against the *szlachta* and their Jewish agents, ultimately wresting the central Dniepr region from Polish power. Khmel'nitskii's attempt to halt the "the merciless bloodletting of the peasants, the result of repression by the Poles and the *pans,*" and to change the fact that "Yids and dogs are respected more than our Christian brothers," claimed commission members, had allowed Cossack leaders and simple folk alike to join together to protect local culture and Orthodoxy on the empire's frontier.[24]

By the late 1860s, the historical commissions had become powerful cultural institutions and political forces in Kiev. The expansion of their activities—and the prestige that came with participation in them—created an insatiable demand for journalists, historians, and teachers in the city, stimulating another wave of migration. In contrast to the early affiliates of the historical commissions, who tended to be noble-born, the new migrants included a number of self-made professionals who were proud of having risen up from the poverty that they believed had been foisted on generations of their ancestors by Poles and Jews. O. I. Levitskii, the son of a parish priest, served as the secretary of the governor-general's local history commission while still in his twenties, beginning a career as an historian, politician, and Ukrainian activist that would last through the 1917 revolution.[25] P. G. Lebedintsev, a parish priest posted in a district city in

Kiev Province, used the notoriety he gained in the historical commissions to advance through the church hierarchy, eventually becoming the first editor of *Kievskie eparkhial'nye vedomosti* (News of Kiev Diocese) and the rector of St. Sophia's Cathedral.[26] Of all the commissions' affiliates, V. Ia. Shul'gin, the son of an itinerant, mid-ranking bureaucrat, leveraged most effectively the respect and acclaim he gained in the local history circles. Determined to cast off "the triple yoke of Catholic clergy, Poles (landlords, rentiers, and estate managers), and Jews" that he believed continued to hang on the backs of the local Orthodox population, he founded Kiev's first daily, *Kievlianin* (*The Kievan*), in 1864.[27] The paper, which remained the city's most popular news organ through 1917, allowed Shul'gin to serve as the official spokesman of the "Orthodox cause"—and the most vociferous opponent of Polish and Jewish interests—in the southwest.[28]

As they used the activities of the historical commissions to rise through the ranks of educated society, Kiev's Little Russian activists aspired to bring the masses with them. Lebedintsev, Levitskii, and others in their circle participated in Sunday schools and popular-education ventures that taught peasants and workers to read in Russian and Ukrainian.[29] The historical commissions reached out to parishes and communes as well, distributing tracts in simple language that described their activities and solicited small donations. Inspired by Shul'gin's example, other activists founded penny papers, such as *Trud* (Labor) and *Drug naroda* (Friend of the People), to educate the barely literate about the scholarly and political agendas of the commissions.[30] All the while, Little Russian activists—themselves recent arrivals in Kiev—sought to claim the city as an Orthodox space. They rechristened streets whose names invoked Polish political figures and military victories and founded museums of Ukrainian culture. They even attempted to erect in the city's central square a statue that depicted a horseback Khmel'nitskii trampling a Polish prince, a Jesuit, and a Jew—a plan that Alexander II vetoed as insensitive and politically inflammatory.[31]

The Costs of Mobility: Social and Political Conflict

In the 1880s, Kiev's Little Russian circles seized on the stunning success of Jewish economic migrants, which they interpreted as proof that the city remained under siege by non-Orthodox interests. Organs like *Kievlianin,* which had warned of the dual threat posed to local civilization by Poles and Jews, began to focus more intently on the allegedly baleful influence of Jews in Kiev's contemporary social and political life. Lamenting the influx of Jews into Kiev high society and the city's best neighborhoods, the paper denounced them as a "*kulak* nation that is strong by virtue of its unity, solidarity, single faith and beliefs, and views and has mastered the art of exploiting all non-Jews for more than ten decades."[32] Kiev penny papers echoed these formulations, presenting the continued disenfranchisement of the region's Orthodox population as a direct result of Jewish entrepreneurial success. *Trud* complained that waivers allowing Jews to acquire land permitted entrepreneurial elites to assume the exploitative seigniorial role of the vanquished *szlachta*.[33] *Drug naroda* exposed price-fixing schemes allegedly cooked up by Jewish sugar barons and complained that the inclusion of the city's multicultural elites in the city duma had allowed "Jews and people . . . with a bad conscience" to "control and misuse local self-governance."[34]

Kiev's Jewish elites did not directly respond to these attacks by Little Russian intellectuals; rather, they sought out state patronage only more aggressively. In 1887, Lev Brodskii, Israel's son, hosted a meeting of the city's major sugar producers, which produced a formal agreement to set production levels and to export quantities exceeding this limit overseas; within five years, 90 percent of the empire's sugar refineries had joined the Kiev cartel.[35] Coupled with new protectionist tariffs and bad harvests in the late 1880s, the cartel's creation resulted in a rapid increase in the price of sugar—and in the sugar barons' profits. The finance minister Count Sergei Witte (who had befriended the Brodskiis while managing the Southwest Railroad from Kiev in the 1870s) intervened at numerous points to protect the Kiev sugar industrialists, whom he viewed as model agents of capitalist development, from domestic and foreign competitors.[36] In 1895, after continued lobbying from the Brodskiis, Witte officially recognized the cartel, levying harsh duties on foreign sugar and setting empire-wide production limits. Sugar speculation and the price-fixing practices of Kiev's sugar kings now gained official sanction from the imperial government, in an arrangement that foreign commentators viewed as a startling example of predatory capitalism.[37]

In the face of increasing criticism—at home and abroad—of their capitalist excesses, Kiev's Jewish mercantile elites sought to highlight their imperial patriotism and sense of *noblesse oblige,* generously funding a variety of charitable causes while showcasing their commitment to the city's continued cultural and infrastructural development.[38] Around the turn of the century, they began to develop the city's utilities networks, which they saw as promising investments and as a means of endowing their city with a modern, European face. The Brodskiis established a private water company, which by 1900 provided connections to four thousand of Kiev's seven thousand properties. Margolin, for his part, founded a transport company, which launched the Russian Empire's first electric tram in 1894 and built a network that comprised thirteen lines by 1904.[39] The Brodskiis and Tereshchenkos—apparently the lone Gentile investors in the city's utility system—controlled an equal number of shares in the sewer company.[40]

The creation of the sugar cartel and the continued expansion of the plutocrats' charitable and economic activities enraged a new generation of Little Russian populist activists. D. I. Pikhno, the son of a *meshchanin* who ultimately became a professor of economics at Kiev University and succeeded Shul'gin as the editor of *Kievlianin,* continued to argue that the interests of local Jewish elites were incompatible with those of the masses.[41] The "Jews and sugar barons" of the Stock Committee, producers' cartels, and utilities companies, he charged, had set artificially high prices for the most basic commodities, blocking upward mobility for millions of peasants.[42] In 1902, Pikhno caused a scene at a Stock Committee meeting devoted to the bread trade. When Lev Brodskii and other Jewish entrepreneurs complained that existing trade agreements provided inadequate protections for the southwest's largest commodity producers, Pikhno countered that state policy should aim to distribute the region's wealth rather than concentrate it in the hands of a few. Before he stormed out of the meeting, the professor denounced the lack of transparency in the committee's activities, complaining that its closed meetings were designed to keep the public ignorant of its decisions.[43]

By the 1890s, populist delegates within the Kiev city duma had joined local intellectuals in denouncing the capitalist city fathers' disregard for the welfare of the Little Russian simple folk. Although the body was dominated by mercantile elites through the 1870s and 1880s, continued attacks on the absenteeism of the city fathers and their narrow class interests eventually permitted petty merchants and Orthodox professionals of the third curia to seize control, continuing the social-mobility process for a new generation of populist politicians. Once elected, these delegates spoke out against irregularities in elections and abuses of power by the city's political elite and expressed dismay at the duma's lack of interest in the welfare of the city's laboring population, devoting special attention to the plight of impoverished neighborhoods on the urban periphery.[44] The newly elected Orthodox delegates singled out for criticism the private utilities companies; rather than endow the city with a modern appearance, the delegates charged, the companies created new distinctions between center and periphery, rich and poor, plutocrats and the "simple folk." The high cost of the water-filtration system developed by the Brodskiis guaranteed the proprietors of the waterworks immense profits but deprived the city's poorest citizens of a potable water supply; Margolin's tram network charged excessively high fares and served only the central areas of the city, where the wealthy congregated; and the electric lights installed throughout the city in the 1890s illuminated the central districts but left the peripheral neighborhoods, with growing crime rates, to languish in darkness.[45] As the physician and duma delegate E. I. Afanas'ev put it, the neglect of the local plutocrats had put working-class residents on the "path to extinction."[46]

Afanas'ev and other populist activists in the duma, including O. I. Levitskii, F. N. Iasnogurskii, the accountant A. L. Tsytovich, and the railroad engineer N. P. Dobrynin, styled themselves as men of the people, denouncing with ever greater intensity Jews' role in the local economy and their historical "oppression" of the local Orthodox population.[47] They began to form issue-based coalitions—which, by the mid-1890s, observers were even calling "parties": a novel concept in a body where voting preferences traditionally had been shaped more by personal allegiances and self-interest than by ideological convictions.[48] Of course, on the eve of the twentieth century, the vast majority of the city's residents remained excluded from the formal political process. But drawing on the historical narrative of oppression crafted by the first generation of Little Russian migrants, Kiev's new generation of populist politicians had begun to craft a coherent political program that combined class and regional consciousness with anticapitalist and anti-Semitic sentiment.

From Conflict to Violence

The imperial state had used a variety of incentives to lure Jewish and Little Russian elites to Kiev, where they vied for economic resources and political power. A small group of Jewish plutocrats had managed to integrate itself into the upper ranks of the city's society. These businessmen established a spirit of accommodation in Kiev's multicultural *beau monde* but also jealously guarded their class privilege, using the city's resources to enhance their wealth and social status. Ethnic Ukrainian entrepreneurs and political activists, resentful of Jewish elites, attacked their "exploitative" practices, positing the deracination of "Jewish capitalists" as a prerequisite to ensuring the upward social mobility of the simple folk. By the turn of the twentieth century, the clash between the two groups would be superimposed against the backdrop of revolutionary politics, as large segments of the tsar's subjects united in what has become known as the liberation movement to call for basic civil rights to be extended to all residents of the empire.

The growing interest in politics, reflected in all segments of society, finally allowed populist opponents of the capitalist order and the local Jewish elite to spread their message to the masses, and groups inspired by their beliefs rapidly proliferated across the southwest. For example, the Union of Russian Patriots, a club that united Orthodox believers from all walks of life behind a populist, regionalist, and anti-Semitic agenda, wrote to the governor-general in August 1905 to complain that Kiev's Orthodox population "has been isolated . . . by the shadow of Yids [*zhidovskoi teni*], which renders us invisible."[49] Denouncing officials' long-running accommodation of Jewish commercial elites, the group expressed its concern that the tsar would be convinced by liberationist forces and "Witte and Company . . . to give the damned Jews [civil] rights."[50] The creation of an equal-rights regime, the group insisted, would only permit local "Yids" to consolidate their political and economic power; if the authorities continued to appease the "enemies" of the Orthodox people at the expense of the laboring masses, the group ominously warned, it might be forced to take matters into its own hands.[51] The activities of such groups imbued the catchphrase of liberation with exclusionary (and even eliminationist) tones. Turning the arguments of many liberationist activists on their heads, Kiev's populist demagogues insisted that the "simple folk" could be liberated not through the civic guarantees offered by a Rechtsstaat (which they alleged was a Jewish ruse further to enslave the simple folk) but only through emancipation from the "Jewish yoke."

Concerned by the growing popularity of groups like the Union of Russian Patriots, Kiev's Jewish elites began to explore political alternatives to the imperial patronage networks on which they traditionally had relied. Their first forays into mass politics, however, were hesitant; recognizing that they stood to lose everything if the liberation movement evolved into a revolution, the plutocrats insisted that change must be gradual and orderly. D. S. Margolin, for example, took it upon himself to visit local synagogues, urging his co-confessionalists struggling for political change to "stand in solidarity with the Christian population and not to incite the population by carrying out illegal disturbances that could raise doubts about [Jews'] faith in the government."[52] Non-Jewish liberationists, too, hastened to contradict the arguments of their antiliberal foes, insisting that the class distinctions that continued to divide the city's residents could best be resolved by democratizing municipal and imperial politics, not by attacking Jews' role in local business and culture.[53]

In response, Kiev's populist duma deputies only intensified their attacks on the leaders of the Jewish community. Little Russian activists pointed out that the same liberal deputies who trumpeted the banner of equality for all recently had voted to provide a series of tax breaks for the Brodskii family.[54] Again, the local demagogues turned liberationist slogans against the liberationists, portraying Jewish entrepreneurs—not police and tsarist bureaucrats—as the true "enemies of the people." When the city duma met in October 1905 to discuss whether to permit a new mill to be constructed in the city, the duma deputy F. N. Iasnogurskii feverishly denounced those who voted against the project; he claimed that they were agents of the Brodskiis, who hoped to establish a monopoly in the milling business.[55] "There is nothing more upsetting than the fact that the duma will not permit the construction of a new mill for the benefit of the capitalist Brodskii. This will slow the development of industry. Why is flour expensive in Kiev? Because the mill is in the hands of the millionaire Brodskii," he cried. Ending his speech with his trademark sarcasm, he sneered, "It's fine that the population drinks water that is dangerous for their health. No, we can't do anything about it."[56]

Kiev's Jewish entrepreneurial elite and populist anti-Semitic activists came into direct conflict in the aftermath of the announcement of the October manifesto. At 9:00 A.M. on 18 October 1905, students of the First Commercial School arrived for class clutching copies of the manifesto. D. S. Margolin and Lev

Brodskii, who served on the school's board of directors, happened to be on the premises that morning for a meeting. The students crowded around the directors, begging for a celebration to mark the historic occasion. Margolin finally assented and arranged a Dniepr cruise for the students. As the directors and teachers accompanied the students to the riverside port, they struggled to keep the group together; the students, who passed celebrants waving red flags, could barely control their excitement. Once the boat pushed off from the pier, the students declared themselves "young republicans," tore the school's banner into pieces, and hoisted a red flag on the boat's mast as they sang, danced, and gave speeches. The teachers struggled to regain control of the students, but to no avail. Finally, Margolin promised the pupils that if they calmed down, he would treat them to a day at his *dacha,* directing the boat's captain to head downriver to his property.[57] Only toward night did the drunken participants of the celebration finally begin wandering back to town.[58]

By the afternoon of 18 October, special editions of *Kievlianin* excoriated the actions of Margolin and Brodskii and repeated rumors that Jewish mercantile elites, no longer content to oppress only Little Russians, intended to seize control of Russia. By early evening, the crowds that had convened at the city duma to cheer the manifesto were transformed into mobs of angry pogromists. The violence and looting began in ethnically mixed, outlying neighborhoods, where Gentile workers and merchants attacked their Jewish neighbors.[59] But in a stunning deviation from earlier pogroms in the city, aristocratic enclaves in central Kiev became the other major center of violence. Proclaiming that the liberation of the Little Russian people could not be accomplished until the "Jewish yoke" had been destroyed, activists and common mobs headed to Kiev's best neighborhoods on 19 October, resolving to attack the "Jewish millionaires."[60] The manors of many of the city's Jewish sugar barons were destroyed that day, along with the central Kiev apartment of D. S. Margolin's son, a liberationist lawyer.[61]

Perhaps the most dramatic events of the entire pogrom unfolded outside the adjacent manors of the Gintsburg and Brodskii families on Bank Street. On the afternoon of 19 October, Aleksander Gintsburg, Horace's son, went to ask the civil governor for protection, while his brother, Vladimir Gintsburg, stayed at home with his son.[62] A crowd of a dozen or so pogromists arrived at the house, dragging Vladimir outside and beating him senseless while others ransacked the property. The student Grigorii Brodskii, Israel Brodskii's grandson, witnessed the scene from his window, venturing outside with a Mauser in one hand and a Browning in the other. The student fired one shot into the air and another into the crowd as they approached the Gintsburgs' property. He then entered the house, shooting the Gintsburgs' butler, who apparently had not joined the *rioters,* as well as two attackers, one of whom later died. By the time that Brodskii exited the home, a policeman was waiting for him. The student confessed to the crime and handed over his guns, as the crowd chanted, "Beat him! That's the murderer!" Another armed member of the Brodskii family was removed from the home by the police.[63] As police and army regiments stood by watching, pogromists then looted the Brodskiis' property.[64]

The violence continued unabated for three days. Finally, on 21 October, the political director of the city police, after meeting with Lev Brodskii, informed the civil governor of his intention to halt the pogrom.[65] By the twenty-second, the police and gendarme divisions that had ignored the violence were fanning out across the city looking for the Brodskiis' billiard cues, which had been stolen during the mayhem.[66] The pogrom had finally come to an end. Leaving 1,800 homes and businesses destroyed, twenty-seven dead, three hundred injured, and 10.5 million rubles of damage, it attained a dubious distinction as the costliest outbreak of street violence in the entire empire in 1905.[67] The most striking casualty of the pogrom, however, was the peace of mind of the city's Jewish elites. The local authorities, whom they traditionally had viewed as their greatest patrons, failed to protect them from rampaging mobs; even the police had turned on them, permitting the destruction of their property and sense of security.

In the aftermath of 1905, relations between the Jewish and Little Russian elites who had settled in Kiev in the wake of the Polish revolt continued to deteriorate.[68] Appealing to abstract principles of justice and equality—and almost exclusively to their fellow social elites—Kiev's isolated liberal voices, unlike their adversaries, never mastered the art of mobilizing constituencies or manipulating the media. By contrast, populist activists continued their grassroots organizing efforts, catering to the masses with a political program that combined nationalist rhetoric, class consciousness, and vicious anti-Semitism. By 1907, Kiev's mass-oriented, right-wing, anti-Semitic political coalition had won a majority in the municipal duma and had seized the city's seat in the state duma; over the next decade, right-wing activists continued to expand their influence by staging public spectacles—from demonstrations to street violence to the notorious Beilis trial—designed to highlight the continuing threat posed by the city's Jewish elites. The growing power of the Kiev right distressed bureaucrats in the southwestern borderlands and St. Petersburg, who darkly warned that the "exceptional intolerance . . . and fanaticism" of the local right complicated the state's efforts to maintain civic peace.[69] Political conflicts created by official intervention in mobility processes had taken on a momentum of their own, which the state could no longer control.

State intervention in human-mobility processes utterly transformed the demographics and political culture of Kiev in the decades following the 1863 revolt. Imperial bureaucrats encouraged Jewish and Little Russian migration to the city as a means of de-Polonizing its economy and culture; they hoped to use the former group to maintain Kiev's robust economic growth, and the latter to claim it as a primordially Orthodox locale. Contrary to bureaucrats' expectation that the new migrants would transform Kiev into an economic powerhouse and a "truly Russian" city, the rapid influx of Jewish and Little Russian subjects created new social and political conflicts. In the wake of the 1905 revolution, these tensions produced a violent, mass-oriented, and anti-Semitic right that dominated local politics, seriously undermined autocratic rule in the city, and distinguished Kiev's political culture from other urban centers, which tended to be strongholds of liberal or socialist thought. Impossible to explain by reference to political or sociological phenomena alone, the rise of the Kiev right was conditioned by official attempts to govern through mobility—and their many unintended consequences.

Notes

1. On the role of officials and intellectuals in proliferating anti-Semitic ideas, see John Doyle Klier, *Imperial Russia's Jewish Question, 1855–1881* (New York: Cambridge University Press, 1995); Hans Rogger, *Jewish Policies and Right-Wing Politics in Imperial Russia* (Los Angeles: University of California Press, 1986). For excellent analyses of the social and political underpinnings of anti-Semitism in nineteenth-century Europe, consult Philip G. Nord, *Paris Shopkeepers and the Politics of Resentment* (Princeton, N.J.: Princeton University Press, 1986); John W. Boyer, *Political Radicalism in Late Imperial Vienna: Origins of the Christian Social Movement, 1848–1897* (Chicago: University of Chicago Press, 1981).

2. V. B. Anan'ich, *Bankirskie doma v Rossii, 1860–1914 gg.* (Leningrad: Nauka, 1991), 39.

3. On Jews' acquisition of Polish-owned property, see Witold Walewski, "Sukrownictwo na Ukrainie," in *Pamiętnik Kijowski,* vol. 2 (London: Nakładem Koła Kijowian, 1959), 179–81; Daniel Beauvois, *La bataille de la terre en Ukraine, 1863–1914: Les Polonais et les conflits socio-ethniques* (Lille: Presses Universitaires de Lille, 1993), 48. On Jewish settlement laws, consult Natan Menachem Meir, "The Jews of Kiev, 1859–1914: Community and Charity in an Imperial Russian City" (Ph.D. dissertation, Columbia University, 2004), 12. Benjamin Nathans describes similar efforts to attract Jewish merchants of the first guild to St. Petersburg. See Benjamin Nathans, *Beyond the Pale: The Jewish Encounter with Late Imperial Russia* (Berkeley: University of California Press, 2002).

4. G. B. Sliozberg, *Dela minuvshikh dnei,* vol. 2 (Paris: Pascal, 1933), 144–56. This document was held in Sliozberg's private archive, and he notes that he does not have a record of the Ministry of Internal Affairs' response.

5. Fanny Alexandra Brodsky, *Smoke Signals: From Eminence to Exile* (London: Radcliffe Press, 1997), 3–5; Victoria Khiterer, "Jewish Life in Kyiv at the Turn of the Twentieth Century," *Ukraina moderna* 10 (2006): 78.

6. Meir, "Jews of Kiev," 42.

7. Vitalii Kovalinskii, *Metsenaty Kieva* (Kiev: Kyi, 1998), 400.

8. Sliozberg, *Dela minuvshikh dnei*, vol. 1, 284; Michael Vetukhiv, "Arnold Davydovych Margolin, 1877–1956," *Annals of the Ukrainian Academy of Arts and Sciences in the United States* 7.1–2 (1959): 1671.

9. The Gintsburg banking house was founded on profits from government-guaranteed investments in private railroads and the realization of land-bank obligations. See Sliozberg, *Dela minuvshikh dnei*, vol. 2, 214.

10. Henri Sliosberg [G. B. Sliozberg], *Baron Horace-O. de Gunzbourg: Sa vie, son oeuvre* (Paris: Pascal, 1933), 18, 33; Walewski, "Sukrownictwo na Ukrainie," 180.

11. "Vedomost' o chisle vydannykh, kupecheskikh promyslovykh i prikazchikh bilety" (1881), Derzhavnyi arkhiv mista Kyeva (hereafter DAK), f. 163, op. 39, d. 211, l. 56; G. Ia. Krasnyi-Admoni, *Materialy dlia istorii antievreiskikh pogromov v Rossii: Vos'midesiatye gody (15 aprelia 1881 g.–29 fevralia 1882 g.)*, vol. 2 (St. Petersburg: Gosudarstvennoe izdatel'stvo, 1923), xx. Although Odessa is often cited as Russia's major center of Jewish commerce, Jews were better represented among the mercantile elite in Kiev than in Odessa, where about half of the first guild merchants were Jews. See Sliozberg, *Dela minuvshikh dnei*, vol. 2, 75; Nicholas V. Iljine, *Odessa Memories* (Seattle: University of Washington Press, 2003), 77.

12. Meir, "Jews of Kiev," 32.

13. Kovalinskii, *Metsenaty Kieva*, 214.

14. Ibid., 339–401.

15. Report of Governor-General A. R. Drentel'n to Kiev City Administration, 25 June 1879, DAK, f. 163, op. 7, d. 743, l. 1. A number of Jewish families, including the Brodskiis, also acquired vast tracts of rural land zoned for industrial use in eastern and southern Ukraine, which featured lavish manor homes and well-manicured park lands in addition to sugar refineries. See Brodsky, *Smoke Signals*, 6–7.

16. Viktoriia Khiterer, *Dokumenty sobrannye evreiskoi istoriko-arkheograficheskoi komissiei* (Kiev: Institut Iudaiki, 1999), 143. These figures do not include the tens of thousands of illegal migrants who, hoping to emulate the success of the Brodskiis, poured into Kiev from surrounding shtetls. The social station of these migrants contrasted greatly with that of the plutocrats. By the last years of the nineteenth century, a mere 15 percent of Kiev's Jews were registered merchants; one Zionist colonization group estimated that nearly 20 percent of the city's Jewish population lived in poverty. See Meir, "Jews of Kiev," 26; "Kiev," in *Evreiskaia entsiklopediia*, vol. 9 (St. Petersburg: Brokgauz-Efron, n.d.), 527.

17. See Nathans, *Beyond the Pale*, 168–86; "Memoire du Baron Alexandre de Gunzburg" (1939), in the author's possession. I am very grateful to Benjamin Nathans for providing me with a copy of this unpublished manuscript.

18. Anan'ich, *Bankirskie doma*, 46, 40; Sliozberg, *Dela minuvshikh dnei*, vol. 2, 219; Boris V. Anan'ich and Sergei G. Beliaev, "St. Petersburg: Banking Center of the Russian Empire," in *Commerce in Russian Urban Culture, 1861–1914*, ed. William Craft Brumfield, Boris V. Anan'ich, and Yuri A. Petrov (Washington, D.C.: Woodrow Wilson Center Press, 2001), 14. The Gintsburgs maintained a close personal relationship with Tsarina Alexandra. Alexandra had first met the family as a child, when they built a railroad for her father, the Prince of Hesse. Alexandra's brother, who became the Prince of Bulgaria,

commissioned the Gintsburgs to build a railroad and national bank in that country. "Memoire du Baron Alexandre de Gunzburg," 26, 35, 38.

19. See N. Kh. Bunge to N. G. Khriakov, 2 March 1870, DAK, f. 226, op. 1, d. 1, l. 100b; Kiev Stock Committee to Bunge, 7 March 1870, DAK, f. 226, op. 1, d. 1, l. 12; *Dvadtsatipiatiletie Kievskoi Birzhi, 1869–1894 g.* (Kiev: S. V. Kul'zhenko, 1895), xvii. The committee included Lazar Brodskii, Israel's son. In 1870, a group of Orthodox merchants asked that Jews be banned from the ranks of the stock exchange's leadership. The president of the exchange passed the question on to the minister of finance and the governor-general, who ruled that Jewish merchants of the first guild, who enjoyed the right to reside in the city, could not be barred from participating in the group's activities at any level. *Dvadtsatipiatiletie Kievskoi Birzhi,* second pagination, 1.

20. Alfred J. Rieber, *Merchants and Entrepreneurs in Imperial Russia* (Chapel Hill: University of North Carolina Press, 1982), 106.

21. Starozhil, *Kiev v vos'midesiatykh godakh* (Kiev: Petr Barskii, 1910), 92. Representatives of the Brodskii, Kogen, and Gintsburg families served in the Kiev city duma. On Jewish involvement in duma elections, see, for example, "Vedomost' o chisle izbiratelei za 1875–79 g.," DAK, f. 163, op. 39, d. 211, l. 51.

22. See Kovalinskii, *Metsenaty Kieva*; Vitalii Kovalinskii, *Sem'ia Tereshchenko* (Kiev: Presa Ukraini, 2003).

23. On the commissions' activities, see "Tsentral'nye arkhivy drevnikh aktovykh knig: Vilenskii i Kievskii," (St. Petersburg: Ministerstvo narodnogo prosveshcheniia, 1883), 37; *Sbornik statei i materialov po istorii iugo-zapadnoi Rossii, izdavaemyi Kommissiei dlia razbora drevnikh aktov, sostoiashchei pri Kievskom, Podol'skom i Volynskom General-Gubernator* (Kiev: N. T. Korchak-Novitskii, 1911); O. I. Levitskii, *Piatidesiatiletie Kievskoi Kommissii dlia razbora drevnikh aktov, 1843–1893: Istoricheskaia zapiska o ee deiatel'nosti* (Kiev: S. V. Kul'zhenko, 1893).

24. M. A. Maksimovich, *Vospominanie o Bogdane Khmel'nitskom* (Kiev: Russkaia beseda, 1857), 68.

25. Levitskii served as president of the Ukrainian Academy of Sciences in the 1920s. On his life and accomplishments, see "Levyts'kyi, Orest," in *Entsyklopediia Ukrainoznavstva,* vol. 4 (Lviv: Molode zhittia, 1994), 1269; M. Hrushevs'kyi, "Orest Levits'kyi," *Ukraina* 1–2 (1924): 199–202.

26. F. I. Titov, "Petr Gavriilovich Lebedintsev," *Kievskoi dukhovnoi akademii* 38.1 (January 1897): 133–75; Nikolai Vasylenko, "Akademyk Orest Ivanovych Levyts'kyi," *Zapysky Sotsiial'no-ekonomichnoho Viddilu Ukrainskoi Akademii Nauk* 1 (1923): lxii.

27. V.Ia. Shul'gin, "Iugo-zapadnyi krai pod upravleniem D. G. Bibikova," *Drevniaia i novaia rossiia* 6 (1879): 89.

28. See "Vitalii Iakovlevich Shul'gin," *Kievlianin* (Kiev: I.I. Zavadskii, 1880), 1–6; "Shul'gin, Vitalii Iakovlevich," in *Biograficheskii slovar' professor i prepodavatelei imperatorskogo universiteta Sv. Vladimira (1834–1884),* ed. V. S. Ikonnikov (Kiev: Imperatorskii Universiteta Sv. Vladimira, 1884), 770.

29. Ignat Zhitets'kyi, "Kyivs'ka Hromada za 60-tykh rokiv," *Ukraina* 1 (1928): 94.

30. On these popular-outreach campaigns, see M. V. Iuzefovich to A. M. Dondukov-Korsakov, 10 February 1870, in DAK, f. 301, op. 1, d. 3, ll. 13–140b.

31. Alexander permitted the figure of the hetman alone, which still stands in front of St. Sophia's Cathedral. The episode is recounted in full detail in Faith C. Hillis, "Between Empire and Nation: Urban Politics, Community, and Violence in Kiev, 1863–1907" (Ph.D. dissertation, Yale University, 2009, 146–63).

32. "Evrei i trudiashchaiasia massa v nashem krae," *Kievlianin,* 20 March 1881, 1. Consult also John D. Klier, "Kievlianin and the Jews: A Decade of Disillusionment, 1864–1873," *Harvard Ukrainian Studies* 5.1 (March 1981): 83–101.

33. *Trud,* 11 March 1881, 2–3.

34. "Zametka nanimaiushchimsia na sakharnye zavody," *Drug naroda,* 1 March 1876, 67.

35. "Sveklasakharnaia normirovka," *Entsiklopedicheskii slovar',* vol. 29 (St. Petersburg: Brokgauz-Efron, 1900), 27. By 1887, the sixty sugar refineries located in Kiev Province produced more than one third of the empire's sugar—a proportion that would double by the turn of the century. See L. F. Volokhov, *Sakharnaia promyshlennost' Rossii v tsifrakh* (Kiev: R. K. Lubkovskii, 1913), 43.

36. V. B. Anan'ich et al., eds., *Iz arkhiva S.Iu. Vitte: Vospominaniia,* vol. 1 (St. Petersburg: Dmitrii Bulanin, 2003), 180–83; *Dvadtsatipiatiletie Kievskoi Birzhi,* 90.

37. See, for example, *Appleton's Annual Cyclopaedia and Register of Important Events of the Year: 1901* (New York: Appleton, 1902), 595.

38. D. S. Margolin regularly attended synagogue, hired private Hebrew tutors for his children, and spoke Russian and Yiddish at home. He insisted, however, that his Jewish faith was completely compatible with his Russian patriotism. He declared it his patriotic duty to buy only Russian-made steamships and instilled in his son a love for the Ukrainian countryside, with its "housetops of straw . . . cherry trees, and . . . golden yellow fields" (qtd. in Starozhil, 189).

39. P. Golubiatnikov, *Spravka o khode dela po rasshireniiu Kievskoi kanalizatsii v chetyrekhletie s 1902 po 1906 god: Prilozheniia* (Kiev: Tipografiia Okruzhnogo Shtaba, 1906), 255–62; P. T. Tron'ko et al., eds., *Istoriia gorodov i sel Ukrainskoi SSR: Kiev* (Kiev: Institut istorii akademii nauk USSR, 1979), 157.

40. "Zasedanie dumy," *Kievlianin,* 14 July 1904, 3.

41. "D. I. Pikhno," in *Biograficheskii slovar' professor i prepodavatelei imperatorskogo universiteta Sv. Vladimira (1834–1884),* ed. V. S. Ikonnikov (Kiev: Imperatorskii Universiteta Sv. Vladimira, 1884), 553.

42. "Sakharnoe proizvodstvo i normirovka," *Kievlianin,* 21 January 1894, 1; *Kievlianin,* 18 February 1883, 2; "Kredit i sel'skoe khoziastvo," *Kievlianin,* 24 February 1883, 1.

43. *Otchet Kievskogo Birzhevogo Komiteta za 1902 god* (Kiev: Frontskevich, 1903), 48–51 (quotation on 51).

44. "Osoboe mnenie," 1889, DAK, f. 163, op. 8. d. 55, l. 524; A. L. Tsytovich to City Duma, 20 August 1889, DAK, f. 163, op. 8. d. 55, l. 795.

45. P. T. Tron'ko et al., eds., *Istoriia gorodov i sel Ukrainskoi SSR: Kiev* (Kiev: Institut istorii akademii nauk USSR, 1979), 158; S. M. Boguslavskii, *Sputnik po g. Kievu* (Kiev: L. V. Khmeliovskii, 1913), 10. Criticism of utilities networks, which denizens of many cities denounced as foreign "cabals" bleeding city residents of their last dime, was widespread across the empire. In most cities, however, these companies were managed by French,

German, and Belgian firms; in Kiev, where prominent local plutocrats, not faceless foreign capitalists, controlled the utilities, anger toward the companies became even more intense. See, for example, D. I. Bagalei and D. P. Miller, *Istoriia goroda Khar'kova za 250 let ego sushchestvovaniia (s 1655-go po 1905-i god)* (Kharkov: M. Zil'berberg i synov'ia, 1912), 397; Patricia Herlihy, *Odessa: A History, 1794–1914* (Cambridge, Mass.: Harvard Ukrainian Research Institute, 1986), 191; John P. McKay, *Pioneers for Profit: Foreign Entrepreneurship and Russian Industrialization, 1885–1913* (Chicago: University of Chicago Press, 1970), 100.

46. "Gorodskie i mestnye izvestiia," *Trud,* 16 March 1881, 1–2.

47. "Zasedanie dumy," *Kievskoe slovo,* 11 August 1891, 3; Garol'd, *Nashi Glasnye: Otkrytki s momental'nymi snimkami nashikh dumtsev* (Kiev: P. K. Lubkovskii, 1906), 47.

48. *Kievskoe slovo,* 10 February 1894, 3.

49. V. Gorbunov and D. Titov to Kiev Governor-General, 3 August 1905, Tsentral'nyi derzhavnyi istorychnyi arkhiv Ukrainy, m. Kyiv (hereafter TsDIAK), f. 442, op. 855, d. 71, l. 28ob.

50. Ibid., l. 28.

51. Ibid., ll. 31–32.

52. Kiev Civil Governor to Ministry of Internal Affairs, 12 August 1905, Gosudarstvennyi arkhiv Rossiiskoi Federatsii (hereafter GARF), f. 102, OO, 1905, d. 1350, ch. 15, l. 38ob.

53. N. F. Stradomskii, *Osnovanie reformy gorodskogo polozheniia* (Kiev: Petr Barskii, 1905), 3.

54. DAK, f. 163, op. 8, d. 11, l. 865.

55. "V dume," *Kievskie otkliki,* 4 October 1905, 3.

56. "Duma," *Kievskie otkliki,* 5 October 1905, 3; "V dume," *Kievskie otkliki,* 4 October 1905, 3.

57. "Eshche o progulke na parakhode," *Kievlianin,* 30 October 1905, 3; GARF, f. 102, OO, 1905, d. 1350, ch. 15, l. 163.

58. *Kievlianin,* 28 October 1905, 3.

59. TsDIAK, f. 442, op. 855, d. 391, ch. 1, l. 311; l. 147.

60. GARF, f. 102, OO, 1905, d. 1350, ch. 15, l. 163.

61. D. S. Margolin to Governor-General Sukhomlinov, 20 October 1905, TsDIAK, f. 442, op. 855, d. 391, ch. 1, l. 179. See also Vice Governor Rafal'skii to Governor-General Sukhomlinov, 21 October 1905, TsDIAK, f. 442, op. 855, d. 391, ch. 1, l. 178.

62. "Kievskii okruzhnyi sud: Delo Grigoriia Brodskogo," *Pravo* 48 (30 November 1907): 2660.

63. Ibid., 2658.

64. Ibid., 2659.

65. Telegraph, Director of the Political Division to Kiev Civil Governor, 21 October 1905, TsDIAK, f. 442, op. 855, d. 391, ch. 1, l. 151.

66. Governor-General's Chancery to Judicial Investigator of the Kiev First District, 22 October 1905, TsDIAK, f. 442, op. 855, d. 391, ch. 1, ll. 168–69.

67. "Obvinitel'nyi akt," *Kievskaia mysl',* 7 December 1907, 4; Zionistischen Hilfsfond in London, "Die Dimensionen der Oktober-pogrome (1905)," *Die Judenpogrome in Russ-*

land, vol. 1 (Cologne: Jüdischer Verlag, 1910), 209. A local commission charged with collecting materials on the pogrom, led by Lev Brodskii, estimated that seven thousand families had been touched by the violence. TsDIAK, f. 1423, op. 1, d. 30, l. 14.

68. By 1905, some of the Little Russian migrants who had relocated to Kiev following the 1863 revolt identified as Ukrainians, while others saw themselves as Russian. If self-proclaimed Ukrainian and Russian nationalists now competed for control of the city, both groups tended to define Jews and Poles as "enemies" of the Russian and Ukrainian people. A small group of local intellectuals, including the historian I. V. Luchitskii, the lawyer and sociologist B. A. Kistiakovskii, and A. D. Margolin (the son of the steamboat magnate), hoped to reconcile national ideas with liberal ideals of inclusion, but outspoken anti-Semites dominated urban politics and the city's nationalist movements. On liberal intellectuals, see Susan Heuman, *Kistiakovsky: The Struggle for National and Constitutional Rights in the Last Years of Tsarism* (Cambridge, Mass.: Harvard University Press, 1998); Victoria Khiterer, "Arnold Davidovich Margolin: Ukrainian-Jewish Jurist, Statesman, and Diplomat," *Revolutionary Russia* 18.2 (2005): 145–67. For a discussion of the relationship between various national groupings and right-wing ideologues, see Hillis, "Between Empire and Nation," chap. 6.

69. Governor-General V. A. Sukhomlinov to Chairman of the Council of Ministers P. A. Stolypin, 14 July 1907, GARF, f. 102, OO, 1905, op. 316, d. 999. ch. 39, t. 2, l. 528. For a similar sentiment, see Chairman of the Council of Ministers Stolypin to the Holy Synod, 28 July 1907, GARF, f. 102, OO, 1905, op. 316, d. 999, ch. 39, t. 2, l. 561.

2

Frontier Urban and Imperial Dreams

The Chinese Eastern Railroad and the Creation of a Russian Global City, 1890–1917

CHIA YIN HSU

Mobility in the context of the Russian Empire's expansion has often been thought of as the "colonization" of frontier land, which the renowned late nineteenth-century Russian historian V. O. Kliuchevskii held to be the "basic fact" of Russian history.[1] Colonization was in turn seen by many Russians as an "internal" colonization, involving largely the migration of peasants.[2] The magnitude of this agrarian movement has tended to obscure the emergence of a new conception of imperial expansion in the last decade of the nineteenth century, which focused on the urbanization of the frontier, on land external to the empire.[3] The articulation of this new conception followed the building of the Siberian Railroad, begun in 1892. Within the framework of the Russian Empire, the Siberian Railroad served as a central instrument of internal agrarian colonization.[4] But its builders imagined it as an agent that could unify Europe and Asia and therefore saw it as having global significance. As such, the railroad inspired an urban vision of frontier development. Massive in scope and cost, this urban vision shaped the building of the Siberian Railroad's final stretch to the Pacific Ocean, known as the Chinese Eastern Railroad (CER).

Railroads were key to the expansion of towns and cities at the core and at the frontier of the Russian Empire. In both cases, urban growth brought by the railroad mostly took the form of the expansion of existing cities rather than the creation of new ones; and the scope and direction of this growth tended to be a secondary result of railroad construction rather than the goal of deliberate planning.[5] The construction of the CER departed from this tendency to let urban expansion develop on its own and marked a new, conscious attempt to engineer urbanization. The railroad's builders envisioned cities planned from scratch as an integral part of the railway's operation. In so doing, they also added an ideal of the globally connected commercial urban center to the "island of almost solid agricultural population"—Kliuchevskii's phrase for the successful instance of agrarian colonization—as the developmental goal of the imperial frontier.[6]

This essay focuses on the urbanization of the empire's frontier initiated by the construction of the CER on a thin strip of land leased by the railroad across the Chinese territory of Manchuria. This urbanization project created a network of cities along the railway line that, I argue, were envisioned not only to rival the major cities in the Pacific Coast region but also to create an international commercial center capable of reshaping the order of global trade.

In this analysis, I follow David Harvey's idea of urban space as a "place of encounters" where money—the "great integrator and unifier across the great diversity of traditional communities and group interests"—is concentrated and circulates freely.[7] By "encounter," Harvey means the coming together and the exchange of money, labor, and commodities in the Marxian sense. The CER's planners intended the railroad and its extended infrastructure to enable the encounter of capital, labor, and commodities; this in fact happened. Taking Harvey's definition of urban space therefore allows me to consider as a whole the railroad, its cities, and the concession zone itself—the site in which the tracks and the cities were laid—as the assemblage that make up the railway's "global city." To describe the aspiration it embodied, rather than the functions it in reality performed, I refer to this assemblage—which included Harbin, the railway's administrative center and largest city—as a "global city." Here I follow Saskia Sassen's definition of such a city as a strategic commanding post for reordering the global flow of labor, commodities, and capital.[8]

Studies of the CER by historians of Russia have mostly fallen into two groups: those dealing with the expansion of the Russian Empire into East Asia, and those that focus on the experience of the Russian population in the leased land that constituted the railway-concession zone.[9] Works in the first group recognize the priority given to the "financial and economic strategy" in the empire's expansion in this region. For example, Dietrich Geyer states that Sergei Witte—the powerful finance minister behind this expansion—"like no other official before him . . . understood the economy as a category of power." Geyer underscores the "visionary aspect" of Witte's economic strategy of "reach[ing] out toward China, Korea, and Japan" through the Siberian Railroad.[10] But, in attending mainly to geopolitical concerns, these works do not engage the issue of human mobility linked to imperial expansion. Works in the second group pay implicit tribute to the population mobility enabled by the CER. But, intent on documenting the life experience of the Russian population in Manchuria, these works do not connect this mobility to imperial expansion.

David Wolff's study of Harbin comes close to bridging the divide between these two literatures. Wolff recognizes an expansionary economic agenda in the building of the CER and ties this agenda to the settlement policies applied to the city. By focusing on Harbin, and by pointing out the guiding "axiom" of the concession zone favoring settlers with occupations in trade and industry, Wolff confirms the urbanizing drive of the railroad project.[11] But Wolff reads Witte's emphasis on economic development as a civilian "liberal" challenge to militarism and sees Harbin as the site of a "liberal" experiment. Asserting that the city became a "haven of tolerance" to which non-Russian subjects of the empire were welcomed, and that its residents enjoyed "improved civil rights and political participation," Wolff contends that Harbin was a "liberal alternative" to the autocracy that "hampered the development of civil society in Russia proper."[12] Wolff's study is defined, in short, by issues internal to the Russian Empire and by the historical break represented by the Russian Revolution in 1917. Despite acknowledging the "competitive colonialism" between Russia, China, and Japan, the work in fact does not treat Russian rule in the region as "colonial."[13]

This essay addresses the global and colonial aspect of Russian expansion into Manchuria as an urbanization project. Engaging Russian views of the Siberian Railroad and the CER as connectors linking Europe and Asia, I find this continental and metaphorical divide to be a critical framing vision for shaping Russian identity and policy goals, and for reordering the relationship between subjects of the Russian and Chinese Empires. I argue that the Russian urban project in Manchuria helped shape Russianness as a European colonial identity. Envisioned as "global cities," Harbin and the CER served as places that concentrated capital investment and dispersed this investment to enable the circulation of labor—in this case, Chinese migrant workers. But while this circulation entailed leveling, Harbin and the CER were envisioned as distinctly Russian places designed to assert Russia's dominance in the region.

This tension between the making of a global city and the making of a Russian city was resolved by a type of segregation that might be called "segregated integration." Following European colonial practices of using local labor, Russian builders of Harbin and the CER opened "Russian Manchuria" to Chinese labor, while containing the integrative potential of this mobility by setting up spatial, legal, and economic infrastructures premised on segregating "natives" from "Europeans." Identifying Russians as Europeans, these modes of segregation also helped to identify Russianness with European colonial privilege in China. In what follows, I describe how this colonial identity—based on the promotion of mobility for the sake of rapid urbanization—was also destabilized as a result of the high degree of mobility enabled by the CER and the construction of the Manchurian global city. The rush of Chinese migrants into Manchuria for railroad work raised doubts regarding the Russianness of "Russian Manchuria." Chinese and Russian interaction among the humbler classes caused European watchers to question Russia's Europeanness. The Russian civilizing mission in Manchuria, in short, allowed a modernity of eroding boundaries to emerge so quickly that Russian claims to the civilizing role often seemed precarious.

Colonial Frontier, Global City

Following China's defeat in the Sino-Japanese War of 1895, the Russian finance minister Witte, representing the Russian Empire, concluded a military-alliance treaty with the Qing government. The treaty drew on Russian access to the European financial market to procure loans for the Qing government to pay war indemnities to Japan. In exchange, Witte obtained from the Chinese government a territorial concession for a Russian railway to be built across Manchuria, on the Chinese side across the Amur River from Russia's Far Eastern frontier. Witte justified building the railway on Chinese territory as "necessary for economic reasons," as this was the "shortest route" connecting the Siberian railroad to Vladivostok on the Pacific Coast. He further justified it on diplomatic and developmental grounds, for a railroad in this region would "benefit both the Chinese and Russian territories through which it passed."[14]

The building of the CER signaled a new conception of Russian frontier development, distinct from the more common notion of agricultural expansion and peasant migration. Agrarian settlement was advocated by Witte himself, who directed the Siberian Railroad to organize peasant migration. But the location of Manchuria outside the formal boundary of the Russian Empire presented to Witte an opportunity for a different strategy, one that promised a level of control over the frontier beyond what could be achieved through peasant settlement. This strategy involved the creation of a commercial "colony," not the continuation of agrarian "colonization."

Like many of his contemporaries, Witte believed that the economic aspect of civilizational progress proceeded according to a set sequence of stages. He distinguished agricultural nations from industrial nations, characterizing the first group as stagnant and the second as endowed with "state power" to "extend its activities to all parts of the world and *establish colonies* [kolonii]."[15] According to this scheme, the critical difference between an advanced nation and one that had not yet reached this stage was control over international trade and the possession of colonies. In a memorandum written in 1899, three years after he oversaw the signing of the CER concession agreement, Witte noted that Russia was an agrarian nation and a "handmaiden" of Western Europe, serving it as "colonial countries" served "their metropolises." To escape this position, the memorandum proposed, Russia must turn to the "Asiatic trade" to make up for its "losses in the European trade" and become "a metropolis herself."[16] Believing that state power could be mobilized to alter the course of civilizational development, Witte also outlined a program for making Russia a "metropolis."

Russian advance into the industrial stage had both a nationalizing and racializing aspect. Seen as a trade route, the Siberian line and its Manchurian extension were proclaimed by Witte as enabling the encounter of different peoples—suggesting the erasure of racial difference. Yet the marking of differences in the local populations as racial was more salient in Witte's view of the encounter. Reporting on his visit to Manchuria in 1902, he observed that the railroad "opens a gate for Europe into [a] hitherto closed-off world" of "numerous tribes of the Mongol race" and promised to bring about a "coming together [*sblizhenie*] of the yellow and white races [*zheltoi i beloi ras*]."[17] For Witte, the building of a Russian railroad in northern China made clear both the salience of race and Russian responsibility in the region. Advancing with the railroad, the Russian people, a "European race [*evropeiskaia rasa*]" separated from "the peoples of Asia," would push the border of Europe to "the endpoint of the Chinese Eastern Railroad" on the Pacific Coast.[18] At the same time, "holding in its hands the road along which this coming together [of races] will take place," Russia had "a serious responsibility" for its consequences.[19] Russia's task, Witte maintained, was to stand "on guard at the gates between Europe and Asia that [the railroad] opened, so that it can regulate and direct this coming together in the direction most favorable for it."[20] Thus the encounter promised by the railroad, though to be encouraged for urban development, was also to be regulated and directed, guided by the racialized divide between Europe and Asia. The railroad, as Witte imagined it, would make visible formerly isolated peoples, highlighting rather than erasing their differences, in spite of his emphasis on the "coming together" [*sblizhenie*] the railroad would effect.

Mapped in 1896, the CER line first ran only in the east-west direction from Vladivostok to the last station of the Siberian Railroad. After the Russian acquisition of the Liaodung Peninsula in 1898,[21] a branch line was added connecting Harbin, at the midpoint of the original line, to the Pacific port terminus of Dal'nii to its south, another projected new city. The concession contract Witte negotiated deemphasized territorial acquisition, the critical factor in agrarian settlement. The railroad-concession zone consisted of a strip of land 220 feet in width for most of the length of line—a "right of way necessary for the operation of the railroad"[22] that bulged out at the major stations[23] to allow for the building of a town or city. The railroad was to be run by a private firm, the Chinese Eastern Railroad Company. Created to bypass treaty restrictions against the

Russian state's involvement in the railroad, the company served as a front for the Finance Ministry and stood for Witte's intention to use the concession for commercial development.[24]

The story of the construction of the railroad, as told by a Finance Ministry publication commemorating it, followed the theme of transformation indicated by Witte: from isolation to the "coming together" of peoples. That is, it told of a transformation from a "closed-off world" to a "place of encounters," bringing together capital, labor, and commodities.

According to this account, Russian engineers arriving in Manchuria to survey the terrain in 1897 found the region "in a state of complete disorganization," its population "uncultured" and "very scarce." The railroad's builders faced "extreme privation" in the early days of exploration and construction work.[25] In spite of this difficult beginning, railroad building proceeded apace. The CER Company recruited engineers and technicians from "back home" for the "distant and un-known Manchuria," and Chinese artisans and workers from nearby Chinese cities.[26] In 1900, the railway hired seventy-five thousand Chinese workers from Tianjin alone. Between 1897 and the completion of the railroad in 1902, the CER at times employed more than two hundred thousand Chinese workers at its construction sites.[27] To bridge the language gap, the railroad company built schools teaching Russian to Chinese workers and sent Russians to Beijing to learn Chinese.[28]

Relatively silent about the functions of the Russo-Chinese Bank, the parent company of the CER formed by Witte with investment extended by French banks and credit backed by the Russian government, the commemorative volume nevertheless indicated the importance of ensuring the flow of a Russian-controlled source of capital into the region.[29] The railroad introduced the ruble and strengthened its value over the local currencies by making it the sole legal tender for railway transport. The Russian currency's "final moment of . . . victory" was guaranteed, the commemorative volume noted, when the CER began service and "dictated the fares to the population" in rubles.[30]

The railroad was not only meant to link the centers of European Russia to the major cities on the CER line—Harbin, Vladivostok, and Dal'nii—but also to connect western European cities to the ports of China, Korea, and Japan.[31] Witte wrote in 1892, four years before the railway concession in Manchuria was secured, of establishing a line reaching the Pacific to shape "communications be-tween Europe and Asia to her [Russia's] advantage" and to gain "control over the entire movement of international commerce in Pacific waters."[32] In his memoirs, written after 1907, Witte continued to argue for the Siberian Railroad's cross-continental significance, suggesting that the routing of its extension through northern Manchuria rendered its importance "world-class."[33] Of negotiating the CER treaty with China, Witte wrote:

[A]t that time our great Siberian road was already approaching the Lake Baikal region [near the Chinese border]. . . . Very naturally the idea came to me to continue the railroad straight to Vladivostok, crossing over Mongolia and the northern part of Manchuria. This would lead to a significant acceleration of construction time. So carried out, the great Siberian road indeed became a world-class [*mirovoi*] transport route connecting Japan and all the Far East with Russia and with Europe.[34]

In a report on his trip to Manchuria in 1902, Witte explained the complementary functions he envisioned for the three largest cities on the railway line—Harbin, Dal'nii, and Vladivostok. Harbin, at the intersection of the east-west line and the southern branch of the railroad reaching down to an ice-free harbor at the Dalian Bay, was to become a commercial center settled by Russian "firms and desirable private persons." Dal'nii, the new port city at the Dalian Bay harbor, was to be set up as a "center of international trade" by keeping its port open. Vladivostok, the older port city at the eastern terminus of the CER line and located on the Russian side of the border, was to combine the functions of Harbin (an "exclusively Russian" commercial city) and Dal'nii (an open port).[35] Witte proposed building an "open harbor" to bring in trade from Europe and Japan and enclosing the harbor by customs checkpoints to prevent the goods of these countries from "penetrating" into the interior of Russia.[36] Thus, for Witte, Harbin, Dal'nii, and Vladivostok were levers he could manipulate—or, as Sassen might call it, "nodal points for the coordination of [global] processes"—to produce the conditions he believed most beneficial to Russia's economic interest.[37]

The CER Company acquired support enterprises, such as coal mining and steamship transport, and opened offices in the major ports of China, Japan, and Korea, anticipating that its activities would reach an international scale.[38] In the first years after the completion of the CER, Witte's confidence regarding the railroad's role was matched by the admiration of foreign observers. A U.S. consul who toured Manchuria in 1903 remarked on the "thirty trains running daily in and out of Harbin" and the "splendid cities . . . springing up along the track." Echoing Witte's hopes for Dal'nii, the consul saw in Harbin a city that would become "in a few years not only the greatest market of Manchuria, but . . . one of the most important cities in the Far East."[39] Visiting Harbin in 1904, the British journalist B. L. Putnam Weale registered the high productivity of its flour mills, which were "fitted with the latest American or European machinery," and "producing stuff superior to American winter wheat flour."[40]

Regarding Dal'nii, an article in the *New York Times* proclaimed the port city to be "more perfectly arranged and more suitably ordered for the purpose in view than any other city in the world"—thanks to the "remarkable nature of the Russian undertaking." Cargo could be unloaded from ships "directly on to cars that will run direct to St. Petersburg." Another U.S. consul quoted in the article found it difficult "to conceive of a port where the economy of handling cargo will excel that of the harbor of Dalny when it is completed." The construction of the city of Dal'nii likewise garnered the article's respect. "The Russian officials who designed Dalny" planted trees and gardens and provided for water supply, electric lights, and electric street cars, to "insure the prosperity, beauty, and agreeableness of the city." Certain that Dal'nii was "destined to be one of the most prosperous ports of Asia," the article concluded with the consul's urging that U.S. merchants consider "settling in the Far East" to make use of the "splendid opportunity for American enterprise" offered by Dal'nii.[41]

Russifying Visions, Europeanizing Measures

Witte saw the railroad as "a means for bringing together the European and Oriental nations," and railway trade and commerce as ensuring the "close-knit coming together of nations [*tesnoe sblizhenie narodov*]" and the elimination of military conflicts.[42] Reflecting this view, the CER commemorative volume emphasized the railroad company's friendly relations with the Chinese authorities, its "unconditional respect for Chinese custom and beliefs," and its "tact and [regard for] humane relations toward the native population [*tuzemnoe naselenie*]."[43] But the CER had also "the highest political . . . significance," not a solely commercial one, according to Witte.[44] The CER was a Russian railroad, in Witte's view, brought into existence "in a foreign uncultured land in the shortest possible time" thanks to the "the great patriotism of the persons linked to this task."[45] As a Russian railroad, the CER had a moral purpose: "[T]o serve as an instrument of moral influence" by demonstrating that Christian culture "was more powerful than the culture of the yellow nations, based on idolatry";[46] and to allow Russia to stand "on guard" to "regulate and direct this coming together [of peoples] in the direction most favorable for it [Russia]."[47] As instantiated by the encounter between Russians and Chinese, regulating and directing the meeting between European and Oriental nations often took the form of segregational measures and practices.

Some forms of segregation were spatial. Harbin, located on the bank of the Sungari River, tied the river traffic to the railroad. The city consisted of several gridded sections. The largest, Novyi Gorod (New Town), included administrative, financial, and cultural districts. The second largest was Pristan, a commercial district delineated by railroad tracks on one side and docks serving Sungari's traffic on the other side.[48] At the center of the city sat the railroad station, built in the art-nouveau style fashionable throughout Europe at the time of its construction. This symbolic center of the city faced an Orthodox cathedral in the Vologda style, the two connected by a grand boulevard through New Town. Across the tracks, a long commercial street, nearly tracing a straight line from the rear of the station to the docks of Sungari, marked the center of Pristan. Outside the concession zone, a Chinese town, Fujiadian, nestled against the concession's boundary line, separated from Pristan and New Town by an extensive railroad workshop and warehouse district.[49]

Dal'nii was divided into distinct "European" and "Chinese" quarters. Banks, museums, churches, and numerous other cultural and financial establishments were planned for the European quarter. In the Chinese quarter was to be built accommodation for Chinese workers, whom Witte found "indispensable" for the construction of the city and the port.[50] The largest of the city's three sections, European Town, lay next to the Administration Town, which was positioned to oversee the docks, the train yard, and the railroad station. Both quarters were criss-crossed by radiating boulevards joined by large plazas. The Chinese Town was set a distance apart. On water, the layout of the port ensured the segregation of Chinese from "foreign" ships. "Docks, piers, and anchorages for Chinese craft are to be constructed in another part of the bay opposite the native city," separate from the two-mile shoreline where "foreign vessels" docked.[51] This separation was probably devised to address the different technologies of Chinese ships and steam-powered "foreign vessels," but it also followed directly from the planned division of the "native city" from the rest of Dal'nii.

Some forms of segregation were demographic and enacted through settlement policies. A number of Russian officials called for populating the railway concession zone with the "Russian element," defined as those who could be counted on to "preserv[e] their [Russian] nationality" in alien environments.[52] Witte chose to select settlers by estate rather than nationality, however, giving preference to the "trading and manufacturing class," which he considered more "energetic, persistent, capable of adapting to new living conditions" than other estates.[53] As a result, the "Russian" settlers of Manchuria turned out to include many non-Russian subjects of the empire—suggesting that the urban space of Harbin and the railway concession zone was also a place of encounter for the empire's nationalities.[54] Wolff reads this encounter of nationalities as reflecting a liberal attitude of tolerance toward non-Russians, which Wolff believes was advocated by Witte and his successor as finance minister, N. I. Kokovtsov.[55] But their view of Russianness pointed more to redrawing the boundaries of inclusion than the making of a "haven of tolerance."[56]

Referring to Harbin's Jewish and Polish subjects of Russia, Kokovtsov stated in 1911 that "in our Far Eastern colony," given that the "fierce battle on the basis of international rivalry holds the first place . . . narrow national differences [uzkonatsionalisticheskie], tribal and religious discord among separate elements of the nation, are wiped away."[57] Kokovtsov's statement marked a conscious inclusion of the empire's non-Russians in the Russian "nation"—for he believed that the empire's subjects who participated in the "international rivalry" would come to realize that they were "representatives, not of one or another particular people . . . but of the state in its entirety."[58] But this openness to embracing non-Russians as "Russian" must also be read against the positioning—called forth by the possession of a "Far Eastern colony"—of Russianness with regard to Europeanness and its presumed antithesis, Chineseness.

In a memorandum on his visit to Manchuria in 1909, Kokovtsov asserted that the "character" of the entire railway zone was "completely Russian":

> Russian language is heard everywhere. Schools follow a curriculum no different from those in the Russian Empire; Russian folk songs welcome distinguished visitors to the area, and resound even in schools of the mixed type, such as the municipal school in Harbin that I visited, whose pupils included representatives of different nationalities [*natsional'nosti*], with the predominance of Jews.[59]

Kokovtsov's view of Russianness suggested an assimilationist attitude regarding the non-Russian subjects of the empire. Regarding the Chinese, Kokovtsov pointed to subordination, rather than assimilation and possible erasure of difference, as the mode of their integration in the concession zone. Speaking of the Chinese, Kokovtsov reported: "Next to all this lives the Chinese population, in one way or another occupying a subordinate place as a simple labor force, directed by us and by various newcomers of the white race [*beloi rasy*]."[60]

Russian settlement plans for the railroad concession likewise led to a reconsideration of the alignment of nations and peoples in Dal'nii. In Harbin, non-Russian subjects of the empire were considered by the Russian state as "Russian." In Dal'nii, Russians were confirmed as European by the city's division into Chinese and European sections. As an open port, Dal'nii, unlike Harbin, was declared a city "free to all nations," supporting the notion of international cooperation. With this arrangement, national differences were "wiped away" in Dal'nii toward the making of an explicitly European identity. Russia's Europeanness was asserted by the location of an Orthodox church at the center of the European Town. But a Catholic church, an "English" church, and an "English" chapel were also to be found in prominent locations there. The city was to be governed not by any particular state but by a town council elected by its rate payers, ensuring, in short, the creation of an international city. However, the composition of the government of this international city would be weighted in favor of Russians and against non-Europeans. As noted by the *New York Times* article on Dal'nii, "[T]he only stipulations in regard to the nationality of the members [of the town council] are that two of them must be Russian subjects, and that not more than two of them can be Chinese or Japanese."[61]

Another form of segregation was jurisdictional. So-called mixed courts (*smeshannie sudy*) were formed by the CER company and given the task of adjudicating disputes between the CER company and subjects of the Qing, and by extension those between Russian and Chinese subjects. These courts in effect introduced a separate judicial system alongside the Chinese to govern Russian subjects in Manchuria and ensured the extraterritoriality of the Russian subjects.[62] This helped entrench Russians' sense of difference from the Chinese in part by celebrating the Russian moral and legal order over the Chinese. A local Russian account of the concession zone called the mixed courts "one of the first cultural initiatives [kul'turnye nachinaniia]" undertaken by Russia in Manchuria, echoing Witte's view that European and Oriental nations would be brought together not only in a material way, but also in a "moral sense" implied by the European mission to uplift.[63] The mixed courts contrasted against the "sad tradition" of corrupt Chinese courts, according to this account. Exercising a "humanizing influence," the author asserted, this court system represented "the threshold to a new, happier era in China," when legal reforms following "the European model" would allow the Chinese to "raise high the unfurled banner of truth, justice, and mercy."[64]

At the turn of the twentieth century, segregation by presumed racial categories was often seen as natural and desirable. The *New York Times* report on Dal'nii referred approvingly to the separate sections of the city and the functional efficiency this separation implied: "One sees by [the city map] that each section has been planned to serve a special purpose. Everything has been segregated."[65] The division of "Europeans" and the "white race" from the "Chinese"—apart from permitting a cautious integration, or "segregated integration," of the Chinese into the Russian-controlled spaces—also promoted the Russifying of non-Russian nationalities of the empire, and the Europeanizing of Russian subjects.

The Uncertain Civilizer

Doubts over Witte's frontier project arose soon after the completion of the CER. Russian internal disagreement over policy direction in the Far East turned against Witte, leading to his dismissal as finance minister in 1903.[66] After his fall from power, what might have been accepted as a strategy of deficit financing came to be seen as simply deficits undermining the viability of the railroad and the urbanization of the frontier. By 1903, as noted by the war minister General A. N. Kuropatkin, the CER had accrued an annual deficit of forty million rubles, close to one thirtieth of the empire's total budget that year.[67] Reports on Dal'nii in 1903 suggested that—in Theodore Von Laue's words—the city was a "conspicuous failure" and "wither[ing] rapidly."[68] Other expenses were criticized. The construction cost of the railway and the two port cities on the southern branch line, Dal'nii and Port Arthur, reached nearly five hundred million rubles by 1904. Witte's protective tariff system for the Far East favored the CER and

Manchuria, especially Dal'nii, but, according to Dietrich Geyer, "crippled" business development in the Russian territories.[69]

But it was Russia's defeat in the Russo-Japanese War in 1905 that fundamentally disrupted Witte's scheme for urbanizing the Far Eastern frontier. With defeat, Russia ceded to Japan the southern branch of the CER and its two port cities, Port Arthur and Dal'nii (renamed Dairen by the Japanese). This loss undid much of the preparatory work invested by Witte in the region and removed the possibility of vindicating his vision through the completion of Dal'nii. Nevertheless, the Portsmouth peace treaty was "comparatively favorable" to the Russian position, as Witte, the treaty's negotiator, recognized.[70] The treaty kept the main branch of the CER and its concession zone, as well as the city of Harbin, under Russian control. Witte attributed this outcome to American sympathy for Russia and their caution with regard to Japan. He also referred to the bonds of "Christian unity" and racial membership between Americans and Russians: "I was able to rouse in the Americans the recognition that we Russians, who are related to them by blood, culture, and religion, had come to compete with members of a race that was alien to them."[71] American sympathy did indeed exist. Even before the end of the war, an essay in the *New York Times* advocated allowing "Russia to remain in possession of North Manchuria." The essay pointed to the fairness and benefit of this resolution. To demand the departure of Russia from Manchuria to satisfy either Chinese or Japanese claims, the essay argued, would be a "forcible dispossession of Russia from the railroad itself, a railroad built with Russia's own money, as far as possible on Russia's own land, and a just source of Russian national pride." To insist on this dispossession "would be a misfortune . . . an indignity," as well as "contrary to the interests of mankind," for "to build the Trans-Siberian was to do good. . . . And [Russia] may be expected to continue the good work . . . through the rugged wilderness that lies between Harbin and Vladivostok. In that work it is to be expected that she will be, as she has been, the pioneer of civilization and the agent of humanity."[72]

Another set of doubts over Witte's project reflected concerns over Russians' relationship to the Chinese and the "yellow race." Despite the endorsement of the *New York Times* writer just mentioned, Russians' capacity to act as civilizers—a capacity seen as intertwined with racial membership—was often questioned. Watching Russian conduct at the level of everyday interactions, European and American observers in Manchuria often saw more affinity between Russians and the Chinese, or Asiatics in general, than the racial and cultural bonds between Russians and the West Witte affirmed.

Reporting on the aftermath of the Boxer Rebellion, an article in the *Times* of London noted that "the Russians, especially the officers, seemed to treat the Chinese with more consideration, friendliness, and familiarity than one is accustomed to see elsewhere."[73] An American author, Albert Beveridge, was "startled" by the "mingled motley humanity" at the Russian border of the Man-churian frontier: "The bronzed Korean, the queued Chinaman, and the blue-eyed, yellow-haired Russian soldier arrange themselves on an open flat-car in a human mosaic of mutual agreeableness."[74] Another U. S. writer, H. J. Whigham, found it "rather curious that Russians—even of the lowest order—should allow themselves to be crowded out by Chinese coolies" on the CER's freight trains, and he noticed with "a similar shock" Cossack women and girls "selling bread and 'kvass' . . . to these same coolies at the various stopping places."[75] Beveridge described the mingling as "picturesque" and cast the Russian's ability to com-municate easily with Chinese and Koreans as an advantage, "a valuable amalgam with which Russian policy knits and fuses alien peoples into the Slav metal."[76] Whigham, "much impressed" by the sight of "white women . . . serving out food and drink to Chinese coolies at a profit," believed this "trifling episode" to be indicative of the "extraordinary power which Russia is able to exert over China."[77] Although interpreted as signs of Russian strength, both writers nonetheless saw these instances as transgressions of boundaries they took to be expected.

Other observers found Russians in Manchuria not only racially ambigu-ous but also disadvantaged because of this ambiguity. Writing just before the Russo-Japanese War, as did Beveridge and Whigham, a British-Dutch journal-ist deemed "the Russian [to be] not so sure of his own superiority" at a time when the "yellow race" was engaged "in a struggle for existence with Euro-peans." This was so because "Russia is only connected with the West and not really of it."[78] B. L. Putnam Weale, a British author whose work was published in 1904 and reprinted in 1907, was appalled by the sight of Russians working under a "Chinaman" on a Russian steamship. Remarking that "it is somehow not good for the white man to be the servant of the yellow," Putnam Weale warned: "[T]he Slav had best beware before he is hopelessly engulfed in the bottomless abyss of Chinese ingenuity and silent diplomacy." Judging Russians' frequent and wide-ranging interactions with the Chinese as dependence and weakness, and certain that "Russia has tackled what is beyond her power" in Manchuria, Putnam Weale pronounced the notion of Russian Manchuria "but an idle dream" and "a myth made possible by gigantic bluff."[79]

Some Russians might have agreed with Putnam Weale that Russian Man-churia was "not really Russia," but from a standpoint internal to the Russian Empire.[80] Unlike Kokovtsov, who saw Russified non-Russian nationalities of the concession zone as "Russian," a 1908 publication signed by "St. Kharbinskii," possibly a self designation as an "Old [*staryi*] Harbiner," insisted that of the Russian subjects in Manchuria, "an enormous percent . . . are not of Russian origin." In Harbin, a good part of the city's Russian citizenry (*gorozhane*) were "Jews or Caucasians," the author continued. Harbin's municipal stock-exchange committee consisted, "to a man, of Jews," and its municipal council, of "Poles,

Polish Jews, and simply Jews." There were, therefore, "almost no real Russians [*russkikh*]" in the railway-concession zone, for the "Russian element is being gradually pushed out of here and replaced by the Poles."[81]

Lurking behind these various assessments of the failure of the Russian urbanizing project was the specter of the yellow peril, enlarged by perceptions of the inflow of Chinese labor to Russian Manchuria and the outflow of Russian rubles to China. Though at times approving,[82] alarm often accompanied Russian and general European observations of a common sight: Chinese workers at construction sites.[83] Chinese workers traveled not only to worksites in Manchuria but also across the border to Lake Baikal and Vladivostok.[84] In 1900, a Russian pamphlet warned of "a triumphal march of the yellow race, specifically the Chinese, into the north and . . . eastern parts of the Russian Empire."[85] Speaking of Harbin's commercial district of Pristan, by 1908 a mixed Russian and Chinese quarter, St. Kharbinskii described the crowd there as "wrong"—with a "European element of thirty thousand nearly dissolved" among two hundred thousand Chinese.[86] By 1909, a Russian essay addressing the "yellow question" cautioned against an "overload of the yellow race" at the frontier territory of Priamur'e.[87] With regard to Russian investments in Manchuria, St. Kharbinskii's question, "Where did [the railroad's] millions go?" was anticipated and answered by Putnam Weale in the guise of an interview with his Russian host in Harbin. According to the British journalist, his host asserted: "The Chinese . . . have got all the money. We have been spending millions, hundreds of millions, and what have we got for it in return?"[88] Noticing that in five years since railroad construction began, "two hundred and fifty thousand Chinese have congregated" in Harbin, Putnam Weale imagined that outside Harbin, twenty million more Chinese "are waiting with Oriental indifference, and are meanwhile garnering in all Russia's gold."[89]

The CER urbanization project came to be seen as a burden to the Russian state after Witte's removal from power and the truncation of the concession zone. Addressing the new military and strategic problems following the Russo-Japanese War and mounting dissatisfaction regarding the real and perceived cost of the CER, the Russian government began a new project to build an alternate extension from the Siberian railroad to Vladivostok.[90] Approved by the duma in 1908, the Amur Railroad was to be built on the Russian side of the Russian-Chinese border. The justificatory statement for the new railroad promised that its construction would be "completed exclusively by the labor of Russian workers."[91] Elaborated in an official publication of the agricultural department, this stipulation of exclusivity meant "without the least participation of the yellows," so that "tens of millions of rubles in wages, instead of disappearing into China, [would remain] in Russia."[92] The inclusion of an account of the Amur Railroad in this publication—put out by the Agricultural Department's Resettlement Section for the purpose of promoting peasant colonization of the frontier—was itself a reply to the urbanization push signaled by the CER. With the construction of the Amur line, the prevailing Russian views of frontier development once more embraced agrarian settlement and peasant migration.

Epilogue

Intertwined with the concession zone's urban expansion was the constant movement of people to and from its cities. It was the presence of these mobile populations that many observers found objectionable about "Russian Manchuria." Before 1917, Chinese seasonal and migrant workers in particular inspired doubts among Russian and European commentators regarding the soundness of Witte's Manchurian frontier project. After 1917, large contingents of refugees fleeing the civil war in Russia elicited remarks on the disorder of the frontier space.

Whatever the context, perceptions of excessive demographic fluidity in the region were probably encouraged by the facts on the ground. Recent arrivals rapidly became the majority of northern Manchuria's population after the CER was opened. In Harbin, where Russians concentrated, population growth was marked by sharp increases followed by quick declines. Located in a region whose population was described as "very scarce" prior to railway construction, Harbin grew to be a city of thirteen thousand by 1900,[93] reaching sixty thousand after the railroad opened in 1903. Of this number, twenty thousand were Russians, and forty thousand Chinese. The city's population increased to one hundred thousand during the Russo-Japanese War but fluctuated between sixty and eighty thousand thereafter.[94] In 1913, the railroad concession overall had 115,000 inhabitants—Russian, Chinese, and others—including the sixty-nine thousand counted for Harbin.[95] The sharpest increase in the number of Russians came in the years around the civil war—from two hundred thousand in 1917 to about four hundred thousand in 1923,[96] by which time northern Manchuria's total population had grown to twelve million.[97] Overlapping with these figures are those indicating a high volume of train travelers in the region. The passenger traffic for the CER rose from 442,000 passengers in 1907 to 1,226,000 in 1911. In the war year of 1916, the civilian traffic consisted of 1,786,000 passengers, and, in 1917, of 2,260,000.[98]

Russian refugees, arriving in trainloads,[99] in fact contributed to a more sustained urban growth in the concession zone.[100] But many accounts focused on the poverty of the Russian refugees and highlighted the pathetic and destabilizing aspect of this new demographic shift. Photographs published in the Harbin municipal journal showed refugee crowds gathering before the city-run shelter.[101] Reports in a Chinese paper in Harbin noted Russian refugees seeking work as "coolies," the old and disabled among them in rags and begging—causing "pity in those who see them"—and the women falling into a life of prostitution that "inspired tears."[102] A Russian writer believed that the presence of Russian refugees made the Chinese aware that Russians could be as destitute as the "coolie," thereby ending "the myth of the power and prestige [*izbrannost*'] of white-skinned people."[103]

In the first phase of Russian frontier development, when the physical buildings and railway infrastructure were being completed, journalistic reports of the concession zone frequently expressed awe over the extent and the rapidity of the transformation of this region. Perceptions of Russian economic strength suggested political power and the legitimacy of its "form of government." The U.S. writer Beveridge, impressed by the "extraordinary" building activities in Harbin, noted that "at Harbin and at Dalni, and, indeed, in other towns in Manchuria, Russia appears to be doing with autocratic instantaneousness what other pioneer peoples do gradually."[104] More explicitly crediting "Russia's form of government" for the Russian accomplishment at the frontier, the 1902 *New York Times* article on Dal'nii opined that "there are . . . certain advantages in connection with an autocracy." According to the article, the city, "a Russian achievement on the east coast of Manchuria," was "an excellent instance." There, "the Emperor Nicholas issues an edict ordering a certain thing to be done. That thing is done, done quickly, and done well, whatever the difficulty of the task."[105] The perceived success of Witte's frontier urban project, in short, translated into vindication of the Russian state as an autocracy.

But after 1917, the CER concession zone, the "Russian achievement" in Manchuria, turned into a visual metaphor of the disadvantage of autocracy. The appearance of Russian refugees in tens of thousands in the concession zone every year into the 1920s presented a localized enactment of the Russian state's disintegration, and with it the dissolution of the state-sponsored project of reordering the peoples and the geographical space of Europe and Asia.

Notes

1. V. O. Kliucheskii, *Sochineniia v deviati tomakh*, vol. 1 (Moscow: Mysl, 1987), 50.

2. Willard Sunderland, "The 'Colonization Question': Visions of Colonization in Late Imperial Russia," *Jahrbücher für Geschichte Osteuropas* 48 (2000): 212, n. 5.

3. See Donald Treadgold, *The Great Siberian Migration: Government and Peasant in Resettlement from Emancipation to the First World War* (Princeton, N.J.: Princeton University Press, 1957); V. M. Kabuzan, *Dal'nevostochnyi krai v XVII–nachale XX vv. (1640–1917)* (Moscow: Nauka, 1985); and Willard Sunderland, *Taming the Wild Field: Colonization and Empire on the Russian Steppe* (Ithaca, N.Y.: Cornell University Press, 2004).

4. See Steven Marks, *Road to Power: The Trans-Siberian Railroad and the Colonization of Asian Russia, 1850—1917* (Ithaca, N.Y.: Cornell University Press, 1991), 153–69.

5. For urban growth and the railroad in European Russia, see Daniel Brower, *The*

Russian City between Tradition and Modernity, 1850–1900 (Berkeley: University of California Press, 1990), chap. 2; Michael F. Hamm, Introduction to *The City in Late Imperial Russia,* ed. Michael F. Hamm (Bloomington: Indiana University Press, 1986). For urban growth and the railroad at the frontier, see Adeeb Khalid, *Politics of Muslim Cultural Reform: Jadidism in Central Asia* (Berkeley: University of California Press, 1998), 73, 77; Seymour Becker, *Russia's Protectorate in Central Asia: Bukhara and Khiva: 1865–1924* (New York: Routledge, 2004), chap. 8; Jeffrey Sahadeo, *Russian Colonial City in Tashkent, 1865–1923* (Bloomington: Indiana University Press, 2007), 156.

6. Kliuchevskii, *Sochineniia v deviati tomakh,* vol. 1, 50.

7. David Harvey, *The Urban Experience* (Baltimore: Johns Hopkins University Press, 1989), 175, 178.

8. Saskia Sassen, *The Global City: New York, London, Tokyo* (Princeton, N.J.: Princeton University Press, 1991), 3. Sassen's use of the term refers to the 1990s. Her work shows how a small handful of cities—New York, Tokyo, and London—emerged as international financial centers following "a fundamental transformation in the geography and composition of international economic transactions" (62). Sassen also seeks to explain the concentration of global investment and financial activities in the three cities in conjunction with the technological possibility for dispersing these activities. Looking at this process of simultaneous concentration and dispersal in reverse, I relate the culmination of this process—exemplified by the global control exercised by these cities—to the starting point of the urbanization envisioned for the CER, which laid down a program for inducing such a process.

9. For the first group, see B. A. Romanov, *Russia in Manchuria (1892–1906),* trans. Susan Wilbur Jones (Ann Arbor, Mich.: J. W. Edwards, 1952); Dietrich Geyer, *Russian Imperialism: The Interaction of Domestic and Foreign Policy, 1860–1914,* trans. Bruce Little (New Haven, Conn.: Yale University Press, 1977); David Schimmelpenninck van der Oye, *Toward the Rising Sun: Russian Ideologies of Empire and the Path to War with Japan* (DeKalb: Northern Illinois University Press, 2001). For the second, see E. P. Taskina, *Neizvestnyi Kharbin* (Moscow: Prometei, 1994); Olga Bakich, "Émigré Identity: The Case of Harbin," *South Atlantic Quarterly* 99.1 (Winter 2000): 51–76; and G. V. Melikhov, *Rossiiskaia emigratsiia v Kitae (1917–1924 gg.)* (Moscow: Institut rossiiskoi istorii RAN, 1997).

10. Geyer, *Russian Imperialism,* 187–88. Geyer follows Romanov in this interpretation.

11. David Wolff, *To the Harbin Station: The Liberal Alternative in Russian Manchuria, 1898–1914* (Stanford, Calif.: Stanford University Press, 1999), 86–87.

12. Ibid., 3, 6, 10.

13. Ibid., 2, 176.

14. S. Iu. Witte, *The Memoirs of Count Witte,* ed. and trans. Sidney Harcave (New York: M. E. Sharpe, 1990), 232.

15. S. Iu. Witte, *Po povodu natsionalizma. Natsional'naia ekonomiia i Fridrikh List,* 2d ed. (St. Petersburg: Brokgauz-Efron, 1912), 25, 66–68. This pamphlet was first published in 1889, the year Witte entered government service. See Theodore Von Laue, *Sergei Witte and the Industrialization of Russia* (New York: Atheneum, 1974), 56, 62.

16. "A Secret Memorandum of Sergei Witte," trans. Theodore Von Laue, *Journal of Modern History* 26 (March–December, 1954): 66–67.

17. In B. B. Glinskii, ed., *Prolog russko-iaponskoi voiny: Materialy iz arkhiva Grafa S. Iu. Vitte* (St. Petersburg: Brokgauz-Efron, 1916), 242.

18. Ibid., 242.

19. Ibid., 190.

20. Ibid.

21. Schimmelpenninck van der Oye, *Toward the Rising Sun*, 156.

22. Witte, *Memoirs of Count Witte*, 233.

23. E. Kh. Nilus, *Istoricheskii obzor Kitaiskoi Vostochnoi zheleznoi dorogi 1896–1923*, vol. 1 (Harbin: Tip. K.V.zh.d., 1923), 64, 410–11; Wolff, *To the Harbin Station*, 28.

24. Witte, *Memoirs of Count Witte*, 232–33.

25. *Kitaiskaia Vostochnaia zhelznaia doroga. Istoricheskii Ocherk* (hereafter KVzhd Istoricheskii Ocherk), vol. 1, ed. Kantseliariei Pravleniia Obshchestva KVzhd. (St. Petersburg: Tipografiia V. F. Kirshbauma, d. M-va Finansov, 1914), 14–16.

26. Ibid., 22, 24, 40, 45.

27. Ibid., 22, 24.

28. Ibid., 18–19.

29. Romanov, *Russia in Manchuria*, 67–69; Witte, *Memoirs of Count Witte*, 229, 234–35.

30. *KVzhd Istoricheskii Ocherk*, vol. 1, 22.

31. Ibid., 189.

32. Witte's report to Nicholas II, 6 November 1892, as qtd. in Romanov, *Russia in Manchuria*, 1–2.

33. Sidney Harcave, Introduction to *The Memoirs of Count Witte*, ed. and trans. Sidney Harcave (New York: M. E. Sharpe, 1990), xvi–xvii.

34. S. Iu. Vitte, *Vospominaniia*, vol. 2 (Tallinn: Skif Aleks, 1994), 46.

35. Witte in Glinskii, *Prolog russko-iaponskoi voiny*, 226–27.

36. Ibid., 238–40.

37. Sassen, *Global City*, 5.

38. *KVzhd Istoricheskii Ocherk*, vol. 1, 111.

39. "The Russians in Manchuria," *Times (London)*, 18 December 1903.

40. B. L. Putnam Weale, *Manchu and Muscovite* (London: MacMillan and Co., 1907), 143–44.

41. "The City That Was Made to Order," *New York Times*, 23 March 1902.

42. Witte, *Memoirs of Count Witte*, 237; Witte in Glinskii, *Prolog russko-iaponskoi voiny*, 215.

43. *KVzhd Istoricheskii Ocherk*, vol. 1, 40, 45.

44. Witte, *Memoirs of Count Witte*, 237.

45. Witte qtd. in *KVzhd Istoricheskii Ocherk*, vol. 1, 112.

46. Witte, *Memoirs of Count Witte*, 237.

47. Witte in Glinskii, *Prolog russko-iaponskoi voiny*, 190.

48. See map insert of Harbin in *KVzhd Istoricheskii Ocherk*, n.p.

49. See maps of Harbin and photographs of the church and train station in Wolff, *To the Harbin Station*, n.p.

50. See map insert for Dal'nii in *KVzhd Istoricheskii Ocherk,* n.p.; "City That Was Made to Order"; Witte in Glinskii, *Prolog russko-iaponskoi voiny,* 227–29.

51. "City That Was Made to Order."

52. Rossiiskii gosudarstvennyi istoricheskii arkhiv (hereafer RGIA): f. 391, op. 2, d. 813, ll. 120b, 1220b–124; f. 391, op. 2, d. 813, l. 160.

53. RGIA, f. 391, op. 2, d. 813, ll. 159, 1600b.

54. The "Russian" population in Harbin, for example, included significant numbers of Germans, Poles, Ukrainians, Jews, Latvians, Lithuanians, and Georgians. Wolff, *To the Harbin Station,* 78.

55. Ibid., 103–9.

56. Wolff's term for Harbin (ibid., 4).

57. N. I. Kokovtsov qtd. in ibid., 107.

58. Kokovtsov qtd. in ibid., 107.

59. GARF, f. 818, op. 1, d. 187 (Dokladnaia zapiska [pechatnaia kopiia] Kokovtsova, ministra finansov Nikolaiu II o Dal'nem vostoke, 17 November 1909), ll. 370b–38.

60. GARF, f. 818, op. 1, d. 187, ll. 370b–38.

61. "City That Was Made to Order."

62. *KVzhd Istoricheskii Ocherk,* vol. 1, 43–44; P. S. Tishenko, *Kitaiskaia Vostochnaia zheleznaia doroga, 1903–1913gg.* (Harbin: N.p., 1914), 203.

63. Ibid.

64. Ibid., 204–5.

65. "City That Was Made to Order."

66. Von Laue, *Sergei Witte,* 237–38, 244, 248; Schimmelpenninck van der Oye, *Toward the Rising Sun,* 180.

67. Andrew Malozemoff, *Russian Far Eastern Policy, 1881–1904: With Special Emphasis on the Causes of the Russo-Japanese War* (Berkeley: University of California Press, 1958), 188–89.

68. Von Laue, *Sergei Witte,* 235.

69. Geyer, *Russian Imperialism,* 210–11.

70. Witte, *Memoirs of Count Witte,* 441.

71. Ibid., 441–42.

72. "'Spheres' in Manchuria," *New York Times,* 19 March 1905.

73. "The Russians in Manchuria: Results of the Occupation," *Times (London),* 22 October 1902.

74. Albert J. Beveridge, *The Russian Advance* (New York: Harper and Bros., 1904), 16.

75. H. J. Whigham, *Manchuria and Korea* (London: Isbister and Co., 1904), 82–83.

76. Beveridge, *Russian Advance,* 140–41.

77. Whigham, *Manchuria and Korea,* 84.

78. Wirt Gerrare, *Greater Russia: The Continental Empire of the Old World* (New York: MacMillan Co., 1904), 235–36. On Gerrare, see R. K. I. Quested, *"Matey" Imperialists? The Tsarist Russians in Manchuria, 1895–1917* (Hong Kong: University of Hong Kong, Centre of Asian Studies, 1982), 126.

79. Putnam Weale, *Manchu and Muscovite,* 68–69, 148–49.

80. Ibid., 67.

81. St. Kharbinskii, *Chto takoe Kitaiskaia Vostochnaia zh. d. i kuda idut ee milliony?* (St. Petersburg: Pechatnoe iskusstvo, 1908), 27, 105.

82. "Coolies work[ing] for a few cents a day" stretched the money invested further than elsewhere, as noted by a U.S. reporter ("City That Was Made to Order").

83. See, for example Beveridge, *Russian Advance,* 28–29.

84. Malozemoff, *Russian Far Eastern Policy,* 189–90, 302 n. 89.

85. I. S. Levitov, *Zheltaia rasa* (St. Petersburg: Tip. Inzhenera G. A. Bernshteina, 1900), qtd. in ibid., 190. Levitov's other works on the "yellow race" are *Zheltaia Rossiia* (Yellow Russia) (St. Petersburg: N.p., 1901), and "Zheltyi Bosfor" (Yellow Bosporus), in *Trudy Obshchestva dlia sodeistviia Russkoi Promyshlennosti i torgvlia* (St. Petersburg: N.p., 1904).

86. St. Kharbinskii, *Chto takoe Kitaiskaia Vostochnaia zh. d.,* 104.

87. A. Panov, "Zheltyi vopros v Priamur'e," *Voprosy kolonizatsii* (St. Petersburg: N.p., 1910), 53.

88. St. Kharbinskii, *Chto takoe Kitaiskaia Vostochnaia zh. d.*; Putnam Weale, *Manchu and Muscovite,* 142–43.

89. Ibid., 148–49.

90. See Chia Yin Hsu, "A Tale of Two Railroads: 'Yellow Labor,' Agrarian Colonization, and the Making of Russianness at the Far Eastern Frontier, 1890s-1910," *Ab Imperio* 3 (2006): 217–53.

91. *Amurskaia doroga. Rechi o nei pravykh v 3-i Gosudarstvennoi Dume* (St. Petersburg: N.p., 1909), 47.

92. *Aziatskaia Rossiia, Tom pervyi: Liudi i poriadki za uralom* (1914; reprint, Cambridge: Oriental Research Partners, 1974), 541.

93. *KVzhd Istoricheskii Ocherk,* vol. 1, 14; Olga Bakich, "A Russian City in China: Harbin before 1917," *Canadian Slavonic Papers* 28.2 (June 1986): 141.

94. Bakich, "Russian City in China," 141–42.

95. Tishenko, *Kitaiskaia vostochnaia zheleznaia doroga,* 197; Bakich, "Russian City in China," 142.

96. Melikhov, *Rossiiskaia emigratsiia v Kitae,* 8, 58, 213.

97. This was the figure for 1921. *North Manchuria and the Chinese Eastern Railway* (Harbin: CER Printing Office, 1924), 10–11.

98. Quested, *"Matey" Imperialists?* 225.

99. *"Yuandong Bao" Zhaibian (1920 nian–1921 nian 2 yue),* vol. 11 (Harbin: Harbin City Government, 1984), 43.

100. For a personal account of Harbin's expansion in the 1920s, see Vs. N. Ivanov, "Kharbin. 20-e gody," in *Russkii Kharbin* (Moscow: Izd-vo MGU, 1998), 13.

101. *Izvestiia Kharbinskago Obshchestvennago Upraveleniia. 1922 god* (Harbin: Tipografiia Kitaiskaoi Vostochnoi zheleznoi dorogi, 1922), photographs, 151–52.

102. *Binjiang Shibao,* 10 September 1924; *Binjiang Shibao,* 18 January 1923.

103. Petr Balakshin, *Final v Kitae,* vol. 1 (San Francisco: Sirius, 1958), 101–2.

104. Beveridge, *Russian Advance,* 66.

105. "City That Was Made to Order."

3

The Origins of Soviet Internal-Migration Policy

Industrialization and the 1930s Rural Exodus

GIJS KESSLER

Soviet migration policy as yet awaits its historiographer. This is surprising, given the fact that the Soviet Union represents an exceptional case in twentieth-century migration history in at least two important respects. In the first place, it is a country that managed to largely isolate itself from global migration flows for most of this century of unprecedented global migration. Second, at the same time, it witnessed mass population displacement and one of the most rapid processes of urbanization in the world. Keeping Soviet citizens in, foreign citizens out, and handling the movements of millions around a vast territory were major policy challenges and defining moments in the development of the Soviet social and political system.

This essay examines the origins of Soviet internal-migration policy. Epitomized by the restrictions on mobility and settlement of the infamous internal-passport system, this policy emerged in the 1930s in response to the challenges posed by the mass movement of peasants set adrift by the collectivization of agriculture towards towns, urban settlements, and industrial areas. Challenging existing views of the introduction of the passport system as a move toward a system of "managed migration," the essay argues that at the time no such agenda existed. Rather than reflecting a premeditated set of ideas and objectives, migration policy of the 1930s evolved as a series of measures meant to address immediate concerns, with all the ambiguities and internal contradictions this involved. Eventually, in the postwar period the passport system would evolve into an instrument of migration and urbanization control, but it is important to realize that this functionality was tagged onto a system that had been introduced with a different set of intentions. Unlike tsarist migration policy, which actively steered population flows to achieve certain ends, such as the de-Polonization of southwestern towns described by Faith Hillis in this volume, or the consolidation of Russian rule in imperial borderlands, Soviet migration policy was initially above all one of containment, meant to prevent certain categories of people from moving into certain areas.[1]

Soviet migration policy was formed during the Great Leap Forward of 1929–32—years of unanticipated mass-population displacement, which put issues of mobility and migration firmly on the political agenda. The key was labor recruitment. These were the years of a premeditated, state-led industrialization drive that started from a carefully prepared five-year development plan, the First Five-Year Plan, but soon transformed into an all-out rush for higher and higher levels of output, bereft of internal coherence and equilibrium and propelled through exhortation and mobilization.[2] In a similar vein, an initial intention in the Five-Year Plan to favor the development of collective forms of agricultural production was transformed into an all-out forcible collectivization of agriculture that aimed to eliminate peasant small-holder agriculture as quickly as possible.[3] In conjunction, all-out collectivization and all-out industrialization caused mass migration, the dominant vector of which ran from village to town. Collectivization and the reign of terror that accompanied it led to mass departure from the village.[4] Breakneck-speed industrial expansion came to rely on a constant increase of labor inputs to raise output, and industrial establishments recruited all urban, rural, and other labor they could lay their hands on.[5] All in all, it is estimated that of the 12.6 million new wage and salary earners who began work between 1929 and 1932, over two-thirds, or about 8.6 million people, were peasants.[6] This is among the most rapid processes of urbanization recorded in history.

The initial Five-Year Plan had not anticipated this expansion of the urban workforce, nor the rural-urban migration that fed it. Urban unemployment had been substantial at the end of the 1920s, and it was assumed that this pool of excess labor would cover industry's needs for the years to come. Indeed, planners had expected urban unemployment to decrease only slowly, and the First Five-Year Plan had envisaged some four hundred thousand jobless still at the end of the plan period.[7] Instead, by the summer of 1930 the Soviet leadership saw itself confronted with a full-blown labor-supply crisis. Urban unemployment had disappeared and reverted into its opposite—while the labor exchanges had still been able to meet 79 percent of all requests for construction workers in May, by August this figure had dropped to a mere 29.5 percent.[8] The specter of a labor shortage had been raised, and it continued to haunt the Soviet leadership throughout the 1930s and later decades. It was to prove one of the hallmarks of the economic system they had built, along with a long list of other shortages that later caused Janós Kornai to speak of the "economics of shortage" in relation to the planned economies of the socialist bloc.[9]

When it first emerged in the early 1930s, the labor shortage was perceived as an imminent threat to the further advance of industrial expansion, and the Soviet leadership scrambled to find a solution to this unanticipated problem. It was in the midst of this crisis that Soviet migration policy was born, as the countryside was the only viable source of additional labor reserves of the magnitude required. Marxist analysts of the 1920s had spoken of a problem of "overpopulation" in the countryside, or rather, rural underemployment, defined in the context of the peasant economy as a disparity between available labor reserves and the need for labor input in agriculture.[10] Fantastic calculations were made to determine the number of "superfluous" hands in the countryside, with estimates ranging from nine to twenty million people.[11] As B. L. Markus, an influential labor theoretician, had written in 1929, these "unused" labor reserves might well be of future use in supplying industry with labor, even if the First Five-Year Plan did not immediately require this.[12] To all evidence, though, the time had come, and recruiting rural labor for industry became a matter of the utmost concern from the summer of 1930 onward.

Tapping Rural Labor Reserves

Throughout the 1930s, the single most important consideration underlying migration policy was the imperative to maintain an uninterrupted flow of rural labor to industry. As has been noted elsewhere, for all its reliance on planning, the Soviet leadership never shifted to a planned, administrative allocation of labor resources.[13] With the important exception of forced labor, the Soviet system essentially relied on market forces and voluntary migration to get labor power where it was needed. This was not a principled position but a highly pragmatic and utilitarian solution, forced upon the authorities by the contingencies of a labor-supply crisis they had failed to anticipate and initially did not know how to handle.

Faced with an acute labor shortage, the countryside, with its mythical millions of idle hands, appeared to offer prospects of instant relief. It also presented problems, though, because migrant labor was widely believed to fuel labor turnover. What resulted was a policy that combined an all-out drive to enlarge rural labor supply to industry with a whole array of measures to minimize supply disturbances and curb labor mobility. The underlying idea behind this essentially self-contradictory policy was to encourage peasants to move to town to work in industry, but then to get them to cease moving as soon as they had entered the urban workforce. Efforts at maximizing the supply of rural labor to industry aimed above all to break the hold of collective farm administrations over their workforce. A June 1931 decree on labor migration (*otkhodnichestvo* or *otkhod*) obliged the collective farms to grant permission to leave to anyone who wanted to do so, and to organize the collective farm work in such a way that people with important industrial skills could be missed at any time of the year. Unfortunately, the decree did not specify how the collective farms were supposed to achieve this.[14]

While stimulating rural-urban migration to secure labor supply to industry, the Soviet leadership did everything within its might to curb labor mobility, so as to minimize labor-supply disturbances and other disruptive effects of un-fettered migration. This found its first expression in attempts at transforming construction, lumber, and other seasonal industries into year-round activi-ties.[15] This campaign against "seasonality" was characteristic of the simplistic economic policies of the time: oblivious of practical restraints, and with an of-fensive touch to it—if the seasonality of production in certain branches of the economy caused problems in the field of labor supply, then seasonality had to go! As Kuibyshev stated it at a meeting of the Vesenkha Presidium in late 1930: "Seasonal fluctuations—spontaneous inflows and outflows of workers—we find absolutely intolerable."[16] Crude calculations by the People's Commissariat of Labor "demonstrated" that the elimination of seasonality would resolve most of the problems with labor supply in construction, because it would spread the demand for labor more evenly over the year, thus avoiding the seasonal peaks during the harvest season, when workers had their hands full in the country-side.[17] On 5 December 1930, oblivious of climate constraints, a decree was issued that ordered all enterprises engaged in construction activities to continue work during the winter and to get the workforce to stay on the job.[18]

The regime's efforts at curbing labor-supply disturbances and worker mobility came together in the repeated campaigns against labor turnover. Labor turnover, or *tekuchest,'* was one of the prime headaches of the leadership during the First Five-Year Plan. Not only was it thought to slow down and disrupt the pace of the industrial buildup, it was also seen as one of the main factors behind the recurrent bottlenecks in labor supply. In the eyes of the regime, labor turnover epitomized the much-condemned *stikhiia,* the spontaneity of economic life, which was held to be unacceptable in a state-controlled socialist economy. The press bulged with shrill descriptions of how labor turnover had led to a general state of flux and had turned factories into "transit yards."[19] The influx of peasant labor from the countryside was seen as one of the prime causes of labor turnover. A 1931 article in the journal *Voprosy truda* flatly blamed labor turnover on the rural element in the urban and industrial workforce. Apart from the fact that they disrupted production by returning to the village in the summer, rural mi-grants also contributed to labor turnover passively, through their "class-alien" and "petit-bourgeois" attitudes, not to mention that they counted among their ranks seemingly endless numbers of "kulaks," "priests," "former White guards," "traders," and other "former people," who were actively "inciting" workers to wander from job to job to "disrupt fulfillment of the plan."[20] Labor migration was linked to labor turnover and increasingly portrayed in a negative light.

Balancing Migration

Soviet internal-migration policy of the early 1930s reveals an increasing unease on the part of the regime with the consequences of the unchecked rural-urban migration it had pushed so hard for to secure labor supply to industry. In the political pressure-cooker of the Great Leap Forward, this unease quickly translated itself into the kind of accusations against migrants we saw in the paragraph above, blaming them for disruption of the construction of socialism as an essentially willful act—in other words, as deliberate wrecking or sabotage. The Bolshevik leadership fundamentally distrusted peasant workers, and this had not a little to do with the fact that they came from villages the regime well knew deeply resented the forced collectivization of agriculture. But it depended on them to keep up the pace of industrial expansion, and tension came to a head in 1932–33 during a social, economic, and political crisis in which migration and population displacement played a pivotal role.[21]

The central issue around which the crisis of 1932–33 revolved was food, and with it, food supply. Collectivization had severely undermined the productive capacity of the agricultural sector at a time when the rapid growth of the urban and industrial population had greatly increased the number of mouths to feed. For a while, the regime managed to hold its ground by operating a strict system of urban rationing and by confiscating a larger and larger part of agricultural production. By late 1932, however, the bottom had been reached. Drought and a peasant refusal in the main grain-growing areas to work any longer for the exploitative collective farm system severely curtailed grain production and procurements, and town and village alike headed for disaster. The urban rationing system collapsed, famine raised its head in the countryside, bread riots and strikes broke out, industrial production stagnated, and starving people roamed the country in search of food.[22]

In the midst of this crisis, the regime's unease about mobility and migration grew into a full-fledged security concern, and the strain in migration policy favoring curbs on population mobility gained the upper hand. At the end of 1932, a system of internal passports and urban residence permits was introduced that aimed to enhance the authorities' insight into migration flows and to strengthen their hand in restricting access to strategically sensitive areas. This passport system essentially remained in place throughout the Soviet period, and it lies at the foundation of the current system of population registration in the Russian Federation.

A persistent notion about the Soviet passport system is that it was introduced to bar the rural population from migrating to the towns and to tie the collective farm population to the land, and as such constituted a first step toward a system of managed migration and restrained urbanization. This reading is based on an apparent analogy to the system of internal passports in place in the tsarist period, which did serve the purpose of keeping peasants attached to the land and the rural community, as well as the projection of the passport system's functionality in the late Soviet period backward in time.[23]

As I have argued elsewhere, this reading is mistaken.[24] The passport system of the 1930s aimed to impose qualitative rather than quantitative restrictions on migration and settlement. It was introduced to rid the urban population of people who were assessed to be a security risk, hangers-on to the urban rationing system, or both, to put in place a system to prevent such people from taking up residence in selected towns and urban areas in the future and, finally, to serve the wider aim of improving urban population registration, which was ramshackle to the point of being nonexistent.

Among these considerations, security concerns were by far the most important. The express aim of the passport system, as formulated by the *Politburo* on 15 November 1932, was to facilitate the cleansing of Moscow, Leningrad, and other large cities of "superfluous people, not involved in production or the work of institutions, as well as of *kulak*—criminal and other antisocial elements hiding in the towns."[25] The details were worked out in an instruction of 14 January 1933 that laid down the rules governing the issuing of passports and residence permits in Moscow, Leningrad, and Kharkov, as well as within a ring of one hundred kilometers around Moscow and Leningrad and fifty kilometers around Kharkov. The instruction consisted of two parts; one part that was meant for publication, and a second, secret part that had to be sent down to the local police administrations.[26] The secret part specified the categories of persons that were to be denied a passport and residence registration (*propiska*) and deprived of the right to live in the areas concerned:

   a) persons who are not involved in production or the work of institutions or schools, and who are not engaged in any other form of socially useful work (with the exception of the disabled and pensioners);

   b) kulaks or dekulakized persons who have fled from the countryside, even if they are employed at enterprises or Soviet institutions;

   c) persons who have arrived from other towns or from the countryside . . . after 1 January 1931 without a formal invitation to work at an institution or

an enterprise, if they are currently without fixed work, or if they are working at an enterprise or institution but are obvious flitters or have been fired
[in the past] for disorganization of production . . . ;

d) persons deprived of the right to vote;
e) all persons with a criminal record;
f) refugees from abroad, with the exception of political emigrants;
g) all family members of persons falling into one of the former categories in as
  far as they are part of the same household.[27]

On 28 April 1933 the passport system was extended to the entire territory of
the Soviet Union, with the exception of areas with rural status, save for a one-
hundred-kilometer strategic zone inwards from the western border of the Soviet
Union.[28]

The passport system was a two-tier system of migration and settlement control
in which "passportized" areas were divided into two categories according to their
strategic importance. Major cities, border zones, and industrial objects made
up the first, so-called regime category, where passports and residence permits
had to be denied to the categories of "unreliable elements" specified in the secret
decree listed above. In all other urban areas, passports and residence permits
were to be handed out to the entire population, and afterward all persons arriving in these areas in the possession of a passport were eligible for a residence
permit. It is important to note that these differences in settlement restrictions
among the two categories were never explicitly and publicly formulated but
instead developed as an ever more intricate network of secret instructions and
regulations operated behind the scenes by the police and NKVD apparatus.[29]

In the regime localities, the actual introduction of the passport system was a
large-scale social-cleansing operation, a purge of the urban masses accumulated
over the preceding years of unfettered migration. The operation continued well
into the late spring, summer, and autumn of 1933 and involved a meticulous
screening of the population for "suspicious" antecedents through neighborhood
committees, workplace commissions, and police personnel. Those "unmasked"
as being ineligible for a passport and residence permit were to pack their belongings and leave the area concerned within ten days.[30]

Even before this purging of the regime cities of the first category had been
concluded, passportization was extended to all urban and semi-urban areas of
the nonregime category. As pointed out above, these towns and settlements were
not to be subjected to the rigid form of social cleansing provided for in the secret
part of the instruction of 14 January 1933. Nonetheless, even in the nonregime
areas the police screened the histories of applicants and "unmasked" a total of
423,438 "socially alien," "fugitive" and "criminal" elements in the course of the
campaign. In a secret report to the Central Executive Committee of August 1934,

the NKVD presented the balance sheet of the passportization campaign. The total number of passports issued was 12,006,987 for the regime category and 14,942,572 for the nonregime areas, thus bringing the total population of the passportized areas that was over sixteen years of age to around twenty-seven million persons, or roughly 20 percent of the estimated 1934 population of the country as a whole. A passport was refused to 384,922 persons, which corresponded to around 3 percent of applications in the regime localities.[31]

During the first half of 1933, the introduction of the passport system appears to have reversed the migration current, at least as far as the urban areas of the regime category were concerned. Apart from the expulsions, unspecified numbers of people who apparently had good reason to expect that they would fail the test left these areas of their own accord. An NKVD report mentions figures of thirty-five thousand for Magnitogorsk, fifty-four thousand for Leningrad, and sixty thousand for Moscow, but it is obvious that these figures are only coarse estimates, given the fact that such forms of migration would evidently go entirely unregistered.[32] At the same time, though, migration to the urban areas of the nonregime category actually intensified. This was because people who left or were evicted from the regime areas went to nonregime areas to try and obtain a passport and residence permit there, but also because migration from the countryside would likely temporarily have been redirected to the nonregime areas as long as the purging operations in the regime areas were in full swing. These disturbances were only temporary, though. By the second half of 1933, rural-urban migration had resumed its course, although at a different order of magnitude than before the 1932–33 crisis.[33]

The lower migration rates were not so much a result of the imposition of the passport system in itself but rather of a change in industrial investment policy, which aimed at achieving a more balanced pace of growth, relying less on constant increases of factor input and more on rises in productivity and intensification of existing capacity. This involved a temporary moratorium on labor recruitment and the imposition of a set of controls to keep further expansion of the urban workforce in sync with the industrial production targets as set out in the plan. In terms of labor policy, this meant improving labor productivity and ridding enterprises of excess workers. For the Second Five-Year Plan as a whole, an increase in the industrial workforce was envisaged that would remain well behind that of the First Five-Year Plan, and in construction, the total workforce would even have to be reduced in absolute terms. Apart from an attempt to hold down the rise of the total-wage bill, this policy of restraint was also an effort to bring down rural-urban migration rates to a level well below the mass exodus from the countryside of the years leading up to the crisis of 1932–33. It was intended that the majority of the five-and-a-half million new workers required by the plan would be recruited from among the nonworking parts of the urban population rather than brought in from the countryside. Total rural-urban migration over the Second Five-Year Plan was initially projected at only three million.[34]

Thus, for the first time since the start of industrialization, the Soviet leadership had explicitly formulated an explicit internal-migration policy. It did not contain any new elements but brought together the considerations that had been governing ad hoc policy making during the first half of the decade into a more or less coherent whole. Labor supply to industry was safeguarded by a series of clauses and exemptions in passport legislation, which ensured that rural recruits for industry could take out passports in the countryside and take up residence in the urban areas when and where required.[35] At the same time, the social screening of arrivals in the urban areas and the obligation to obtain a residence permit aimed to prevent unchecked migration and the "infiltration" of strategic urban areas by "unreliable" elements and potential rioters. What had been born out of ad hoc concerns during the all-out drive for industrial expansion of the First Five-Year Plan had now crystallized into an identifiable policy.

Industry Comes First

After the summer of 1933, economic recovery set in, urban and industrial employment picked up again, and so did rural-urban migration rates. By mid-1935, the urbanization quota of four million people eventually set for the whole of the Second Five-Year Plan had already been reached, and the State Planning Commission (Gosplan) predicted considerable "overfulfillment of the plan" if rural-urban migration continued at the current rates.[36] But by 1935 this was no longer a matter of concern for the authorities. The economy was thriving, the country had left behind the unstable and chaotic years of the industrial take-off of the First Five-Year Plan, migrant arrivals in strategic urban areas were filtered for the presence of potentially subversive elements, and, perhaps even most importantly, the urban rationing system had been abolished, which meant that the authorities no longer bore direct responsibility for feeding the urban population and were therefore less concerned with the pace of its increase. As a sign of the times, Stalin boasted at a meeting of Outstanding Combine Operators and Central Committee members in December 1935 that "the population of the towns . . . is growing at least twice as fast as in the old days."[37]

One of the consequences of this loss of urgency was that the passport system was never properly finalized as had been intended. As soon as the main strategic towns and areas had been cleansed of "socially unreliable elements" and the crisis of 1932–33 had abated, the passport system lost its priority status, and the attention of the country's leadership switched to other matters. The active involvement of the central leadership in the passport system effectively ended with the decree of 28 April 1933, which extended the workings of the passport system to all urban, semi-urban, industrial, and otherwise strategic areas and introduced the two-tier system of regime and nonregime areas. This left the police and the OGPU with what amounted to a half-finished system of population registration. The law only regulated the issuing of passports, which was to be selective in regime areas and nonselective in nonregime areas. But no procedures were defined for handling the registration of new arrivals once the system was in place, and it was never defined which settlement restrictions were to be in force in the regime areas.

This lack of central guidance gave rise to widespread confusion and grassroots improvisation by local police authorities in the issuing of residence permits in regime areas. Not only were they left without the criteria, they also lacked part of the instruments to screen arrivals for the presence of the "socially unreliable elements" that had to be prevented from infiltrating these areas. New arrivals were to be in the possession of a passport issued at the place of former residence, but this passport did not contain the necessary information to determine whether the bearer was eligible for taking up residence in a regime area or not. If the passport had been issued in another regime area, the police could be fairly sure that the person concerned had been thoroughly checked and found to be reliable during the phase of actual passportization. But this was not the case for arrivals from nonregime areas, where passports were issued to all applicants, regardless of social background. For a variety of reasons, any incriminating information on applicants revealed during passportization in these areas was not entered into the passport but into a shadow system of card catalogs maintained by the police.[38] For handling residence applications in the regime areas, the idea was that the police would contact their counterparts in the locality where the passport had been issued to check whether any incriminating information on this person was stored in the local card catalog and, consequently, whether the person should be refused a residence permit. But with millions of people moving around the country, this was a task that could not have been achieved even under the best of circumstances.

During the 1930s, such complicated administrative procedures relying on horizontal lines of communication between regions were way beyond the Soviet state's capabilities, and this effectively meant that one of the core aims of the passport system—namely, safeguarding strategic areas from "infiltration" by potentially subversive elements—was not met. This had important consequences, both for the regime's attitude to migration and mobility and for the further evolution of the passport system.

In a letter to the Council of People's Commissars in December 1935, Genrikh Yagoda, head of the OGPU, signaled the fact that, because of the absence of any incriminating information in the passport itself, "socially alien" and "harmful elements," as well as convicts having finished their terms, were able to worm their way into regime areas by taking out "clean" passports in nonregime areas and subsequently moving on to regime areas.[39] The main remedy applied to counteract this seeping "infiltration" was the constant and incremental extension of the regime category to include a growing number of urban, industrial, and otherwise strategically important areas, because this opened the door to the conduct of social-cleansing operations to weed out undesirables in these areas.

As has been shown by Paul Hagenloh and David Shearer, such purging campaigns of passportized areas became the predominant policing tactic during the mid-1930s, eventually feeding into the mass operations against "socially marginal elements" conducted on the basis of the infamous order 00447 within the framework of the Great Terror of 1936–38.[40] In this light, the failure of the passport system to effectively monitor and filter migration flows appears as one of the factors feeding the regime's unease about the building-up of a "fifth column," which has been identified as the main motivating power behind the Terror.[41]

At the same time, the continuing expansion of the regime category also gradually exerted its toll on the supply of labor to industry. The original regime category, as introduced in 1933, had included only Moscow, Leningrad, Kharkov, and their immediate surroundings, but by the end of the decade it encompassed 175 towns out of a total of 931 (18 percent), and 460 out of a total 3,526 districts (13 percent).[42] By force of the instruction of 14 January 1933, these regime areas were closed to all persons with a criminal record, as well as to any relatives belonging to the same household. Considering the levels of state repression and the concomitant growth of the number of inmates and ex-inmates in the course of the 1930s, this alone must have been a sizeable part of the population by the end of the decade. Add to this all the other categories of "unwanted elements" specified in the instruction of January 1933, and one likely ends up with a share of the population that was not eligible for settlement in the regime areas numbering into the millions of people. This cannot but have had a substantial impact on the labor supply. The two aims of the passport system as identified above—namely, to allow for the necessary levels of immigration to the passportized areas while filtering this inflow to prevent "undesirables" from slipping in along with the "desirables"—had come into conflict with each other. The system had become like a snake that bites its own tail, and eventually this resulted in a major overhaul towards the end of the decade, triggered by war preparations and renewed concern over labor supply to industry.

With Japan having invaded China in 1937, and Nazi Germany becoming ever more aggressive in Europe, the Third Five-Year Plan, which started in 1938, again accelerated investment, particularly in defense and heavy industry. As the country began to prepare for a possible war, industrial expansion was speeded up, and economic resources were increasingly diverted to the defense sector.[43] To supply the extra workforce required by this speedup in investment, the Third Five-Year Plan envisaged the recruitment of 3.2 million permanent and an additional four million temporary or seasonal workers from the countryside over the coming five years,[44] at a time when rural-urban migration rates had in fact started to decline. Data from the archives of the Central Statistical Administration reveal that net urbanization for 1937 was well below the levels recorded for the first half of the decade, and this downward trend continued through 1938 and 1939.[45] As a result, the recruitment targets for 1938 were not met, and for the first time since 1933, levels of industrial employment actually fell below plan.[46] This continued into the following year. In the first quarter of 1939, ferrous metallurgy was forty thousand workers short of the planned targets, nonferrous metallurgy was short twenty-five thousand, and the textile industry forty-seven thousand. On average, only 15 percent of recruitment targets had been fulfilled.[47]

In this situation, concern over labor supply to industry made a quick comeback as the overriding consideration shaping migration policy. In July 1938, a permanent commission was established within the framework of the Sovnarkom SSSR, which had to coordinate the organized recruitment of labor in the collective farms on a national level.[48] Lapsing into old habits, a second set of measures aimed at strengthening labor discipline in order to stabilize the industrial workforce and reduce labor turnover. On 20 December 1938, workbooks were introduced, which were issued by plant management and which accompanied the employee from plant to plant.[49] New employees had to present it to their employer before being allowed to take up work. The decree was meant to reduce labor turnover by giving employers a greater hold over their workforce, since they could withhold the workbooks of those they were reluctant to let go. On 28 December 1938, a decree was issued that placed new legal obstacles in the way of workers who wanted to leave their jobs voluntarily and introduced severe penalties for breaches of work-discipline.[50]

Most importantly, however, the regime moved to eliminate all impediments to the flow of rural labor to industry in what can essentially be interpreted as a revival of the internal-migration policy that had been in place up to the crisis of 1932–33. A decree of 27 May 1939 on the "Bazaarification [*razbazarivanie*] of collective farmlands" signaled widespread abuse of collective farmland for individual farming on the private plots collective farmers were entitled to. These plots were meant for small-scale market gardening and subsidiary agriculture and subject to strict limitations in size.[51] The decree claimed these were widely violated. As a result, the individual household economy had come to lose its subsidiary character and had in some cases even grown into the main source of income for the collective farm population. It ordered all land being individually used by collective farmers in excess of the norms to be returned to the collective farms. The use of collective farmland for pasture or haymaking by individual collective farmers was also expressly forbidden.[52]

The intent of the decree was clear—to prune down collective farmers' efforts on their private plots. It is usually portrayed as an attempt to bolster peasants' involvement in collective farmwork, but actual production data, also available to the authorities at the time, strongly suggest that peasants' work on the collective farms did not suffer much from their efforts on the private plot.[53] It makes more sense, instead, to interpret the attack on the private plot in the light of the regime's efforts to boost labor supply to industry. At the end of 1938, Gosplan had launched an investigation into the reasons for the failure to meet the recruitment target for that year. The conclusions of this investigation were forwarded to the Council of People's Commissars on 22 February 1939. What had been found was that an absolute shortage of labor in the countryside was not the problem. On the contrary, the collective farms harbored significant unused labor reserves, and large numbers of collective farmers worked little if at all on the collective farm. Therefore, the report concluded, if the recruitment plan had remained unfulfilled, this could only be ascribed to the fact that collective farmers preferred to stay home instead of going to work in industry; the report attributed this preference to the gradual increase in rural living standards over the preceding year.[54] It was precisely this that the decree of May 1939 was meant to "correct" by making life in the countryside less attractive.

In September 1940, finally, the existing passport laws were completely overhauled, and a new Passport Statute was adopted that considerably reduced the limitations on settlement that had existed under the previous legislation. The decree split up the regime localities into two categories with different limitations on settlement. The strict limitations of the first category, which had been in force in all regime towns before 1940, were now to be applied only in Moscow, Leningrad, Kiev, and other republican capitals, a couple of seaside resorts and health resorts in the Crimea and the North Caucasus (where the country's leaders had their dachas), plus the border zones of the country. Most conspicuously absent in the first category were the main industrial centers, which all fell into the second category, from now on closed only to people convicted for counterrevolutionary or criminal offences.[55]

Everything having been done to enlarge total supply, the infamous decree of June 1940 made quitting and absenteeism criminal offences to be punished through the courts. For willfully quitting one's job without the permission of the enterprise director, a worker was to be tried and, if found guilty, to receive a prison sentence of from two to four months.[56] It was meant to be the definitive answer to the problem of labor turnover, and it closed the circle. The regime had returned to an internal migration policy that again combined the essentially contradictory elements of stimulating rural-urban migration and discouraging labor mobility, but the curbs were much more severe this time. Nevertheless, the authorities continued to rely on the use of market-type forces to effectuate the transfer of rural labor to urban industry and construction and stopped short of introducing outright administrative allocation of labor.

Studying the origin and evolution of Soviet internal-migration policy reveals two essential aspects of Stalinist policy making. In the first place, it was improvisational in character, at least in areas of policy making that did not relate to high-priority, strategic issues. Industrial expansion and internal and external state security were the main concerns of the Soviet leadership during the 1930s and were the subject of deliberate planning and policy development; most other issues were subservient to these goals and were resolved on a pragmatic, largely ad hoc basis. Closely related to this was a second aspect of Stalinist policy making, at least in these low-priority areas: its cyclical character. Alternating between two concerns, migration policy tended to repeat the same solutions to similar problems with a frequency that roughly coincided with that of the Five-Year Plans. The start of a Five-Year Plan heralded short-lived policy initiatives in the one or the other direction, which subsequently petered out and were left to run a course determined largely by contingency.

This combination of improvisation and repetition tended to shape essential elements of the Soviet system in ways that had never been planned and had never been the subject of any fundamental debate. The regime's distrust of the peasants translated into distrust of labor migrants, which translated into general distrust of migrants and mobility. The passport system embodied this distrust, and once in place, its institutional dynamics reproduced concern over mobility and migration, because they fitted badly with the administrative system that had been created. Migration was a necessary evil, but also a constant source of tension and anxiety, and this contributed to a tendency to resort to ever harsher measures to prevent these uncontrollable flows from jeopardizing the realization of the Bolshevik leadership's key policies. Governing a nation in flux was not only a major challenge but also a formative experience with a lasting impact on the nature of Soviet rule.

Notes

1. On the use of religious dissenters for settling imperial borderlands in the South Caucasus, see Nicholas Breyfogle, "The Possibilities of Empire: Russian Sectarian Migration to South Caucasia and the Refashioning of Social Boundaries," in *Migration and Membership Regimes in Global and Historical Perspective,* ed. Ulbe Bosma, Gijs Kessler, and Leo Lucassen (Boston: Brill, forthcoming).

2. Moshe Lewin has called this "the disappearance of planning in the plan." See Moshe Lewin, *Russia-USSR-Russia* (New York: New Press, 1995), chap. 5.

3. Moshe Lewin, *The Making of the Soviet System: Essays in the Social History of Interwar Russia* (London: Methuen, 1985), 105–7.

4. Sheila Fitzpatrick, *Stalin's Peasants: Resistance and Survival in the Russian Village after Collectivization* (New York: Oxford University Press, 1994), 80–95.

5. Paul R. Gregory, *Before Command: An Economic History of Russia from Emancipation to the First Five-Year Plan* (Princeton, N.J.: Princeton University Press, 1994), 130.

6. R. W. Davies et al., eds., *The Economic Transformation of the Soviet Union, 1913–1945* (Cambridge: Cambridge University Press, 1994), 101.

7. G. T. Grinko, *The Five-Year Plan of the Soviet Union: A Political Interpretation* (London: Martin Lawrence Ltd., 1930), 123.

8. R. W. Davies, *The Soviet Economy in Turmoil* (London: Macmillan, 1989), 359–60.

9. János Kornai, *Economics of Shortage* (Stockholm: Institute for International Economic Studies, University of Stockholm, 1979).

10. Lev E. Mints, *Agrarnoe perenaselenie i rynok truda v SSSR* (Moscow: Gos. Izd., 1929).

11. A. Libkind, "Proletarskie promysly v krest'ianskom khoziaistve," *Statisticheskoe obozrenie* 5 (1928): 26–30.

12. B. Markus, *Osnovnye voprosy truda v piatiletke* (Moscow: Gos. Izd., 1929), 31–32.

13. John Barber, "The Development of Soviet Employment and Labour Policy, 1930–41," in *Labour and Employment in the USSR,* ed. David Lane (New York: New York University Press, 1986), 63.

14. Gosudarstvennyi Arkhiv Rossiiskoi Federatsii (hereafter GARF), f. r-5446 (SNK SSSR), op. 12, d. 1725, ll. 168–69; Barber, "Development of Soviet Employment," 52. For the text of the decree of 30 June 1931, see *Sobranie zakonov i rasporiazhenii Raboche-Krest'ianskogo pravitel'stva SSSR* (hereafter *SZ SSSR*) 42 (1931): art. 286.

15. This campaign has been treated in more detail in Gijs Kessler, "Krest'ianskaia migratsiia v Rossiiskoi imperii i Sovetskom soiuze. Otkhodnichestvo i vykhod iz sela," in *Sotsial'naia istoriia. Ezhegodnik, 1998/99* (Moscow: ROSSPEN, 1999), 327–29.

16. M. Rakovskii, "Sotssorevnovanie i tekuchest' rabochei sily," *Puti Industrializatsii* 15–16 (1930): 32.

17. GARF, f. r-5446 (SNK SSSR), op. 12, d. 1737, l. 13.

18. Ibid., l. 2.

19. *Voprosy truda* 6(1930): 23–28; *Voprosy truda* 3–4 (1931): 68–71.

20. Z. Mordukhovich, "Real'nye mery bor'by s tekuchest'iu," *Voprosy truda* 3–4 (1931): 65–76.

21. Davies, R. W., *Crisis and Progress in the Soviet Economy, 1931–1933* (Basingstoke, U.K.: Macmillan, 1996)

22. On the refusal of the peasant population to work for the state, see D'ann R. Penner, "Stalin and the Ital'ianka of 1932–1933 in the Don region," *Cahiers du Monde russe* 39.1–2 (1998): 27–68. On urban rationing, see Elena Osokina, *Za fasadom "stalinskogo izobiliia." Raspredelenie i rynok v snabzhenii naseleniia v gody industrializatsii, 1927–1941* (Moscow: ROSSPEN, 1998). On the collapse of the rationing system in 1932, see Barbara Falk, *Sowjetische Städte in der Hungersnot 1932–33. Staatliche Ernährungspolitik und Städtisches Alltagsleben,* vol. 38, Beiträge zur Geschichte Osteuropas (Cologne: Böhlau

Verlag, 2005). On the big strike of 1932 in the textile industry of the Ivanovo region, see Jeffrey J. Rossman, *Worker Resistance under Stalin: Class and Revolution on the Shop Floor,* vol. 96, Russian Research Center Studies (Cambridge, Mass.: Harvard University Press, 2005), 207–30.

23. On the functionality of the tsarist passport system and its implementation, see Jeffrey Burds, "The Social Control of Peasant Labor in Russia: The Response of Village Communities to Labor Migration in the Central Industrial Region, 1861–1905," in *Peasant Economy, Culture, and Politics of European Russia, 1800–1921,* ed. Esther Kingston-Mann and Timothy Mixter (Princeton, N.J.: Princeton University Press, 1991). The Soviet passport system evolved into an instrument of a policy of managed migration only in 1956, when quantitative rather than qualitative settlement restrictions were introduced for a total of seventy-one cities. See Cynthia Buckley, "The Myth of Managed Migration: Migration Control and Market in the Soviet Period," *Slavic Review* 54.4 (1995): 905–6.

24. Gijs Kessler, "The Passport System and State Control over Population Flows in the Soviet Union, 1932–1940," *Cahiers du Monde russe* 42.2–4 (2001): 482–83.

25. "'Izmeneniia pasportnoi sistemy nosiat printsipial'no vazhnyi kharakter': Kak sozdavalas' i razvivalas' pasportnaia sistema v strane," *Istochnik, Vestnik arkhiva prezidenta rossiiskoi federatsii* 6 (1997): 104.

26. *SZ SSSR* 3 (1933): art. 22; GARF, f. r-5446 (SNK SSSR), op. 14a, d. 740, ll. 101–35.

27. Gosudarstvennyi arkhiv Sverdlovskoi oblasti (hereafter GASO), f. r-854 (URKM UNKVD po Sverdlovskoi oblasti), op. 3, d. 113, l. 11.

28. *SZ SSSR* 28 (1933): art. 168

29. Kessler, "Passport System," 502–3.

30. *SZ SSSR* 3 (1933): art. 22.

31. Nicolas Werth and Gaël Moullec, eds., *Rapports secrets soviétiques* (Paris: Gallimard, 1994), 45–47. Population estimate taken from Davies et al., *Economic Transformation,* 274.

32. Werth and Moullec, *Rapports secrets soviétiques,* 27–34.

33. Based on data in Rossiiskii gosudarstvennyi arkhiv ekonomiki (hereafter RGAE), f. 1562 (TsSU SSSR), op. 329, d. 131, l. 4; f. 4372 (GOSPLAN SSSR), op. 32, d. 139, l. 2.

34. RGAE, f. 4372 (GOSPLAN SSSR), op. 31, d. 396, ll. 1–28.

35. Gijs Kessler, "The Peasant and the Town: Rural-Urban Migration in the Soviet Union, 1929–40" (Ph.D. dissertation, European University Institute, 2001), 184–85, 219.

36. RGAE, f. 4372 (GOSPLAN SSSR), op. 32, d. 139, l. 38.

37. Qtd. in V. B. Zhiromskaia et al., *Polveka pod grifom "sekretno." Vsesoiuznaia perepis' naseleniia 1937 goda* (Moscow: Nauka, 1996), 29.

38. Nathalie Moine, "Passeportisation, statistique des migrations et contrôle de l'identité sociale," *Cahiers du Monde russe* 38.4 (1997): 595–96; Paul M. Hagenloh, "'Socially Harmful Elements' and the Great Terror," in *Stalinism: New Directions,* ed. Sheila Fitzpatrick (London: Routledge, 2000), 297.

39. GARF, f. r-5446 (SNK SSSR), op. 18a, d. 845, ll. 31–32.

40. Paul M. Hagenloh, "'Chekist in Essence, Chekist in Spirit': Regular and Political Police in the 1930s," *Cahiers du Monde russe* 42.2–4 (2001): 469; David R. Shearer,

"Social Disorder, Mass Repression, and the NKVD during the 1930s," *Cahiers du Monde russe* 42.2–4 (2001): 529–32.

41. O. V. Khlevniuk, *Politbiuro. Mekhanizmy politicheskoi vlasti v 1930-e gody* (Moscow: ROSSPEN, 1996), 194–95.

42. Kessler, "Passport System," 495.

43. Alec Nove, *An Economic History of the USSR* (London: Penguin, 1969), 247–48.

44. RGAE, f. 4372 (Gosplan SSSR), op. 36, d. 351b, l. 7.

45. RGAE, f. 1562 (TsSU SSSR), op. 20, d. 171, ll. 8–9. Data for 1928–35 were published in *Trud v SSSR: Statisticheskii spravochnik* (Moscow: TsUNKhU Gosplana SSSR, 1936), 7.

46. Donald A. Filtzer, *Soviet Workers and Stalinist Industrialization: The Formation of Modern Soviet Production Relations, 1928–1941* (London: Pluto, 1986), 127.

47. RGAE, f. 4372 (Gosplan SSSR), op. 37, d. 1030, l. 4.

48. *Sobranie postanovlenii i rasporiazhenii pravitel'stva SSSR (SPiR SSSR)* 34 (1938): art. 208.

49. *SPiR SSSR* 58 (1938): art. 329

50. Filtzer, *Soviet Workers and Stalinist Industrialization*, 233.

51. On the private plot and its role in the rural economy of the 1930s, see Gijs Kessler, "The 1932–1933 Crisis and Its Aftermath beyond the Epicenters of Famine: The Urals Region," in *Hunger by Design: The Great Ukrainian Famine and Its Soviet Context*, ed. Halyna Hryn, Harvard Papers in Ukrainian Studies (Cambridge, Mass.: Ukrainian Research Institute, Harvard University, 2008), 123–26.

52. Institut Marksa-Engelsa-Lenina-Stalina pri TsK KPSS, *KPSS v rezoliutsiiakh i resheniiakh s"ezdov, konferentsii i plenumov TsK*, vol. 2, 1925–53 (Moscow: Gosudarstvennoe izdatel'stvo politicheskoi literatury, 1953), 939–45.

53. Davies et al., *Economic Transformation*, 286–89.

54. RGAE, f. 4372 (Gosplan SSSR), op. 36, d. 351b, ll. 7, 18–20.

55. *SPiR SSSR* 24 (1940): art. 591; GARF, f. r-9401 (NKVD SSSR), op. 12, d. 233, tom 1, ll. 1–65; Moine, "Passeportisation," 597.

56. Filtzer, *Soviet Workers and Stalinist Industrialization*, chap. 9.

4

Migration Controls in Soviet and Post-Soviet Moscow

From "Closed City" to "Illegal City"

MATTHEW LIGHT

The post-Soviet period has seen Moscow transformed into a hub of domestic and international migration, and the former Soviet capital has become an increasingly multiethnic metropolis. Yet, the governance of migration to contemporary Moscow has been marked by the city government's overt and covert attempts to limit the rights of new residents of the city.

This essay analyzes significant differences between Soviet and post-Soviet residence policies in the city. It is based on a comparison of historical materials and information gleaned from interviews and other field research conducted in Moscow in 2003–4 and 2005–6. Soviet migration policies were highly centralized and overtly repressive: the Soviet government restricted residence in Moscow to promote national policy objectives, such as rationing of housing and consumer goods, as well as population surveillance. While this central, all-Union system has collapsed, it has not been replaced by a regime of free and orderly migration; the city government now seeks to limit the rights of migrants and harasses many non-Russian ethnic groups. Moreover, techniques of controlling migration have also changed. In Soviet Moscow, residence controls were integrated into the administration of a functioning police state. In post-Soviet Moscow, the city faces a much larger pool of potential migrants and keeps them in check by deploying a police force whose propensity for abuse and corruption has dramatically increased since the Soviet period.

Post-Soviet Moscow's residence policies have created a de facto urban citizenship that is implemented through tacit municipal policies and enforced by police and other city officials. This de facto Moscow citizenship reflects the economic and political chasm that separates the capital city from the rest of Russia. It also reflects post-Soviet political realities, in which the fiscal incentives for Moscow to restrict entry have increased, and the Kremlin has been largely unwilling to protect the rights of migrants in the capital. For an individual Russian or other post-Soviet citizen who moves to Moscow, all this means that the right to live in the metropolis of Eurasia has become more tenuous, as well as highly dependent on official, or unofficial, toleration by the authorities. Contemporary Moscow resembles less the "closed city" of the Soviet era than it does an "illegal city"—a kind of metropolis found in contemporary developing countries in which a large portion of the population is unwelcome and subject to official sanctions for their mere presence.

Historical Context: Traditional Governance and Changing Realities of Migration to Moscow

In all three phases of the recent Russian state—imperial, Soviet, and post-Soviet—migration to Moscow has been highly regulated. In the late imperial period, complex residence rules were applied to the country's two capitals, Moscow and St. Petersburg, whether to limit settlement by disfavored groups or to encourage settlement by some favored ones (such as foreign specialists and entrepreneurs).[1] Indeed, as Faith Hillis argues in chapter 1 of this volume, the imperial government also deployed migration policy in other major cities in support of specific policy goals, as in its attempts to "de-Polonize" Kiev by encouraging Jewish and Ukrainian settlement in the city.

Soviet policies on residence in Moscow, like tsarist ones, made special provisions for specific categories of potential migrants. However, Soviet-era Moscow residence controls formed part of a monumental bureaucratic effort to control population mobility in the USSR, and they ultimately achieved a level of systematization never attained before the Revolution. Gijs Kessler, in chapter 3 of this volume, analyzes the creation of Soviet internal-migration controls in the 1930s and argues that they should be understood as an ad hoc process that responded to twin, contradictory imperatives: the absolute need to guarantee an adequate flow of labor from the countryside into the factories of the rapidly industrializing USSR, and the government's desire to filter new urban residents for political reliability and overall desirability. Kessler offers a much-needed reminder that systems of migration control, including the Soviet one, do not come into being fully formed, as part of some master plan; they reflect affirmative policy goals, sometimes including the encouragement of desired forms of mobility, and not simply a desire to restrict all mobility. With this caveat in mind, this essay is primarily concerned to establish and delineate contrasts between Soviet migration policies as they existed in the last decades of the USSR and those that took shape in the post-Soviet period. For this purpose, a certain degree of stylization of the Soviet migration system is necessary and inevitable.

The institutions and techniques of late-Soviet internal-migration control have been described extensively in existing scholarly literature.[2] The main administrative device for the regulation of internal migration was the so-called internal passport, an identity document that entitled the bearer to reside in most urban areas. Urban residents were also required to obtain a document known as a *propiska,* often translated as "residence permit," which authorized them to live in a particular city and at a particular address. The Soviet web of residence controls thus came to be known as "the passport-*propiska* system." Moreover, major cities and some other sensitive regions were designated "regime areas" in which residence was subject to additional restrictions.

Regulation of settlement in Moscow constituted a special case even within this restricted category of "regime cities." Soviet policies on grants of Moscow *propiska* were intended to limit the number of new residents, to regulate their characteristics, and to maintain effective police surveillance of the population. As the Soviet capital and official showcase of world socialism, Moscow received urban amenities, infrastructure, and consumer goods that were unparalleled elsewhere in the country.[3] Limiting the city's population growth was in effect a way to ration these amenities.[4]

Soviet restrictions on migration to Moscow also had an explicitly political function. Thus, from the early 1930s, police were instructed to deny *propiska* in Moscow (and a few other key cities) to *kulaks,* "class enemies," ex-convicts, willfully unemployed "parasites," and other disfavored social groups.[5] For someone moving to Moscow from outside the city, an application for a new Moscow *propiska* automatically triggered a police investigation of the applicant—a kind of security clearance. In addition, even someone holding a valid Moscow *propiska* was subject to eviction if he or she was found occupying particular living quarters other than those listed on the *propiska.* This policy enforced the landlord's (i.e., the state's) control of the use of its property and also forced citizens to reside where they were registered, thus ensuring that the police could always find them.

The Soviet government used direct and indirect methods to implement policies on Moscow residence.[6] The main *direct* mechanism was police enforcement of the passport-*propiska* system. Compared with today's, the relatively effective and honest police force of Soviet Moscow facilitated such enforcement. While there was significant unauthorized residence in the city, the blatantly criminal methods of moving to Moscow (such as bribes to officials, forged documents, and clandestine residence in the city) were less widespread during the Soviet period; less confrontational methods (such as fictitious marriages to *propiska*-holders, which conferred a *propiska* on the new spouse) were more common. Actually bribing officials to obtain the right documents, or to overlook their absence, entailed a high risk of detection and punishment.[7] Moreover, the police were aided by apartment-building managers, known as *upravdomy*, who reported on unauthorized residents; other informants and anonymous denunciations also aided the police.[8]

The Soviet government also used *indirect* methods of migration control involving the city's housing stock and the labor market. Since most people received living quarters through their employer, obtaining housing was dependent on having a legitimate job in the city.[9] As for employment, because of the city's perennial labor shortage, "temporary" workers known as *limitchiki* were admitted to Moscow without the right to a permanent *propiska* in the city.[10] Although they were Soviet citizens, the *limitchiki* were essentially internal guest workers, not unlike the foreign guest workers used by Western countries in the postwar decades.

In addition to government controls over migration, background demographic conditions favored Soviet policies to limit the growth of Moscow. One was the relatively limited supply of potential migrants, at least in contrast to the post-Soviet period. Migrants to Moscow during the early Soviet period were mainly peasants from the villages of Central European Russia.[11] Unlike today, Central Asia and the Caucasus contributed relatively few migrants to Soviet Moscow. Ironically, although Moscow was the capital of a multiethnic state, the city's population remained overwhelmingly ethnically Russian through the end of Soviet rule.

In the contemporary period, these supporting factors have been reversed, and post-Soviet migration controls operate in a larger, more diverse, and richer Moscow than before. All these changes impede efforts to restrict migration into the city. Thus, in the thirteen years between the 1989 and 2002 censuses, even as Russia's population declined, Moscow's recorded population increased from 8.5 to almost 10.5 million—growth that is entirely attributable to net in-migration from Russia and other ex-Soviet republics. Moreover, Moscow is now a center of undocumented international migration. In the early 2000s, an estimated one million undocumented foreign-labor migrants (mostly from the CIS countries) resided in the city, constituting about 10 percent of its population.[12]

Moscow's attractiveness to migrants is explained by pull and push factors. Since the fall of the Soviet Union, Moscow has become the financial center of the post-Soviet region. The city's relative wealth has actually increased, compared with the rest of Russia and the post-Soviet region more generally. Moscow's income per capita is higher than in any other region and almost four times higher than the national average.[13] The city also boasts a relatively tight labor market.[14] Thus, Moscow is no longer a socialist capital but a wealthy financial and business center that attracts unemployed people from its impoverished hinterland. Not for nothing do Russians call Moscow "a state within a state": its standard of living is more similar to that of some European Union member states, such as Greece or Portugal, than to Russia's other provinces.

Internal demographic factors also create a demand for labor migrants. Because of Russia's shrinking population and the city's own low birthrate, Moscow must "import" new workers from outside Russia, especially from Central Asia.[15] At the same time, post-Soviet political turmoil and economic collapse in much of Russia and the rest of the former Soviet Union (FSU) have drawn many nonethnic Russians into long-distance migration. Because Moscow is the main destination for these non-Russians, it has become more multiethnic than ever before in its history. In addition, many of these labor migrants are undocumented, and Moscow now has a large population of such unauthorized foreign nationals. To take only a few examples, of the estimated fifty to one hundred thousand Moldovan citizens residing in Russia illegally, three quarters are believed to live in Moscow or its region.[16] The city now also boasts large populations from the South Caucasus and Central Asia. While the exact population statistics are disputed, it is clear that many are undocumented.[17] In short, Moscow has become a multicultural immigrant metropolis, yet this transformation has been met with deep ambivalence by the city's existing population and the municipal government.

Migrants fill clear ethnic and migrant niches in the economy. Foreign guest workers work in a range of low-wage jobs in outdoor markets and unlicensed factories. Tajiks and other Central Asians are concentrated in heavy construction work, often living in appalling conditions at construction sites.[18] Migrants to Moscow also create their own self-sustaining informal economy. Some forms of business—such as the markets where many Muscovites shop for groceries, inexpensive clothing, and home wares—are dominated by ethnic cartels, which sometimes use force to maintain their control.[19] It is important to note that non-Russian migrants do not dominate all organized crime in Moscow. However, the growth of such an informal migrant economy means that migration to Moscow cannot be managed effectively by regulating formal employment, in contrast to the Soviet period.[20]

Moscow's migration boom raises the question of who benefits from it, which in turn helps explain how it is regulated. Some private actors clearly profit, such as employers and owners of rental housing properties. Yet, migrants themselves face severe exploitation. The pervasive use of undocumented immigrants in entire segments of the economy, notably construction, has led to repressive labor practices, overcrowded living quarters, and other forms of squalor. Moreover, the city government itself, as a public provider of social services, claims that increased migration presents it with fiscal problems. Compared to most if not all other Russian regions, Moscow provides superior public services, such as health care and education.[21] At the same time, Moscow is the most substantial regional "donor" to the federal budget, meaning that the city contributes indirectly to the budgets of other regions and funding services used by their residents. In addition, the bulk of the city's tax base depends on the oil and gas companies headquartered there, rather than on taxes on individuals and small businesses.[22] In consequence, the Moscow city government perceives new residents (at least poor ones) as a drain on the public purse because they require services while providing little additional tax revenue in return.[23]

In short, Moscow needs migrant labor, but its government does not want to accept the social charges that come with the mostly poor people who provide this labor. The next section outlines the city's response to this dilemma, which has primarily focused on limiting the rights of migrants.

The City Government's Response to Post-Soviet Migration: Accept the Rich, Discourage the Rest

Under the Russian constitution, all Russian citizens have the right to reside anywhere in Russia, and the regulation of mobility is a matter of federal jurisdiction. Citizens are still required to hold, and keep with them, their "internal passports," and to register their place of residence (known as "permanent registration") or place of stay ("temporary registration") with the police. Such "registration," however, is now supposed to be purely for purposes of information—not a privilege to be withheld by the authorities. In particular, the regulation of internal and external migration is constitutionally subject to exclusive federal jurisdiction, and the country's regions (including Moscow) do not have the legal right to restrict mobility, whether of citizens or foreigners.

Yet, despite the Russian government's official allegiance to the principle of freedom of movement and the supposedly "informational" character of registration, Moscow has restricted registration through various explicit and tacit municipal policies. The city has also encumbered access to temporary residence, while simultaneously stepping up pressure on the unregistered population, in effect "illegalizing" such people, even if they are Russian citizens. The following discussion describes these municipal policies and assesses their significance.

A path-breaking study charted Moscow's efforts to restrict migration in the 1990s.[24] At one point, the city attempted to impose exorbitant fees on temporary registration in order to place it beyond the reach of many migrants. The registration fee was graduated depending on whether the migrant was arriving from the Moscow region, elsewhere in Russia, or outside Russia.[25] This policy, however, was struck down by Russia's Constitutional Court in 1998. Moscow then began relying on other restrictive mechanisms that it hoped would withstand judicial scrutiny.

Thus, after the 1999 explosions in Moscow apartment buildings that were attributed to Chechen terrorist attacks, Mayor Luzhkov issued decrees that registrants must produce proof of employment, tax receipts, and a residential lease in order to receive a temporary permit.[26] Since many landlords refuse to provide tenants with a lease (often because they are afraid of extortion by the city administration or police), the tenants remain unregistered. The migrant—potentially a Russian citizen—then finds that his or her very presence in the city becomes a de facto violation of the law. Such a person cannot engage in many everyday legal acts, such as signing a contract—even to work.[27]

The city also sought to impose a municipal penalty of expulsion for violations of its registration rules. This penalty is a violation of Russian law, under which only "administrative" fines may be imposed for violations of the registration requirement.[28] In addition, for a time the city also attempted to use minimum-housing-space requirements to limit registration in apartments, even if the apartment was privately owned and the owner was attempting to register his or her own family members. It also all but denied medical care and education to persons without Moscow permanent registration, even Russian citizens with registration in other regions. These requirements were, however, struck down in 2000 by order of a city court upon a complaint filed by the legal aid organization Grazhdanskoe Sodeistvie (Civil Support).[29]

In addition, the national system of residential registration, which distinguishes between permanent and temporary registration, has led to extremely perverse outcomes in Moscow, mainly because of the role of real-estate ownership in securing permanent registration. Neither the national policy nor the city's 2004 residence-registration rules, as codified by a decree of the Moscow government, formally require that a registrant own real estate in Moscow to receive permanent registration there.[30] In practice, however, property owners are usually willing to provide permanent registration at their property only to their own close relatives. Even if a landlord is willing to cooperate in the registration process, the tenant's registration is automatically limited to the period of the lease. While such a distinction exists in other regions, given Moscow's role as the migration center of the country and the gap between Moscow real-estate prices and those in other parts of Russia, its consequences are particularly serious for Russian citizens from elsewhere wishing to relocate to Moscow. Even if a Russian citizen sells his or her apartment in another region, he or she frequently finds it impossible to acquire property in Moscow and is therefore doomed to temporary registration (or no registration).

This section has addressed efforts by the government of Moscow to regulate residence in the city and how these efforts have affected people's right to live and work in the Russian capital. In practice, however, the ability to exercise a right depends not only on legal texts or even court decisions interpreting them but also on day-to-day enforcement practices. The next section outlines some of the abuses that restrictive in-migration policies in Moscow have spawned and argues that such abuses at least to some extent take place with the tacit acquiescence of the city and federal authorities.

Consequences of Moscow Migration Restrictions in the Post-Soviet Period: Corruption, Ethnic Discrimination, and the State's Response

In the Soviet period, migration was controlled through proactive, administrative techniques based on the regulation of workplace, social services, and housing. In the post-Soviet period, it is controlled by reactive police techniques that have been accompanied by mass corruption, ethnic discrimination, and physical violence. These abuses, in turn, have pushed the Russian government toward some tentative and partial efforts at reform of migration policy.

With the privatization of housing and the disappearance of the *upravdomy* (apartment-building superintendents), the city's ability to use housing for migration enforcement has been drastically curtailed.[31] In response, the Moscow government has shifted increasingly to more reactive and unsystematic methods of enforcing policy that basically involve finding unregistered persons in flagrante delicto. Three methods in particular have been deployed: police checks of people's identity documents in public places; raids on premises (such as construction sites) harboring unregistered Russian citizens or undocumented foreign guest workers; and deployment of law-enforcement personnel at transit hubs.

While all these methods existed in the Soviet Union, the systematic, routine deployment of police in public spaces to conduct document sweeps is a post-Soviet phenomenon. The practice seems to have begun in 1993 (a date that corresponds closely to the attempts at liberalization of Russia's internal-mobility laws) and intensified in 1997.[32] Such checks are now a regular feature of Moscow life. They occur on the street and especially in contained spaces such as metro and railway stations that combine a constant flow of pedestrians with limited exits. These methods represent an extralegal extension of police power to investigate crimes. Indeed, according to a lawyer working for one of Russia's leading migrant organizations, the Forum of Migrant Organizations, they are flagrant violations of Russian law.[33] The police also conduct raids against sites where undocumented migrants are known to be concentrated, such as the trailers and construction sites where most of Moscow's Tajik construction workers reside during their stays in the city. Police raids are often accompanied by brazen attempts at extortion, and they are sometimes even orchestrated by employers as a way of disciplining recalcitrant laborers.[34]

While all migration-control systems are susceptible to rights abuse and corruption, in Moscow such corruption has taken on a highly systemic character and frequently involves networks of law enforcement and private businesses operating in tandem. For example, there are businesses that provide identity documents (such as Russian passports, visas, migration cards, or registration stamps) in exchange for payment. By definition, this kind of business requires official wrongdoing—some official has to supply the documents. Advertisements for businesses that provide official documents are publicly displayed in places such as subway cars, complete with phone numbers and other contact details, apparently without any fear of police investigation. Sometimes the businesses actually record the client's registration in official databases, usually in exchange for a higher fee. According to one respondent, a call to one of these businesses elicited the information that for a price of five hundred rubles, the registration provided would be genuine—that is, recorded in the city's computer database.[35] A related form of corruption is police extortion to overlook migration and residence violations. For example, a police officer may stop a person (even a Russian citizen) in a metro station and find that he or she lacks Moscow registration, and then receive a bribe to release the "suspect."

Finally, some people also pay bribes so that police and other officials will actually enforce the law. Thus, employers of undocumented workers arrange police raids on their premises to remove troublesome or insubordinate foreign workers (who can then be deported), and thereby intimidate other employees. This method of labor coercion is said to be common on construction sites and in unlicensed factories.[36]

Official corruption in migration enforcement is accompanied by the targeting of people on ethnic grounds. Perhaps the most glaring example of ethnically based abuse involves the ethnic Chechen population of Moscow, which numbers "several hundred thousand," according to unnamed Russian government sources quoted by the United Nations. It has been virtually impossible for most of the Chechen community to obtain either permanent or temporary registration in Moscow. Even when such registration is granted, Chechens are often subject to a special requirement that it be renewed monthly.[37]

The position of Chechens in Moscow has become increasingly fraught during the post-Soviet period, during which the Chechen population of the city has grown, even in the face of continuing official and popular hostility to their presence. This hostility can be linked to the separatist movement in Chechnya, with which Russian federal forces fought two brief wars, in 1995–96 and 1999–2000, and which has also involved terrorist attacks in Moscow and other parts of Russia. After each such attack, Chechen residents of the city have been subjected to particularly severe abuse. Thus, after the bombings of a Moscow metro station and apartment buildings in August and September 1999 and the renewal of hostilities in Chechnya later that year, the Moscow authorities carried out mass detentions and arrests of Chechens (as well as persons belonging to the closely related Ingush ethnic group) as the federal government stood by.[38] A similar pattern of intensifying harassment of Chechens has occurred after each major terrorist incident in Moscow up to the present.[39]

This evidence suggests that the Moscow government is attempting to discourage permanent Chechen resettlement in Moscow. According to the same source, Moscow authorities have admitted in private conversations that the arrest sweeps and refusal to register Chechens had been ordered by the city government.[40] The U.N. High Commissioner for Refugees reports that Russian authorities say openly that Chechen internally displaced persons are a "destabilizing factor" in their host regions.[41] Interviews in Moscow support the conclusion that the Moscow government shares the federal authorities' desire to prevent the formation of a permanent Chechen community in Moscow.[42]

Members of other Caucasian ethnic groups in Moscow, including Armenians and Azeris, face similar (albeit less extreme) police harassment, as do all visible minorities—and indeed, to a lesser extent, anyone (including Slavic-looking Russians) who appears to be from out of town. As I have argued in detail elsewhere, such practices stem from a combination of factors: opportunistic corruption by police officers (which is stimulated by the collapse of police salaries in the post-Soviet period); the unwillingness of ordinary Muscovites and the city government to accept the creation of a permanently multiethnic milieu in the city; and, on the part of the city and national administrations, unwillingness to address the problems of corruption and abuse within the police.[43] Ironically, brazen police abuse of citizens in public was less common in the Soviet Union than today. Thus, some aspects of the city government's policies—such as the harassment of Caucasian people, especially Chechens— seem designed to limit the transformation of the city from an overwhelmingly Russian city into a more ethnically diverse one.

The city government has created a system of migration enforcement in which corruption and abuse are tacitly permitted in order to limit residence rights in Moscow, including the rights of Russian citizens. But since the city government lacks the administrative tools of the Soviet police state, the strategy for achieving these objectives has essentially relied on mass police harassment and abuse of migrants.

Since the Moscow government does not have the constitutional power to limit migration, the question naturally arises: How has the Russian federal government responded to Moscow's legal (and extralegal) overreaching? In this regard, the situation is complex, but in general, during the presidencies of Boris Yeltsin (1991–99) and Vladimir Putin (1999–2008), the federal executive appeared willing to tolerate many violations of migrants' rights. And while Russian courts sometimes issued rulings intended to curb such rights violations, they achieved only limited success in correcting them. More recently, however, there have been some indications that the Kremlin has begun to reconsider its approach to migration issues and to police corruption and malfeasance.

The post-Soviet system of Moscow migration practices took shape in the 1990s, during the Yeltsin presidency. Although President (now Prime Minister) Putin publicly declared his goal of bringing regional policies into conformity with national legislation, representatives of human-rights organizations have argued that during his presidency, the federal government reduced its effective, as opposed to rhetorical, support for migrant rights in Moscow.[44]

It is true that during the Yeltsin and Putin presidencies there were occasions when the federal authorities forced the city to retreat. These generally came when city policies encroached too brazenly on federal authority. Thus, Moscow failed to secure passage of a bill introduced into the national Parliament that would have explicitly limited freedom of migration to Moscow and given the city the legal power to regulate entry to the city.[45] In 2002, a new federal statute, the Law on the Legal Status of Foreign Nationals, forced Moscow's administration into greater *superficial* conformity with federal laws. For example, the municipal agency called the Committee on Migration was forced to disband following the transfer of the Federal Migration Service to the Ministry of Interior (although it was later reconstituted under a more innocuous name). The federal government also forced Moscow to reduce the fines it was imposing on employers for unlawful use of foreign labor to comply with a new national law regulating this "administrative violation," and jurisdiction over enforcement was transferred from the city executive (the mayor and his subordinates) to the courts.[46] Yet, these federal efforts to curtail Moscow's migration policies were essentially cosmetic; they were targeted at eliminating open constitutional impropriety but did not address the core problems of a municipal government whose policy objectives infringed on federal jurisdiction over migration, in concert with a corrupted law-enforcement apparatus.

The field research for this essay was completed in 2006, however, and the Russian federal government has since begun to demonstrate more concern about the proliferation of corruption and illegality in migration enforcement—not only in Moscow, but presumably especially there. In particular, the government has enacted some liberalizing changes in Russia's migration policies that have led to improved conditions for at least some migrants, including in Moscow.

This policy shift has included measures to bring at least some CIS guest workers out of the "shadow economy" and into the realm of legitimate employment, some of which have been accomplished by presidential decrees and some by new legislation or reforms to existing laws. Specifically, the government has simplified the application procedure for work permits, eased requirements for temporary registration, facilitated adjustment of immigration status to temporary residence, and begun charging employers significant fines for violating immigration rules.[47] Taken together, these reforms were intended to promote legality in the market for CIS migrant labor by facilitating compliance and by penalizing noncompliance. While more research would be needed to establish this point, the reforms also seem targeted specifically at the most abusive practices of the Moscow government and employers.

Yet, although the Russian government's reforms have led to the legalization of many CIS guest workers and curbed at least some of the exploitation associated with an undocumented labor force, they have not halted many other abusive practices associated with migration enforcement in Moscow, including the harassment of members of Caucasian ethnic groups and the registration racket.[48] As of 2011, the Russian government has announced plans to restructure the Ministry of Interior, which is responsible for the police and most other law enforcement in Russia. It remains to be seen whether the reforms that are introduced will prevent abuses of individual rights, or only cement the control of the Kremlin over regional police administration.

Thus, to date the Russian government is apparently still unwilling to confront the underlying causes of such practices in Moscow—a city whose policies, whether or not they are openly acknowledged, limit the rights of migrants, in large part with the help of a police force that derives illicit benefits from these policies. Moscow's transformation to immigrant metropolis thus remains contested at the federal and at the municipal levels.

Conclusion: Residence in Moscow and the Meaning of Municipal Citizenship

What has emerged from this contestation over Moscow residence rights is a peculiar kind of de facto municipal citizenship. In this brief conclusion, I will assess the meaning of this citizenship and the rights that are associated with it in the context of both international comparisons and in that of Russia's own history. Residence controls in contemporary Moscow are distinct from those of Soviet Moscow. Indeed, they are in some ways more similar to the immigration policies of a contemporary western state, and to the system of population management in Third World metropolises, than they are to any Soviet model.

With its determination to filter potential residents and award permanent registration only to desirable applicants, the Moscow city government has been conducting what looks like an immigration policy. John Torpey has argued that the combination of relatively strict barriers to external entry (immigration) and relatively open internal migration is the characteristic feature of twentieth-century regimes of mobility in liberal states.[49] In other words, while national governments filter potential immigrants, a person who already holds national citizenship should be entitled to establish legal permanent residence in any part of the national territory. As in the Soviet Union, registration policy in contemporary Russia, and especially in Moscow, violates this principle of internal free choice of residence. But whereas the Soviet Union restricted Moscow residence for ultimately political reasons connected with the hegemony of the Soviet Communist party, contemporary Moscow does so in large part for the city government's own reasons. In particular, the distinction between temporary and permanent registration, combined with the effective requirement of property ownership for permanent registration, implies a distinction between prosperous new arrivals and all other Russian citizens. The former (those who can afford real property in Moscow) now enjoy a genuine freedom to move to Moscow without administrative authorization that the Soviet Union never allowed. The latter (other Russian citizens and FSU guest workers) find themselves denied the effective right to a permanent status in the capital.

Moscow's filtration of potential residents by wealth resembles the policies of many western states—for example, the United States and Canada—many of which at various times have adopted policies to facilitate immigration by wealthy individuals prepared to make substantial investments in their new country.[50] But these are national governments selecting immigrants, not a municipal government denying residence rights to current citizens and lawfully resident foreigners. One can debate the ethics and utility of the United States' and other governments' preference for rich immigrants. However, the Moscow government's overt and implicit residence policies are qualitatively different in that they call into question the value and significance of Russia's own national citizenship and the authority of Russia's federal government over migration control. The fact that Moscow's government is pursuing such a policy vividly illustrates the economic and political chasm between the city and its "hinterland," including the other former republics of the USSR as well as other regions of the Russian Federation. At least part of what is at stake for Moscow's city government is the city's ability to avoid responsibility for the social needs of new residents, even if they are Russian citizens.

Whereas national immigration-policy preferences for wealthy "investors" are codified in *explicit* statutes, however, Moscow's residence-limitation policies are necessarily implicit—their restrictive character is not officially acknowledged. Moreover, to some extent, they are actually enforced by extralegal or illegal means, such as police harassment, at the municipal rather than the national level. In this respect, contemporary Moscow bears comparison with large cities in developing countries, in which a high proportion of the population resides in unauthorized settlements, often consisting of self-built, substandard housing.[51] The growth of such "illegal cities" has led to ongoing disputes about the rights of their residents to recognition of their land tenure and access to urban services that in some ways evoke those of Moscow.

Yet, while Moscow's post-Soviet migrant influx has been accompanied by increasing use of unauthorized sites for housing (such as the trailers where Central Asian guest workers live), Moscow's residence disputes are primarily about the legal status of *persons* rather than *structures,* and ultimately about people's right to live (or simply to be) in particular locations. In this respect, Moscow's current situation is perhaps most similar to that of urban centers in other middle-income countries that have recently experienced a major political transition. For example, the "pass laws" of Apartheid South Africa systematically restricted the mobility of the country's black majority, in particular excluding them from residential areas reserved for whites. In post-Apartheid South Africa the pass laws are no more, and South Africa has become a multiracial democracy in which most political power is held by black citizens. Yet, even today, black urban settlement continues to be concentrated in informal settlements at the urban periphery that are far removed from the wealthy enclaves inhabited by whites. This persistence of spatial separation between the races has been attributed in part to "a host of other ostensibly race-neutral provisions [of land-use regulation] that effectively perpetuate racial segregation."[52] Moreover, following the transition to majority rule, the country has seen a rapid expansion of private security services, which are retained primarily by white South Africans to police residences, business establishments such as shops and restaurants, and even public streets in predominantly white areas, thus perversely reinforcing whites' privileged access to desirable spaces and indeed security, even in the new South Africa.[53]

While Moscow is not ringed with migrant shantytowns, it could fairly be described as an "illegal city," for a substantial number of Moscow residents face the declared or tacit hostility of the city government to their claims for civil rights, if not their very presence. Such residents must navigate the streets of a city whose police force has been given virtually free rein to harass them. Moreover, the experience of racial isolation and differentiated policing in post-Apartheid South Africa suggests a further important aspect of Moscow's transformation from "closed city" into "illegal city." As in South African cities, contemporary Moscow's migration policies are in large part a local response to the broader national political transition from Soviet rule—and indeed, as in South Africa, this response actually vitiates the intended political significance of that transition. Just as in South Africa, those who are not welcome to live in the city are nonetheless solicited to provide their labor, albeit on highly unfavorable terms. In this respect, the nonregistered population of Moscow resembles the Soviet-era *limitchiki,* although their temporary status is maintained through informal pressure and harassment rather than formal regulation of their status.

In an irony of the post-Soviet transition, the contrast between the Soviet and post-Soviet control of migration is not entirely in the latter's favor. While migration into Soviet Moscow was tightly controlled, for authorized residents there was probably more security of status and transparency, predictability, and probity of enforcement than is the case today. In contemporary Moscow, migration flows in the city have not been regularized, as was anticipated, but rather "irregularized" and subjected to an array of extralegal and infralegal obstructions that obfuscate and undermine the formal freedom of movement conferred by the Russian constitution and Russian law. As a result, the conferral of residence rights has become more haphazard, their retention more insecure, and their contestation more violent than in the Soviet past.

Notes

This essay is adapted from my dissertation, "Regional Migration Policies in Post-Soviet Russia" (Yale University, 2006), and is based in part on field research conducted 2003–4 and 2005–6. The second of these visits was supported by an Individual Advanced Research Opportunities fellowship from IREX, the International Research and Exchanges Board. I am grateful to Mikhail Denisenko and the other researchers and staff of the Centre of Population Studies, Faculty of Economics, Moscow State University, for their hospitality and institutional support during my stay in Moscow. I also thank Mariana Valverde and Peter H. Solomon of the Centre of Criminology, University of Toronto, for valuable comments on earlier versions of this essay. Portions of this essay previously appeared in Matthew Light, "Policing Migration in Soviet and Post-Soviet Moscow," *Post-Soviet Affairs* 26.4 (2010): 275–313.

1. Mervyn Matthews, *The Passport Society: Controlling Movement in Russia and the USSR* (Boulder, Colo.: Westview Press, 1993), 7.

2. For a survey of the Soviet migration-control system, see ibid. For a study of the police administration of the system, see Louise I. Shelley, *Policing Soviet Society: The Evolution of State Control* (London: Routledge, 1996).

3. Valentina Moiseenko, Viktor Perevedentsev, and Natal'ia Voronina, *Moskovskii region: Migratsiia i migratsionnaia politika* (Moscow: Carnegie Center, 1999).

4. Cynthia Buckley, "The Myth of Managed Migration: Migration Control and Market in the Soviet Period," *Slavic Review* 54.4 (1995): 896–916.

5. Gijs Kessler, "The Passport System and State Control over Population Flows in the Soviet Union, 1932–1940," *Cahiers du monde russe* 42.2–4 (2001): 477–503. See also chap. 3 of this volume.

6. Cecil J. Houston, "Administrative Control of Migration to Moscow, 1959–1975," *Canadian Geographer* 23.1 (1979): 32–44.

7. Ibid., 38.

8. Shelley, *Policing Soviet Society,* 122–23.

9. Timothy J. Colton, *Moscow: Governing the Socialist Metropolis* (Cambridge, Mass.: Harvard University Press, 1995), 500.

10. Houston, "Administrative Control," 41.

11. David L. Hoffman, *Peasant Metropolis: Social Identities in Moscow, 1929–1941* (Ithaca, N.Y.: Cornell University Press, 1994).

12. International Organization for Migration, "Russian Federation: New Research Revealed on Irregular Migration," *IOM in Eastern Europe and Central Asia* 11 (April–June 2003): 8; Vitalii Kurennoi, "Inogda my namerenno idem na uzhestochenie nakazanii . . .," *Otechestvennye zapiski* 4.19 (2004): 117–25.

13. Moscow (Russian Federation), *Postanovlenie Pravitel'stva Moskvy No. 189-PP,* 6 April 2004; Vladimir Popov, "Reform Strategies and Economic Performance of Russia's Regions," *World Development* 29.5 (2001): 865–86.

14. "In 2000 the proportion of the labor force that was unemployed in Moscow City, at 3.8 percent, was lower than elsewhere in the Russian Federation, with the exception of the remote Evenk Autonomous Okrug" (Imogen Bell, *The Territories of the Russian Federation* [London: Europa Publications Limited, 2003], 271). By way of comparison, the unemployment rate was four times higher in nearby Vladimir Oblast (Kurennoi, "Inogda my namerenno").

15. Moiseenko, Perevedentsev, and Voronina, *Moskovskii region,* 39.

16. International Organization for Migration, "Russian Federation."

17. A leader of one of Moscow's numerous Armenian organizations claimed that there are two million people of Armenian origin in Russia, of whom 850,000 to one million reside in the Moscow area, contrary to the official figure of one hundred thousand. Of the Moscow Armenians, he claims that five hundred thousand are undocumented (author's interview with Smbat Karakhanyan, Moscow, June 2004). Likewise, while the Azerbaijan embassy claims that about six hundred thousand Azeris reside in Moscow, of whom three hundred thousand are Russian citizens, community representatives cite a higher total figure of eight hundred thousand, a lower citizen figure of only one hundred thousand, and an unspecified number of undocumented (Arif Seifullaevich Usunov, "Trudovaia emigratsiia iz Azerbaidzhana: Strategii integratsii v rynki truda i riski," in *Trudovaia migratsiia v SNG: Sotsial'nye i ekonomicheskie effekty,* ed. Z. A. Zayonchkovskaya [Moscow: Tsentr izucheniia problem vynuzhdennoi migratsii v SNG, 2003], 125–26). The International Organization for Labor estimates 1.2 million Tajiks in Russia, most of whom live in the Moscow region; 40 percent of the Moscow Tajiks are said to be undocumented (International Organization for Labor, *Sotsial'nyi status rabotnikov iz Tadzhikistana v stroitel'noi otrasli v Moskve i v Moskovskoi oblasti* [Geneva: International Organization for Labor, 2006], 33).

18. International Organization for Labor, *Sotsial'nyi status rabotnikov iz Tadzhikistana.*

19. During the 1990s and early 2000s, for example, Azeri and Chechen cartels battled for control of grocery markets (Unusov, *Trudovaia emigratsiia iz Azerbaidzhana,* 122–30).

20. Zhanna Zayonchkovskaya, "Recent Migration Trends in Russia," in *Population under Duress: The Geodemography of Post-Soviet Russia,* ed. G. J. Demko, G. Ioffe, and Zh. Zayonchkovskaya (Boulder, Colo: Westview Press, 1999), 107–36.

21. Judyth L. Twigg, "Russian Health Care Reform at the Regional Level: Status and Impact," *Post-Soviet Geography and Economics* 42.3 (2001): 202–19; Christophe Raison, "Regionalisation et crise sanitaire en Russie," *Revue d'études comparative Est-Ouest* 29.3

(1998): 207–39; Galina Cerednicenko, "L'Ecole secondaire russe en mutation (d'apres la situation a Moscou)," *Revue d'etudes comparative Est-Ouest* 31.3 (2000): 99–125.

22. Oleg Alexandrov, "Centre and Periphery," in *Russian Regions and Regionalism: Strength through Weakness,* ed. G. P. Herd and Anne Aldis (London: Routledge, 2003), 247.

23. A representative of the city has noted, in particular, the ubiquitous evasion of taxes and fees on the part of market shopkeepers and peddlers. Ksenia Larina, "Interview with Sergei Smidovich," Radio Ekho Moskvy, January 11, 2003. Interviewed by another journalist, Smidovich has also claimed that undocumented labor migrants pay no taxes or social charges into the city's budget, and that they represent a burden on social-welfare expenditures (Kurennoi, "Inogda my namerenno").

24. Damian S. Schaible, "Life in Russia's 'Closed City': Moscow's Movement Restrictions and the Rule of Law," *New York University Law Review* 76 (2001): 344–73.

25. V. Mukomel' and E. Pain, *Vynuzhdennye migranty v tsentral'noi Rossii: Pravovye osnovy i praktika regulirovaniia vynuzhdennykh migratsii v sub"ektakh Rossiiskoi Federatsii* (Moscow: Inograf, 1999), 66.

26. Moiseenko, Perevedentsev, and Voronina, *Moskovskii region.*

27. Riders of the Moscow metro are familiar with job advertisements that typically announce openings for "Muscovites and residents of the nearby suburbs." It is, in fact, a requirement—in violation of Russian labor law—that someone employed in this capacity must be permanently registered in Moscow or the nearby Moscow Oblast.

28. Schaible, "Life in Russia's 'Closed City.'"

29. Svetlana Alekseevna Gannushkina and J. Chardina, *Discrimination on the Basis of Place of Residence and Ethnic Origin in Moscow and the Moscow Region* (Moscow: Human Rights Center Memorial, 2002). As a result of the court's decision, the Moscow city government issued a decree ordering its public-health clinics and hospitals to provide at least some form of medical care to Russian citizens holding temporary registration in the city. Moscow (Russian Federation), *Postanovlenie pravitel'stvo Moskvy No. 241–28* (as amended 28 November 2000; 1999).

30. Moscow, *Postanovlenie Pravitel'stvo Moskvy No. 189-PP* (2004).

31. Svetlana Alekseevna Gannushkina, personal communication with the author, Moscow, 10 May 2004; Vyacheslav Petrovich Rozhkov, personal communication with the author, Moscow, 12 March 2004.

32. Gannushkina and Chardina, "Discrimination on the Basis of Place," 18.

33. "Absolutely all document checks on the street are unlawful, as the police have no grounds to suspect citizens of committing a violation of the law. Therefore they have no legal grounds to stop people on the street. . . . Instead of catching criminals, the police have established a general raid [*oblava*] on unregistered persons" (author's interview with Evgenii Bobrov, Moscow, June 2004).

34. International Organization for Labor, *Sotsial'nyi status rabotnikov.* Ironically, one Tajik diplomat suggests that Tajik workers stay on their construction sites in part because of fear of police surveillance of public places (Muxkhammad Mshrafovich Egamzod, Press Secretary, Embassy of Tadjikistan, personal communication with the

author, Moscow, 4 June 2004). If this is true, it also indicates the success of the Moscow police in creating a threatening presence in public.

35. Gannushkina, personal communication.

36. Elena Tiuriukanova et al., *Prinuditel'nyi trud v sovremennoi Rossii: Nereguliruemaia migratsiia i torgovlia liud'mi* (Moscow: International Labor Organization, 2004).

37. United Nations, *UNHCR Paper on Asylum Seekers from the Russian Federation in the Context of the Situation in Chechnya* (Geneva: U.N. High Commissioner for Refugees, 2003).

38. "Events showed not only the helplessness of the federal authorities in the face of grave violations of the law by regional authorities, but also an explicit reluctance to counteract these violations, and in a number of instances, direct support by the federal bodies, particularly in cases of violation of the right to freedom of movement and systematic discrimination on ethnic grounds" (Gannushkina and Chardina, "Discrimination on the Basis of Place," 5).

39. Thus, after the Dubrovka theater siege in 2002, document sweeps in public places were stepped up, with the result that "[d]uring these months it became dangerous for Chechens to simply go out into the street" (ibid., 17).

40. Ibid., 15, 20, 31.

41. U.S. Committee for Refugees, *World Refugee Survey 2003 Country Report: Russian Federation*; accessed 30 October 2011, http://www.refugees.org.

42. This view was expressed by a legal officer of the UNHCR (Yuri Bortnikov, personal communication with the author, Moscow, 15 March 2004) and by an anonymous police officer. The latter justifies this unofficial policy on the grounds that the Chechen population is disproportionately involved in organized crime and financial misconduct and also uses the proceeds of its business activities to support Chechen separatist guerillas.

43. Light, "Regional Migration Policies." The issue of police corruption is explored in depth in Light, "Policing Migration in Soviet and Post-Soviet Moscow."

44. Gannushkina and Chardina, "Discrimination on the Basis of Place," 109–11.

45. Mukomel' and Pain, *Vynuzhdennye migratsii,* 73.

46. Oleg Miliukov, "Migratsiia, informatsiia, registratsiia," *Moskovskaia promyshlennaia gazeta,* 22–28 August 2002.

47. Decree No. 681 of the Russian Federation Government, "On the order of issuing permit documents for foreign citizens working temporarily in the Russian Federation," 15 November 2006; "On the migration registry of foreign nationals and stateless persons," Rossiiskoi Federatsii," *Rossiiskaia gazeta,* 16 November 2006. My summary of penalties and fines is based on data presented by Human Rights Watch, "'Are You Happy to Cheat Us?': Exploitation of Migrant Construction Workers in Russia," February 2009; accessed 30 October 2011, http://www.hrw.org/sites/default/files/reports/russia0209web_0.pdf.

48. For a more detailed analysis of the effects of national policy changes on police practices, see Light, "Policing Migration in Soviet and Post-Soviet Moscow."

49. John Torpey, *The Invention of the Passport: Surveillance, Citizenship, and the State* (Cambridge: Cambridge University Press, 2000).

50. The United States created a preferred "investor" category in pursuit of wealthy Asian

immigrants, such as those who left Hong Kong in anticipation of the Chinese takeover in 1997. See Aihwa Ong, *Flexible Citizenship: The Cultural Logics of Transnationality* (Durham, N.C.: Duke University Press, 1999).

51. Edésio Fernandes and Ann Varley, eds., *Illegal Cities: Law and Urban Change in Developing Countries* (London: Zed Books, 1998).

52. Stephen Berrisford, "Law and Urban Change in the New South Africa," in *Illegal Cities: Law and Urban Change in Developing Countries,* ed. Edésio Fernandes and Ann Varley (London: Zed Books, 1998), 214–16.

53. Michael Kempa and Anne-Marie Singh, "Private Security, Political Economy, and the Policing of Race: Probing Global Hypotheses through the Case of South Africa," *Theoretical Criminology* 12.3 (2008): 333–54.

PART II

Social Horizons

[blank page 100]

Preface

WILLARD SUNDERLAND

In *Dead Souls,* one of Nikolai Gogol's eccentric noblemen pronounces proudly: "The Russian *muzhik* can adapt himself to . . . any environment. . . . Pack him off to Kamchatka with a pair of mittens and it won't be long before he slaps his hands together, grabs an ax, and heads off to chop down some timber for his new hut."[1]

This is the kind of claim that one normally takes with a grain of salt, but as Anatoly Remnev makes clear in his essay in this section, educated Russians in the nineteenth century (much like their counterparts in the United States) enjoyed imagining their country folk as hardy pioneers with a natural knack for colonizing new places. Gogol could have had the gullible and self-important landlords in his story tell even taller tales about indomitable Russian peasant colonists and it wouldn't have been a problem.

What's interesting about this national mythology, however, is that we see it first emerge not in the late Imperial period, when mass resettlements were actually unfolding, but rather in the 1840s, when Gogol's great novel appeared—some twenty years before the end of serfdom, when it was still illegal for any peasant, including so-called state peasants living on government lands, to move even one village over without permission. What an irony! The Russians are great colonizers. They subdue far-off lands, including chilly Kamchatka. Yet they do all this despite not being supposed to move. While Gogol didn't address this particular paradox, this is exactly the type of absurd situation he was a master at portraying.

Curious contradictions like this have always been part of the Russian landscape. The Russians have a remarkable history of movement. Even under serfdom, they moved in multiple directions in sizeable numbers, as did non-Russian peoples of the old empire. Yet it is also true that they often barely moved at all.

Even in the midst of the remarkable surge of mass mobility that was transforming the country in the late nineteenth century, for example, well over 90 percent of all of the peasants in the empire were recorded by the Imperial census of 1897 as living in the district (*uezd*) of their birth.[2] Official policy at different times has played an obvious role in keeping people in place, but so too have less official habits and institutions, such as the peasant commune. Part of the challenge of understanding how movement "worked" in the Russian context is thus a matter of explaining how it took place and why it didn't, as well as exploring the many meanings that have been associated with it in Russian society. Indeed, the recurring tension that we find between moving and not moving, between imagining going and committing to staying put, defines the true horizon of mobility in the Russian experience, and this applies to all the actors involved in the equation: governments, observers, and settlers alike.

One general conclusion emerges from the four engaging essays in this section: mobility and immobility are deeply intertwined in Russian space. Indeed, we rarely find one without the other. And in large part this is because both have continuously had their uses, for Russia's rulers as well as its would-be migrants. For the state, movement and stasis have each been—and continue to be—fields of power. The long-running habit of trying to root people in place, whether through serfdom or the Soviet and post-Soviet practice of residential registration (*propiska*), has allowed the government to try to tie down labor and distribute social privilege. Meanwhile, its equally long habit of forcing or luring people to move from place to place has allowed the government to promote economic development and various imperial objectives in the borderlands, while also giving ordinary people at least limited room to better their condition through geographic mobility.

The Russian state, by and large, has tried to have it both ways when it comes to mobility and immobility. Serfdom arose as a response to hard truths of geography and demography. The country was too big, and the people too few. Consequently, the peasants had to be rooted in place, the nobles argued, or they would simply pick up and move away, taking their precious labor with them. In the same way, because Russia was so vast and so thinly populated, the state was perennially faced with having to push people to move in certain directions—to the vulnerable borders of the south during the late Muscovite era, to the new capital of St. Petersburg under Peter the Great, or to the Virgin Lands of Soviet Kazakhstan, among countless other destinations. And over the centuries it relied on relatively free as well as coercive methods for doing so.

Little of this is unique to the Russian context, but the continuities are striking nonetheless. From a state perspective, the basic problem of Russian power hasn't changed much in five hundred years. The country has been consistently enormous and just as persistently (relatively) underpopulated. As a result, the rulers of the state have repeatedly had to weigh out their needs, balancing degrees of immobility and mobility as required to serve their purposes.

In each of the essays here, we see aspects of these forces at work. Eileen Kane shows us the tsarist government's close involvement with organizing the Muslim hajj. On the face of it, we might assume that a conservative Orthodox empire like Russia would be hesitant to do anything to contribute to the regular shuttling of large numbers of Muslims across its borders. But Kane shows us that rather than avoiding or repressing the hajj, the state supported it in order to look after the interests of Russian business, while at the same time solidifying good relations with the empire's Muslim community. By 1908, Premier Stolypin had even appointed a well-connected Muslim entrepreneur from Tashkent as the "head of the Muslim pilgrimage in Russia." The new position didn't last long, but the initiative behind it reminds us of the state's willingness to use movement, even movement it didn't otherwise endorse, as a means of advancing its goals.

In Siberia in the same period, the government's efforts to promote massive resettlement "beyond the Urals" was driven by a similar sort of practical thinking. As Remnev shows, by the late Imperial period resettlement had became attractive from the state's perspective because it seemed to kill two birds with one stone. On the one hand, it alleviated land pressure in the overcrowded heartland of the country. On the other hand, it promoted the economy and security of the frontier. The pursuit of one sort of stability thus seemed to fit neatly into another, like two pieces snapping together in a puzzle. And this was the sort of snap every state minister loved to hear.

Yet Remnev underscores another truth about movement in the Russian context: tsarist officials may have promoted resettlement on a mass scale during the age of the Great Siberian Migration, but they didn't necessarily like everything they saw happening as a result. Indeed, it is fair to say that movement has always been met with unease on the part of Russia's rulers. Movement is expensive and chaotic. It introduces instability. When people move, they become hard to track or simply behave badly. Perhaps most importantly, the state was always a little leery of movement because it always had a hard time controlling it. Serfdom was supposed to immobilize people, yet peasants still ran away. By contrast, the intricate resettlement system of the late Imperial era was designed to move people around, yet it never came close to containing the full dynamism of the process. As Remnev shows, even legal peasant migrants read things their own way and diverted from the paths laid out for them. Plus, they were poor and repeatedly failed to conform to official expectations of what they were supposed to do, either as national subject-citizens or as farmers.

Another useful point underscored by the essays here is the central role played by ordinary people in the mobility/immobility conundrum. While the Russian state has long insisted on its prerogatives to determine who can move and who must not, its terms have never provided the whole story. Instead, decisions about movement and nonmovement in Russia as elsewhere have usually been shaped by a dynamic relationship between the state or some other form of outside power and individual and communal agency. People move, and the state responds. People then shape their next movement or nonmovement on the basis of these new state interventions, and the cycle continues.

The details of the dynamic are complex, of course, and vary considerably from one social milieu and period to the next. In fact, the essays here remind us how diverse the terrain can be, in particular with regard to migration. Some individuals and communities choose to migrate, usually under the influence of some degree of pressure from either their economic situation or from state politics. Others find themselves forced to move. Still others might have every economic motivation for moving but instead choose to stay in place. As these "nonmigrants" see it, while they might be free to migrate, there is no reason to do so because they can't see anything better out there. Why go to all the trouble of moving?

We find this immobility of choice nicely described in Elena Tyuryukanova's essay, which takes us to contemporary Iaroslavl', a province just north of Moscow. In past times, the region was a center of textile manufacturing, but the industry has long since died, and the area is in the midst of what may be a permanent downturn. Yet as Tyuryukanova shows, few Iaroslavlians so far seem interested in leaving. In part, this is because the Russian government has done little to make out-migration affordable or attractive. In this sense, people are staying in Iaroslavl' because they are stuck. Yet they are also staying because they want to. Things might be bad at home, but the Iaroslavlians have assumed, perhaps rightly, that conditions are no better anywhere else either. In other words, home is good, or at least good enough. The decision to migrate or not migrate in this case is located squarely in mentality. State power can affect this mentality, but it is hardly an all-determining factor.

Jeff Sahadeo's essay on non-Russian migrants to Moscow and Leningrad in the last Soviet decades gives us a similar perspective on the nonstate milieu of migration, though from the opposite side. As Sahadeo points out, his informants had extremely diverse experiences, some of which coincided with state goals and ideology, while others did not. Yet even when state and migrant objectives ran together, the meeting was often on the migrants' terms. For example, many of the migrants Sahadeo interviewed expressed a subtly different interpretation of the Friendship of Peoples (*Druzhba Narodov*) ideal than the one offered to them by the state. In the migrants' experience, to be multinational was a practical matter of everyday life, not a cheery slogan, and as such it could be alternately disorienting and empowering. The migrants thus embraced parts of the ideology but left others out, making ideology conform to real life rather than the other way around.

When we put these essays together, we find a state-society dynamic that is predictable and surprising at the same time. The state is clearly involved in promoting and shaping movement, including movement we might otherwise assume it didn't want to encourage, such as the Muslim hajj. At the same time, despite the powers at their disposal, the tsarist and the Soviet governments faced persistent obstacles in making migrants and travelers do what they wanted. In fact, the diverse people moving in these essays clearly have plans of their own, which means in certain cases opting *not* to move when they otherwise objectively should, and in others taking advantage of the state's language and structures of migration but filling the language with their own, sometimes quite different meanings. In other words, the worlds of state power and the movement of ordinary people are inextricably intertwined, but they don't fit together neatly.

One response to this bundle of paradoxes is to throw up one's hands and bemoan the fact that things aren't more straightforward. But even as we might wish things were simpler, we should take comfort from the fact that these complexities cannot be simplified too much, for a certain amount of ambiguity and inconsistency is inherent to the mobility horizon. When migrants set out or state planners scheme, things rarely go as planned. In fact, even when people choose not to move, their reasons for staying put are often less intuitive than we might assume. We can see the multifaceted and often contradictory political, social, and cultural impacts of mass migrations most clearly when we place them in the context of the recurring tension between mobility and immobility—between staying and going—that runs throughout the modern Russian experience, from the late Imperial period to today. This is what the essays in this section help us to do.

Notes

1. Nikolai Gogol, *Dead Souls* (New York: Modern Library, 1965), 177.

2. Robert John Kaiser, *The Geography of Nationalism in Russia and the USSR* (Princeton, N.J.: Princeton University Press, 1994), 51–53. The exceptions, not surprisingly, were districts in the settler zones of southern Russia, the North Caucasus, and Siberia. The Baltic provinces and Poland also saw relatively higher rates of mobility than the Russian heartland.

[blank page 106]

5

Odessa as a Hajj Hub, 1880s–1910s

EILEEN KANE

One unexpected result of Russia's modernization drive after the Crimean War was that the empire became a crossroads of the hajj, the annual Muslim pilgrimage to Mecca. This was part of the global remapping of hajj routes along modern rail and steamship lines, a spontaneous process that accelerated after the opening of the Suez Canal in 1869.[1] Starting in the 1850s, the Russian state funded the development of two commercial fleets: the Russian Society of Steam Navigation and Trade (ROPiT), and the Volunteer Fleet. Both provided steamship service between Black Sea ports and the Far East, with stops along the way in the Mediterranean, the Red Sea, and the Persian Gulf.[2] In the 1880s, the state expanded its railroad system into the Caucasus and Central Asia, eventually making it possible to get from Tashkent to Odessa by train in eight and a half days.[3] Muslims with access to these lines of modern transport—from Russia as well as Afghanistan, China, Persia, and Bukhara—were quick to see in them a faster, less expensive way of making the hajj. By the early 1900s, thousands every year were turning away from ancient overland routes through Persia and India to take Russian trains and steamships to Mecca.[4] With this shift in traffic patterns, new hajj hubs gradually emerged across Russia's southern borderlands, and Odessa was among the most important of these.

Known as "Adis" among Turkic-speakers, Odessa by the early twentieth century was the center of the Black Sea hajj traffic leaving Russia. State-led efforts to organize hajj transport helped bring as many as twenty-five thousand Muslim pilgrims through Odessa every year.[5] Even in a city of half a million people, crowds this big must have been hard to miss.[6] And yet they show up nowhere in the historiography. Why is that? In part it has to do with the way Odessa's history is often framed—as a Jewish city, a site of labor unrest, a cultural center, a frontier town—the result being a series of narrowly focused studies that collectively reinforce a sense of Odessa's uniqueness, with less attention paid to its increasing connectedness to other parts of the empire and its role as a mass-transit hub in the era of modernization.[7] Also at work here is the general problem of neglect of Islam: the missing hajj story from Odessa's past is another example of how Muslims are often left out of the larger narrative of Russian history, particularly when it comes to parts of the empire where they did not historically predominate. Finally, there is a methodological issue: many traditional sources on Odessa, such as Russian-language newspapers, guidebooks, and European travel memoirs, are largely silent on the hajj traffic. Nowhere, for instance, is it mentioned in the famous Baedeker and Moskvich guides to the city from the early 1900s.[8]

Reconstructing Odessa's history as a hajj hub requires us to look beyond the usual sources on the city. Of particular importance are the various Muslim newspapers published in late Imperial Russia, and the dozens of hajj memoirs written by Russian Muslims in these years; both genres offer rich detail on the pilgrim traffic through Odessa.[9] At the same time, by returning to traditional sources with fresh eyes, we can discern traces of this history. A grainy photo appears in the pages of *Odesskie novosti,* one of Odessa's mainstream newspapers, of two Tashkent natives posing at Odessa's railroad station, just back from Mecca and heading home; and thick folders of correspondence on the hajj turn up in Odessa's Imperial-era archives, in easy-to-miss files labeled simply "Pilgrims." Piecing together sources like these allows us see Odessa anew, as a place transformed in the era of mass mobility into an international center of Muslim pilgrimage.[10]

In this essay, I explore hajj season in Odessa, focusing on state efforts to streamline the pilgrim traffic by supporting construction of a full-service "hajj complex" (*khadzhikhana*) in the port. Beyond trying to illuminate a little-known dimension of Odessa's history, my larger goal is to show how state officials tried to harness the economic potential of the mass hajj traffic to further Russia's modernization. This idea will not fit with prevailing views about the tsarist regime as suspicious of and always trying to stop Muslims from moving around or going abroad, especially as anxieties about pan-Islamism mounted in the early twentieth century.[11] Such views, while common, reflect only one side of a complicated debate within the late Imperial regime about the relationship between Muslim mobility and empire building. The archives of the Odessa city-governor offer a starting point for considering other sides to this debate; in the pages that follow, I will use these archives to explore how officials saw problems and opportunities in the growing hajj traffic. I will also bring into my analysis articles and advertisements from *Turkistan wilayatining gazeti,* Tashkent's main Turkic-language newspaper, that illustrate the use of mass media by Russian steamship companies to encourage Central Asian Muslims to make the hajj by way of Odessa and other Black Sea ports.

Modernization and Mass Pilgrimage

The history of Russia's modernization has often been told through a Marxist lens, in terms of cities, factories, and workers, leading inexorably to socialist revolution.[12] In recent years, historians of Russia have joined with other scholars of modern Europe to explore how modernization led also to increased religiosity and new forms of religious observance. Much of this new work focuses on how railroads and steamships gave rise to mass Christian pilgrimages within Europe and Russia, to places like the Marian shrine at Lourdes, a French town in the foothills of the Pyrenees, and Solovki, a fifteenth-century Orthodox monastery complex on an island in the White Sea.[13] Parallel to this scholarship, though rarely brought into dialogue with it, there is also an emerging body of work on the mass hajj as a by-product of European imperialism, which brought modern transportation networks to Muslim regions across Asia and Africa.[14]

From Algeria to Russia to Indonesia, railroads and steamships revolutionized the Muslim pilgrimage to Mecca, transforming it from a small-scale phenomenon performed mainly by the wealthy and well-connected along land routes and on sailing vessels into a mass, steam-powered event dominated by the poor. The political and economic effects of this transformation were dramatic and global. Eager to tap into this huge new market, European steamship companies expanded their fleets and opened new lines to the Red Sea and the Persian Gulf. Fearing cholera epidemics and the spread of "fanatical" Islamic teachings from Arabia, European colonial officials undertook projects to monitor and support the flow of pilgrims to Mecca and back to the colonies, while the European powers formed an international sanitary conference (precursor to the World Health Organization) to address the problem of cholera being spread along hajj routes and into Europe.[15] At the same time, port cities around the world became bustling new transit centers for the hajj traffic—places like Algiers, Jeddah, Singapore, Bombay, as well as Odessa—while ancient inland caravan cities, abandoned by pilgrims, lost prestige and revenues. Damascus was one such place: having served since ancient times as center of the Syrian caravan, one of the three main Meccan caravans sponsored by Islamic kings and sultans, its once-flourishing economy declined with the opening of the Suez Canal and shift of hajj traffic to the seas.[16]

Historians, echoing colonial officials' anxieties about cholera and pan-Islamism, have generally presented the hajj in the decades leading up to World War I as a source of "twin infection."[17] Framed in geopolitical terms, the hajj's ground-level social, political, and economic dimensions have largely been overlooked, along with critical questions about the pilgrims themselves.[18] In Russia, as elsewhere, hajj pilgrims transformed the places they traveled through, often taking local officials by surprise while also generating new economic opportunities and relationships and debates about how to manage the little-understood phenomenon of the pilgrimage. Nowhere was this more the case than in turn-of-the-century Odessa. While other Russian ports in the Black Sea were also used by Muslim pilgrims, none in this period saw the same volume of traffic as Odessa. This made sense, given Odessa's leading role in Russian trade and transportation on the Black Sea: steamships left the city several times a day for Istanbul and beyond, and rail lines directly connected it to spots all across the empire.

Drawn by the convenience of travel, large numbers of Mecca-bound Muslim pilgrims started gathering in Odessa every year by the 1880s, attracting the attention of the Sharif of Mecca, who began sending envoys to the city to help coordinate the annual movement of pilgrims to the Hejaz.[19] Improvements in transportation soon made these numbers even greater. In 1903, direct Odessa-Jeddah service was introduced on Russian steamships; this made it possible for Muslim pilgrims to get from the Black Sea to Red Sea ports without changing ships.[20] And in 1906 a rail line was finished linking Tashkent to Orenburg and on to Odessa. By 1908 the Ministry of Transport was organizing special "hajj cars" for rail service between Tashkent and Odessa, and by 1909 the Volunteer Fleet was running "Hejaz steamships" out of Odessa exclusively for Muslim pilgrims.[21]

Hajj Season in Odessa

The hajj traffic dramatically altered Odessa's human landscape, filling the streets with crowds of Muslim men (women and children were less common), most of them poor, exhausted, and dirty from a week spent crammed into a poorly ventilated train car. On their backs they carried huge sacks stuffed with necessities for the weeks-long journey: blankets, carpets, cups, pots and pans, stores of rusk (*sukhar'*), fruits and vegetables, and metal locks and samovars to sell in Arabian markets.[22] Most spoke no Russian and were at the mercy of self-styled "hajj agents" that swarmed their arriving trains. Consistent with the fixed timing of the hajj by the Islamic calendar, these crowds were intensely seasonal: they formed in Odessa suddenly, over a span of a few months, and disappeared as quickly, boarding steamships a month or so ahead of the scheduled rituals in Arabia (the date of which shifted back eleven days each year, in line with the lunar cycles). For locals looking on, the initial effect must have been something like seeing the carnival come to town: costumed figures parading through the streets and speaking in strange tongues, the air thick with smells of rotting food and unwashed bodies, paper tickets littering the streets, shady types lurking in the margins, before—POOF—the crowds cleared and the whole thing was over.

However short-lived hajj season in Odessa was, it had become an integral, if also controversial, part of the city's economic and political life by the early twentieth century. Entire industries sprung up to serve the crowds: bakeries producing "Sart" breads, firms hiring out Turkic-speaking interpreters, travel agencies offering cut rates on steamers to Arabia, and criminal rings (found always and everywhere the lucrative hajj crowds moved) hawking everything from fake Chinese passports to tickets on nonexistent steamers.[23] Local hotels refashioned themselves during the season as "hajj inns," and homeowners rented out furnished rooms to pilgrims, who might spend several weeks in Odessa getting their passports in order and waiting for a spot on a ship. The local mullah, Sabirzhan Safarov, made lots of money doing burials of would-be pilgrims in the Muslim cemetery near the railway station. And while a large Muslim labor force was imported from Tashkent—for translating, slaughtering livestock, and preparing "Muslim" foods—plenty of local Jews and Christians also made their living off the hajj traffic. All of this created headaches for local police and sanitary officials, who struggled to get a handle on the growing crowds.[24]

For the majority of Muslim pilgrims that traveled third-class to Odessa, getting there could be an ordeal. Russia's new rail lines were notoriously inefficient and unregulated and not designed for Muslim needs. Across southern Russia, crowds of pilgrims would gather at new railway "stations"—which were often nothing more than a sign posted alongside the tracks—where they would sit and wait for days in the open air, enduring blazing sun, rainstorms, and cold, with no access to food or water. Penza and Samara were supposed to be two of the worst transfer stations on pilgrims' itineraries: through them trains from Siberia would pass, already overflowing with passengers and without stopping for the miserable crowds. When a train with space finally did pull up, as many as sixty pilgrims might pile into a car designed for forty and spend the next several days trapped in squalor. Standing, half-sitting, sprawled on luggage racks and in the passageways of stuffy cars, men were mixed in among women, and people got sick in the car; there were no private lavatories, there was no fresh water, and no open space for prayer. Food was also a problem. Between Tashkent and Istanbul, pilgrims had trouble finding anything they could eat: at train stops across Russia, peasants lined up along the tracks selling pork sausages, lard (*salo*), and baked goods made from mystery animal fats, all of it forbidden by Muslim dietary laws. Faced with going hungry or eating the rotting food in their sacks, many became sick during the journey from disease or food poisoning. Arriving in Odessa exhausted and disoriented, pilgrims were easy prey for the scores of pickpockets and thieves that eagerly awaited their arrival.[25]

A Plan for Organizing the Hajj

This was the awful state of affairs presented by Said Gani Saidazimbaev in a report on the hajj he took to St. Petersburg in the winter of 1908. A rich Tashkent businessman in tight with the Russian administration there, Saidazimbaev also had powerful friends in the state duma who helped him gain access to various government offices during his visit to the capital.[26] Saidazimbaev's dismal view of the Russian hajj was not news to state officials: it basically squared with the dozens of other reports the government had received over the years, from Russian officials and eyewitnesses to the hajj traffic. For decades, Russian consuls in Istanbul, Beirut, and Jeddah had been sending the foreign ministry accounts of abuse suffered by Russia's Muslims en route to Mecca—getting fleeced by steamship captains, locked into airless holds and denied food aboard ROPiT ships, attacked by Bedouins during the overland trek from Jeddah to Mecca— and proposing new state measures to protect them.[27] The Russian Ministry of Internal Affairs had been hearing similar things from the doctors and spies it sent into Arabia to research the sanitary dimensions of the hajj.[28] The Russian press periodically ran pieces about the perils Russia's Muslims faced in making the hajj: one article, published in the newspaper *Novoe vremia* in 1908, urged the government to intervene and save Muslim pilgrims from the "predatory claws of the Jews, Greeks, and Armenians" who were ripping them off in Odessa and Sevastopol."[29]

In his report, Saidazimbaev argued that modernization had made a mess of the hajj in Russia and that most Muslim pilgrims were "simple" and "unsophisticated," lacking the resources to navigate the journey on their own and in need of a leader to guide them. He offered himself as the best candidate for the job. He proposed an ambitious and "rational" reorganization of the hajj in Russia for the benefit "not only of Muslim pilgrims, but also the state coffers of the Russian Empire." He claimed that poor travel conditions throughout Russia, along with rumors about special "privileges" awaiting pilgrims along land routes through India and Persia, were making some pilgrims turn back to the old land routes, thus depriving Russia of much-needed revenues. Improving conditions on rail cars and steamships, he argued, would keep the lucrative hajj traffic circulating within the empire, thus enriching Russian railroad and steamship companies.[30]

Modeled on British efforts to organize the hajj in India through Thomas Cook, Saidazimbaev's plan called for a state-backed monopoly, directed by him, that would coordinate and oversee all aspects of the pilgrim traffic across the empire and charge pilgrims a flat rate for a single ticket to get them from home to Odessa to Jeddah and back.[31] His plan aimed to eliminate the multiethnic group of middlemen already providing services to pilgrims in Odessa; Saidazimbaev dismissed them all as "predatory cabals" and crooks and proposed instead to create instead a single full-service "hajj complex" (*khadzhikhana*) in the port that provided dormitory-like, gender-segregated accommodations, separate hospitals for men and women, a "disinfection" facility, prayer room, barber, bathhouse, kitchens, shops selling *halal* foods, visa services, and steamship ticket sales, all under one roof.[32]

The Odessa hajj complex was supposed to be the end point in a network of hajj facilities that Saidazimbaev proposed building along Russian rail routes used by Muslims. These were to go up all across Central Asia, as well as in Penza, Samara, and Kharkov, and were designed to resemble traditional caravanserais, providing water, food, trading stalls, a teahouse, a prayer hall, and gender-segregated shelter for Muslim travelers. Odessa's was to be the biggest, with capacity for three thousand pilgrims and a modern sanitary facility up to international quarantine standards. Saidazimbaev's plan also called for an overhaul of the transport of Muslim pilgrims through Russia and from Odessa. Similar to how special train cars were designed to transport the many sick pilgrims to the healing shrine at Lourdes, Saidazimbaev proposed that "hajj cars" be created by Russian railroad companies, with gender-segregated compartments, open space for prayer, and fresh water available for ablutions and washing clothes. These train cars were to be staffed with a crew of Muslim "guides" to assist pilgrims on the journey, as would a fleet of steamships specially renovated for Muslim pilgrims.[33]

Saidazimbaev's plan met enthusiastic support in St. Petersburg. In February 1908, A. G. Niedermiller, the chair of the Committee of the Volunteer Fleet, signed an exclusive deal with Saidazimbaev, promising him a fleet of specially outfitted steamships to transport pilgrims from Odessa to Jeddah over the next three hajj seasons and a 15 percent commission on the price of each pilgrim ticket he sold. Niedermiller also gave Saidazimbaev a five-thousand-ruble interest-free loan to build a pilgrim complex adjacent to the Tashkent railroad station, complete with an office selling Volunteer Fleet tickets. In return, Saidazimbaev promised to deal only with the Volunteer Fleet and to "attract pilgrims to these steamships in the largest possible numbers." Saidazimbaev claimed already to own a building in Odessa's port, which he would convert into a sanitary facility to "disinfect" pilgrims prior to their boarding the Volunteer Fleet ships; this was not true and would later become a point of contention in Saidazimbaev's dealings with the Odessa authorities.[34]

In March 1908, Petr Stolypin—who was both minister of internal affairs and prime minister of Russia from 1906 to 1911—named Saidazimbaev "head of the Muslim pilgrimage in Russia." This was a new position; while various Russian ministries had been involved for decades in facilitating aspects of the hajj, no single institution or individual had ever been put in charge of the entire pilgrimage. In mid-March, the Ministry of Internal Affairs circulated an announcement to the empire's governors and city-governors informing them of Stolypin's appointment of Saidazimbaev—"to organize the pilgrimage from Russia to Mecca, and solve the many problems associated with it"—and asking them to get local officials to help him. By June, Saidazimbaev had also, with the help of the minister of transport, persuaded a congress of representatives of the Russian railroads to designate up to one thousand third-class train cars as "hajj cars" for use along the fourteen different train lines used by Muslims across the empire during hajj season. Beyond this, the Minister of Transport gave Saidazimbaev permission to organize provisions centers for hajj pilgrims at major train stations along their routes, and the minister of finance helped him petition the port authorities in Odessa for a lease of land to build his hajj complex.[35]

How do we account for Saidazimbaev's extraordinary success in getting state support for his hajj plan? His connections in the government clearly helped. Niedermiller, for one, mentioned that Saidazimbaev had come "highly recommended" to the Volunteer Fleet by several duma members.[36] Saidazimbaev's timing was also good. With the opening of the Trans-Siberian railroad in 1903, the Volunteer Fleet had lost much of its business ferrying goods and people between Odessa and the Far East. The fleet suffered further losses after the Russo-Japanese War in 1905, when trade between Odessa and the Far East came to a standstill.[37] Seeking new ways to fill its ships, the fleet looked to the competitive and ever-expanding market of transporting pilgrims to Jerusalem and Mecca: in 1907 it began direct service from Odessa to Beirut and Jeddah, the main ports used by Christian and Muslim pilgrims. In this context, Saidazimbaev's plan must have seemed to Niedermiller a unique opportunity to outmaneuver competing foreign steamship companies, British companies especially, in capitalizing on Russia's hajj traffic.

Stolypin had his own reasons for supporting Saidazimbaev's plan, all related to his desire for imperial stability in the shadow of the 1905 revolution. Perhaps best known for his brutal repression of revolutionary groups and radical land reforms, Stolypin was also committed to religious toleration as a guarantor of social order, something that often led to tensions with his more conservative colleagues and the tsar himself.[38] This commitment, together with the government's stepped-up efforts to fight cholera and other infectious diseases associated with the hajj, led Stolypin in 1907 to issue *Rules on the Transport by Ship of Muslim Pilgrims from Black Sea Ports to the Hejaz and Back*. Issued in the aftermath of a massive cholera outbreak in 1907 that had killed some twenty thousand in Arabia alone, and distributed to officials in all of Russia's Black Sea ports, the *Rules* give a clear sense of the cramped and unsanitary conditions pilgrims had long been suffering aboard steamships: they required ships to provide adequate drinking water and food, access to clean toilets (at least one toilet per hundred passengers, and gender-segregated), an onboard disinfection room and fully equipped medical clinic, ventilation and regular cleaning of below-deck space, and at least 1.5 square meters of space per pilgrim.[39]

Besides imposing new restrictions and requirements on steamship companies, the *Rules* greatly expanded the role of Odessa's local officials in regulating the hajj traffic. The *Rules* established the city as the main port of exit for Muslim pilgrims leaving Russia (Feodosiia, which already had an established quarantine system, was made the port of return) and created a Port Pilgrimage Commission in Odessa. Headed by the Odessa city-governor and including local sanitary, trade, and customs officials and Russian steamship-company representatives, the commission's basic duties were to set ticket prices on steamships carrying Muslim pilgrims, ensure their sanitary screening in the port, inspect and issue certificates to steamships approved for hajj transport, and appoint doctors to hajj ships.[40] Stolypin's appointment of Saidazimbaev should be seen in the context of the Ministry of Interior's larger project, already well under way in late 1907, to bring the hajj traffic under centralized state control and surveillance. At the same time, as Stolypin's correspondence with the Odessa authorities makes clear, it was also an attempt to increase revenues for Russian steamship companies by having them replace foreign companies that had long dominated Black Sea hajj transport.

The *Khadzhikhana* in Odessa

In June 1908 Saidazimbaev arrived in Odessa to prepare for that year's hajj traffic. With the season due to start in September, and resistance to his plans cropping up almost immediately, it quickly became clear he had to scale back some of his plans. The first major issue Saidazimbaev faced was where to house his hajj complex: not only was there no time to build a new structure, but his request for a piece of land in the quarantine area of the port had embroiled him in a feud involving the Odessa city-governor, ROPiT representatives, and local customs officials and businessmen who also had claims to the spot.[41] While Niedermiller lobbied the Odessa city-governor, I. N. Tolmachev, to decide things in Saidazimbaev's favor, Saidazimbaev went in search of a temporary rental to serve as that year's *khadzhikhana*.

With Tolmachev's help and for 7,500 rubles, he managed to rent the partly vacant local House of Industry (*Dom trudoliubiia*), a two-story stone building flanked by one-story wings in the industrial Peresyp neighborhood adjacent to the port.[42] Saidazimbaev got use of the building from August through December (the projected hajj-departure season that year) on the condition that the House of Industry's baker continue to occupy one wing of the building. This deal made creative use of a work-relief institution that had been set up—along with dozens of other houses of industry across Russian cities starting in the 1890s—to provide food and shelter to homeless and unemployed workers.[43] The building was not ideal: with space for only 1,400 people, it was not big enough to house the crowds expected that year. It also needed extensive renovations, which Saidazimbaev got started on immediately.

Paying out of pocket, Saidazimbaev quickly put up a makeshift hajj complex organized around the House of Industry. Attached to the building, an outpatient clinic and separate men's and women's hospitals were built, and an old bathhouse was renovated to include two steam-disinfection facilities, outfit-ted in consultation with the doctor in charge of Odessa's medical observation station. In the building's courtyard a mosque was constructed with space for four hundred. Just outside, special for "Kirgiz pilgrims," ten tents were pitched (donated by troops of the Odessa military district) alongside outdoor ovens for cooking (*ochagi*). A row of shops was built across the street, selling meat, groceries, and dry goods needed for the trip (cooking pans, drinking mugs, samovars, steamer rugs, suitcases, blankets, etc.). In this space Saidazimbaev also installed a Turkestani barber, offering free shaves and haircuts. In vacant buildings up the street a teahouse and a bakery selling Sart breads and cakes were opened. Inside the House of Industry, six large halls were lit with kerosene lamps and divided according to levels of disinfection: downstairs was open space filled with iron bunks, and upstairs were "hotel rooms" with signs on the door indicating the number of pilgrims in each room and where they were in the disinfection process (Just Arrived, Completed Disinfection Process in the Bathhouse, Under Five-Day Observation, or Finished with Observation).

Impersonal, efficient, and state-of-the-art, the disinfection facility was the cen-terpiece of Saidazimbaev's hajj complex. He carefully built it in accordance with international quarantine requirements, including an ultramodern "Japanese-system" steam room, the first of its kind in Russia. He hoped it would establish Odessa as the sole government-sanctioned port of departure for Muslim pil-grims, thus bringing the hajj traffic under his monopoly. His proud description of the facility, laid out in a twenty-three-page report on the 1908 hajj for the Ministry of Internal Affairs, gives some sense of what the disinfection experi-ence was like for pilgrims.

Overseen by a staff of Muslim attendants, disinfection was a mass, highly or-ganized process that took place two or three times a day, between 7:00 A.M. and 4:00 P.M. After depositing their clothes and belongings for steam disinfection in a separate room, seventy-five naked men were herded into a long, narrow room with clean white plaster walls and a cement floor covered with a lattice mat, lined with individual showers along both walls and steam pipes sticking out of the walls. Each shower had a basin with cold and hot faucets, a piece of bast, and a bar of soap; above each shower was a number, which pilgrims matched to the number on metal tags worn around their necks. Many also wore a clear, rubberized bag around their necks, issued by attendants to hold their valuables. Upon completion of the disinfection process (which Saidazimbaev refrained from describing in detail) and after dressing, pilgrims were given a final tag to put around their necks: a cardboard sign reading, "Underwent Disinfection and Observation, on such-and-such day and month."[44]

What were the results of Saidazimbaev's efforts to streamline Odessa's hajj traffic in 1908? Reporting to the Ministry of Internal Affairs, Saidazimbaev declared it a huge success "for both the government and for pilgrims." He described his efficient handling of nearly seven thousand pilgrims (less than half the number expected, due to a cholera outbreak that year in Russia). Nearly half came from Turkestan, and another 25 percent from China; all were registered in the *khadzhikhana's* logbook, put through disinfection, and sent to Jeddah on five Volunteer Fleet vessels certified for hajj transport by the local authorities. Saidazimbaev reported no signs of cholera and only six deaths; despite attempts by "enemies" to discredit him and sabotage his plan, he claimed strong support from the pilgrims themselves, as seen in the fan letters several apparently wrote to the Ministry of Internal Affairs.[45]

The archives of the Odessa city-governor do not bear out Saidazimbaev's view of things: they reveal widespread resistance to Saidazimbaev and his plan, ending in the Ministry of Internal Affairs cutting ties with him. Viewed in a comparative context, it is tempting to see Saidazimbaev's failure to organize the hajj as inevitable. Faced with uncooperative pilgrims and yearly losses, Thomas Cook had finally given up trying to organize the hajj in India, and colonial officials elsewhere struggled to find a way to control the hajj traffic without alienating Muslim populations.[46] But there were also local dynamics, specific to Odessa and to Russia, that perhaps doomed Saidazimbaev's plan from the start.

ROPiT never supported the plan because it stood only to lose from it: for years it had been the sole Russian company transporting Muslim pilgrims from Russia, and now it was blocked out entirely. ROPiT responded by launching plans to open a competing hajj facility in Odessa, while also encouraging pilgrims to use the one it already operated in Sevastopol; this created confusion for port officials and city-governor Tolmachev and undermined the goal of concentrating hajj pilgrims in a single facility. Also opposed to Saidazimbaev's plan were the many local merchants and businesspeople that rightly saw it as a threat to their economic interests: people like Rylka Zekhster, a young Jewish widow who supported herself and seven children by renting furnished rooms to "Tatar pilgrims." Fearing that her business would soon be shut down, she wrote to Tolmachev in August 1908, assuring him that she ran an honest business and was not a "swindler" and that the local mullah would vouch for her. Another opponent was Petr Gurzhi, a retired ship captain–turned-businessman who had seen his own ambitious plan for building a hajj complex in Odessa dashed when Saidazimbaev came along. Though persuaded by the city-governor to cooperate with Saidazimbaev, Gurzhi seethed with resentment and missed no opportunity to badmouth him to the local authorities.[47]

Many pilgrims also resented Saidazimbaev, for reasons that are easy to understand. His plan involved force every step of the way. Armed gendarmes, provided by Tolmachev, met pilgrims' trains and "escorted" them to the hajj complex, where they were locked in and not allowed to leave.[48] Several episodes of unrest in the hajj complex, explained away by Saidazimbaev as deliberate "provocation" by his enemies, may well have been resistance to the prisonlike conditions or the humiliating experience of "disinfection." Of particular note is a pamphlet that an outraged Saidazimbaev found circulating among the pilgrims: a group of pilgrims was depicted in chains, being dragged by Saidazimbaev from the door of the *khadzhikhana* to a waiting Volunteer Fleet ship in the port. This, too, Saidazimbaev dismissed as a smear campaign by his jealous rivals. And yet the story told in this drawing bears striking resemblance to other stories reported by pilgrims in Muslim newspapers around this time, about new uncertainties and horrors brought by quarantine procedures and other measures introduced in the name of modernizing and "improving" the hajj.[49]

Rumors of Saidazimbaev's heavyhandedness seem to have cost him Stolypin's support. Oblivious to the complex economic dynamics of the hajj traffic in Odessa, and having bought Saidazimbaev's characterization of pilgrims as a "simple" and inexperienced bunch, Stolypin had envisioned the Odessa *khadzhikhana* as a safe haven for Muslim pilgrims, who would "naturally" find their way there and feel tremendous gratitude toward the government. He was therefore indignant when he heard in November about Muslim pilgrims being forced into the *khadzhikhana* and onto Volunteer Fleet ships: he immediately wrote to Tolmachev, reminding him that pilgrims must be "free to choose" where they stayed and which ships they boarded, and asking him to stop all use of coercion. Stolypin was further dismayed to learn that Saidazimbaev had made a secret deal to send pilgrims on Egyptian steamers, pocketing a huge advance and violating his promise to Stolypin to use only Russian steamships.[50]

Saidazimbaev's Legacies

Though Saidazimbaev had great plans for the 1909 hajj season in Odessa, he had disappeared from the scene by the time it came around. Gone also was the government's plan for centralizing the hajj through Odessa: instead there emerged multiple, competing firms that cooperated with the railroads, ROPiT, and the Volunteer Fleet in organizing the hajj traffic through Odessa, Sevastopol, and Batumi. In fall 1909, Petr Gurzhi, Saidazimbaev's old rival, joined with Odessa's mullah Safarov and several former employees of Saidazimbaev to form the Society for the Transport of Muslim Pilgrims, which arranged lodging for pilgrims in Odessa hotels, ran special "Hejaz steamships" during hajj season, and sold tickets in Odessa and in the empire's Muslim regions, with plans to open an office in Tashkent.[51] Gurzhi's company competed that year with a St. Petersburg–based firm hired by the Volunteer Fleet to coordinate its hajj services and sell steamship tickets in Tashkent, Kashgar, Baku, Batumi, Sevastopol,' and Odessa.[52] By 1910, ROPiT and the Volunteer Fleet were running ads for their Hejaz Steamships in Tashkent's main newspaper. "Esteemed hajjis" were offered a variety of choices: ROPiT's ships went from Sevastopol or Feodosiia to Beirut, while the Volunteer Fleet ran service from Odessa to Beirut, Yanbu, and Jeddah.[53] In fine print, at the bottom of a Volunteer Fleet ad from August 1910, ran this disclaimer: "Said Gani Saidazimbaev has nothing to do with the services of the Volunteer Fleet."[54]

And so Saidazimbaev left a mixed legacy. Clearly discredited in the eyes of many by his efforts to organize the hajj, he nonetheless advanced a number of ideas that gave shape to a new kind of hajj experience in Russia, one in which the government and private industry did more to meet the needs of Muslim pilgrims. After 1908, Russian steamship companies built hajj facilities not only in Odessa but all around the Black Sea, providing space where Muslims could rest and pray while they waited for their ship to leave port.[55] And in 1910, the Ministry of Transportation introduced new, direct (*besperesadochnaia*) rail service between Tashkent and Odessa especially for Turkestani Muslims; now, for the first time, it was possible to make this journey without changing trains. An article published in *Turkistan wilayatining gazeti* in February 1910 described the two options newly available to pilgrims: they could either take a postal train that provided first-, second-, or third-class service and took eight-and-a-half days to reach Odessa, or go fourth-class on a freight train that took twelve days.[56]

As for the *khadzhikhana* Saidazimbaev had set up in the House of Industry, this continued to serve as Odessa's central lodging place for hajj pilgrims up to World War I. Outside hajj season, the building came in handy during cholera outbreaks, equipped as it was with the city's most modern steam-disinfection facility. In June 1910, *Odesskie novosti* reported that the city government had evacuated hundreds of residents from contaminated neighborhoods and sent them to the "specially equipped 'khadzhi-khane,'" where they received food, lodging, and medical treatment.[57]

Conclusions

What do we gain from reconstructing the history of Odessa's brief role as an international hajj hub? Considered within the body of work on late Imperial Russia's modernization, it offers a new vantage point from which to understand the dynamics of this process. Industrialization, urban growth, the emergence of a working class, the rise of nationalism and revolutionary movements—these are all central, well-documented pieces of the story of Russia's modernization that hold the focus mainly on Russia's western, European regions. Scholars are less accustomed to thinking about modernization in the broader geographical context of the empire and as part of Russia's colonization of southern and eastern borderlands.

State planners in St. Petersburg may have ordered railroads built into Central Asia as a way to export European culture and troops to Asiatic borderlands, but this did not stop the people living there from putting these railroads to their own uses.[58] By investing in railroads and steamship navigation, the tsarist regime helped facilitate Muslim mobility within the empire, bringing its Muslim subjects into closer contact with the wider Muslim world. The effects of this went beyond small circles of elites and intellectuals, who enjoyed more efficient travel abroad and easier access to foreign publications; long-distance travel was now open to Muslims of all segments of society, many thousands of whom began to make the annual pilgrimage to Mecca, traveling on trains and steamships alongside Muslims from China, Afghanistan, and Persia. Having made mass Muslim mobility a reality, the drivers of Russia's modernization next sought to profit from it, by harnessing the economic benefits of the hajj for Russia's struggling steamship companies.

There are broader lessons to take away from this history. Temporary and circular forms of movement like religious pilgrimages can have enormous influence on historical processes, and yet they feature little in histories of human mobility, which tend to deal primarily with migration. By seeing Odessa's emergence as a hajj hub, historians can also begin to see Russia's conquests of Muslim lands as more than an acquisition of new territories and peoples but as a process that brought dramatic changes empire-wide and in Russia's relations with the outside world. In this regard, Odessa can serve as a starting point for exploring how, in the era of mass mobility, the circulation of hajj traffic through the Russian Empire created pockets of Muslim settlements outside predominantly Muslim borderlands, led to unprecedented mixing of peoples of different backgrounds, forged new patterns of economic activity, and helped shape the development of Russia's transit routes. Invisible threads of cross-regional contacts and influence thus become visible through the lens of the hajj, revealing how a focus on mobility yields new insights into Russia's imperial evolution.

Notes

For useful comments on earlier drafts of this essay, I thank John Randolph, Gene Avrutin, Patricia Herlihy, Bob Crews, the Eurasian Studies Working Group at Stanford University, Fred Paxton, and the history department's fall 2009 senior-thesis class at Connecticut College. I am also grateful to the National Council for Eurasian and East European Research and the International Research and Exchanges Board for supporting research in Tbilisi and Odessa included in this essay.

1. See C. A. Bayly, *The Birth of the Modern World, 1780–1914: Global Connections and Comparisons* (Malden, Mass.: Wiley-Blackwell, 2003): 351–57; F. E. Peters, *The Hajj: The Muslim Pilgrimage to Mecca and the Holy Places* (Princeton, N.J.: Princeton University Press, 1994), 266–315.

2. The Russian state created ROPiT in 1856, and it nationalized the Volunteer Fleet (founded in 1878 by a group of Russian tea merchants) in 1883. See S. I. Ilovaiskii, *Istoricheskii ocherk piatidesiatiletiia Russkogo obshchestva parokhodstva i torgovli* (Odessa: Tip. Iuzhno-russkago obshchestva pechatnago diela, 1907); M. Poggenpol,' *Ocherk vozniknoveniia i deiatel'nosti Dobrovol'nago Flota za vremia XXV-ti letniago ego sushchestvovaniia* (St. Petersburg: Tip. A. Benke, 1903), 113; and Thomas C. Sorenson, "The End of the Volunteer Fleet: Some Evidence on the Scope of Pobedonostsev's Power in Russia," *Slavic Review* 34.1 (March 1975): 131–37.

3. Derzhavnyi Arkhiv Odes'koi Oblasti (hereafter DAOO), f. 2, op. 2, d. 3391, ll. 76–77. On railroad construction in Russia's southern and eastern borderlands, see Derek W. Spring, "Railways and Economic Development in Turkestan before 1917," in *Russian Transport: An Historical and Geographical Survey,* by Leslie Symons and Colin White (London: Collins Educational, 1975); and W. E. Wheeler, "The Control of Land Routes: Railways in Central Asia," *Journal of the Royal Central Asian Society* 21 (1934): 585–608.

4. S. E. Grigor'ev, "Rossiiskie palomniki v sviatykh gorodakh Aravii v kontse XIX–nachale XX v." in *Istoriografiia i istochnikovedenie istorii stran Azii i Afriki,* ed. N. N. D'iakov (St. Petersburg: Izd. S.-Peterburgskogo universiteta, 1999), 88–110; S. E. Grigor'ev, "Al-Hujjāj al-Rūs ilá Makkah al-Mukarrimah wa-al-Madīnah al-Munawwarah fī awākhir al-qarn al-tāsi' 'ashr wa-bidāyat al-qarn al-'ishrīn," *al-Wathīqah* 32 (July 1997): 106–38; and Yaghim Rizfan, *Al-Hajj qabla mi'at sanah: al-rihlah al-sirrīyah lil-dābit al-Rūsī 'Abd al-'Azīz Dawlatshīn ilá Makkah al-Mukarrimah, 1898–1899: al-sira' al-dawlī 'alá al-Jazīrah al-'Arabīyah wa-al-'ālam al-Islāmī: riwāyah wasfīyah badi'ah lil-tārīkh wa-al-jughrāfīyā wa-al-ijtimā' wa-al-idārah* (Beirut: Dār al-Taqrīb, 1993).

5. DAOO, f. 2, op. 2, d. 3391, ll. 400b–42. See also M. Menshikov, "Uvazhenie k Islamu," *Novoe vremia,* 25 November 1908, 1.

6. In 1897, Odessa's population was nearly half a million; by 1914 it was 630,000. See Patricia Herlihy, *Odessa: A History, 1794–1914* (Cambridge, Mass.: Harvard Ukrainian Research Institute, 1986), 233.

7. For a broad social and economic study of tsarist-era Odessa—the first history of the city written in any language—see ibid. For more narrowly focused studies, see E. G. Plesskaia-Zebol'd, *Odesskie nemtsy, 1803–1920* (Odessa: Izd. TES, 1999); M. Polishchuk, *Evrei Odessy i Novorossii: Sotsial'no-politicheskaia istoriia evreev Odessy i drugikh gorodov v Novorossii, 1881—1904* (Moscow: Mosty kul'tury, 2002); Roshanna P. Sylvester, *Tales of Old Odessa: Crime and Civility in a City of Thieves* (DeKalb: Northern Illinois University Press, 2005); Robert Weinberg, *The Revolution of 1905 in Odessa: Blood on the Steps* (Bloomington: Indiana University Press, 1993); and Steven J. Zipperstein, *The Jews of Odessa: A Cultural History, 1794–1881* (Stanford, Calif.: Stanford University Press, 1985).

8. This is not so surprising, given what Baedeker and Moskvich were selling (an adventure/vacation) and their target audiences (middle-class Europeans and Russians). See Karl Baedeker, *Baedeker's Russia, 1914* (London: George Allen and Unwin, Ltd., 1914); Grigorii Moskvich, *Illiustrirovannyi prakticheskii putevoditel' po Odessie,* 4th ed. (Odessa: Tip. Tekhnik, 1908); and D. Vainer, *Illiustrirovannyi putevoditel' "Odessa"* (Odessa: Tip. B. Sapozhnikova, 1900).

9. For hajj memoirs, see R. Berdiev, *Sayahatnama, 1909/1327* (Astrakhan: Tip. T-go D-ma A. Umerov i Ko., 1911); and Sh. Ishaev, "Mekka—sviashchennyi gorod musul'man (rasskaz palomnika)," *Sredneaziatskii vestnik* (November 1896): 60–81, and (December 1896): 45–83. See also "S palomnikami do Dzheddi i obratno," *Turkistān wilāyatining gazeti*, 2 February 1914, 1; "Poezdka odnogo tuzemtsa palomnika v Mekku," *Turkistān wilāyatining gazeti*, 23 February 1914, 2; and "Pis'mo Mully Alima o puteshestvii v Mekku," *Turkistān wilāyatining gazeti*, 25 March 1910, 1.

10. In these same years, Odessa became a center also of Orthodox pilgrimage from Russia to Jerusalem—a story that has yet to be told by historians—resulting in the construction of new facilities attached to Orthodox monasteries to house and feed the crowds of pilgrims. ROPiT guidebooks in the early 1900s included an entire back section for Orthodox pilgrims traveling through Odessa, providing information on steamship-ticket prices, details on necessary travel documents, and a detailed list of accommodations for Russian Orthodox pilgrims in Odessa, Mt. Athos, Nazareth, and Jerusalem. See, for example, *Putevoditel' Russkago obshchestva parokhodstva i torgovli, 1911 god* (Odessa: Tip. Aktsionernago Iuzhno-Russkago obshchestva pechiatnago dela, 1911): 466–73.

11. On tsarist officials' anxieties about the hajj, see Daniel Brower, "Russian Roads to Mecca: Religious Tolerance and Muslim Pilgrimage in the Russian Empire," *Slavic Review* 55.3 (Fall 1996): 567–84: Robert Crews, *For Prophet and Tsar: Islam and Empire in Russia and Central Asia* (Cambridge, Mass.: Harvard University Press, 2006): 72–74; and Adeeb Khalid, *The Politics of Muslim Cultural Reform: Jadidism in Central Asia* (Berkeley: University of California Press, 1998), 52.

12. See, for example, Hans Rogger, *Russia in the Age of Modernisation and Revolution, 1881–1917* (New York: Longman, 1983), 100–61.

13. See, for example, Ruth Harris, *Lourdes: Body and Spirit in the Secular Age* (New York: Viking Penguin, 1999); Suzanne K. Kaufman, *Consuming Visions: Mass Culture and the Lourdes Shrine* (Ithaca, N.Y.: Cornell University Press, 2005); Roy R. Robson, *Solovki: The Story of Russia Told through Its Most Remarkable Islands* (New Haven, Conn.: Yale University Press, 2004): 170–85; Roy R. Robson, "Transforming Solovki: Pilgrim Narratives, Modernization, and Late Imperial Monastic Life," in *Sacred Stories: Religion and Spirituality in Modern Russia,* ed. Mark D. Steinberg and Heather J. Coleman (Bloomington: Indiana University Press, 2007): 44–60; and Christine D. Worobec, "The Unintended Consequences of a Surge in Orthodox Pilgrimages in Late Imperial Russia," *Russian History* 36 (2009): 62–76.

14. Sugata Bose, *A Hundred Horizons: The Indian Ocean in the Age of Global Empire* (Cambridge, Mass.: Harvard University Press, 2006): 193–242; Brower, "Russian Roads to Mecca"; Laurent Escande, "D'Alger à la Mecque: L'administration française et le contrôle du pèlerinage (1894–1962)," *Revue d'histoire maghrebine* 26 (1999): 277–92; Michael F. Laffan, *Islamic Nationhood and Colonial Indonesia: The Umma below the Winds* (New York: Routledge/Curzon, 2003); Michael Christopher Low, "Empire and the Hajj: Pilgrims, Plagues, and Pan-Islam under British Surveillance, 1865–1926" (Master's thesis, Georgia State University, 2007); Gregory Mann and Baz Lecocq, "Between Empire, Umma, and the Muslim Third World: The French Union and African Pilgrims

to Mecca, 1946–1958," *Comparative Studies of South Asia, Africa, and the Middle East* 27.2 (2007): 365–81; Takashi Oishi, "Friction and Rivalry over Pious Mobility: British Colonial Management of the Hajj and Reaction to It by Indian Muslims, 1870–1920," in *The Influence of Human Mobility in Muslim Societies,* ed. Hidemitsu Kuroki (London: Kegan Paul International, 2003): 151–75; and William R. Roff, "Sanitation and Security: The Imperial Powers and the Nineteenth-Century Hajj," *Arabian Studies* 6 (1982): 143–60.

15. Peters, *The Hajj,* 266–315; and David Edwin Long, *The Hajj Today: A Survey of the Contemporary Pilgrimage to Makkah* (Albany: State University of New York Press, 1979), 69–75.

16. Abdul-Karim Rafeq, "Damascus and the Pilgrim Caravan," in *Modernity and Culture: From the Mediterranean to the Indian Ocean,* ed. Leila Tarazi Fawaz and C. A. Bayly (New York: Columbia University Press, 2002), 130–43. In part hoping to revive Damascus's role as a hajj center, the Ottoman sultan in the 1900s started construction on the Hejaz Railway, projected to run between Damascus and Yemen (it reached Medina in 1908, as far as it would go). See James Nicholson, *The Hejaz Railway* (London: Stacey International, 2005); and *Hicaz Demiryolu: Istanbul'dan Medine'ye bir Tarih Belgeseli* (Istanbul: Albaraka Türk Yayinlari, 1999).

17. The phrase comes from Roff, "Sanitation and Security."

18. Historians of Christian pilgrimage in modern Europe have shown far more interest in the ground-level experience of the pilgrims themselves, exploring questions about their religious beliefs and practices, attitudes toward modern technologies and medicine, experience of illness, the food they ate, the cost of their tickets, the souvenirs they bought, and their economic importance to the communities intersected by new hajj routes. See Harris, *Lourdes;* and Kaufman, *Consuming Visions.*

19. Hafez Farmayan and Elton L. Daniel, ed. and trans., *A Shi'ite Pilgrimage to Mecca, 1885–1886: The* Safarnameh *of Mirza Mohammad Hosayn Farahani* (Austin: University of Texas Press, 1990), 183–84.

20. ROPiT introduced a Persian Line with service to Jeddah in 1903, and the Volunteer Fleet introduced service to Beirut and Jeddah in 1907. On the ROPiT line, see "Ob ustanovlenii srochnykh parokhodnykh reisov mezhdu Odessoi i portami Persidskogo zaliva i Bassoroi," No. 22767 in *Polnoe sobranie zakonov Rossiiskoi imperii,* 3d ed. (St. Petersburg: Gosudarstvennaia tipografiia, 1885–1916); and *Putevoditel' Russkogo obshchestva parokhodstva i torgovli* (Odessa: Tip. Aktsionernago Iuzhno-Russkago Obshchestva pechatnago diela, 1911), 105. See also Aleksandr Adamov, *Irak arabskii: Bassorskoi vilaiet v ego proshlom i nastoiaschem* (St. Petersburg: Tip. Glav. Upr. Udielov, 1912), 475; Grigor'ev, "Rossiiskie palomniki," 93; and *Otchet Shtabs-Kapitana Davletshina o komandirovke v Khidzhaz* (St. Petersburg: Voennaia tipografiia, 1899), 90.

21. Spring, "Railways and Economic Development in Turkestan," 51; DAOO, f. 2, op. 2, d. 3391, ll. 76, 253; and DAOO, f. 2, op. 2, d. 3471, ll. 17–17ob, 20.

22. Ishaev, "Mekka—sviashchennyi gorod musul'man (rasskaz palomnika)," 46.

23. *Turkistān wilāyatining gazeti,* 19 August 1910; 2 February 1914.

24. DAOO, f. 2, op. 3, d. 3471, l. 11; DAOO, f. 2, op. 3, d. 3391, ll. 600b, 122.

25. DAOO, f. 2, op. 2, d. 3391, ll. 76–82, 273–74.

26. DAOO, f. 2, op. 2, d. 3391, l. 95ob; Menshikov, "Uvazhenie k Islamu."

27. See, for example, the 1903 report from Russia's Jeddah consul to the ambassa-dor in Istanbul. Rossiiskii gosudarstevnnyi arkhiv voenno-morskogo flota (hereafter RGAVMF), f. 417, op. 1, d. 2757, ll. 2–8.

28. See, for example, D. Zabolotnyi, *Otchet o komandirovke v Dzheddu* (St. Petersburg: Tip. V. Kirshbauma, 1897); and *Otchet Shtabs-Kapitana Davletshina.*

29. Menshikov, "Uvazhenie k Islamu."

30. DAOO, f. 2, op. 2, d. 3391, ll. 78–81.

31. On Thomas Cook in India, see Low, "Empire and the Hajj," 65–71; and *The Mecca Pilgrimage: Appointment by the Government of India of Thos. Cook and Son as Agents for the Control of the Movements of Mahomedan Pilgrims from All Parts of India to Jeddah for Mecca, Medina, etc., and Back* (London: Printed for Private Circulation, 1886).

32. DAOO, f. 2, op. 2, d. 3391, ll. 78–80.

33. DAOO, f. 2, op. 2, d. 3391, l. 79, 274. On the Lourdes train cars, see Kaufman, *Consuming Visions,* 37.

34. DAOO, f. 2, op. 2, d. 3391, ll. 83–85.

35. DAOO, f. 2, op. 2, d. 3391, ll. 64, 82; 79–790b, 274ob; 800b, 276.

36. DAOO, f. 2, op. 2, d. 3391, l. 95ob. See also Menshikov, "Uvazhenie k Islamu."

37. Herlihy, *Odessa,* 107, 203; Stuart Thompstone, "Tsarist Russia's Investment in Transport," *Journal of Transport History* 19.1 (March 1998): 63; RGAVMF, f. 417, op. 1, d. 2757, l. 3ob.

38. Abraham Ascher, *P. A. Stolypin: The Search for Stability in Late Imperial Russia* (Stanford, Calif.: Stanford University Press, 2001), 296–97; and Paul Werth, "Empire, Religious Freedom, and the Legal Regulation of 'Mixed' Marriage in Imperial Russia," *Journal of Modern History* 80 (June 2008): 328.

39. See *Pravila perevozki na sudakh palomnikov-musul'man iz Chernomorskikh portov v Gedzhasa i obratno* (St. Petersburg: Pervaia tsentral'naia vostochnaia elektropechatnia, 1908). In 1897, Tsar Nicholas II established the Commission on Measures for Prevention and Struggle against the Plague, Cholera, and Yellow Fever. Around that time, the tsarist government began sending Russian doctors and spies into Arabia to collect information about conditions on hajj ships and the spread of disease. In 1904, the Chief Medical In-spectorate (under the Ministry of Internal Affairs) began drafting rules for monitoring Russia's Muslim pilgrims abroad to control the spread of cholera. DAOO, f. 2, op. 2, d. 3391, l. 90; Zabolotnyi, *Otchet o komandirovke v Dzheddu*; and *Otchet Shtabs-Kapitana Davletshina.*

40. DAOO, f. 2, op. 2, d. 3391, l. 128–290b.

41. DAOO, f. 2, op. 2, d. 3391, ll. 62, 870b, 91–950b, 125–250b.

42. DAOO, f. 2, op. 2, d. 3391, l. 110.

43. Adele Lindenmeyr, *Poverty Is Not a Vice: Charity, Society, and the State in Imperial Russia* (Princeton, N.J.; Princeton University Press, 1996), 168–95.

44. DAOO, f. 2, op. 2, d. 3391, ll. 276–77.

45. DAOO, f. 2, op. 2, d. 3991, l. 279.

46. Low, "Empire and the Hajj," 65–71.

47. DAOO, f. 2, op. 2, d. 3391, ll. 121–22.

48. DAOO, f. 2, op. 2, d. 3391, l. 203.

49. See, for example, *Turkistān wilāyatining gazeti,* 2 February 1914, 1.

50. DAOO, f. 2, op. 2, d. 3391, ll. 204–5; 2020b.

51. DAOO, f. 2, op. 2, d. 3471.

52. *Turkistān wilāyatining gazeti,* 12 August 1910.

53. *Turkistān wilāyatining gazeti,* 22 September 1911.

54. *Turkistān wilāyatining gazeti,* 19 August 1910.

55. As of 1910, ROPiT was advertising a *kervansarai* and *mesjid* for Muslim pilgrims in Sevastopol and Feodosiia, and as of 1913, the Ministry of Internal Affairs was planning to build a *khadzhikhana* in Batumi. *Turkistān wilāyatining gazeti,* 8 September 1910; Central State Historical Archive, Tbilisi, f. 13, op. 1, d. 501 (1913).

56. *Turkistān wilāyatining gazeti,* 26 February 1910.

57. *Odesskie novosti* 8136 (10 June 1910): 3; *Odesskie novosti* 8138 (12 June 1910): 2.

58. Spring, "Railways and Economic Development in Turkestan," 46.

6

Russians as Colonists at the Empire's Asian Borders

Optimistic Prognoses and Pessimistic Assessments

ANATOLYI REMNEV

Translated by Anastasiya Lakhtikova

Large volumes have been written on the migration of Russian peasants to the east, as well as on the colonizing politics of the Russian Empire in the nineteenth to early twentieth centuries. I would like to focus on the optimistic prognoses and pessimistic assessments offered by a number of observers who took part in the migration processes, as well as on the political and ideological consequences of these judgments.[1] Emphasizing the "voluntary" and "popular" nature of the Cossack and peasant movement to the east, many prominent Imperial Russian historians, geographers, ethnographers, and economists have argued that "the Russian peasant for the most part was a colonizer" and claimed that the population of the land east of the Urals was unauthorized and sometimes even against the law. The government, they argued, appropriated the results of the migratory creativity of the simple Russian people. At the same time, they celebrated the adaptive abilities of Russians, their cultural compatibility and peace-loving attitude toward other peoples. The territorial homogeneity of the empire seemed to allow an alternative to a colonial interpretation of the dynamics between the "center" and the "Asian periphery": namely, the idea that the "Russian land" had spontaneously spread by virtue of popular migratory movement from west to east.

Armed with western theories of "civilization" and "progress," Russian intellectuals (especially those prepared to cultivate a distanced cooperation with the authorities) not only refused to see their own actions as exploitative and unjust but also insisted on trying to overcome the "backwardness" they believed to be characteristic of Asian peoples and Russian peasants alike. This seemed to promise that the empire could reframe the old question of "power and the people," enlisting positive peasant support for official politics and the empire's ideological claims. Moreover, it was expected that the overt turning away from "colonialism" would decrease the potential of ethnic and religious separatist movements. The empire hoped to find a peaceful way of "merging" people into a single state community, one "great Russian nation," by uniting the population with sentiments of dynastic loyalty, official patriotism, Russian national citizenship, and allegiance to Russian culture and language.

Official governance of and support for migratory movement attracted a great deal of criticism, not only with regard to logistical and financial questions but because of their relation to other, much more important social and cultural issues. Migratory movement forced the prevailing populist (*narodnik*) discourse—which dominated the radical intelligentsia and was familiar to a significant number of state officials—to face a number of uncomfortable questions. How should Russians understand the social rebirth of the idealized Russian peasant man (*muzhik*) as a colonist, as well as the new social relations peasants had to establish when they reached the culturally alien territory of Asian Russia? The Russian peasant, idealized by the *narodniks,* was socially reborn as a colonist and had to establish new social relations when he reached the culturally alien territory of Asian Russia. Often affiliated with the various branches of the Russian Geographical Society, many exiled populist revolutionaries were involved in ethnographic and migration research and found themselves in demand by the administration as research consultants and advisers. Siberian regionalists and the emerging national intelligentsia formed an elite group in this local community of experts. Mass resettlement not only encouraged social activists—who normally kept their distance from the bureaucracy—to cooperate with the authorities; it also made them rethink their view of the Russian peasant, who suddenly began to be seen not only as a victim but also as a predator in relation to the environment and to indigenous peoples.

Imperial Optimism about Transforming "Alien" Land into "Russian" Land

In the region east of the Urals, the tsarist government practically gave up on serfdom as a system of securing new land for the empire. It did not use landowners as a colonizing and cultural element (as it did in southern Russia and Ukraine and the western region) and instead relied primarily on Cossacks and peasants. Cossacks and peasants, however, were not dedicated agents of the imperial power, advocates of an exalted "civilizing" mission, nor Christian missionaries, though all these missions were ascribed to them by others, who sought thereby to give peasant and Cossack[2] migration an ideological coloring and to include them in the resolution of the geopolitical and nationalistic objectives.[3] As usual, peasants were remote from a conscious recognition of their supposed imperial and cultural missions; in effect, they functioned as "nonimperial imperialists," remaining pragmatic in their views on indigenous populations and preoccupied mainly with the quantity and quality of land.[4] Most imperial experts agreed, however, that only these peasants could become a force capable of unifying Russia's vast political territory, merging its periphery with the Russian state core and pushing the ethnographic border between Europe and Asia further east.[5]

Expert students and proponents of resettlement belonged to different political movements, social strata, and professional groups, but they were surprisingly similar in their assessments. Thus Prince Alexandr Illarionovich Vasil'chikov, a prominent *zemstvo* activist, emphasized that, in contrast to America,

> Russian settlers neither exterminated anyone, nor forced anyone out; they occupied only vacant lands and settled among the non-Russians [*inorodtsy*], slowly assimilating them and marking everyone with the seal of their own ethnicity and allegiance to the tsar. . . . Russian colonizers advanced in cartels and communes, unarmed, carrying only their scythes and axes, but their progress was unrestrained and incessant, always in the same eastward direction.[6]

"This mighty popular movement . . . forced the government not only to abandon the idea of stopping this movement or limiting its regulation, but also to lead it," confirms the historian Matvei Kuz'mich Liubavskii.[7] Officials in charge of resettlement considered the active "Siberian squatter" as an ideal type of frontier settler:

> He is a special type of a man: strong, healthy, brave; most of all he loves independence from people, for him nature serves as substitute. He looks for places distant from any settlement, cultivates a piece of land that no one—neither people nor the government—has cared for yet . . . and suddenly, as soon as the settlements approach his plot, he abandons this farm built with his own heroic labors and moves on as though his providential role was to conquer nature.[8]

In this manner, concluded Leonid Mitrophanovich Bolkhovitinov, the colonel of the General Staff, the resettlement of landless peasants from the European parts of Russia could be used to populate the "peripheral wastes," thereby reinforcing Russia's eastern borders in a "fusion of colonization and resettlement."[9]

Official bureaucrats in charge of resettlement—who, by the end of the nineteenth and early twentieth centuries, directed imperial social and economic objectives at the periphery—also viewed the problem of migration within the interpretive frame of Russia's supposed civilizing mission in Asia. They imagined resettlement as a means to reconcile government service with their own populist worldview, which they now projected not only onto the still "backward" Russian peasants but also onto the primordially "wild" natives. Moreover, the government and the intelligentsia (often united in the persons of village or resettlement bureaucrats, doctors, and teachers) agreed that though the Siberian "non-Russians" and Steppe nomads were a "half-civilized" people, they were capable of development, and the proximity of Russians would become an important stimulus for their "civilization" or "culturalization." This formula, it seemed, gave the empire a chance not only to find in the resettlement movement the resolution of economic and social problems but also a chance to create a new political paradigm. At its core, there was the idea of the common people's "peaceful conquest" of new lands for their own use and the establishment, hand in hand with this, of a new "Russian civic spirit."

At this point in history, it was believed that the main engine of colonization was not the "raw element" of peasant flight from the state but the state itself. The government would regulate popular movement, create a protective infrastructure for Russian settlers, and use law to stimulate and manage the location of the Russian settlements.[10] Lands developed by the Russian plowman would belong to Russia. Russians, of course, were not strangers to the urge of escaping from the zone of state influence, but spontaneously, it seems, they could fulfill a function that was perfectly suitable to the empire—by bringing Russian culture into the depths of Asia, civilizing the local "horde," and, as peasants themselves put it, by "winning the land for the Russian tsar." All that would be left to the diplomats would be to "formalize this conquest."[11] This image of the Russian explorer, with his brave and unrestrained urge toward new lands, was created either in the mold of a Spanish conquistador or as a squatter of the American frontier, racing toward the new location with a plow, a shotgun, and a knife tucked into his boot. All this created the preconditions, it was believed, for the ideological combination of free popular migration, state colonization, and imperial expansion. It also corresponded to official hopes to create a "popular autocracy" in Russia, in which a patriarchal government acted as the people's guardian and received popular loyalty in return.

In the peasant-migrant consciousness, the resettlement east of the Urals could be perceived as a strategic goal set by the monarch that united peasant and state interests. This lent the migratory ambitions of peasants a particular legitimacy. Despite the bureaucratic prohibitions, the settler strongly believed that by moving east of the Urals he was doing the "tsar's business." The folklore of the Russian East preserves echoes of the peasants' desire for the land and the "tricks" they used to get it.[12] The peasants proclaimed openly in Siberia and the steppe territory (Stepnoi Krai) that the land belonged to the state and that they too belonged to the state—"consequently this land is ours."[13] The Kazakh exemption from military service ("they do not serve the tsar") also provided an additional reason to encroach on the best Kazakh lands and to demand them as a starting "stake" for Russian settlements.[14] For example, one of the district chiefs wrote to the Akmolin governor, "It is positively impossible to persuade them [the peasants] that there is no free land left for settlements, as to all the arguments they answer: 'We have come . . ., and consequently, we have the right to settle.'"[15]

The extensive nature of Russian farming and the demographic explosion of the post-reform period increased the migratory motivation of the Russian peasant, creating a unique "agricultural imperialism," as it was aptly dubbed by the philosopher Nikolai Fedorovich Fedorov.[16] For many years, popular consciousness associated the empire's physical size with its political magnificence.

Simultaneously, mental exploration of the new territory advanced along with its appropriation as "Russian land." The concept "ours" (*nashe*), as Claudia Weis has noted, which had deep roots in the popular consciousness, provides a key paradigm for understanding the structure of the Russian Empire at this time and its annexation of its borderlands, Siberia in particular.[17] Having settled on the new land, the settlers offered their own methods of symbolically fixing their ownership. On his trip around Ussuriiskii region in 1867–69, Nikolai Mikhailovich Przheval'skii noted with satisfaction that peasants brought along "to the distant strange land" their native habits and popular beliefs, and that they were quickly ceasing to feel homesick, saying: "What's for us there? There's not enough land, everything is cramped, and here, see, what spaciousness; live where you wish, plough where you want, there is also plenty of forest, fish, and multitudes of different creatures—what else could one wish for? If God grants us, we'll settle, recover, have plenty of everything, *and then we'll make Russia here as well.*"[18] The main markers fixing something as "Russian land" were Russian Orthodox churches, ploughed fields, and Russian settlements with graveyards, the gravestones, like the churches, topped by crosses.

The Russian Orthodox church was supposed to cement the heterogeneous Russian community on the Asian periphery. The peasants perceived "Russian land" as a "Christian kingdom," populated by Orthodox believers. The popular consciousness understood Ermak (the first Cossack "conqueror" of Siberia), Khabarov, Dezhnev, and Poiarkov as specifically Siberian Russian heroes; and peasants revered saints, icons, popular places of religious pilgrimages, and monasteries. Ermak, who combined the image of "Cossack freeman" and "agent of the tsar," became an emblematic historical figure in the reimagination of Siberia's annexation. There were even attempts to canonize him.

Russian toponymy became another indicator of the "Russianization" (*obrusenie*) of the colonized territory.[19] Starting in the middle of the nineteenth century, the empire began to take special interest in the names of towns, thereby forming a unique topographic text for each territory to be included in imperial and national discourses, with the intention of blending national and imperial motifs in the popular consciousness. Toponymy became a symbolic means of securing the right to possess the land with all its natural resources. Through names, the geographic landscape could be made to match the new cultural landscape, and thereby demonstrate to local populations that the territory belonged to Russia.

Mikhail Nikiforovich Katkov, an influential political writer and the ideologist of Russia's "Russification," saw the main value in this to be its role in making the Russian nation a political whole. This was, for him, a meta-objective for Russian peasant migration. Since the 1860s, he had been formulating this new national goal of creating a "whole and single" Russia, with a central national core surrounded by peripheral lands. Eastward migratory movement not only broadened the geography of the Russians' settlement but was also supposed to consolidate Russians into a nation. Katkov saw a "healthy Russian type" emerging on the Russian periphery, where various ethnic elements mixed under the structuring influence of Russian culture and common economic interests. For him, this "type" represented everything "purely, nationally Russian," as it expanded "Mother Russia's" limits.

Doubts about Cossacks and Peasants as Colonizers and "Russianizers"

According to the theories just described, the growth of the Russian population in the empire's Asian territory should have successfully begun to "merge" the periphery with the center of the country. In fact, however, peasant resettlement created new problems for the government, making social, national, and confessional disagreements even worse. It also became clear that the colonial project of Russianization would not be equally effective for all parts of the periphery. Rostislav Andreevich Fadeev, a general and conservative commentator, considered the Russian resettlement of Novorossiia, Povolzh'e, Priural'e, Siberia, and the northern Caucausus historically successful, but he was much less optimistic in regard to Transcaucasia and Turkestan. He felt that the latter could not "accommodate the sizeable masses of transplanted Russians needed to transform the area into Russia ethnographically; for a very long time these territories will remain Russian outposts in Asia, with all the inevitable consequences of such a possession."[20]

However, as the Polish uprising of 1863 aptly demonstrated, the empire needed many more Russians, Ukrainians, and Belorussians in its western borderlands as well, to reinforce "the Russian foundation" there. Indeed, the autocracy had to suspend operation of the Ministry of the Interior's directive "About the Order of Peasant Resettlement to the Free Lands" (1868).[21] "We are moving into Asia so as to give foreigners maximum freedom to colonize our European territory!" Katkov's own *Russkii Vestnik* (Russian herald) declared sarcastically, already picturing the "Germanization" of western Russian lands."[22] In the 1890s, Governor Victor Vilgelmovich von Val' expressed his concern that "the quiet and peaceful Belorussian population will be substituted by the Lettish, and that with the decrease of the Belorussian population the Russian character of the Vitebsk province will weaken."[23] The same concerns were expressed in 1903 by the minister of the interior Viacheslav Konstantinovich Pleve, who observed that "it is mainly Russian peasants who are moving away from territories populated primarily by non-Russian ethnicities." He pointed out the absence of a focused policy meant to "reinforce Russian ethnicity in regions primarily populated by other non-Russian ethnicities" and noted that the migrants only went reluctantly to the Caucasus, Turkestan, the Amur Territory (Priamurskii Krai)—"territories that for political reasons especially need the influx of a Russian population."[24] Later, Petr Arkad'evich Stolypin, the proponent of the active relocation of peasants east of the Urals, would come to fear that migration east could weaken the western periphery, stating that "in the West, excessive relocation creates numerous pores and holes that are quickly filled in by the foreign colonizers."[25]

Even in Asian Russia, earlier optimistic hopes that eastward migration would play a leading role in creating and reinforcing a "united and undivided" Russia underwent serious revision and came to exist side-by-side with pessimistic assessments of the culture-bearing potential of Cossacks and peasants.

Cossacks had been part of the Russian eastern expansion and reinforcement of the imperial periphery for a long time. However, having lost their former freedoms by the beginning of the nineteenth century, they became, in essence, military settlers situated along the Asian border. The state accorded them legal status as a special class and gave them huge tracts of land. However, the unsuccessful Crimean War, military reform, and the expansion of the Asian borders in the east and south raised new doubts about their efficacy as a military force. Even so, the empire didn't have the means to substitute the Cossacks with a regular army and police. (This would have required radical changes in the military infrastructure of the Asian peripheries and posed a whole spectrum of social and economic problems.) Doubts also remained about the political stability of the periphery, and it was felt that Cossacks, as permanent residents, were at least motivated to conduct external and internal police actions on behalf of the empire.

If in Siberia the Cossacks were considered to have already completed their role, and thus might be demoted to the status of peasants or reduced to a small supplemental police force in the North, the Cossacks' future on the steppe and in Far Eastern regions was more complex. This issue was particularly sensitive with regard to the Ural, Orenburg, and Siberian Cossack hosts. These were now located far from the imperial borders, but this same Kazakh steppe seemed to have a chance of becoming an inner "periphery." After the suppression of Kenesar Kasymov's 1840s uprising on the Kazakh plains, it became obvious that policy in regard to the Kazakhs' land rights might have to be significantly adjusted, and that a developed network of peasant settlements on the steppe would be more effective in "pacifying" the Kazakhs than occasional Cossack posts.[26] The peasant on the plains east of the Urals expressed lively interest as to whether Kirgiz land or Bashkir forests would be given to Russians; if so, wouldn't the Cossacks become "unneeded" there?

Peasants acknowledged the historic achievements of the Cossacks: if earlier "the Bashkirs rebelled, Kirghizs disobeyed," now it was "quiet." Yet they believed that Cossacks now only "crowded" the peasants, whereas they would be of better use fighting along the eastern Chinese border, to which they should be relocated.[27] In Omsk, officials suggested decreasing the size of the Siberian Cossack army and liquidating the Cossack defense posts. The Orenburg frontier line was also considered to have lost its military function. The local governor-general Alexandr Pavlovich Bezak proposed to liquidate the Ural and Orenburg Cossack armies, though this suggestion was rejected as premature.[28] With the exception of Semireche, the authorities did not use Cossack military and economic colonization in Turkestan.

In the Far East, even more so than on the steppe, the empire was not ready to dismiss the services of the Cossacks as warriors and farmers. There was no one who could take their place, especially in the beginning. Peasant colonization in the Far East advanced slowly, and the upkeep of a regular army turned out to be extremely expensive in the absence of the necessary economic infrastructure and developed service and transportations lines. Cossack colonization on the Amur was different from other territories because of a stringent regulatory regime that negatively affected economic productivity. Critics of Cossack colonization argued that the forced resettlement of Cossacks, under the guardianship of the state, created an apathetic population that was accustomed to being cared for. As Przheval'skii reported, during the initial years the majority of Cossacks languished in poverty; they were demoralized and expressed open animosity to the new environment.[29]

At the turn of the nineteenth century, the question of Cossack colonization was raised again in connection with the so-called yellow peril. Local authorities constantly demanded the reinforcement of the Russian Cossack population in the Amur Territory. Realizing the economic unsustainability of the regular army, the regional governor-general Sergei Mikhailovich Dukhovskoi secured a huge additional land grant for the Cossacks.

Despite the absolute growth of the Cossack population in the Amur Territory, the flow of peasants into the region was constantly increasing. It was they who, in the beginning of the twentieth century, began to determine the character of the Far Eastern periphery. Yet the 270-acre "Dukhovskoi allotment" included the most fertile arable lands, where peasants were prohibited from settling. A land commission, working in the region from 1901 to 1903 and headed by Anatolii Nikolaevich Kulomzin, concluded that "the so-called Cossack colonization" had no grounds to be called a "colonization," since it actually contradicted the main objectives of colonization: namely, populating empty areas and turning them into arable lands.[30] Subsequently, the Cossacks played only a secondary role in the interior minister P. A. Stolypin's agricultural policy, and their land rights were considered to be detrimental to mass peasant resettlement.[31]

The most unexpected thing that emerged from debates in government committees and on the pages of scientific and popular publications were the doubts regarding the Cossack's farming, as well as military, abilities. Critics asserted that Cossacks mostly did not work their lands, preferring to lease them out and lead a life of idleness.[32] Giving scientific legitimacy to this view, ethnographers described the look of the Cossack posts as "dull," calling the streets "incorrect," the houses "carelessly" built, and the Cossacks themselves poor housekeepers who did not seem to care about "outward order." The general conclusion drawn from such reports, as a rule, went like this: "The peasant is undoubtedly a more positive type, and in terms of his economic power he is stronger and more desirable in the pacified territory than the Cossack."[33]

Critics also worried about the complex relations developing between the Cossacks and peasant settlers. Although they acknowledged their social and ethnic similarities with the peasants, it was believed that the Cossacks nonetheless held themselves apart from the general peasant population. As Alexandr Nikolaevich Sedel'nikov, a specialist on Western Siberia and the steppe territory, described the Cossack attitude in one popular science magazine: "He views himself first of all as the 'tsar's servant,' is proud of his privileged status, looks down on the peasant, whom he derogatively calls '*muzhik*,' and treats the Kazakh with contempt, calls him 'dog' and habitually takes advantage of him or abuses him verbally."[34]

Among other things, some questioned whether transplanted Cossacks were preserving their "Russianness" and their ability to provide a positive image of Russians for the native population. In northern and northeastern Asia, according to many who traveled there, the Cossacks had lost their former military prowess, had a negligent attitude to their service, on occasion did not even speak Russian, and had completely assimilated with the local population. It was not accidental that observers who worried about Russians "going native" on the Asian periphery often pointed to Cossack-pioneers and their offspring. This opinion spread to cover all the Cossacks of the eastern periphery. Lending his scientific authority to such conclusions, Nikolai Przheval'skii made this general statement: "Assimilation is going in an undesirable direction here. It is the Cossacks who adopt the language and customs of their non-Russian neighbors, passing onto them nothing of their own. The Cossack at home shows off in a Chinese coat, speaks Mongolian or Kirghiz, prefers tea to any other food, and the nomads' dairy food. Even his physiognomy has degenerated and more often than not resembles his ethnic neighbor."[35] At the same time, Cossack laziness and many other negative behavioral and character traits were announced to be the consequence of the natives' regressive influence. The most troubling thing was that even among themselves the Cossacks had started speaking local languages, and their children acquired Russian with difficulty.

In their capacity as military and police, the Cossacks' complicity in local administrations' abuse of power did not help advance a positive image of the Cossack as a representative of the Russian people, either.[36] Populist discourse typically accused the Cossacks of exploiting other ethnicities. In this context, Cossacks who actively employed non-Russians and even peasant-settlers as wage laborers could be viewed as exploiters (*kulaks*) in public opinion. Indeed, Cossacks felt quite at home on the steppe and were ready to conquer the nomads' land and jealously guard it from their new competitors, the peasant-settlers. All this confused a system of social, economic, and legal relations that was already rather complicated and resulted in greater upheavals in regions that the imperial government had thought were completely "pacified."

Such criticism, however, did not amount to the complete denial of the Cossacks' historical merits and their potential military importance in the region. At the time, the argument was about changing the colonizing priorities to the peasants' advantage. As a result, Cossacks were able to retain their light cavalry and border-patrol functions. The Cossacks turned out to be useful as police and as the middle- and lower-level administration because, as one official explained, "having lived since childhood in constant interaction with the nearest neighbors to their settlements and farms, the Kirghiz, they know well the Kirghiz way of nomadic life and also can speak the Kirghiz language." They therefore could provide a link "between the district administration and the Kirghiz people, finding out—because of their craftiness and knowledge of the language and lifestyle—the secret intentions and aspirations of the Muslim community."[37]

Thus, Cossacks acquired the reputation of being reliable agents for unmediated and constant surveillance over the nomads.

In the late nineteenth century and early twentieth century, the government's political priorities on the Asian periphery turned from the narrow task of populating land by anyone—even economically "weak," populations, religiously "alien" old believers and sectarians, or even by convicts—to a broader political vision: the creation of an economically stable and culturally dominant Russian population that could firmly consolidate the empire. At the same time, the populist intelligentsia in Asian Russia, especially those who had anything to do with resettlement and could influence government policy, preferred to regard Russian peasants as "backward," in need of acquiring higher standards of culture and requiring state oversight. They worried about the settlers' ability to organize efficient homesteads upon arrival, which carried as its consequence a possible shortage of arable land.[38]

Resettlement to the Asian periphery complicated long-standing perceptions of "the people" (*narod*) in Russian culture, due to conflicts between the new settlers and the old-timers, and between the peasants and the non-Russians (*inorodtsy*). Publications about settlers were suddenly filled not only with "pain" for their wandering but also with "sadness" for newly observed features in their character, which included a "hungry desire to grab the best piece of land, fear about the final decision about which land to choose, a frothing hurry when rushing from one unsatisfactory place to another."[39] Admiration of the settlers' "courage" and their colonizing energy gave way to negative opinions of their willfulness, propensity for wandering, depredation of natural resources, and lack of any restraint in exploiting the native population. Alexandr Arkad'evich Kaufman, one of the most authoritative experts in the resettlement business, publicly criticized "*muzhik*-loving authors," with their argumentation borrowed from the "ultrapopulist dictionary," and pointed out that the resettlement process was chiefly of an "invasive and predatory nature."[40] Under settler pressure, the local administration had to acknowledge the unauthorized seizure of property and attempted to somehow assure orderliness in the settlers' land rights. However, it was no longer possible to contain the resettlement surge. More and more new settlers overwhelmed not only the other ethnicities but also Russian old-timers, who now found themselves to be the wronged party.

The newly arrived settlers manifested "an amazing absence of common interests, among members of one community." Initially, because of weak self-governance, peasant settlers could not create stable communal infrastructures of governance, justice, and, most importantly, mutual aid. The differences between the settlers themselves, as well as the strange new context in which they found themselves, did not help peasant communes to knit together either.[41] Having assumed a high mission on the peripheries, Russian peasants sought not only to make up for moving and resettling expenses but to continue receiving rewards for their role as national colonizers. These ideas sometimes promoted parasitical attitudes that contributed to the settlers' economic and cultural apathy, as they "lost the habit of any communal responsibilities, such as opening new schools, hospitals, creating community reserves, building of roads, public administration, building of churches, and caring for orphans and invalids; even the fee for the priest's occasional service they considered the government's responsibility."[42]

The appearance of impoverished peasants—pushed out of European Russia primarily by economic conditions—on Russia's Asian peripheries in no way furthered public acknowledgment of the status some planned for them. It was officially recognized that newly arrived settlers' farming capabilities were even lower than those of the local population. Settlers were not prepared to speedily adapt their farming methods to the new climate, and in general they seemed to lack the ingenuity and independence initially expected of them. Naturally enough, settlers tended to seek the same conditions for their farms and households that they had experienced in their homeland; and if, for the lack of the necessary knowledge, determination, perseverance, and funds, they did not find them, they quickly lost their patience and faith in their abilities and abandoned the land to which they had little attachment.

The authorities did not encourage peasants' alienation from farming and their transformation into city dwellers, as this contradicted the ideological directive oriented around the peasant-farmer's potential. All the same, Russian settlers did not resume their steady, settled lifestyle and because of that did not care for the land, so that when their allotments exhausted themselves, they rented something else or moved onto the new resettlement allotment. Miraculous stories about "extraordinarily rich lands" in Siberia—and the printing of popular brochures enticing them to move east of the Urals—provoked peasants to constantly desire to find better land. As a result, it seemed, peasant colonization was not resulting in the creation of the "homogenous thick Russian population" but in a mass of people in Siberia "wandering around the districts aimlessly and pointlessly." Predatory destruction of forest by peasants often was accompanied by statements like, "There's plenty for our lifetime."[43]

Cautiously, trying not to make umbrella statements, journalists began to describe a special type of "land predator," "loafer," or "grabber" who had nothing in common with the "essential plowman." Regression among harvests and agronomic strategies, the lowering of the land's productivity, chronic famine, the loss of communal traditions, and reverse migration became common phenomena accompanying peasant resettlement and acclimatization in the new territories. Those who described this process in social and economic terms preferred to see reasons for the negative phenomena exclusively in the financial sphere: lack of finances for resettlement, inconvenient lands, lack of hands on farms, and lack of livestock and equipment. Some predicted that resettlement to Siberia could "put breaks" on Russia's development, however. "In Siberia farming methods become less cultured, homesteaders and even landowners turn into common laborers, attachment to church and school weakens, and a roving, roguish spirit develops."[44]

Officials were forced to admit that the Russian peasant had not become a model for nomads who were transitioning to farming. The nomads "borrowed the predatory attitude to the land that Russians, unfortunately, manifested in foreign lands."[45] The regionalist (*oblastnik*) Petr Mikhailovich Golovachev wrote, "It has to be noted that the spiritual, moral side of the Kirghiz does not change for the better after living side-by-side with Russians, that is, with Cossacks (who are lazy, ignorant, and greedy) and with the settlers from Russia, whom the Kirghiz views as enemies who would deprive him of his best lands."[46] This sort of disappointment in the Russian people's colonizing potential became common, though it was somewhat hidden by writers' customary sympathy for the people and the criticism of governmental lethargy, which continued to fill the majority of publications about resettlement.

Meanwhile, the settlers went for more and more new land that "does not require either special knowledge, or energy that they do not have; it often happens that they have already visited the mythical 'Chinese Wedge,' and Western Siberia, and Akmolin district; some of them have managed to grab a little piece of new land, exhaust it, and some of them are still wandering looking for the 'promised land.'"[47] That is why, Aleksandr Kaufman argued, the colonial potential of Siberia could not be measured solely by the amount of suitable land but should be assessed by the quality of the settlers as well. Things would be better, he believed, if these settlers were not Russian peasant farmers but "old believers or sectarians, or Letts and German colonists, or Chinese and Koreans, who assign astonishingly little value to their own labor and possess a thousand-year-old tradition of intensive, almost garden-like agriculture."[48]

These critical assessments of the "cultural powerlessness" of Russian peasants provoked a search for enemies, as well as attempts to identify religious and cultural competitors. For example, a nationalistic spirit of struggle with foreign oppression in Asian Russia turned into a phobia of German farming that, supposedly, threatened Russia's mission on the periphery.[49] Tatars were described as dangerous competitors against the Russianization of the Kazakh steppes in Turkestan.[50] Muslims of non-Kazakh origin were prohibited from purchasing land in the steppes. The Jewish threat was not forgotten either, as not only "naïve" natives but also Russian peasants could get into economic bondage to them.[51] "Such a baby-nation," Vladimir Liudvigovich Dedlov stated in his Siberian travelog, "so morally weak; that is why it is so easy for the Germans, the Armenians, and the Middle Eastern natives, who are more cultured and have a more pronounced identity, to manage them. This is why the government has to protect them; otherwise they will be crushed."[52] (This provides another example of an author calling for more intimate, paternalistic relations between imperial power and the Russian people).

Old-Timers and Settlers: "Ours" as "Others"

Mass peasant migration to the peripheries drew attention not only to the economic but also to the religious and moral condition of Russians. There was a growing concern that Russians, outside their habitual social and cultural context, would easily succumb to foreign influence and lose connection with their native Russia. On the Asian peripheries, Russians' preservation of Orthodoxy was of serious concern, first and foremost to religious leaders. Dreams that Orthodox believers would attract natives to Christianity by their example did not materialize. Authorities were set on edge by the numbers of schismatics in Siberia, as well as by Islamic and Lamaist influences. Contemporaries observed that in frequent and close interactions with adherents of different faiths, Russians "became somewhat indifferent to their faith."[53] A special report on the state of the religion in Siberia prepared by the office of the Committee of Ministers emphasized a special need to unite spiritual life on the Siberian periphery with that of the central provinces "by reinforcing Russian Orthodoxy, Russian ethnicity, and civic spirit in that land."[54]

According to government officials, setting such an important goal was warranted by Siberian idiosyncrasies such as old-timers' religious indifferentism and the diverse ethnic and confessional makeup of the population. To stop the process by which settlers were being alienated from "old" Russia and to restore in them a Russianness that the government could recognize and understand, it was necessary to conduct cultural work among these migrants. Anatolii Nikolaevich Kulomzin, the executive officer of the Siberian Railway Committee, insisted on urgent measures aimed at the convergence of Siberia with Russia and encouraged his colleagues to spend generously on schools and Orthodox churches, so that the Siberian wouldn't grow "wild."[55] In 1894, a special fund named after Emperor Alexander III was instituted to collect money for building churches and schools for the settlers. After his visit to Siberia in 1910, Minister Stolypin noted with guarded optimism the growing number of Orthodox churches and schools in the region, inferring that now "the danger of the settlers' moral degradation will be less threatening."[56]

Local authorities often found themselves in a situation where the national imperative to spread Orthodoxy clashed with colonization objectives. Old-believer and sectarian settlements combined an appealing stability with a high degree of farming efficiency but caused concerns from the ideological point of view. (Often, the farming ability and religiosity of old believers was estimated higher than that of the official church followers.[57]) In the end, the imperial government could not work out an unambiguous position in relation to those "persecuted for their faith," leaving the question of confessional sectarianism within the Russian nation open and in the hands of local authorities. The old believers' political loyalty to the empire was acknowledged in the Northwest territories, in Transcaucasia, as well as in the borderland territories of Asian Russia.[58] In no way did the conservatism of their religious life influence the economic inclinations of old-believer colonizers; in new conditions they modernized their farming methods and tools, mastered new trades, and cultivated new crops.

Officials viewed the "low" level of culture among the Russian settlers and old-timers—which seemed to decrease the cultural divide between them and the local peoples—as a threat; it implied that these people were more likely to lose their Russianness than to make the periphery Russian. In this manner, Russian peasant migration to the empire's peripheries and to a new and foreign linguistic and religious environment became a serious test of the Russians' cultural resiliency and adherence to Orthodoxy. Their acculturation could result not only in a change of cultural identity but also in the loss of Russian anthropological features. Voices began to rise, bemoaning the threat of the potential "tungization," "yakutization," "tatarization," "buryatization," or "kirghization" of the Russian people.[59] Popular journals stated that, as a result of these processes, Russians in Siberia decreased in height, diminished in physical strength and fertility, lost their customs, faith, and language, and transitioned "from a higher culture to a lower one"—from farming to cattle husbandry and hunting, from building their traditional *izbas* (log huts) to constructing *chums* (animal-skin tents), and so on.[60] And although this phenomenon was not ubiquitous and was noticeable only in "marginal" groups of the Russian old-timer population far from the major centers of the resettlement, this type of "chimerical ethnography" attracted heightened public attention. [61] Ethnographers contributed to such fearful agitation the most. These men were mostly regionalist (*oblastnik*) and exiled populists who, examining the situation through ideological lenses, sought out deviations in the Russian ethnic, cultural, and anthropological features of the Siberian old-timer population. Nikolai Mikhailovich Iadrintsev, the leader of the Siberian social movement (*oblastnichestvo*), went so far as to prepare a special research program aimed at thorough collection and analysis of data related to how other ethnicities influenced Russians, indicating the cases of physical and mental deterioration of the latter. Travelers and scientists (i.e. professional writers) hurried to share their discoveries of the loss of Russianness at the imperial Asian peripheries, lending these reports social, cultural, and even political importance.

The peasant settlers' predatory treatment of the environment and the exploitative strategies they used against the other ethnicities caused some concern in the government and irritated populist-leaning members of the intelligentsia. Based on such "facts," Georgii Konstantinovich Gins, a resettlement official, came to the following general conclusion (which at least partially saved the face of populist mythology by underscoring the harmful influence of the Asian environment): "When inflamed by the spirit of conquerors, the Russian peasants not infrequently lose their *inherent goodheartedness,* and along with it their childish good-natured smile so beloved by Lev Nikolaevich Tolstoi, who failed to spot this smile amongst the metropolitan proletariat. They get infected with the thirst for profit so widespread on the peripheries among the half-civilized population; they get accustomed to exploiting, get unaccustomed to hospitality—and often they *become unrecognizable.*"[62] Dedlov (as Mikhail Petrovich Pogodin did in his time) thought the Russian people "perhaps an odd people" and had to "quite sincerely and regretfully confess that they were a bad people." He also mentioned Fedor Mikhailovich Dostoevsky, who characterized the Russian intelligentsia thusly: "Russian people are bad, but their ideals are great."[63]

The common image of Siberia as "peasant Eldorado," a "*muzhik* kingdom" of sorts, free from landowners—created, in part, much earlier by the exiled Decembrists—had been built upon by the populist press as an embodiment of its communal socialist ideal. However, as soon as populists faced Siberian reality, many of them quickly forgot their socialist illusions concerning the Siberian peasant. Sergei Iakovlevich Elpat'evskii, a convicted populist revolutionary, was shocked by what he saw in Siberia: "Among the various elements populating a Siberian village, only one is lacking—the Russian. . . . 'Russian' is invisible and unheard of; one has no sense of Russia in Siberia."[64] The same was written by such authoritative authors as the exiled populists I. G. Pryzhov, N. M. Astyrev, N. G. Korolenko, and the Siberian-born A. P. Shchapov. Gleb Ivanovich Uspenskii, one of the most influential intellectuals of the time, was amazed during his trip to "damned Siberia" at how much the "self-willed Siberian," with his "pride," passion for "freedom," tendency to grab things "aggressively," and self-reliance ("if God wouldn't give, we'll take it ourselves!"), was unlike the Russian peasant.[65] He writes of frequent conflicts of "our folks with the Siberians."[66] The Siberian, in his turn, wondered not only about the "Russians'" greed for land but also about their frequent references to the "soul" and constant reliance on God. At this point in history, the Siberian explorers' progress was understood as motivated mainly by avarice and robbery. The legacy of the region as an exile for criminals was also an important part of the formation of an immoral image of the Siberian old-timer.

Since the early 1890s, metropolitan publications had been filled with descriptions written by all kinds of travelers, disseminating the image of the Siberan as a cultural anomaly. Summing up these stereotypes dominating public opinion, the Polish scholar V. Bronislavskii, who spent several years in Siberia, described them in the following way: "Accidental explorers of Siberia attempt to make us believe that the Siberian is spoiled to the marrow of his bone, that he worships brute force, seeing in it man's purpose, that, in a word, he has inherited all the predatory instincts from the first pioneers." Meanwhile, according to Bronislavskii, populist-sympathizing writers faced a dilemma: "The threadbare, destitute, unfortunate exile should have aroused compassion and even perhaps sympathy; in reality, the spiritually offended and indignant visitor of this land of 'miracles and oddities' felt for the Siberian quite different sentiments. Strangely enough, the responsibility for the ugly organization of the Siberian civic life fell upon the Siberian."[67] Siberian separatists were not strangers to populist sentiments and attempts to make "pilgrimages into Siberia," either; yet much faster than their European colleagues, they rid themselves of idealistic views of peasants. Their reports were more realistic, but in this situation the sympathies lay with the old-timer Siberians.

The St. Petersburg newspaper *Sibir'* (Siberia), issued between 1897 and 1898, played an important role here. There were well-known people on its staff: G. N. Potanin, D. M. and P. H. Golovachiov, V. I. Vagin, S. Ia. Elpat'evskii, M. V. Zagoskin, A. A. Kaufman, D. A. Klements, V. M. Krutovskii, D. N. Mamin-Sibiriak, G. A. Machtet, N. L. Skalozubov, and V. L. Seroshevskii. These men represented a variety of political views. However, they were united by the belief that Russian peasant-settlers were not able to perform their cultural mission, in relation to Siberian old-timers and the cattle-breeding Kirghiz, whom they were supposed to initiate into farming. The peasant-settlers were in need of education and introduction to advanced farming methods, because they were "extremely conservative and unaccustomed to learn anything."

The idealized image of the " well-fed contentment" of the Siberian peasants did not satisfy the intelligentsia anymore, wrote one of the authorities on peasant life, the *narodnik* Nikolai Mikhailovich Astyrev. This image was too distant from their own ideals about the Russian peasant, as created and celebrated in great Russian literature—the same literature that had attracted many populists to the cause of serving the people. Astyrev's pen (with reference to ethnographic research and his own observations) produced a portrait of "the Siberian" who acquired a certain wealth but became a "dry materialist," forgot his history, lost his formerly good moral qualities, and even became indifferent to religion. This Siberian was in the habit of respecting the power of money; he had become independent and self-reliant, pragmatic like an American. He was neither musical nor poetic, indifferent to school, though more literate than his brother in European Russia. This literacy, however, did not broaden his "mental horizons" but served only utilitarian purposes.

Most importantly and disappointingly, this was a Siberian who had lost those attractive features of the poor but potentially spiritually rich Russian peasant whom populists so adored and praised, regardless of whether they were in power or opposed to it. This Siberian, Astyrev wrote, "has no idea about the peasant's cross, the peasant's lot that his distant relatives, left to endure the laborer's fate in European Russia, have." The peasant community in Siberia did not retain its traditional name *mir* (world), preferring to call itself a "society" (*obshchestvo*), which robbed it of "that shade of idealism that can still be observed in Russia" and that agrees more with the administrative term "rural community."[68]

Metaphors replaced the former epithets: "Siberia is not the anchor of salvation for Russia"; "Siberia is Russia's daughter who is in every way similar to her mother."[69] When in 1905 the ruling authorities discussed the issue of peasant representation to the state council (Duma), they insisted on privileges for the inner provinces, stating that the peasant deputies from Siberia, Turkestan, and the steppe territory "will not aid in development of the state."[70]

Even Stolypin, who had done so much for the economic and cultural development of Siberia, insisted that the momentum should not be lost, "otherwise, unconsciously and uncontrollably, a huge rough and democratic country will emerge that will soon squash European Russia."[71] His suspension of the introduction of the elective district council (*zemstvo*) in Siberia was not accidental. He was worried that the old-timers would take the leading positions and would resist the resettlement movement. As Kaufman later stated, "The *zemstvo* is good for only one thing—for trying to shut the door on further settlement of the territory."[72] He declared the lands east of the Urals "people's property," which contradicted the separatist and nationalist slogans "Siberia for the Siberians," "Kirghizia for the Kirghiz," and "Buriatiia for the Buriats."[73]

Kaufman also claimed that Amur peasants looked like Americans and not Russian *muzhiks*.[74] This Siberian Yankee is a "materialist to the marrow of his bones" who doesn't care about the "cursed questions" occupying the Russian peasant; there is no one braver than he; he has "neither servility, nor fear of the uniform in him; he knows his worth, knows his rights and, if need be, can defend them. Severe climate taught him to rely only upon himself and cultivated inventiveness and self-assuredness. A skeptic in his soul, he meticulously follows all rituals, but looks at the clergy in the same way he looks at the administration, with hidden contempt." Submissive against his will, the Siberian tried to buy his freedom from the officials and often was ready to protest and take revenge for an offense—to "break the bosses' ribs in a tight spot or send a bullet through his head."[75]

In 1913, Gins, who would live to see the revolution and the civil war, defined the situation born of mass peasant resettlement to the Asian borderland (the frontier between the nomad and the settled worlds) not only as an opposition between the people and the authorities, but also as a "process of the population's silent inner struggle with itself."[76] If critics often imagined the empire as playing only a provocative or aggressive role in the life of Russia's people, here it seemed that the government also served to contain and control the dark instincts that came to the surface when "the bosses left" (as Vasilii Rozanov put it). Free from the restraining and regulating guardianship of the empire, the peasant population fell upon the other ethnicities with an unheard-of fury, capable of demolishing the populist myths about the Russian peasant.[77]

Conclusion

These various interpretations of peasant colonization allow us to better understand how this colonization came to be included in imperial theories and ambitions for the Russianization of the empire; what paradigms dominated the treatment of this theme; and the place this colonization occupied in ambitions to create a "united and undivided Russia."[78] While the scope and aims of various theories obviously differed, they were homogenized by a similar civilizational rhetoric and a shared conviction in the extreme importance of the Russian peasant's role in political, economic, social, cultural, and mental expansion of "Russian land." It was believed that Russian population growth in Asian parts of the empire would further the process of "merging" of the periphery with the center of the country; however, peasant resettlement created new problems for the authorities and exacerbated social, national, and religious controversies.

On the one hand, the settlers often did not take into account the norms of traditional land use, while the feeling of national and cultural dominance could be reinforced by state support. Desires for an internal Russian national consolidation could prevail in these communities and get reinforced by a feeling of superiority; though, in reality, it was not always supported by actual cultural and economic achievements. On the other hand, the Russian peasant-settlers themselves were often viewed as "backward," and their "cultural impotence" produced doubt as to their ability to carry on a civilizing mission. Cossacks, who were accused of not only lacking a civilizing potential but of losing their Russianness, fell under suspicion as well. Even if one allows for the inflation of the scope of this "cultural impotence" and loss of Russianness, one has to take into consideration that they gravely concerned the imperial powers and seriously breached their ideological constructs. The simultaneously coexisting optimistic and pessimistic views about Russian colonization reflected mainly a difference in opinion about the future of "Russia's task in Asia" rather than the real state of the Russian peasantry in the region. These differences not only forced a revision of certain imperial ideological postulates but also undermined the intelligentsia's populist beliefs.

Notes

1. See my previous work on this subject: Anatolyi Remnev, "Rossiia i Sibir' v meniaiushchemsia prostranstve imperii, XIX–nachalo XX veka," in *Rossiiskaia imperiia v sravnitel'noi perspective,* ed. Alexei I. Miller (Moscow: Novoe izdatel'stvo, 2004), 286–319. See also Anatolyi Remnev and Natalia G. Suvorova, "Russkoe delo na aziatskikh okrainakh: 'Russkost' pod ugrozoi ili 'somnitel'nye kul'turtregery,'" *Ab Imperio* 2 (2008): 157–222; Anatolyi Remnev and Natalia G. Suvorova, "'Obrusenie' aziatskikh okrain Rossiiskoi imperii: Optimizm i pessimizm russkoi kolonizatsii," *Istoricheskie zapiski* 11.129 (2008): 132–79; Anatolyi Remnev, "Asian Russia: Colonization and 'Russification' in the Imperial Geography of the Nineteenth to Early Twentieth Centuries" in *Asiatic Russia: Imperial Power in Regional and International Contexts,* ed. Tomohiko Uyama (London: Routledge, 2011).

2. Unlike the first Cossack settlers of Siberia, who were free individuals, in the nineteenth century Cossacks in Asian Russia were under state administration and became a military and administrative resource for the empire, uniting military and agricultural functions.

3. Nicholas Breyfogle, "Kontakt kak sozdanie. Russkie sektanty i zhiteli Zakavkaz'ia v XIX v.," *Diaspory* 4 (2002): 185, 188.

4. Willard Sunderland, "Peasant Pioneering: Russian Settlers Describe Colonization and the Eastern Frontier, 1880s–1910," *Journal of Social History* 24.3 (2001): 895–922.

5. Petr P. Semenov, "Znachenie Rossii v kolonizatsionnom dvizhenii evropeiskikh narodov," *Izvestiia Imperatorskogo Russkogo geograficheskogo obshchestva* 28.4 (1892): 354.

6. Aleksandr I. Vasil'chikov, *Zemlevladenie i zemledelie v Rossii i v drugikh evropeiskikh gosudarstvakh,* vol. 2 (St. Petersburg: Tipografiia M. Stasiulevicha, 1876), 926–27.

7. M. K. Liubavskii, *Obzor istorii Russkoi kolonizatsii s drevneishikh vremen i do XX veka* (Moscow: Izdatel'stvo Moskovskogo universiteta, 1996), 474.

8. Vladimir F. Romanov, "Starorezhimnyi chinovnik (iz lichnykh vospominanii ot shkoly do emigratsii. 1874–1920 gg.," Gosudarstvennyi Arkhiv Rossiiskoi Federatsii (hereafter GARF), f. P-5881, op. 2, d. 598, ll. 261–62.

9. Leonid M. Bolkhovitinov, "Kolonizatory Dal'nego Vostoka," *Velikaia Rossiia: Sbornik statei po voennym i obshchestvennym voprosam,* vol. 1 (Moscow: Redaktor-izdatel' Vladimir P. Riabushinskii, 1910), 222.

10. Irina V. Erofeeva, "Slavianskoe naselenie Vostochnogo Kazakhstana v XVIII–XX vv.: Migratsionnoe dvizhenie, stadii sotsiokul'turnoi evoliutsii, problemy reemigratsii," in *Etnicheskii natsionalizm i gosudarstvennoe stroitel'stvo,* ed. Yuri G. Alexandrov (Moscow: Institut vostokovedenia Rossiiskoi Akademii Nauk, 2001), 333.

11. Evgenii F. Shmurlo, "Russkie poseleniia za iuzhnym Altaiskim khrebtom na kitaiskoi granitse," *Zapiski Zapadno-Sibirskogo otdela Imperatorskogo Russkogo geograficheskogo obshchestva,* vol. 25 (Omsk: Tipografiia okruzhnogo shtaba, 1898), 62. Svetlana Lur'e describes this process of the peasants "running away" from the state as a "cat-and-mouse" game. See Svetlana V. Lur'e, *Istoricheskaia etnologiia* (Moscow: Aspekt Press, 1997), 161–69.

12. Vadim V. Trepavlov, *"Belyi Tsar": obraz monarkha i predstavleniia o poddanstve u narodov Rossii XV-XVIII vv.* (Moscow: Vostochnaia literatura, 2007), 123–24.

13. Gleb I. Uspenskii, "Pis'ma pereselentsev (Zametki tekushchei narodnoi zhizni)," in *Polnoe Sobranie Sochinenii,* vol. 12 (Moscow: Akademiia nauk USSR, 1953), 294.

14. Rossiiskii gosudarstvennyi voenno-istoricheskii arkhiv (hereafter RGVIA), f. 400, op.1, d. 2952, l. 141.

15. Tsentral'nyi gosudarstvennyi arkhiv Respubliki Kazakhstan, f. 369, op. 1, d. 4591, l.30.

16. Nikolai F. Fedorov, *Sochineniia* (Moscow: Izdatel'stvo "Mysl'," 1982), 110, 286, 335, 378.

17. Claudia Weiss, "'Nash': Appropriating Siberia for the Russian Empire," *Sibirica* 5.1 (Spring 2006): 141–55.

18. Nikolai M. Przheval'skii, *Puteshestvie v Ussuriiskom krae, 1867–1869* (Moscow: OGIZ, 1947), 70.

19. I discuss this subject in more detail in my article "Imperiia rasshiriaetsia na vostok: 'Toponimicheskii natsionalizm' v simvolicheskom prostranstve Aziatskoi Rossii XIX–nachala XX veka," in *Ofiary imperium. Imperia jako ofiary. 44 spojrzenia,* ed. Andrzei Nowak (Warsaw: Instytut Pamieci Narodowej, Instytut Historii Polskiej Nauk, 2010), 153–58.

20. Rostislav A. Fadeev, "Zapiska ob upravlenii aziatskimi okrainami," in *Kavkazskaia voina* (Moscow: Eksmo, 2003), 276.

21. *Ocherki istorii Belorusov v Sibiri v XIX–XX vv.,* ed. Mikail P. Kostiuk and Vladimir A. Lamin (Novosibirsk: Izdatel'stvo Novosibirskogo gosudarstvennogo universiteta, 2001), 60.

22. "Sovremennaia letopis' (*Moskovskie Vedomosti* 342)," *Russkii vestnik* 12 (1882): 999.

23. "Zapiska general-maiora fon Valia 'Otvety na voprosy o krest'ianskikh pereseleniiakh' 1890-e gg)," GARF, f. 586, op. 1, d. 393, l. 5.

24. "Zapiska Pleve 'Sovermennoe polozhenie pereselencheskogo dela' (dekabr' 1903). Chernovik," GARF, f. 586, d. 404, ll. 17, 35.

25. *Zapiska predsedatelia Soveta ministrov i glavnokomanduiushchego zemleustroistvom i zemledeliem o poezdke v Sibir' i povolzh'e v 1910 g.* (St. Petersburg: Tipografiia A.S. Suvorina, 1911), 81.

26. "Po proektu polozheniia Kirgizskoi Stepnoi komissii ob upravlenii kirgizskimi stepiami (1868g.)," RGVIA, f. 400, op. 1, d. 120.

27. Vladimir Dedlov-King, *Pereselentsy na novye mesta: Panorama Sibiri* (Moscow: N.p., 2008), 45.

28. Tatiana K. Makhrova, *Kazachestvo Urala i vlast'* (Moscow: Izdatel'stvo "Globus," 2004), 75.

29. Nikolai M. Przheval'skii, *Puteshestvie v Ussuriiskom krae,* 226–27.

30. "Izvlechenie iz zhurnalov obrazovannoi v Khabarovske v 1909 g. Komissii po kolonizatsionnomu delu," Arkhiv vneshnei politiki Rossiiskoi imperii, f. *Tikhookeanskii stol,* op. 487, d. 762, l. 472.

31. Vladimir M. Kabuzan, *Dal'nevostochnyi krai v XVII–nachale XX vv. (1640–1917).*

Istoriko-demograficheskii ocherk (Moscow: Izdatel'stvo "Nauka," 1985), 151; Leonid L. Rybakovskii, *Naselenie Dal'nego Vostoka za 150 let* (Moscow: Izdatel'stvo "Nauka," 1990), 21.

32. "1895 g. December 30. Otchet Semirechenskogo gubernatora o naselenii, vkliuchaia kazachestvo, i khoziaistvennoi deiatel'nosti v Semirechenskoi oblasti," in *Kazach'i voiska Aziatskoi Rossii v XVIII–nachale XX veka (Astrakhanskoe, Orenburgskoe, Sibirskoe, Semirechenskoe, Ural'skoe)*, ed. Nailia E. Bekmakhanova (Moscow: Istitut Rossiskoi istorii Rossiskoi Akademii Nauk, 2000), 273–74.

33. Aleksandr N. Sedel'nikov, "Raspredelenie naseleniia Kirgizskogo kraia po territorii, ego etnograficheskii sostav, byt i kul'tura," *Rossiia. Polnoe geograficheskoe opisanie nashego otechestva,* vol. 18, ed. Veniamin P. Semenov-Tian-Shanskii (St. Petersburg: Izdatel'stvo Al'fred F. Devrien, 1903), 198.

34. Ibid., 188.

35. Nikolai M. Przheval'skii, "O vozmozhnoi voine s Kitaem (Urga, 22 oktiabria 1880 g.)," in *Sbornik geograficheskikh, topograficheskikh i statisticheskikh materialov po Azii,* vol. 1 (St. Petersburg: Voenno-uchenyi komitet General'nogo shtaba, 1889), 299–300.

36. V. I. Kuz'minykh, "Obraz russkogo kazaka v fol'klore narodov Severo-Vostochnoi Sibiri," in *Uralo-Sibirskoe kazachestvo v panorame vekov* (Tomsk: Izdatel'stvo Tomskogo universiteta, 1994), 32–39.

37. "Pis'mo ispolniaiushchego dolzhnost' stepnogo general-gubernatora Sannikova ministru vnutrennikh del, 12 iiulia 1900 g," RGVIA, f. 400, op. 1, d. 2952, l. 137.

38. Aleksandr A. Kaufman, "Voprosy pereseleniia: I. Pereselenie i kolonizatsiia (Rech' na dispute)," *Russkaia mysl'* 6 (1895): 346.

39. Victor K. Shne, "Pereselenie v Semipalatinskuiu oblast,'" *Stepnoi Krai* 76 (19 October 1895).

40. Aleksandr A. Kaufman, "Nash Dal'nii Vostok i ego kolonzatsiia," *Russkaia Mysl'* 12 (1909): 57.

41. A. I. Ivanov, "Russkaia kolonizatsiia v Turkestanskom krae," *Russkii vestnik* 11–12 (1890): 245.

42. *Sbornik glavneishikh ofitsial'nykh dokumentov po upravleniiu Vostochnoi Sibiriu,* vol. 2 (Irkutsk: N.p., 1884), 14.

43. *Iubileinyi sbornik Zapadno-Sibirskogo otdela Imperatorskogo Russkogo geograficheskogo obshchestva* (Omsk: Tipografiia okruzhnogo shtaba, 1902), 103.

44. Dedlov-King, *Pereselentsy na novye mesta,* 326–27.

45. "Zapiska [Zemskogo otdela MVD] po voprosu o sodeistvii kochevnikam kirgizam k perekhodu v osedloe sostoianie," Tsentral'nyi Gosudarstvennyi arkhiv Respubliki Kazakhstan (hereafter TsGA RK), f. 64, op. 1, d. 647, l. 8.

46. Petr M. Golovachev, *Sibir, Priroda, Liudi, Zhizn'* (Moscow: Izdatel'stvo Iu. I Bazanovoi, 1902), 136.

47. Russkii, "K voprosu o kolonizatsii kirgizskikh stepei (Golos iz Turgaiskoi oblasti)," *Sibir',* 20 June 1897.

48. Alexandr A. Kaufman, "Kolonizatsiia Sibiri v ee nastoiashchem i budushchem," *Sibirskie voprosy* 1 (1905): 175.

49. Dmitrii I. Rezun and Mikhail V. Shilovskii, *Sibir', konets XVI–nachalo XX v.: Frontir*

v kontekste etnosotsial'nykh i etnokul'turnykh protsessov (Novosibirsk: Izdatel'stvo "Sova," 2005), 16. See also Petr P. Vibe, *Nemetskie kolonii v Sibiri: Sotsial'no-economicheskii aspekt* (Omsk: Izdatel'skii dom "Nauka," 2007).

50. See Anatolii Remnev, "Tatary v kazakhskoi stepi: Soratniki i soperniki Rossiiskoi imperii," *Vestnik Evrazii* 4.34 (2006): 5–31.

51. *Vsepoddaneishii otchet Stepnogo general-gubernatora za 1910 g.* (Omsk: N.p., 1910), 21.

52. Dedlov-King, *Pereselentsy na novye mesta*, 330.

53. Vasilii Kir'iakov, *Ocherki po istorii pereselencheskogo dvizheniia v Sibir' (V sviazi s istoriei zaseleniia Sibiri)* (Moscow: N.p., 1902), 327.

54. "Tserkovnoe delo v raione Sibirskoi zheleznoi dorogi," in *Rossiia. Komitet Sibirskoi zheleznoi dorogi (Materialy),* vol. 1 (St. Petersburg: Kantseliaria Komiteta Ministrov, 1894), 116.

55. Anatolyi N. Kulomzin, *Perezhitoe,* RGIA. f. 1642, op. 1, d. 204, l. 107; d. 202, l. 37.

56. "Zapiska predsedatelia Soveta," 124.

57. *Vsepoddaneishii otchet po Tomskoi gubernii za 1879 g,* Gosudarstvennyi arkhiv Omskoi oblasti, f. 3, op. 10, d. 17047, ll. 170–71.

58. Nicholas Breyfogle, *Heretics and Colonizers: Forgings Russia's Empire in the South Caucasus* (Ithaca, N.Y.: Cornell University Press, 2005); F. F. Bolonev, *Staroobriadtsy Zabaikal'ia v XVIII–XX vv* (Novosibirsk: Izdatel'stvo "Fevral'," 1994).

59. See Willard Sunderland, "Russkie prevrashchaiutsia v iakutov? 'Obynorodchivanie' i problemy russkoi natsional'noi identichnosti na Severe Sibiri, 1870–1914," in *Rossiiskaia imperiia v zarubezhnoi istoriografii. Raboty poslednikh let,* ed. Paul Werth, Petr S. Kabytov, Alexei I. Miller (Moscow: Novoe izdatel'stvo, 2005), 199–227.

60. "Novye knigi, Nikolai M. Iadrintsev, Sibir' kak koloniia, K iubileiu trekhsotletiia," *Otechestvennye zapiski* 5 (1882): 113.

61. A review of Nikolai M. Iadrintsev's *Sibir' kak koloniia* (Siberia as a colony), for example, cited such exaggerations of ethnographers and impressionable "tourists." See Semen M. Kapustin, "Zerkalo Rossii" *Russkaia Mysl'* 1 (1883): 1–37.

62. Georgii K. Gins, "V Kirgizskikh aulakh (Ocherki iz poezdki po Semirech'iu)," *Istoricheskii vestnik* 10 (1913): 331–32.

63. Dedlov-King, *Pereselentsy na novye mesta*, 51.

64. Sergei I. El'patevskii, "Chuzhaia zemlia" in *Strana bez Granits,* vol. 1 (Tiumen: SoftDizain, 1998), 133.

65. Gleb I. Uspenskii, "Pis'mo Gleba I. Uspenskogo Nikolaiiu I. Naumovu (Omsk, 30 iiulia 1888 g.)," in *Polnoe sobranie sochinenii,* vol. 14 (Moscow: Akademia nauk USSR, 1953), 154.

66. In 1882, Ivan G. Pryzhov, earlier than Uspenskii and much more critically, wrote about how Russian people became completely barbarous in Siberia, and how the Siberian population "is too often, if not always, dumb and angry," happy to "devour a traveler or, as they say here, 'the Russian' [*rossiiskii*]." See Ivan G. Pryzhov, *26 moskovskikh prorokov, iurodivykh, dur i durakov i drugie trudy po russkoi istorii i etnografii* (Moscow: Izdatel'stvo "Intrada," 1996), 181.

67. V. Bronislavskii, "Sushchestvuet li sibirskaia narodnost'" *Sibir'* 13 June 1897.

68. Nikolai M. Astyrev, "Ocherki byta naseleniia Vostochnoi Sibiri" *Russkaia mysl'* 10 (1890): 94.

69. Nataliia N. Rodigina, "Obraz Sibiri v russkoi zhurnal'noi presse XIX–nachala XX v.: Osnovnye itogi izucheniia," in *Obraz Sibiri v obshchestvennom soznanii rossiian XVIII–nachala XXI v.*, ed. Vladimir A. Zverev (Novosibirsk: Izdatel'stvo Novosibirskogo gosudarstvennogo pedagogicheskogo universiteta, 2006), 99–100.

70. Rafail S. Ganelin, *Rossiiskoe samoderzhavie v 1905 godu. Reformy i revoliutsiia* (St. Petersburg: Izdatel'stvo "Nauka," 1991), 178.

71. "Pis'mo Petra A. Stolypina Nikolaiu II, 26 sentiabria, 1910 g," in *Petr A. Stolypin: Perepiska* (Moscow: Rossiiskaia politicheskaia entsiklopediia, 2004), 62.

72. Kaufman, "Nash Dal'nii Vostok," 65.

73. Kaufman, "Kolinzatsiia Sibiri," 171.

74. Aleksandr A. Kaufman, *Po novym mestam (ocherki i putevye zametki)1901–1903* (St. Petersburg: N.p., 1905), 46, 48.

75. V. Aleksandrov, "Argun' i Priargun'e. Putevye zametki i ocherki." *Vestnik Evropy* 9 (1904): 283.

76. Georgii K. Gins, *Pereselenie i kolonizatsiia* (St. Petersburg: N.p., 1913), 28.

77. Elbek-Dorzhi Rinchino, "Velikaia revoliutsiia i inorodcheskaia problema v Sibiri [Chita, 1918]," *Dokumenty, stat'i, pis'ma* (Ulan-Ude: Ministerstvo pechati Respubliki Buriatii, 1994), 43–44, 55–62.

78. Alfred J. Rieber, "Colonizing Eurasia," in *Peopling the Russian Periphery: Borderland Colonization in Eurasian History,* ed. Nicholas Breyfogle, Abby Schrader, and Willard Sunderland (New York: Routledge, 2007) 269, 272.

7

Druzhba Narodov or Second-Class Citizenship?

Soviet Asian Migrants in a Postcolonial World

JEFF SAHADEO

The title of a glossy 1982 publication proclaimed, *Moscow: A Capital for Everyone*. Only Slavs or Balts, however, smiled for photos in the book's pages.[1] Brief mentions of citizens from Asian regions of the USSR were limited to those who came to study, on work exchanges, or to organize cultural festivals. They could "get their start" in the capital, but the compilers of this and similar volumes expected them, as well as foreign students at Petrice Lumumba Friendship University, to return home to pursue professional or family lives.[2] As they lectured or studied at institutes of higher learning, worked as medical or technical professionals, or, often without official permission, conducted trade in downtown and suburban markets, hundreds of thousands, including Tatars, Azeris, and Uzbeks, remained cloaked in the "two capitals" of Leningrad and Moscow. Along with other minorities, they were denied rights to cultural organizations or to educate children in their national language. At the same time, as new arrivals from former colonial regions of other European states gathered in ethnic ghettos in the metropoles and faced open hostility, many Soviet migrants remember their experiences with fondness, considering themselves proud citizens and arguing that the "friendship of peoples" (*druzhba narodov*) promoted by the regime accurately reflected the harmony they experienced at the heart of the USSR.

Intercultural contact emerged as a central event in defining identity and status in the Soviet Union. Migrant experiences in navigating new environments, as well as policies and attitudes flowing from host societies, offer critical insights into official and popular conceptions of nation, culture, race, and a multiethnic society. As Rogers Brubaker has argued, interethnic mixing produces ambiguous results, strengthening some boundary markers and weakening others.[3] A focus on migrants' lived experiences offers a window toward comparisons with other European states. This essay places the Soviet Union within a global trend of migration from former colonies to Western urban cores in the late twentieth century.[4] Institutional and structural differences remained important; unlike the looser ties formed by Great Britain with its former colonies, for example, the Soviet Union existed as a centralized state with policies to support and develop marginal regions and create a society where national inequalities, though not national distinctiveness, would be submerged under a single "Soviet people." Certain inequities similar to those in Western states nonetheless persisted, affecting the character and volume of migration from the USSR's peripheries. Ambivalence characterized the welcome of newcomers who brought vital skills but different appearances and cultures.

Migrants overwhelmingly appreciated the opportunities they found at the center of the Soviet Union. Russians and non-Russians alike expressed support for Soviet ideas and policies of internationalism. Efforts to stress unity prompted an official avoidance of the term "race" in favor of underlining benign cultural differences between nations. Francine Hirsch takes seriously Soviet claims that the recognition, or in many cases creation, of national groups was a precursor in the march toward equality, to produce a seamless merger (*sliianie*) in a modern socialist state.[5] Differences of color and culture nonetheless tested adherence to equal citizenship and the slogan of *druzhba narodov*.[6] The avoidance of the term "race" does not prevent national distinctions from containing, in the words of Kwame Appiah, "a racial essence."[7] George Fredrickson applies the concept of race to a belief that "significant differences between human groups or communities . . . in visible characteristics or putative ancestry are unchangeable."[8] Eric Weitz has maintained that Soviet policy racialized nationhood, endowing each nation with ostensibly primordial characteristics, from appearance to culture and ways of life.[9] Constructions of hierarchies followed nation building; Terry Martin has noted how the Russian-dominated Soviet state began in the late 1930s to grant the Russian nation a status as "first among equals."[10]

Consciousness of hierarchies and difference spilled into private discourse and street-level encounters, with peoples from the North and South Caucasus, Central Asia, and the Asian regions of the Russian Soviet Federated Socialist Republic (RSFSR) labeled "black" (*chernye*). In addition to being grouped together by racial epithets built upon imperial legacies that defined these peoples against an advanced, white, European Russian population,[11] similarities of treatment in the official realm and commonalities of migrant experiences lead me for the purposes of this essay to merge these groups as "Soviet Asians."[12] This shorthand, however, should not be seen as homogenizing various ethnic, social, and other groups therein.

Migration and the ambiguous reception of nonwhite migrants in former colonial capitals characterizes the fluidity and power imbalances of the postcolonial era.[13] Beyond a simple labeling of the period following the end of European formal empires, the term "postcolonialism" remains the subject of debate. Ania Loomba has argued that the postcolonial involves the contestation of colonial domination.[14] But she recognizes, as does Robert Young, that postcolonialism must account for colonialism's continued legacies. Economic and political links survived the end of empire. Former colonies with differing histories and cultures remained fused into an economic path directed from outside.[15] Intensifying migration from late twentieth-century Western and Soviet peripheries testifies to the strength, if not the strengthening, of core-periphery inequalities along colonial trajectories.[16]

Postcolonial theories can, I argue, alter the debate over the degree to which the Soviet Union constituted an imperial or colonial state. Although a full discussion of the concept lies beyond the scope of this essay, postcolonialism's ambiguities can contain the complexity, and seeming contradictions, of Soviet rule over a multiethnic society that emerged from the tsarist empire. Yuri Slezkine led recent scholars in recognizing the duality of "chronic ethnophilia" and Russian dominance in the USSR.[17] Subsequent studies have exposed continuities and changes from the tsarist era, as well as inconsistencies within Soviet ideology and practice toward minorities and the borderlands. The debate over the essence of the Soviet national state has become polarized, however, with the USSR either being characterized as an imperial or "colonial empire"[18] or a new, universalist socialist entity.[19] Adrienne Edgar, working between these poles, still addresses the issue in either/or terms in a recent study of interwar policies towards Turkmen women, arguing that "Soviet policy. . . . although not imperial in intention, was nonetheless imperial in effect."[20]

Moving beyond the interwar period (the overwhelming focus of scholars interested in questions of empire or colonialism in the USSR) offers new directions. Lines of comparison can be opened with Western states, which in the post-1945 era claimed, like the USSR a generation before, to have shed their imperial skin. In addition to probing similarities and differences of concurrent migration and racism, we have access to a greater variety of sources. Oral interviews and surveys offer ground-level insights into experiences of intercultural contact. This essay draws on twenty-two interviews of ethnic minorities from 2004 to 2007.[21] Oral histories provide particular methodological challenges. History becomes structured and restructured in people's minds; in particular, I and my research assistants confronted a powerful sense of nostalgia for the Soviet

Union, especially given xenophobia in contemporary Russia.[22] Respondents reverted to stereotyping along lines of ethnicity and class, though the stereotypes they use can be telling. Their most vivid testimony occurred when discussing personal experiences of intercultural contact. At the same time, perspective and a changing world led some to consider their own experiences in a broader global and historical perspective.[23]

Soviet and post-Soviet social scientists have also provided valuable survey and interview material. Galina Starovoitova's work on Leningrad's ethnic minorities spurred the subdiscipline of "ethnosociology."[24] Soviet scholars cited in this essay viewed large multiethnic cities as vital engines of integration in the formation of a new Soviet people. "Backward" (*otstal'nye*) nationalities were seen to profit from mobility, with villagers moving to district or republican capitals, and national elites experiencing life in the heart of the USSR.[25] Intimate interethnic contact harmonized ways of life, with intermarriage the ultimate proof of the "merger of nations."[26] Oral histories and qualitative surveys expose the dynamism of the adaptation process, the importance of individual mentalities and behavior, as well as the uniqueness of a Soviet system within a late twentieth-century postcolonial world.

Migrants and Migration

Stalinist policies altered the multinational character of Leningrad and Moscow, home to over one hundred thousand Tatars as well as smaller groups from the Caucasus and Central Asia in the 1930s.[27] In what Terry Martin calls the "Russification of the RSFSR," municipal authorities closed all non-Russian national schools, periodicals, and cultural organizations in 1937; none reopened before the glasnost era.[28] Arrests of those suspected of spying for foreign powers, outmigration, and wartime deaths decimated Leningrad and Moscow's minorities. Postwar opportunities to live in the USSR's "showcase cities" nonetheless attracted Soviet Asian migrants once more; the 1959 census registered 80,500 Tatars, and over five thousand Armenians, Mordvins, Georgians, and Chuvash in Moscow.[29] Several thousand Soviet Muslims, along with foreigners, were attending services in Moscow's one official mosque in the late 1960s.[30]

Postwar migration to reconstruct major cities linked the Soviet Union to other European states. Whereas the Soviets relied upon rural Russians alongside Tatars and others, British legislators looked abroad. Hopeful of perpetuating colonial ties after the impending end of formal empire, they passed the Nationality Act of 1948.[31] The act confirmed unrestricted entry and full political and social rights to residents of British-held colonial territories. Migrants overwhelmingly chose London as their destination; from 1951–66, the West Indian migrant population alone in the city grew from seventeen thousand to 269,000.[32] By the end of the 1960s, eight hundred thousand migrants from the "new commonwealth" (former British territories excluding Canada, New Zealand, Australia, and South Africa) assumed residence in the British capital.[33] Even after British politicians placed restrictions on migration, numbers of former colonials grew in a multiethnic London.[34]

As human flows from peripheries to cores of former Western empires mushroomed, Soviet planners trumpeted their management of movement. A "scientific, predictable, and planned" process differentiated socialist from capitalist economies.[35] Investment in the economies of non-Russian republics, which were partners in a single state rather than cast away former colonies and a *propiska* (permit) system required for residence in Leningrad, Moscow, and other cities gave authorities powerful tools to control resettlement. Significant arrivals to the USSR's heartland from Azerbaijan and Central Asian republics, beginning in the 1960s, were composed primarily of administrators, intellectuals, and students, targeted elites for whom a stay in Moscow was a symbol of prestige.[36] The 1970 Soviet census noted nonetheless that Central Asians as a whole were becoming more likely than those in other regions to migrate outside their own republics, with the RSFSR as their primary destination.[37] Demographic and structural inequities—principally higher birth rates and lower levels of industrialization in southern regions—that replicated those in former Western colonies led some demographers to predict that migration northwards would become a "major influence upon Soviet society."[38] From 1970 to 1989, the numbers of Kyrgyz, Tajik, Turkmen, and Uzbeks registered as living in Russia increased from 140,000 to 248,000—insufficient to be a major social influence, but growth to be sure. By 1989, all-Union census figures counted over thirty thousand Central Asians in Leningrad and Moscow, in addition to over thirty thousand from Azerbaijan. Tatars officially remained the largest non-European group in the "two capitals," with combined numbers of over two hundred thousand.[39] Migration rates from Asian regions of the USSR to Moscow were two to three times higher than from European areas in the last decade of the USSR.[40] Census statistics likely undercounted minorities, relying on self-identification and missing those residing without official permission.[41] Olga Vendina notes that Soviet Asians constituted a substantial portion of the 20 percent non-Russian population in Moscow's core by the end of the Soviet era.[42]

In our interviews, educated migrants, the target of managed movement to the USSR's "showcase cities," expressed satisfaction at assuming residence in the "center of our part of the world."[43] Families and friends appreciated the status that accompanied their relocation to Leningrad or Moscow. Even a temporary stay broadened future career prospects, especially for students. Annual competitions among Central Asian youth for a few thousand spots in institutes of higher education and technical schools were intense. Opportunities for advancement and the sense of prestige at living in the capital of a global power were not restricted to the USSR. Reflecting on his own experience, the Jamaican intellectual Stuart Hall recalls how, "as they hauled down the [British] flag, we got on the banana boat and set sail for the hub of the world."[44] In the USSR, students and professionals alike noted not only the prestige of degrees from Leningrad and Moscow but also the liberty of study and work environments, freer from censorship and with greater access to intellectual materials.[45] Access to consumer goods was also significantly better than at home. Many grew attached to the vitality of urban life. Culture, the arts, science fairs, and museums were available to new arrivals, and not only those who constituted the educated strata. One migrant who failed her university entrance exams and worked in a vegetable market recalled a "cultural liaison" in her dormitory distributing tickets to performances.[46]

Even as economic "push" factors for migration differed in the early postwar era, models of economic development linked the USSR and Western empires. Communists replicated tsarist and other European imperial patterns in using their periphery as a pool for raw resources. Even at the height of "ethnophilia" in the 1920s, the primary Soviet goal in Central Asia was to restore its cotton economy to supply central Russian factories.[47] The skilled professional and industrial labor force in the region remained predominantly European throughout the Soviet period.[48] As a consequence, European outmigrations back to the core, another postcolonial global pattern replicated in the Soviet Union in the 1970s and 1980s as investment in former colonial regions declined, caused significant damage to local economies. Although I would argue that these legacies play a significant role in massive contemporary migration to the Russian Federation,[49] the Soviet economic system stemmed an outward flow. Nancy Lubin found that central planning encouraged collective farm managers to hoard labor, so that ever-increasing numbers of agricultural workers still had jobs and social support. Given relatively low wage differentials, Central Asians beyond upwardly mobile urban strata had less incentive to migrate northward than those in former colonies of Western powers, whose already poor economic systems had been significantly disrupted by formal decolonization.[50]

As labor shortages appeared in the RSFSR in the 1970s, the relative immobility of Central Asian agricultural workers emerged as an official concern. Natural population growth, averaging about four children per family, outpaced employment opportunities.[51] As yields of cotton, dependent on nutrient-killing pesticides and marginal soil, declined, the state Commission of Labor and Social Problems promoted efforts to send Central Asians to technical-vocational schools in the RSFSR for training in service and industrial sectors of the economy, in demand particularly in the Far East.[52] This campaign enjoyed little success, even as youth unemployment in the Ferghana Valley reached 25 percent in the 1980s.[53]

At the same time, rural residents from the Caucasus, who were not targeted for migration, grew increasingly mobile, with major Russian cities as their primary destinations.[54] Villagers exploited slackening state supervision over collective farms to concentrate production on private plots. Low transport costs and established diaspora connections encouraged farmers to sell their products—citrus fruits, melons, vegetables, and flowers—in central Russia. Profits, especially for goods sold in Moscow, were substantial.[55] Georgians and Azeris, among others, became highly visible figures in the public life of Russian capitals, selling their wares in markets or outside metro stations.[56] Azeris took control of the flower-selling market from Balts and Ukrainians.[57] Many of these migrants came without official permission, living with friends and relatives; however, a *propiska* could be obtained through various semilegal means, including bribing passport officials.[58] Economic opportunities, adding to declining investment also apparent in the Caucasus in the USSR's last decades, increased incentives for migration to Leningrad and Moscow.

Other Soviet Asians sought work on construction sites and municipal projects in the "two capitals." Enterprises recruited migrants for jobs that the local population considered undesirable. They became known as "*limitchiki,*" hired on a contract of up to three years, with a temporary resident permit that would be revoked once employment ended. [59] Often unskilled workers—or, in the case of one Uzbek informant, hired straight from military service—*limitchiki,* excluded from the regular housing queue, crowded into state dormitories. For those who sought career advancement but lacked the connections or education to gain permanent residence in Leningrad or Moscow, the status of a *limitchik,* which included rural Russians as well, had its advantages.

Accommodation and the Host Society

All of these new arrivals faced the challenge of adapting to the host society. Local Russians' contacts with these migrants, and migrant perceptions of these contacts, differed on official and unofficial levels, across profession, class, and status, and according to personal willingness to integrate in a multinational city. Internationalist ideals allowed Soviet Asians a degree of comfort not always experienced by former colonials in other European capitals. Violence against African students and racist remarks on the streets of Leningrad and Moscow to Soviet "blacks" nonetheless refute official representations of a mature Communist society free of prejudice.[60] The presence of multiple ethnic groups confirmed Russia's status as the leading nation of a global superpower, but migrants' different characteristics and apparent privileges prompted disquietude.[61]

Interviews and surveys with migrants registered to live in Leningrad and Moscow displayed overall satisfaction with municipal officials. Tajiks who remained in Leningrad after their studies said that they were assigned "normal" apartments. In the work environment, migrants expressed comfort and relative confidence that their minority status did not impede career advancement or relationships with colleagues. Party status was considered a more important factor in mobility, though migrants recognized the CPSU as Russian-dominated.[62] One survey of Caucasus migrants in Moscow taken immediately following the USSR's collapse showed relatively low numbers claiming that their ethnicity significantly damaged career prospects, with Georgians at 16 percent, compared to 6 percent of Armenians and Azeris.[63] An Uzbek migrant stated that professors and employers privileged non-Russian students, taking seriously the role of "elder brother."[64]

Soviet officials selectively trumpeted the integration of former colonials, now proud citizens, alongside students and workers from the developing world and African Americans seeking to escape racial prejudice.[65] To delegations from Asia, Africa, and Latin America, Moscow was the "city of the friendship of peoples [*druzhba narodov*]" and a center of Leninist national politics.[66] Muslim diplomats visited Moscow's only mosque and met with leaders of the official Islamic establishment.[67] Otherwise, however, official publications, from guidebooks to demographic studies ignored Soviet Asians. The comprehensive annual statistical publication *Moscow in Numbers* broke down residents by district, occupation, class, gender, and other groupings, but did not include ethnicity, a category compiled only during the decennial all-union Soviet censuses.[68] Slavic faces dominated Soviet television, especially but not only in urban centers of the RSFSR.[69] Less privileged *limitchiki* remained concealed in republic laws and official discourse.[70] Soviet Asian migrants were woefully underrepresented at all-Union-level state and party organizations in Moscow, not to mention the local levels in major Russian cities.[71]

How do we interpret these absences? Absolute numbers of former colonial minorities remained smaller than in Paris or London. Soviet education policies ensured that overwhelming majorities of migrants spoke Russian well.[72] Continued restrictions on non-Russian schools, publications, and cultural associations reduced minorities' public visibility. State-assigned housing restricted the appearance of concentrated ethnic districts, although well-established minorities such as Georgians and Armenians clustered around certain cultural markers.[73] At the same time, I would argue that Soviet officials and academics saw modern cities—especially but not uniquely those in the Russian core—as inherently European. According to *Moscow: A Capital for Everyone,* city residents were expected to display a "high degree of culture and consciousness," characteristics equated with Europeans, or Europeanness, as the author was certainly not referring to the essentialized cultures of Asian peoples developed through Soviet nationalities policy.[74] Meredith Roman has argued that the colorful festivals of national cultures that marked the most prominent official appearances of Asian minorities in Moscow fixed a hierarchy that placed them as premodern foils to the advanced Russians.[75] Even as scholars vaunted the urban environment's importance for the creation of a "Soviet people," Asian minorities were excluded from the discourse of development of the USSR's showcase cities.

Growing Russian nationalism following the Second World War contributed to racist expressions and acts, although the nature of the relationship between nationalism and racism remains poorly understood.[76] Alexander Yanov quotes one 1965 nationalist Komsomol document that called for a "voice of the blood" and a "cult of ancestors" to be worshipped in Russia.[77] John Bushnell reports that leading party members' sons became involved with nationalist groups.[78] African students, whose numbers increased significantly in 1960s Moscow, reported frequent assaults and police harassment; one murder prompted an unsanctioned 1963 demonstration of several hundred Africans in Red Square.[79] Physical attacks on Soviet Asians are absent from the vast majority of migrant accounts, which helps to account for the predominant perception of equal citizenship within a host Slavic society.

At the same time as these attacks on Africans, the term "blacks" (*chernye*) became more frequently applied to Soviet Asian minorities.[80] Emil Draitser traces the epithet to the immediate postwar era, but its origins and evolutions— as well as its links to racist expressions in Europe and the United States, which were also undergoing south-north migration—remain far from clear. By the late 1960s, when my informants recall hearing the term, perceptions of Soviet Asian migration were becoming linked to highly visible traders. Ethnic humor at that period focused on Georgians, who sullied through involvement in "dirty" capitalist dealings not only themselves, but also their pure, white Slavic hosts.[81] Linking color and economic endeavor to racialize ethnic relationships dates back to the tsarist period, when Russians asserted that their distance from capital gain made them a superior people.[82] As in postcolonial Europe, Russians feared that migrants' enterprise would lead migrants to surpass them on the social ladder. One informant told Rasma Karklins that "the blacks want to take over everywhere."[83] Officials began to deal more harshly with "black" migrants, sweeping them from markets and train stations in advance of the 1980 Olympics.[84] Richard Rowland noted that Muscovite Russians preferred housing in regions dominated by their own ethnicity or Tatars over those with higher concentrations of Caucasians or Central Asians.[85] Changes in the urban "contact zone" led the host society to reevaluate its sense of national identity, as well as its conceptions of multiculturalism and internationalism.[86]

Soviet Asian students' or professionals' experiences in public spaces conditioned their overall evaluation of the "friendship of peoples." Some stated that "racism never existed at all" or, even after years of living in Leningrad and Moscow, that they witnessed no behavior in any form or forum that could be characterized as prejudiced.[87] Others reported hearing the epithets "blacks" or *churkoi* (monkey) and chants of "non-Russian go home" or, in one case "our children cannot get a higher education because of you."[88] One Uzbek claimed the treatment he received on Leningrad's streets drove him to leave, so he would no longer "feel like an *untermensch*."[89] Another who remained claimed that although he considered Russia and Uzbekistan "parts of one country," he never felt himself to be more than a "temporary guest."[90] A Buryat informant separated street-level insults from her professional life, where she was treated as an "equal Soviet citizen."[91]

Problems, as well as the presence, of ethnic minorities in Leningrad and Moscow remained concealed at the same time as the British government developed antiracist legislative acts.[92] Certain provisions of these acts—in housing and employment, for example—were in domains where Soviet minorities expressed strong satisfaction with their own government. At the same time, the pre-glasnost Soviet leadership's continued ban on national organizations prevented the minority participation in public life that emerged in Western capitals, where various ethnicities gained media voices and a political presence. *Druzhba narodov* continued to be expressed through cultural artifacts that highlighted a hierarchical separation between nations.[93]

Glasnost offered unprecedented opportunities for minorities to organize, but also for street-level racism to penetrate popular media. In 1988, members of a Russian fascist group spoke live on Moscow television of the threat of growing Central Asian populations and the potential for "mongrelization" of the Russian nation.[94] A burgeoning right-wing glasnost press spewed racist invective. Before the publication of the 1989 census, however, language primarily targeted Jews. Only in 1990 does a concerted effort link the "illness" and "degeneration" of the Russian nation to the influx of "southerners," who stole jobs and led Russians to take up alcoholism, drugs, and prostitution.[95] The Republican People's party named "pushy" blacks as a factor leading to the potential genocide of Russians.[96] Yet many of these publications feared that the loss of the periphery would end Russia's status as the leading nation of a superpower. As shortages and uncertainties worsened during perestroika, popular opinion expressed significant discomfort with minorities, particularly from the Caucasus: a 1992 survey by Moscow State University's Center for the Study of Public Opinion reported that 46 percent of native Muscovites reported negative feelings toward Azeris, 40 percent toward Chechens, 34 percent toward Armenians, and 33 percent toward Georgians and Gypsies. Only 8 percent recorded negative feelings toward Jews, and even fewer toward other white minorities.[97]

Interethnic liaisons, in Leningrad and Moscow as well as in London, served as a flashpoint for nationalist sentiment. In London, postwar racial disharmony grew at a faster pace, as greater numbers of migrants, many impoverished and lacking language skills, integrated less seamlessly. Anger among poor whites at perceived privileges given newcomers and competition for employment and housing heightened by the mid-1950s.[98] Conceptions of Englishness and Britishness shifted from imperial pride to privileging white Europeanness.[99] An attack on a mixed-race couple by young whites catalyzed a riot in a London district in 1958 that involved knives and petrol bombs.[100] In 1962, British politicians placed the first limits on migrants from former colonies. Simultaneously, Moscow witnessed incidents of racial violence against male African students who associated with Russian women.[101] As Sascha Goluboff has argued, notions of race always privilege purity and hence become inevitably gendered, with women as a threat to separation.[102]

Racial insults resulted from Soviet Asians associating with Russians in romantic situations or public spaces. One informant reported a Buryat friend with a Russian suitor hearing outside a movie theater: "Shame on you to walk with such a monkey. You should find a Russian girl for making love."[103] Tatars noted tension when the host population perceived an improper mixing of national groups, from children of different ethnicities playing together to teachers and students discovering someone in their classroom was the product of a mixed marriage.[104] Samizdat material attacked mixed marriages for "random hybridization."[105] G. I. Zainkina and E. V. Foteeva have criticized Soviet sociologists and demographers for viewing interethnic marriages solely as ultimate evidence of success on the path toward the "merger of nations" when social problems with these unions were apparent.[106]

Identity and Adaptation

Soviet Asian migrants expressed willingness to make certain sacrifices in order to live in the "sacred center" of Moscow or the cultural and educational hotbed of Leningrad.[107] "Spatial stratification" played a large role in my informants' sense of Soviet hierarchies.[108] A desire to live in these cities obviated fears of the State Council for Religious Affairs, which, seeing growing ethnic tension in 1950s–60s Europe, worried that Soviet Muslims might turn to culture or religion to mobilize against the regime. The council noted that Moscow's Muslims had only one mosque and cemetery, despite the fact that 90 percent of Tatars preferred to bury their dead according to Islamic custom.[109] Bans on cultural and national-based organizations had the potential to spur unofficial anti-Soviet groupings.[110] A 1992 Moscow State University survey showed that Moscow's minorities, even as they accepted certain limitations to live in the all-Union capital, claimed that these bans hindered their integration.[111] During glasnost, minorities formed cultural organizations and opened ethnic shops and restaurants as organizational opportunities arose.[112]

Strategies of adaptation and accommodation are central to the migrant experience. Differing according to individual and group, across status, class, and gender, these strategies determine associations, comfort levels, and desired or real lengths of stay in a foreign environment. Some seek a high degree of cultural and personal assimilation; others, professional but not cultural integration; still others minimize nonessential contacts with majority populations. The Soviet experience of common citizenship produced numerous migrants in interviews who saw no borders separating them from "their" capital, with Leningrad and Moscow serving as the realization of *druzhba narodov,* offering complete equality to all citizens of the USSR.[113] I. V Arutiunian's study of the Armenian community noted nonetheless that a perception of being privileged in Moscow did not always equal personal satisfaction. Armenians adjusted personal surroundings to re-create their own culture in the capital. Yet only 25 percent expressed complete contentment with their culture and lifestyle, and many felt isolated from networks of power and privilege.[114] One Uzbek informant who relished the education that he received in Moscow expressed dissatisfaction that only Slavs went to Western Europe on academic or research travel, with Central Asians being sent to Arabic or African countries.[115]

Integration into Soviet Leningrad and Moscow altered elements minorities considered central to their own national identity, but did not, even among those in mixed marriages, significantly transform the strength of identification with a nation. This puzzled some Soviet sociologists who sought progress towards a unified "Soviet people." Arutiunian noted that 88 percent of Armenians (including those from mixed marriages) who had lived a full generation in Moscow and 97 percent of those who arrived more recently considered themselves "full" Armenians. Different factors tied them to their home nation: recent arrivals identified language; "old-timers" (*starozhiltsy*), Russian speakers having lived in Moscow for a generation or more, retained a sense of belonging to Armenia's "historical fate," including memories of the genocide.[116] Given high levels of Armenian integration into Moscow, Arutiunian posited a "limited connection between self-identity and behavior."[117]

Important markers of "home" culture considered in some post-Soviet surveys elucidate a connection between national identity and behavior. For some, ethnic cuisine guarded a sense of home.[118] In a study of Leningrad Armenians, Olga Brednikova and Elena Chikadze note holiday celebrations as key to ethnic attachment.[119] Tatars, another highly integrated minority, had a considerably different view of history than the host population. They angrily refuted the so-called progressive nature of Russian imperial expansion as taught in Soviet schools.[120] Others in my interviews claimed national and cultural superiority through linking Russians to various negative traits: lack of respect towards elders, ignorance, drunkenness, and promiscuity.[121] In the Moscow State University survey, clear majorities of minority groups (including those in mixed marriages) preferred to rear their children according to "national traditions," led by Georgians (90 percent) and Uzbeks (80 percent).[122] Although the holding of traditions remained consistent with Soviet multinationalism, intercultural contact led to self-identification through a distancing from the Russian "big brother."

Migrants' minority status prompted difficult decisions regarding incorporation. Tension surrounded the choice of nationality for passports of children born in Leningrad and Moscow. Respondents expressed frustration as they realized the social and political advantages—potential avoidance of harassment and a clearer path to advancement—if their children could be declared ethnically Russian, even if neither parent felt attached to the majority culture.[123] Such discussions were not limited to mixed-marriage families; evidence suggests that, as with *propiska* regulations, migrants had discovered means of declaring children Russian even if this was the nationality of neither parent.[124] The naming of the child was a charged process, as parents would calculate how skin and hair color would evolve.[125] People with ethnic names who did not fit their appearances faced sarcasm from not only strangers but also colleagues and officials. Minorities who could pass for Russian would take on a Russian diminutive: Kamil, for example, would become Kolya.[126]

The professional and cultural attractions of Leningrad and Moscow softened the feelings of self-described non-Russian patriots or nationalists. One Georgian claimed that he easily integrated into Moscow despite the occasional street-level insult, but he preferred to associate with other Georgians. He recalled the arts, ballets, and theaters but stressed that enjoyment of these "traditionally Russian" arts did not equate to support for the USSR. One Armenian claimed that his own success in Leningrad enforced his view that "all Russians are ignorant." The city, with its natural beauty and cultural opportunities, nonetheless made it almost as attractive as Yerevan. This informant, as well as others, went out of their way in interviews to discuss "opportunities" with Russian women as one of the great temptations of life at the heart of the USSR. Other informants stated matter-of-factly that their experiences confirmed what they already knew about Soviet life: that "native" nationalities are favored in their home republic, and that in the long term, life for them would be easier if they returned.

Excitement about ascending to residence in Leningrad and Moscow was tempered with the realization of strict spatial hierarchies compelling migrants' presence if they hoped to join Soviet cultural, social, or intellectual elites.[127] Elsewhere in the world, colonial core-periphery legacies also conditioned migrant paths. As Stuart Hall has noted, former colonials realized that exploiting postcolonial opportunities, including upward mobility within one's own republics or countries, continued to necessitate a stay in European capitals, where the "play of power" occurred.[128] Many elite migrants appreciated the power as well as the culture of the postcolonial capitals; the Kyrgyz author Chingiz Aitmatov recently argued that "Moscow contributed enormously to the development of our country."[129] One Azeri informant spoke of his pride in residing at the heart of a "great empire."[130] A Kyrgyz intellectual who remained at home criticized the cultural dimension of spatial inequality, noting her need for frequent travel to Moscow, claiming, "How can one live without books?"[131]

Integration into multinational Soviet Leningrad and Moscow complicated relationships within and across minority groups. Within ethnic communities, generational divides proved important. Long-term residents often held patronizing attitudes toward, or isolated themselves from, new, especially rural, arrivals. The latter provided an uncomfortable reminder of how "denationalized" the established community had become, despite strong national self-identification.[132] Starovoitova noted a major line between Leningrad Tatars who spoke Russian and those who spoke Tatar at home. The Russian-speaking group, more oriented toward integration, was less interested in keeping links with conationals or new arrivals; 90 percent approved of mixed marriages, for example, versus 53 percent for the Tatar speakers.[133] Certain other markers, like those who ate pork, divided Muslim minorities. At the same time, ethnic communities established *zemliachestvo,* or kin/ethnic-based support groups, to assist new arrivals in finding housing and employment as well as providing cultural support.[134] Select Leningrad and Moscow minorities expressed greater antagonism toward other minorities than the host society. Armenians, Azeris, and Georgians preferred to work with Russians rather than each other.[135] Long-term residents of virtually all national groups in a 1997–98 survey agreed with Russians that Jews were Moscow's dominant national group during the Soviet period.[136]

Individual migrant experiences and cross-cultural encounters in Leningrad and Moscow alternately enforced and undermined state goals. Migrants appreciated the privileges of living in the USSR's "showcase cities," taking advantage of cultural and professional opportunities and sheltered by multinationalism in official dealings and at the workplace. But restrictions on national organizations and a high level of integration did not catalyze the creation of a "Soviet people." State efforts to manage migration foundered as opportunities in the south narrowed. Glasnost allowed public expression of nationalist and racist discourses heightened by the increased presence of southern traders. At the same time, *druzhba narodov* remains an important component of identity, especially given contemporary racism. As one Kazakh scientist nostalgically stated, dismissing the idea of racism or national tension in the Soviet period: "I have always been a Soviet citizen, and I still am one."[137]

Extensive development projects on the Soviet periphery produced important variations on the migrant experience from those in western, industrial, postcolonial states. Lesser differentiations of wealth, universal citizenship, widespread, if uneven, social services, and a lack of borders allowed a relative freedom to move, or not to move, within the USSR, as compared to the new British commonwealth, for example. The open and volatile racial tensions that prompted British politicians to limit dark-skinned migrants did not materialize in central Soviet Russian cities. At the same time, in the USSR as well as the United Kingdom and its former nonsettler colonies, the play of power and the heart of the industrial economy remained in the European core. As John Rex has argued, migrant minorities faced implicit or explicit requirements to display loyalty to the central state, accept the practices of the host government and society, and acknowledge the privileged aspects of its culture.[138] The *propiska* and the category of *limitchik* embodied Soviet efforts to control populations of its privileged cities. Soviet Asian migrants faced challenges and limitations, particularly if they sought to remain permanently instead of returning home to effuse, as the regime intended, loyalty to a benevolent regime and newfound skills to conationals in their home republics.

Significant work remains to be done to contextualize the Soviet experience of south-north or east-west migration within larger international trends. France, with its assimilatory goal of universal citizenship, may provide a useful comparative path.[139] This research points to factors other than color or race in determining the nature of migrant experiences in Leningrad and Moscow. In an ostensibly classless society, class played an important role. Whereas Soviet Asian professionals integrated relatively smoothly, the appearance of traders and manual workers sparked popular frustration and racist feelings, which some of my informants blamed on lower-class, nonprofessional Russians. My male informants' stress on "adventures" with Russian women demands investigation into issues of masculinity, and larger issues of gender have not been addressed here. A fundamental question remains: given the apparent lack of violence and significant levels of comfort among dark-skinned migrants in Leningrad and Moscow as compared to London and Paris, what about the Soviet system produced this? For while I have shown, in agreement with Meredith Roman, that the system carried seeds of racism, it also produced a sense of tolerance that did not transfer into post-Soviet life.

Broader comparisons and arguments should not subsume the richness of individual experiences. Oral histories show that migrants of similar backgrounds, faced with roughly similar environments and challenges, thought and acted in significantly different ways. Decisions regarding the extent to which migrants adapt, whether in London or Moscow, remain highly charged and personal, reflecting present and potential self-identities. This personal dimension constitutes a critical factor in telling the story of identity, power, and Soviet migration in a global context.

Notes

1. E. B. Bernaskoni, ed., *Moskva: Dlia vsekh stolitsa* (Moscow: Moskovskii rabochii, 1982).

2. R. Dement'eva, "Serdtse Rodiny nashei," in *Moskva: Dlia vsekh stolitsa,* ed. E. B. Bernaskoni (Moscow: Moskovskii robochii, 1982), 17–33. See also *Moskva: Vchera i segodnia* (Moscow: Moskovskii rabochii, 1978); and I. U. Aleksandrovskii, *Moskva: Dialog putevoditel'* (Moscow: Moskovskii rabochii, 1983).

3. Rogers Brubaker, "The 'Diaspora' Diaspora," *Ethnic and Racial Studies* 28.1 (2005): 3–7.

4. On the core-periphery structure of the global economy, see, for example, Immanuel Wallerstein, *The Capitalist World-Economy: Essays* (New York: Cambridge University Press, 1979).

5. Francine Hirsch, *Empire of Nations: Ethnographic Knowledge and the Making of the Soviet Union* (Ithaca, N.Y.: Cornell University Press, 2005).

6. On the relationship between nationalities and a "Soviet people," see *Razvitie natsional'nykh otnoshenii v SSSR* (Moscow: Izdatel'stvo politicheskoi literatury, 1986), 123.

7. Kwame Anthony Appiah, "Racisms," in *Anatomy of Racism,* ed. David Theo Goldberg (Minneapolis: University of Minnesota Press, 1990), 1–5. For a discussion of Appiah's ideas in a post-Soviet context, see Sascha Goluboff, *Jewish Russians: Upheavals in a Moscow Synagogue* (Philadelphia: University of Pennsylvania Press, 2004).

8. Nancy Foner and George Fredrickson, "Immigration, Race, and Ethnicity in the United States: Social Constructions and Social Relations," in *Not Just Black or White: Historical and Contemporary Perspectives on Immigration, Race, and Ethnicity in the United States,* ed. Nancy Foner and George Fredrickson (New York: Russell Sage Foundation, 2004), 2.

9. Eric D. Weitz, "Racial Politics without the Concept of Race: Reevaluating Soviet Ethnic and National Purges" *Slavic Review* 61.1 (2002): 3. On "Stalinist Primordialism" and how the Soviets presented national differences, see Terry Martin, *The Affirmative Action Empire: Nations and Nationalism in the Soviet Union, 1932–1939* (Ithaca, N.Y.: Cornell University Press, 2001). On how these categories resonated, see Z. V. Sikevich, *Peterburzhtsy: Etnosotsial'nye aspekty massogo soznaniiia* (St. Petersburg: Sankt-Petersburgskii gosudarstvennyi universitet, 1995).

10. Martin, *Affirmative Action Empire,* 442–50.

11. On these legacies from the Russian east, see Yuri Slezkine, *Arctic Mirrors: Russia and the Small Peoples of the North* (Ithaca, N.Y.: Cornell University Press, 1994); in the Caucasus, see Susan Layton, *Russian Literature and Empire: The Conquest of the Caucasus from Pushkin to Tolstoy* (Cambridge: Cambridge University Press, 1994); in Central Asia, see Jeff Sahadeo, *Russian Colonial Society in Tashkent, 1856–1923* (Bloomington: Indiana University Press, 2007).

12. Some—particularly Georgians and Armenians, and those of mixed heritage—may justifiably claim a "non-Asian" status on the basis of history, ethnicity, or religion. I believe nonetheless that the term has utility for this study's purposes.

13. On the range of influences stemming from migration from former colonies, see Paul Gilroy, *Black Atlantic: Modernity and Double Consciousness* (Cambridge, Mass.: Harvard University Press, 1993). On the challenges of identifying and interpreting diaspora experiences, see James Clifford, "Diasporas," *Cultural Anthropology* 9.3 (1994): 302–38; and William Safran, "Diasporas in Modern Societies: Myths of Homeland and Return" *Diaspora* 1.1 (1991): 83–99.

14. Ania Loomba, *Colonialism/Postcolonialism* (London: Routledge, 1998), 12.

15. Robert Young, *Postcolonialism: A Historical Introduction* (Oxford: Blackwell, 2001), 4–5.

16. John McLeod, *Beginning Postcolonialism* (Manchester: Manchester University Press, 2000); see also Barbara Bush, *Imperialism and Postcolonialism* (Harlow: Pearson, 2006).

17. Yuri Slezkine, "The USSR as a Communal Apartment, or How the Soviet State Promoted Ethnic Particularism," *Slavic Review* 53.2 (1994): 414–52.

18. Douglas Northrop, *Veiled Empire: Gender and Power in Stalinist Central Asia* (Ithaca, N.Y.: Cornell University Press, 2004), 22. See also Paula Michaels, *Curative Powers: Medicine and Empire in Stalin's Central Asia* (Pittsburgh: University of Pittsburgh Press, 2003).

19. Adeeb Khalid sees a "mobilizational state" seeking to lift the disadvantaged from backwardness. Adeeb Khalid, "Backwardness and the Quest for Civilization: Early Soviet Central Asia in Comparative Perspective" *Slavic Review* 65.2 (2006): 251. See also Marianne Kamp, *The New Women in Uzbekistan: Islam, Modernity, and Unveiling under Communism* (Seattle: University of Washington Press, 2006). Peter A. Blitstein argues that if "the Soviet Union was a colonial project, then it was so distinctive to determine the question of whether it was worth calling it such." Peter A. Blitstein, "Cultural Diversity and the Interwar Conjuncture: Soviet Nationality Policy in a Comparative Context" *Slavic Review* 65.2 (2006): 293.

20. Adrienne Edgar, "Bolshevism, Patriarchy, and the Nation: The Soviet 'Emancipation' of Muslim Women in Pan-Islamic Perspective," *Slavic Review* 65.2 (2006): 272.

21. Some of these interviews were conducted by me, and others by my graduate assistants, Lissa Greenspoon and Shakhnozah Matnazarova. Interviews and follow-up questions were done in person, over the phone, and by email. Respondents were drawn via "snowball method" from North America and the former Soviet Union. Interviews primarily consisted of those who came to the cities as students or professionals. Names of interviewees are pseudonyms.

22. Svetlana Boym, *The Future of Nostalgia* (New York: Basic Books, 2001).

23. Alistair Thomson, "Making the Most of Memories: The Empirical and Subjective Value of Oral History," in *Transactions of the Royal Historical Society,* 6th ser., vol. 9 (1999): 291.

24. Galina Starovoitova, *Etnicheskaia gruppa v sovremennom sovetskom gorode; sotsiologicheskie ocherki* (Leningrad: Nauka, 1987).

25. N. A. Aktov, ed., *Sovetskii gorod: Sotsial'naia struktura* (Moscow: Mysl', 1988).

26. Rasma Karklins, *Ethnic Relations in the USSR: The View from Below* (Boston: Allen and Unwin, 1987), 154.

27. N. S. Goncharova, "Tatarskoe naselenie Moskvy. Gendernye aspekt," in *Gendernye*

problemy v obshchestvennykh naukakh, ed. I. M. Semashko (Moscow: RAN, Instit. etno. antro im. N.N, Miklykho-Maklaia, 2001), 203.

28. Martin, *Affirmative Action Empire,* 406–13.

29. *Itogi vsesoiuznoi perepisi 1959 goda RSFSR* (Moscow: Gosstatizdat, 1962), 316.

30. Yaacov Ro'i notes reports of forty thousand gathering for Eid celebrations. Yaacov Ro'i, *Islam in the Soviet Union: From the Second World War to Gorbachev* (New York: Columbia University Press, 2000), 75n.

31. On the act, see Romain Garbaye, "British Citizens and Ethnic Minorities in the Post-war Era: From Xenophobic Agitation to Multiethnic Government," *Immigrants and Minorities* 22.2–3 (2003): 299.

32. Nancy Foner, *In a New Land: A Comparative View of Immigration* (New York: New York University Press, 2005), 132.

33. Garbaye, "British Citizens and Ethnic Minorities," 300.

34. Nonwhite minorities composed 25 percent of the population of the inner city in 1991, a number that had grown to 34 percent by 2000. Chris Hamnett, *Unequal City: London in the Global Arena* (London: Routledge, 2003), 108–11.

35. Cynthia Buckley, "The Myth of Managed Migration: Migration Control and Market in the Soviet Period," *Slavic Review* 54.4 (1995): 904–5.

36. Meredith Roman, "Making Caucasians Black: Moscow since the Fall of Communism and the Racialization of non-Russians," *Journal of Communist Studies and Transition Politics* 18.2 (2002): 6.

37. *Vsesoiuznaia perepis' naseleniia 1970 goda: Sbornik statei* (Moscow: Statistika, 1976), 248–49.

38. Richard A. Lewis, Richard. H. Rowland, and Ralph S. Clem, *Nationality and Population Change in Russia and the USSR: An Evaluation of Census Data, 1897–1970* (New York: Praeger, 1976), 354–81.

39. Statisticheskii Komitet Sodruzhestva Nezavisimykh Gosudarstv, *Itogi vsesoiuznoi perepisi naseleniia 1989 g.,* vol. 7, pt. 1 (Moscow: Statistika, 1991).

40. Vera Glubova, "Zaboty mnogonatsional'nogo goroda," *Arkhitektura i stroitel'stva Moskvy* 9 (1989): 8.

41. Barbara Anderson and Brian Silver, "Estimating Russification of Ethnic Identity among the Non-Russians of the USSR," *Demography* 20.4 (1983): 461–89.

42. Olga Vendina, "Social Polarization and Ethnic Segregation in Moscow," *Eurasian Geography and Economics* 43.3 (2002): 228.

43. Interview with Shuhrat Ikramov, 12 March 2007.

44. Stuart Hall, "The Local and the Global: Globalization and Identity," in *Culture, Globalization, and the World-System: Contemporary Conditions for the Representation of Identity,* ed. A. D. King (Basingstoke, U.K.: McMillan, 1991), 24.

45. Interview with Shuhrat Ikramov, 12 March 2007.

46. Interview with Aryuna Khamangova, 12 February 2007.

47. Sahadeo, *Russian Colonial Society,* chap. 8. Lenin overruled arguments from Communists in the region, who pleaded for the establishment of a local industrial base to modernize Central Asia. On similarities between western and Soviet models of exploitation of the periphery, see John Comaroff, "Humanity, Ethnicity, Nationality: Conceptual

and Comparative Perspectives on the USSR," *Theory and Society* 23.1 (1994): 47–78; and Kate Brown, "Gridded Lives: Why Kazakhstan and Montana are Nearly the Same Place," *American Historical Review* 106.1 (2001): 17–48.

48. Nancy Lubin, *Labor and Nationality in Soviet Central Asia: An Uneasy Compromise* (Princeton, N.J.: Princeton University Press, 1984), 205.

49. Jeff Sahadeo, "'The Legacy of the Friendship of Peoples: Russia's Ethnic Problems Have Soviet Roots," *Russia Profile* 7.4 (August–September 2007): 22–24.

50. Lubin, *Labor and Nationality,* 128.

51. Ibid., 25–51.

52. Murray Feshbach, "Prospects for Outmigration from Central Asia and Kazakhstan in the Next Decade," *Soviet Economy in a Time of Change* (Washington: U.S. Government Printing Office, 1979), 662.

53. Most Central Asians returned to their republics as soon as, if not before, the work or study programs ended. William Fierman, "Central Asian Youth and Migration," in *Soviet Central Asia: The Failed Transformation,* ed. William Fierman (Boulder, Colo.: Westview, 1991), 257, 268.

54. L. V. Makarova et al., *Regional'nye osobennosti migratsionnykh protsessov SSSR* (Moscow: Nauka, 1986), 86.

55. Arif Iusupov, "Azerbaizhandtsy v Rossii-smena imidzha i sotsial'inykh rolei," *Diaspory* 1 (2001): 113.

56. Emil A. Draitser, *Taking Penguins to the Movies: Ethnic Humor in Russia* (Detroit: Wayne State Universiry Press, 1998), 36. Several interviewees recall the presence of Caucasians at urban markets.

57. Iusupov, "Azerbaizhandtsy v Rossii-smena imidzha," 114.

58. Buckley, "Myth of Managed Migration," 908.

59. Dietrich Andre Loeber, "*Limitchiki*: On the Legal Status of Migrant Workers in Large Soviet Cities," *Soviet Union/Union Sovietique* 11.3 (1984): 301–8.

60. On the Soviet desire to display this image, see Roman, *Making Caucasians Black,* 2.

61. On the pride associated with being part of a superpower, see ibid., 7; on internationalism, see Hilary Pilkington, *Migration, Displacement, and Identity in Post-Soviet Russia* (London: Rouledge, 1998).

62. Oksana Karpenko, "Byt' 'natsional'nym': Strakh poteriat' i strakh poteriatsia, Na primere tatar St. Peterburga," in *Konstruirovanie Etnichnosti: Etnicheskie obshchiny Sankt-Peterburga,* ed. V. Vornokova and I. Osvald (St. Petersburg: Izdatel'stvo "Dmitry Bulanin," 1998), 37–97.

63. Liubov Ostapenko and Irina Subbotina, "Problemy Sotsial'no-ekonomicheskii adaptsii vykhodtsev iz zakavkaz'ia v Moskve," *Diaspory* 1 (2000): 50.

64. Interview with Murad Imamaliev, 8 February 2007.

65. Kate A. Baldwin, *Beyond the Color Line and the Iron Curtain: Reading Encounters between Black and Red, 1922–1963* (Durham, N.C.: Duke University Press, 2002).

66. Dement'eva, "Serdtse Rodiny nashei," 17; Vydro, 29.

67. See, for example, "Guests of Soviet Muslims from the Yemen Arab Republic," *Muslims of the Soviet East* 1 (1985): 16.

68. V. M. Moiseenko, *Naselenie Moskvy: Proshloe, nastoiashchee, budushchee* (Mos-

cow: Izdatel'stvo Moskovskogo Universiteta, 1992); *Moskva v tsifrakh za gody Sovetskoi vlasti: Statisticheskii sbornik* (Moscow: Statisticheskoe upravlenie, 1980–89).

69. Ellen Mickiewicz and Dawn Plumb Jamison, "Ethnicity and the Soviet Television News," in *Mass Culture and Perestroika in the Soviet Union,* ed. Masha Siefert (Oxford: Oxford University Press, 1991), 154–58.

70. Loeber, *"Limitchiki,"* 301.

71. Stephen L. Burg, "Central Asian Political Participation," in *The USSR and the Muslim World,* ed. Yaacov Roi (London: Allen and Unwin, 1984), 53.

72. Starovoitova reports that over 95 percent of Leningrad Tatars and Armenians spoke Russian "freely." Starovoitova, *Etnicheskaia gruppa,* 96.

73. Glubova, "Zaboty mnogonatsional'nogo goroda," 8.

74. Dement'eva, "Serdtse Rodiny nashei," 32.

75. Roman, "Making Caucasians Black," 5–7.

76. See, for example, John Dunlop, *The Faces of Contemporary Russian Nationalism* (Princeton, N.J.: Princeton University Press, 1983); Daniel Rancour-Laferriere, *Russian Nationalism from an Interdisciplinary Perspective: Imagining Russia* (Lewiston, N.Y.: E. Mellen Press, 2000).

77. Alexander Yanov, *The Russian New Right* (Berkeley: University of California Press, 1978), 170–72.

78. John Bushnell, *Moscow Graffiti: Language and Subculture* (Boston: Unwin Hyman, 1990), 157.

79. Julie Hessler, "Death of an African Student in Moscow: Race, Politics, and the Cold War," *Cahiers du monde russe* 47.1–2 (2006): 33.

80. Draitser, *Taking Penguins,* 108; interview with Marat Tursunbaev, 15 May 2007.

81. Draitser, *Taking Penguins,* 41.

82. Sahadeo, *Russian Colonial Society in Tashkent,* chap. 5.

83. Karklins, *Ethnic Relations,* 92.

84. Conversation with Diane P. Koenker, Urbana, Ill., Fall 1994.

85. Richard Rowland, "Nationality Population Distribution, Redistribution, and Degree of Separation in Moscow, 1979–1989," *Nationalities Papers* 26.4 (1998): 705–21.

86. On the "contact zone," see Mary Louise Pratt, *Imperial Eyes: Studies in Travel Writing and Transculturation* (London: Routledge, 1992).

87. Interview with Zhamila Sadybekova, 23 May 2007.

88. Interview with Aryuna Khamagova, 12 February 2007.

89. Interview with Marat Tursunbaev, 15 May 2007.

90. Interview with Shuhrat Ikramov, 12 March 2007.

91. Interview with Aryuna Khamagova, 12 February 2007.

92. Garbaye, "British Citizens and Ethnic Minorities," 306–9.

93. Roman, "Making Caucasians Black," 5–6.

94. Bushnell, *Moscow Graffiti,* 152.

95. *Golos Rossii* (Natsional'no-Respublikanskaia Partiia Rossii, Leningrad) 1.6 (1991).

96. *Nashe vremia* 5 (1991): 4.

97. Aleksandr Verkhovskii, Anatolii Papp, and Vladimir Pribylovskii, *Politicheskii ekstremizm v Rossii* (Moscow: Izdatel'stvo 'Institut eksperimental'noi sotsiologii,' 1996), 13.

98. Kathleen Paul, *Whitewashing Britain: Race and Citizenship in the Postwar Era* (Ithaca, N.Y.: Cornell University Press, 1997), 131–69.

99. C. Harris, "Images of Blacks in Britain, 1930–1960," in *Race and Social Policy*, ed. S. Allen and M. Macey (London: Social and Economic Research Council, 1988), 53.

100. John Solomos, *Race and Racism in Britain*, 3d ed. (Basingstoke, U.K.: Palgrave, 2003), 54–55

101. Hessler, "Death of an African Student," 36.

102. Goluboff, *Jewish Russians*, 123; see also Ann Laura Stoler, "Making Empire Respectable: The Politics of Race and Sexual Morality in Twentieth-Century Colonial Cultures," *American Ethnologist* 16.4 (1989): 634–61.

103. Interview with Aryuna Khamagova, 12 February 2007.

104. Karpenko, "Byt' 'natsional'nym,'" 49.

105. S. Enders Wimbush, "Great Russians and the Soviet State: The Dilemmas of Ethnic Dominance," in *Soviet Nationality Policy and Practices*, ed. Jeremy Azrael (New York: Praeger, 1978), 354.

106. G. I. Zainkina and E. V. Foteeva, "Mezhnatsional'nyi brak v massovom soznanii," *Vestnik Rossisskoi Akademii Nauk* 66.4 (1996): 296.

107. Interviews with Murad Imamaliev, 8 February 2007; Shuhrat Ikramov, 12 March 2007; Aryuna Khamagova, 12 February 2007.

108. Hilary Pilkington, "The Future Is Ours: Youth Culture in Russia, 1953 to the Present," in *Russian Cultural Studies*, ed. Catriona Kelly and David Shepherd (Oxford: Oxford University Press, 1998), 378.

109. Yaacov Roi, *Islam in the Soviet Union: From the Second World War to Gorbachev* (New York: Columbia University Press, 2000), 707.

110. Ibid., 653.

111. G. Belaieva, D. Draguskii, and L. Zotova, "Mnogonatsional'nyi mir Moskvy," *Druzhba narodov* 4 (1993): 138. The survey included 447 members of Moscow's minorities, 60 percent of whom had higher education.

112. Ibid; Glubova, "Zaboty mnogonatsional'nogo goroda," 8.

113. Interviews with Zhamila Sadybekova, 23 May 2007; Oidin Nosirova, 15 May 2007.

114. I. V. Arutiunian, "Armiane-Moskvichi: Sotsial'nyi Portret po materialam etnosotsiologicheskago issledovanie," *Sovetskoe Etnografiia* 2 (1991): 8.

115. Interview with Shuhrat Ikramov, 12 March 2007.

116. Arutiunian, "Armiane-Moskvichi," 13–14.

117. Ibid., 13.

118. Interview with Oidin Nosirova, 15 May 2007.

119. Olga Brednikova and Elena Chikadze, "Armiane St. Peterburga: Kar'ery etnichnosti," in *Konstruirovanie etnichnosti: Etnicheskie obshchiny Sankt-Peterburga*, ed. V. Vornokov and I. Osval'd (St. Petersburg: Izdatel'stvo "Dmitry Bulanin," 1998), 230.

120. Sikevich, *Peterburzhtsy*, 124.

121. Interviews with Zurab Iashvili, 23 January 2007; Rafael Voskanyan, 20 December 2006. See also Sikevich, *Peterburzhtsy*, 124.

122. Beliaeva, Dragunskii, and Zotova, "Mnogonatsional'nyi mir Moskvy," 138.

123. Ibid., 147–48.

124. Vendina, "Social Polarization," 227.

125. Karpenko, "Byt' 'natsional'nym,'" 48.

126. Ibid.

127. Interview with Elmira Jumagulov, 31 July 2007.

128. Hall, "Local and the Global," 24.

129. Interview with Chingiz Aitmatov, "Dialogue with the Islamic World," 24 May 2007; accessed 25 August 2007, www.qantara.de/webcom/show_article.php/_c-310/_nr-426/i.html.

130. Interview with Murad Imamaliev, 8 February 2007.

131. Interview with Anara Zakirov, 2 August 2007.

132. Arutiunian, "Armiane-Moskvichi," 11; see also Brednikova and Chikadze, "Armiane St. Peterburga," 246.

133. Starovoitova, *Etnicheskaia gruppa,* 97.

134. Vendina, "Social Polarization," 229.

135. Ostapenko and Subbotina, "Problemy sotsial'no-ekonomicheskii," 53.

136. Beliaeva, Draguskii, and Zotova, "Mnogonatsional'nyi mir Moskvy," 147–48.

137. Interview with Zhamila Sadybekova, 23 May 2007.

138. John Rex, *Ethnic Minorities in the Modern Nation-State* (London: MacMillan, 1996), 237.

139. On the French experience, see Paul A. Silverstein, *Algeria in France: Transpolitics, Race, Nation* (Bloomington: Indiana University Press, 2004); Gary Wilder, *The French Imperial-State: Negritude and Colonial Humanism between the Two World Wars* (Chicago: University of Chicago Press, 2005); Dominic Thomas, *Black France: Colonialism, Immigration, and Transnationalism* (Bloomington: Indiana University Press, 2007).

8

"Job Wanted! (No) Relocation, Please!"

Barriers to Geographical Mobility in Post-Soviet Russia

ELENA TYURYUKANOVA

Translated by Anastasiya Lakhtikova

In the system of democratic freedoms, the right to relocate freely is one of the basic inalienable human rights. Contemporary liberal democracy acknowledges restraints only on international, not domestic, movement. Restraints on mobility within national borders are considered to be a gross infringement on human rights.

In Russia today there is little information about how people exercise their right to free movement around the country. In the Soviet period, a system of residence permits (*propiska*) restricted popular and labor mobility within the state. Governance of population movements was based on an authorization system; a serious excuse was required to change one's place of residence or leave it temporarily. This provided authorities with the kind of control over people they desired.

Today, it would seem, such administrative barriers have been lifted. People are required to register their places of residence for informational purposes only; otherwise, most formal restrictions are a thing of the past. However, questions remain about how people are exercising—or failing to exercise—their newfound freedom to move and to choose their place of work.

How, and to what degree, do local social conditions attract or repulse people, stimulate or restrain their social and migratory activity in contemporary Russia? How free are people today to relocate, in practice? What restrains them and how? How do people understand, invoke, and exercise their right to unrestricted mobility? How deeply has the idea of free migration entered the mentality of

Russian society? These are the questions I will try to answer in this essay by analyzing actual experiences, behavior, and thoughts. My essay is based on research I conducted from 1998 to 2008 at the Center for Migration Studies in Moscow, with the financial support of the MacArthur Foundation.

Methodology and Data

In Russia, migration is only beginning to be understood as an active realization of the right to free mobility.[1] Such an understanding informs international investigations of the phenomenon, where scholars are increasingly interested in questions of choice. For example, the distinguished researcher John Salt notes that most migration theories have completely ignored the absolute majority of population, which does not participate directly in migration processes. Tomas Hammar explores why only a relatively small portion of the population participates in migration.[2]

The Constitution of the Russian Federation guarantees the right to free mobility within the state. The 1993 law "On Exiting and Entering the Russian Federation" abolished exit visas and guaranteed the right to unrestricted travel out of the country. However, the legal recognition of certain rights does not automatically mean that the population has the ability to exercise them; de jure recognition does not mean rights are demanded and exercised de facto. This breach between official recognition and the actual exercise of rights in many ways reflects the current state of affairs in regard to migration in Russia.[3]

In the 1990s, basic social and civic rights, such as the right to freedom of mobility, were gradually pushed to the periphery of the social consciousness by the weight of economic hardship. The population as a whole did not really exercise them. As a result, it is imperative not only to study migration as such, along with its directions, motives, and migrant populations, but also to examine the factors and reasons underlying the refusal to migrate. Such immobility—as a social phenomenon, as a sign of how positions in society are becoming increasingly determined by considerations of space (and the circumstances of local societies)—is a disturbing symptom, from the point of view of social progress.[4] Here I wish to focus on the question of why the freedom to move remained unclaimed in Russia between 1990 and 2000.

My research is based on a qualitative methodology and the analysis of case studies built through interviews. These interviews took place in Iaroslav region (the town of Rybinsk) and in Ivanovo (Ivanovo region). Each conversation illuminates a specific case and a specific social experience associated with the exercise (or the choice not to exercise) the right to free mobility. This is a so-called theoretical sample in which "the decisive question is not the representativity of the respondents, but the representativity of the concepts discussed."[5] Although seeking a broad respondent sample is important, here our aim is to make our results credible by sampling diverse models of migratory behavior and understandings rather than focusing on representative demographic groups.

I am also drawing data from a selective, structured interview survey of job seekers that was conducted from June to September 2004. The survey took place at job-placement services in central and peripheral towns of the Ivanovo and Iaroslav regions. The sample comprises 436 people. These regions were selected as representatives of the unsatisfactory job-placement situation in Central Russia. Hypothetically, we predicted that the unemployed and those dissatisfied with their jobs could relatively easily move from these regions to neighboring ones, where the employment situation was better. We also predicted that poverty and the extreme lack of local opportunity (80 percent of those surveyed were unemployed for more than half a year) should provide strong incentives for the migratory-behavior models. As we shall see, our findings challenged these hypotheses.

Factors For and Against Migration

In contemporary Russia, a number of factors stimulate, or slow down, free migration. Stimulants include the development of a market economy, the growth of job and real-estate markets, differentiation of income and standards of living in various regions within Russia and between Russia and other countries, regional differences between labor markets, development of the banking system and credit policy, increased information flows, and the formation of the middle class.[6] Factors slowing the migratory activity of the population include weakness and instability of the market infrastructures, social stresses, poverty, general shrinking of production, growing pressure on regional job markets, historically acquired behavior patterns encouraging a "sedentary" lifestyle, and information vacuums.

This second group of factors—factors that depress mobility—generally predominated in Russia in the 1990s to the present. At the same time, push factors favoring migration became powerful in several regions and cities of Russia (for example, in Rybinsk, where I conducted my research). Here we may list serious crises in production, business shutdowns, shortage of jobs, scarcity of educational institutions, poor condition of the old housing stock, and sluggish construction of new housing. Despite all this, however, the migration activity of the population remained low. Why?

Our interviews suggested the following reasons:

1. A conscious and well-articulated desire to live in a town (Rybinsk, in our case), despite acknowledged difficulties;

2. Uncertainty that life will be better in a new place ("There is nowhere to go; it's the same everywhere");
3. Lack of the skills and social activity needed to search for new housing; lack of information about job markets, housing, and so on;[7]
4. Refusal to admit the failure of the efforts at the current place of residence (there is a stereotype that migration is the result of a major failure);
5. Other negative stereotypes associated with migration;
6. Hopes for speedy improvement in the future.

Housing is an important factor tying a person to a specific location. At this time, developments in the real-estate market do not really change anything in this situation, as the majority of the population cannot find any acceptable entrance to this market, especially when this requires crossing local borders (those of a city or a region).

Naturally, a good job holds a person on the spot. However, amazingly, lack of a job does not lead to heightened mobility; on the contrary, low migratory activity is characteristic of the unemployed. As a rule, those who have lost a job or those trying to find a better one do so right where they are—in their own town. The reasons for this are rather obvious.[8]

First of all, it is difficult to look for a job out of town. People do not know how to do it because there is no customary practice for such activities. As a result, if such a search occurs, it is channeled informally—either people look through relatives and friends, or they go where they have been before. As a rule, state and private placement services work only locally, limiting the sphere of their activities by a specific region. Thus a simple and rather inexpensive change—establishment of reciprocal ties and the daily exchange of data between regional placement services—could offer clients jobs outside of their own city's limits, thereby stimulating geographical mobility of labor.

Second, it is rather difficult to settle on a new spot, especially when the move involves a family with children. One has to find not only housing but also schools. A behavioral pattern formed under the socialist system of total employment: "I work where I live." This pattern—which may be contrasted to the Western model of "I live where my job is"—still rules the public consciousness of Russians.

People associate moving with hopes for change in their social or family status, with a qualitative leap in their budget or in their professional career. Migration is an important lever in social mobility.[9] Therefore, as a rule, low migrant activity symbolizes a broader lack of social dynamism, which is characteristic of Russia throughout the 1990s and early 2000s.

For the majority of the population, the economic consequences of the new regime (widespread poverty) reduced to naught the liberal freedoms (freedom of mobility among them) that had been granted to the population by that same government. The lack of opportunities for independent economic activity within the newly sprouted labor and real-estate markets turned such freedoms, including the freedom to choose one's residence, into fiction. As a result, the new freedoms remain unclaimed by significant segments of the population. This contributes to the perception that the new regime that has granted these opportunities is itself useless or unnecessary. People begin to reject it or silently distance themselves from it, becoming socially apathetic and abstaining. Interviewing the citizens of Rybinsk in the late 1990s, one could often sense inertia and passivity, which are the consequences of social disorientation and confusion. Having found no place of their own in the new society, having no use for the new opportunities, people estrange themselves from this society. Heretofore, the state and party gave rigid directive to people's actions—people knew what to do to be successful. In the new conditions of political crisis, however, this direction was no longer there, which led to general disorientation and social apathy and encouraged social disengagement and the dissolution of civic identity.[10] This situation is only starting to improve; its consequences will be perceptible for a long time to come.

"Where Should I Live?": Free Choice Remains Far Away

Such questions as, Where is my homeland? Why do I live in this specific place? How do I relate to the city or place of my residence? and, Where would I like to live? seem rather simple at first sight. However, it is not always easy to get answers to these questions in an interview. As a rule, people have a hard time explaining why they live where they do.

> A few times we were about to move, but, you see, fate left us here to live, it just happened that way.

Judging by the answers we received to these and similar questions, it seems that respondents had not reflected upon them deeply. Yet almost unconsciously they have become a part of each person's identity.

> We live here because our parents' traditions live on. Our parents used to live here, now their children live here, and so on.

One sign of the unconscious treatment of such questions is respondents' frequent use of rhetorical (or semantic) clichés in answering them: *here is my motherland; my parents used to live here; my relatives are buried here.*

Sometimes it seems that respondents inherit their place of residence like they inherit their last name, and it never occurs to them to change it. To a great extent this is the consequence of the Soviet situation, where housing or land was distributed "from above," by government decree, which allowed easy manipulation of people's movement. Multiple institutions in the USSR supported this system, which included residence permits, labor conscription, and guest-worker quotas (*limit*).

Though it would seem that contemporary shifts in society and economy should be breaking down patterns formed under totalitarianism, today's situation preserves the ideology of "attachment to place."

> We are simply sitting here without stirring, he [her husband] and I; we live in poverty and will stay that way for life unless we move somewhere else.

In the early twenty-first century, "attachment to place" is a dominant behavioral model, at least in local societies like the one I am studying. In this way, the recently authorized freedom to choose one's residence has remained unclaimed because of the lack of socially acceptable mechanisms for its realization.

The model of permanent "attachment to place" is characteristic of the indigenous population and of migrants—people who already have had the experience of migration. The situation described in the following passage is typical for those who move to a new place of residence and have to adapt to their new environment:

> I came to Rybinsk as a young specialist. It was hard at first—poor conditions, no housing, no friends. So I was constantly thinking about leaving. I always somehow thought that I would leave, because I didn't like living here. But I kept on postponing the move. And all this dragged on so long that I just stayed here. Before I knew it, I was a ten-year Rybinsk resident. And it is still the same; still my heart tells me that I want to leave for Nizhnii Novgorod, for example, where I went to school. But to drop everything and leave and start all over again is hard, and it's a shame to have wasted so much time here [in Rybinsk].

At first, the new place is often perceived as alien. Then the seeming animosity fades away, but full integration is attained only if a person becomes part of familial, social, professional, and group networks. If a woman who is practically free (no family or good job) realizes that she cannot find locally what she wants, and even knows where she wants to live, why doesn't she move? The problem is that it is so hard to arrange a move in the conditions of underdeveloped real-estate and labor markets (starting with finding information and finishing with finding accommodation in a new location) that the effort and expense seem to be greater than the vague benefits of the move.[11]

Psychological barriers are strong as well. When it is customary to be tied to one place, change of residence location is perceived not as something normal but as a sign of failure. A person spends so much energy and time (sometimes decades) to settle down comfortably in a new location that subsequent moves are perceived as an acknowledgment that these efforts have been wasted.

As a rule, rather than starting something new, people prefer investing their energy and resources in the "life project" they have already begun, even if it might not be exactly what they want. This general rule includes the choice of residence location. However, healthy conservatism in many cases easily morphs into inertia, an inability and lack of desire to make active decisions and to change something radically. As a result, people become slaves to their circumstances. The spread of social inertia in 1990s Russian society was undoubtedly reinforced by economic hardships, social instability, and identity crisis. By the mid-2000s in many regions this situation had barely begun to improve. In contemporary Russia in the early 2010s, migration behavior is becoming more active, but the barriers are still there.

"In Search of a Living": Labor Migration

This section deals with migratory labor—temporary moves to other regions of Russia or abroad to work and earn money. Work-related mobility should be an important part of Russia's development, given the extremely unequal nature of local labor markets. Yet since the 1990s, such mobility has been low because of the general economic crisis, reduction of production, unemployment, the underdevelopment of real-estate and financial markets and of the credit system, as well as poor information flows.

All this leads to the dominance of the traditional behavioral model in mass consciousness. This model is based on primacy of residence over employment, on seeking employment exclusively at the residence location, and on changing jobs as a consequence of changing of residence, and not vice versa. State and social infrastructures sustain this situation because they do not aim to support labor-mobility models.

And yet internal labor mobility has always existed in Russia, and this includes the 1990s. From one interview:

> From here people go to Moscow to earn money. Wages are different there. Here, a million is a huge income. We do not have such wages in our town. In the mass media, lately, there is some information about companies offering employment abroad. However, those who use their services are very few. There are great risks. People are afraid to be deceived.

In what follows I summarize a "straw poll" survey of those seeking employment through placement services in some Russian regions.

Overview Data on Migratory Activity

- Approximately 60 percent of those surveyed were born and lived all their life in a town where the survey was conducted (Rybinsk: 75 percent; Iaroslavl':

60 percent; Ivanovo: 55 percent); these people have not changed their residence location even once.

- Twenty-one percentof the respondents changed their residence location at least once, 10 percent twice, and 8 percent three or more times.
- On the average, 78 percent of the respondents have lived in their town for over ten years.
- Under 15 percent of respondents left their hometown for reasons of temporary employment in Moscow or some other large Russian city at least once.
- Six percent of respondents had children in college in some other town (13 percent are planning to send their children out of town to study; 32 percent would like to be able to do so).

All these numbers point to low migratory activity. Apparently this is the result of the serious barriers that limit people's movement and narrow their opportunities.

The Place of Migration within Job Searches

- About 80 percent of the respondents limit their job search by the administrative borders of their town; 5 percent by the neighboring regional centers with their territories within Russia; and only 3 percent are ready to consider options all over Russia and abroad.

The latter two groups consist of mostly young people with average age of about thirty years. The average age of all respondents is thirty-eight.

- Forty percent of the respondents would prefer a poorer job at home to a good job in Moscow or in some other city.

Answering the question, "Why are you looking for a job within the town limits?" most respondents (71 percent) stated that they do not wish to move, and 6 percent said that they do not have any other options.

Some respondents (15 percent) think that employment services should offer jobs in other regions of Russia and abroad; 32 percent think that the state should create more opportunities for free popular movement, and 43 percent believe that the state should provide initial support for those who move. However, 39 percent of respondents think that the state should help people stay where they are rather than encouraging movement.

Other indices of popular attitudes to migration are not very positive either, and those of real ambition are even less.

- Fifty-one percent will stay and work in their own town; 21 percent will be looking for an alternative place of residence only if the situation at home becomes unbearable; 16 percent could work temporarily out of town, if they had such an opportunity; 6 percent are planning to move but are not doing anything about it; and 1 percent are ready to move or are definitely moving. On the whole, 73 percent are not planning to move (83 percent in Iaroslavl'; 78 percent in Rybinsk; 75 percent in Ivanovo; 60 percent in Zavolzhsk; 51 percent in Iuzha).

The Meanings of Migration Rights

Forty-three percent of respondents think that there is freedom of movement in Russia, while 13 percent think that there isn't. Perhaps most interestingly, a large number of people (43 percent) had trouble answering this question, indicating that these questions have not been the subject of extensive consideration. People often do not think about the possibility of a temporary or a permanent move, thinking of their residence location as something predetermined, inherited from the previous generations, like their last name. Fifty-eight percent of respondents think that one should live where one is born and has grown up; 33 percent think that those who move around a lot are "without roots"; 21 percent insist that people's moving around creates unrest in society, and therefore, the less they move the better; and 25 percent think that everything is the same everywhere, and therefore it's not worthwhile to look for something better. By contrast, 38 percent adhere to cosmopolitan ideas (it does not matter where one lives; the main thing is that one has a nice job and good living conditions); 26 percent think that people should move about more and look for a better place to be; 54 percent think that only the most active and motivated of people move.

People have varying opinions as to what the main institutional obstacle to free movement in Russia is: only 12 percent of the respondents voted for simplification or abolition of registration for Russian citizens; 14 percent are for more strict registration procedures for out-of-country migrants. Twenty-one percent think that the state should ensure Russian citizen's rights over the immigrants,' and the same number (20 percent) think that all people should be equal regardless of their place of residence or citizenship.

Local attitudes toward migrants also vary: 23 percent are positively inclined; 6 percent are negatively inclined (Ivanovo: 9 percent; Iuzha: 10 percent; Zavolzhsk: 2 percent; Rybinsk: 3 percent; Iaroslavl': 6 percent); 49 percent are neutral; and for 18 percent, it is important "where they [migrants] come from."

To overcome the barriers limiting geographical movement, a consistent set of legal and institutional measures will be necessary, aimed at helping people realize their plans and at broadening educational and financial opportunities. Such measures include the simplification of administrative procedures necessary for choosing a new place of residence; strict adherence to the informational (rather than restrictive) intent of all registration procedures; development of information services for all potential migrants, job-information access, and availability of housing; consulting and legal services; implementation of new mechanisms, such as insurance, credit plans, and so on, that stimulate popular mobility. It is essential to support educational migration. Special programs should be implemented locally. Some of the above-listed services and mechanisms can be commercial, offering a set of business services assisting migration organization; others should be supplied by the government, in the name of a more effective use of labor resources and of creating conditions for citizens to realize their potential.

"Stocking Up": 1990s Commercial Shuttle Migration

During the 1990s, unprecedented numbers of traders functioned as human shuttles (*chelnoki*), traveling within the country and abroad to make large purchases of goods to be resold when they came home.

From an interview with a director of a tourist agency:

> Starting from 1989, we organized many so-called shop tours to Poland and Turkey. Now they are significantly fewer. The "shuttle" traders usually take a bus and go to Moscow. They stock up at bulk markets; it is cheaper than going abroad.

In terms of absolute numbers, it is difficult to evaluate the scope of this phenomenon in the country as a whole and in a specific town. However, it certainly had a great influence on the lives of those who did the shuttling and those who consumed the offered merchandise.

Scholars have no unanimous opinion about this activity. It seems that local governments had more trouble than profit from the shuttle traders. However, a rationalistic reasoning about them prevailed—if people use the shuttle traders' services, then they need them.

From an interview:

> This trade is profitable both to the shuttle traders and ordinary citizens, consumers of their goods, to the poor more than others, as they [the traders] have cheap goods. If they didn't have this business going, the poor would have a harder time surviving, as everything is much more expensive in the stores.

There has been and still is significant public demand for the shuttle traders' activity—primarily, shuttle traders serve the needs of the not very wealthy population, which is to say the majority in the 1990s as well as in contemporary society. During the length of our investigation in Rybinsk, people bought all their food and necessary items on the shuttle traders' market. One can hardly think of the social role of such self-employment as negative, especially since the regime itself excluded these people from participation in the official economy. Providing a decent living for themselves through their own activity and enterprise, these people are helping millions of poor Russians to survive, including socially defenseless groups failed by the government.

The enormous numbers of people involved in this business as sellers, carriers, middlemen, and so on indicate that the shuttling business is the kind of enterprise that allowed great numbers of people to quickly readjust to the market economy and gave them a chance—the only chance for many of them—to be successful. Often it is not even success but a means of survival that is at stake.

From an interview at a marketplace:

> I am a single mother. This market is the only way for me to feed my child and save myself from death. We have just enough income to buy food, and this only if we are very frugal. Even racketeers don't bother our sort—they know that there'll be nothing for them to take.

At that time, the shuttle traders and sellers were practically excluded from society. They didn't ask for anything from the government but existed as a huge social group organized "from below."

What happened to all these people by the end of the 2000s? Small businesses are in a difficult situation because of rigid tax policies and free-market competition. Despite this, upon acquiring certain business skills, many of these people moved on to the wholesale trade; others became workers for hire (mostly as shop assistants), while yet others opened commercial enterprises and became entrepreneurs. Many of them joined the ranks of the emerging Russian middle class.

Conclusion

Today, people's awareness of their right to freedom of mobility is still emerging as an innovation. The spread of this new paradigm into popular consciousness is hindered by three major barriers. The first barrier is formed by economic and social stresses that all too recently pushed the population out of its normal daily existence and subjected it to extreme conditions (this was characteristic of the 1990s).[12] The second barrier is the perseverance of ingrained stereotypes and traditional models of behavior. Supported, in effect, by the unstable economy, this legacy is dissolving very slowly. The third barrier is the absolute absence of midlevel institutions that enable and ease migratory activity and encourage active models of migration (this still persists in the early 2010s).

Nonetheless, one would like to believe that an understanding of migration as a realization of the right to free mobility is slowly but surely taking hold. In Russia today, because of its traditions of centralization, these processes are more noticeable in the capitals and large cities. The period of economic growth of in the first decade of the twenty-first century has contributed to an increase of free mobility of people over the territory of the Russian Federation, as well as to the new concept of internal migration. In the future, perhaps, this new understanding of migration as an active factor in social mobility will promote new models of migratory behavior and new institutions for the implementation of these models.

Appendix: Results of the Sample Poll among the Unemployed

Characteristics of the Sample

REGIONS

Region/ Town	Share in the total volume of the sample
Iaroslav Region	
Iaroslavl'	23 percent
Rybinsk	23 percent
Ivanov Region	
Ivanovo	33 percent
Zavolzhsk	10 percent
Iuzha	11 percent
Total (N = 435 questionnaires)	100 percent

THE RESPONDENTS' GENDER

Female	68 percent
Male	32 percent

Average age: thirty-eight years

ECONOMIC WELL-BEING OF RESPONDENTS

Good	2 percent
Average	49 percent
Bad	42 percent
Very bad	7 percent

EMPLOYMENT

No employment	80 percent
Have temporary employment or occasional earnings	20 percent

PLACE OF BIRTH

The same town where the poll took place (Rybinsk: 75 percent; Iaroslavl': 60 percent; Ivanovo: 55 percent)	64 percent
In some other Russian location	26 percent
In the countries of the former USSR	9 percent
Outside of the USSR	1 percent

Mobility in Former Years

HOW MANY TIMES AFTER SIXTEEN YEARS OF AGE HAVE
YOU CHANGED RESIDENCE (FOR A YEAR OR LONGER)?

None	61 percent
One	21 percent
Two	10 percent
Three or more	8 percent

Seventy-eight percent of respondents have lived in the town for over ten years.

WHERE HAVE YOU BEEN (OUTSIDE OF RESIDENCE)
DURING THE LAST TEN YEARS

Temporary work in Moscow	8 percent
Temporary work in the regional center	6 percent
In CIS to visit relatives	19 percent
In CIS for a vacation	6 percent
Outside of the former USSR for a visit	6 percent
Outside of the former USSR as a tourist	11 percent
Nowhere	44 percent

MOBILITY OF THE RESPONDENTS' CHILDREN
(ASSOCIATED WITH EDUCATION)

Children studied in some other town	6 percent
Are planning to send children study in some other town	13 percent
Would like to send their children to study in some other town but have no means to do so	32 percent

LOCATION OF JOB SEARCH

	Before	Now
Only in one's own town	78 percent	81 percent
Within the region	9 percent	6 percent
Within the neighboring regions	5 percent	5 percent
All over Russia*	4 percent	3 percent
In the Russian Federation and abroad**	2 percent	3 percent
No answer	2 percent	2 percent

* average age: twenty-nine years (average age of the poll: thirty-eight)
** average age: thirty-two years.

WHY ARE YOU LOOKING FOR A JOB ONLY
WITHIN YOUR TOWN LIMITS?

Don't want to leave	71 percent
No other options	6 percent
Other	6 percent

WHAT OPTIONS IN JOB SEARCH SHOULD
PLACEMENT SERVICES OFFER?

Within the town	26 percent
Within the town and region	19 percent
Within the neighboring regions	5 percent
All over Russia	14 percent
In Russia and abroad	15 percent
Cannot say	19 percent

Migration Tendencies and Preferences

ALTERNATIVE PREFERENCES

Preference 1	
Work "here" is bad	39 percent
There is a good job in Moscow or elsewhere	61 percent
Preference 2	
Work "here" is good	89 percent
There is a good job in Moscow or elsewhere	11 percent

GENERAL TENDENCIES IN RELATION TO A MOVE

I will live and work only in my own town	51 percent
I will be looking for another place to live if the situation here becomes really bad	21 percent
I could work in some other town temporarily	16 percent
One has to flee this place, but I am not ready to move at this time	7 percent
I'm ready to move	1 percent

MIGRATIONAL PLANS 1

I'm moving for sure	1.4 percent
I'm planning to move but at this time am not doing anything in this respect	6 percent
I'm not planning to move	73 percent
(Iaroslavl': 83 percent; Rybinsk: 78 percent; Ivanovo: 75 percent; Zavolzhsk: 60 percent; Iuzha: 51 percent)	
I don't know	17 percent

MIGRATIONAL PLANS 2

	"Yes" for sure	Possible	"No" for sure
Move permanently within the region	2 percent	16 percent	68 percent
Move permanently to another region	2 percent	17 percent	58 percent
Move permanently within the former USSR	1 percent	4 percent	71 percent
Move permanently abroad	1 percent	5 percent	70 percent
Move temporarily (over one year)	2 percent	17 percent	52 percent

IS THERE FREEDOM OF MOBILITY IN RUSSIA?

Yes	43 percent
No	13 percent
It's hard to say	44 percent

COSMOPOLITANS OR PATRIOTS

One has to live where one is born and raised	58 percent
One has to move around more, look for a better place	26 percent
It's the same everywhere; there is no reason to look for something better	25 percent
Our people are too attached to the place of their residence	59 percent
Those who move around a lot are "rootless" people	33 percent
Only the most active and motivated move	54 percent
Migration causes unrest in society; therefore the smaller it is, the better	21 percent
It doesn't matter where one lives as long as the job and living conditions are good	38 percent

WHAT'S YOUR ATTITUDE TOWARD PEOPLE WHO COME FROM OTHER REGIONS?

Rather positive	23 percent
Rather negative	6 percent
(Ivanovo: 9 percent; Iuzha: 10 percent; Zavolzhsk: 2 percent; Rybinsk:3 percent; Iaroslavl': 6 percent)	
Neutral	49 percent
It depends on where they come from	18 percent

HOW SHOULD THE STATE TREAT PEOPLE WHO
CHANGE THEIR RESIDENCE?

Create more possibilities for the free migration of people	32 percent
Help to overcome initial difficulties on the new place	43 percent
They should help people to live where they live, not help them to move	39 percent
One should simplify or abolish registration for Russian citizens	12 percent
The registration rules for migrants from other countries should be stricter	14 percent
The state shouldn't interfere; migration is a person's private business	10 percent
The state should secure Russian citizens' priorities over the migrants (from elsewhere)	21 percent
All people should be treated equally regardless of where they live	20 percent

Notes

1. See, for example, Y. Andrienko and S. Guriev, "Determinants of Interregional Mobility in Russia: Evidence from Panel Data," *Economics of Transition* 12.1 (2004): 1–27.

2. J. Salt, " Reconceptualizing Migration and Migration Space," *Administrative Science Quarterly* 12 (September 1967): 225–52; J. Salt, "Reconceptualizing Migration and Migration Space," Paper presented at the International Conference on Central and Eastern Europe: New Migration Space, Pultusk, Poland, December 1997; T. Hammar, "Development and Immobility," in *Causes of International Migration,* ed. R. van der Erf and L. Heering (Luxembourg: Eurostat, 1995), 173–86.

3. Zh. A. Zaionchkovskaia and N. N. Nozdrina, "Migratsionnyi opyt regional'nykh tsentrov Rossii," *Problemy prognozirovaniia* 4 (2008): 98–112.

4. V. Popov, "Passportnaia sistema sovetskogo krepostnichestva," *Novyi mir* 6 (1996): 194; Iu. F. Florinskaia, "Vlianie material'nogo polozheniia i zhilishchnykh uslovii na mobil'nost' rossiiskogo naseleniia," *Problemy prognozirovaniia* 6 (2008): 140–55; Timothy Heleniak, *Migration Dilemmas Haunt Post-Soviet Russia* (Washington, D.C.: Migration Policy Institute, 2002); L. B. Karachurina and N. V. Mkrtchian, "Demograficheskie i sotsial'no-ekonomicheskie faktory dinamiki migratsionnoi aktivnosti naseleniia Rossii: sovremennaia situatsiia i perspektivy," in *Nauchnye trudy: Institut narodnokhoziaistvennogo prognozirovaniia RAN,* ed. A. G. Korovin (Moscow: MAKS Press, 2008): 571–604.

5. Juliet Corbin and Anselm Strauss, "Grounded Theory Research: Procedures, Canons, and Evaluative Criteria," in *Qualitative Sociology* 13.1 (1990): 3–21.

6. R. Faini, J. de Melo, and K. Zimmerman, *Migration: The Controversies and the Evidence* (London: CEPR, 1999).

7. Iu. F. Florinskaia and T. G. Roshchina, "Migratsionnye namereniia vypusknikov shkol iz malykh gorodov Rossii," in *Rossiiskaia molodezh': Problemy i resheniia* (Moscow: Tsentr sotsial'nogo prognozirovaniia, 2005), 402.

8. N. V. Mkrtchian, "Gotovy li bezrabotnye ekhat' za rabotoi v drugie regiony," in *Migratsiia i demograficheskii krizis v Rossii.,* ed. Zh. A. Zaionchkovskaia and E. V. Tiuriurkanova (Moscow: MAKS Press, 2010), 80.

9. V. P. Krasnoslobodtsev, "Sel'skie 'miry' Rossii i migratsiia," in *Demoskop Weekly,* 10–23 January 2005, 185–86.

10. See, for example, I. Diskin, "Rossiiskaia model' sotsial'noi transformatsii," *Pro et Contra* 4.3 (Summer 1999): 15.

11. Zhanna Zaionchkovskaia and Nikita Mkrtchian, "Vnutrenniaia migratsiia v Rossii: Pravovaia praktika," in *Migratsionnaia situatsiia v regionakh Rossii,* vol. 4, ed. Zhanna Zaionchkovskaia (Moscow: Tsentr migratsionnykh issledovanii, 2007), 70.

12. N. M. Rimashevkaia, ed., *Rossiia 10 let reform: XI ezhegodnyi doklad* (Moscow: Institut sotsial'no-ekonomicheskikh problem narodonaseleniia, 2002), 49.

PART III

Model Mobility

[blank page 190]

Preface

ANNE LOUNSBERY

The essays in this section call our attention to the fact that there are many possible relationships between mobility and autonomy. Tourists, deportees, "business travelers," soldiers on the march, athletes in wheelchairs, migrant laborers, "rootless cosmopolitans"—all are marked as mobile, but in each case this mobility implies a very different set of circumstances and meanings. The same goes for immobility: prisoners, collective farm workers without passports, disabled people in state-run *internaty*, a peasant woman who has never left her village—immobility, too, can imply a wide range of relationships to power and to a state that is working hard to control people's movements.

The essays fall roughly into two groups, chronologically and thematically. Alexandra Bekasova and Benjamin Schenk examine the impact of coach travel and railroads, two technologies of mobility that were new to nineteenth-century Russia. Their work raises questions about how these new ways of covering ground shaped—or may have shaped—travelers' perceptions of space, especially their perceptions of the Russian nation/empire. Diane Koenker's and Sarah Phillips's work is more focused on the possible relationships between mobility and individual freedom, examining, for example, the state's efforts (not always successful) to harness movement for its own purposes. By drawing our attention to tropes that have been used to associate moving through space with being "free," Koenker and Phillips not only shed light on mobility in the Soviet and post-Soviet periods, they also work to develop nuanced ideas of what might constitute real personal agency in a complex modern society. In fact, all four essays help us to think about the connection—sometimes real, sometimes imaginary or even spurious—between being mobile and being modern.

Bekasova's and Schenk's contributions point to key parallels between commercial coach travel (which developed in Russia beginning in the 1820s) and railway travel (which became possible in the second half of the century). Both coaches and trains opened up vague prospects of class mixing and some form of "equality": Bekasova notes that coach regulations distributed in 1835 affirmed the rights of "all ranks, ages, and both sexes [to] travel in stagecoaches," and as early as the 1820s Pavel Svin'in lauded the coach system as part of "government efforts to ensure equal distribution of public benefits among inhabitants of all estates and classes." And while Schenk's analysis suggests that the class mixing enabled by public modes of transportation may have been more imagined than real, the rhetoric of equality and national unity that often attended discussions of public transport suggests that these new ways of moving through space—by redefining what was close and what was far, what was connected and what was isolated—did more than alter spatial perceptions; they also afforded new ways of imagining social relations (as is underlined, for example, by the number of literary texts in which meditations on these new technologies play an integral role, from Gogol through Chekhov and beyond).

Bekasova's analysis reminds us that railways were not the first or only context in which Russians experienced "modern" time, the kind of structured time requiring them to accommodate themselves to schedules, clocks, conductors' watches, and specific fares for set distances. Schenk's work extends these insights, examining ways in which the railway system and its regulations aimed to standardize what was in reality the heterogeneous, messy, multiethnic space of the Russian Empire. Maps hanging in railway stations showed the empire as "homogeneous white space, uninterrupted by internal political, geographical, or cultural borders and bound together by a network of black lines stretching from the network's center in Moscow to the country's distant peripheries." No matter where one was, a bell was rung three times before every train's departure, and railway schedules indicated all arrivals and departures according to Petersburg time (the same principle holds today, of course, but with Moscow setting the hour).

Negotiating this new geography—learning to see space and time as standardized and measurable—became a hallmark of being modern. In Goncharov's *Oblomov* (1859), for example, the clearest markers of backwardness are spatial isolation and a premodern way of imagining distance, space, and time. When Oblomov is obliged to travel, he does so on his own schedule and in his own "big old-fashioned coach, amidst feather beds, chests, trunks, hams, loaves, all sorts of roasted and cooked beef and poultry."[1] Where Oblomov comes from—the village of Oblomovka—time is measured not by clocks but by seasons, church holidays, and dinner hours, while space is not measurable at all. As a result, the villagers see "the world far away" as "unknown countries, inhabited by monsters

. . . and farther way away still, darkness; and at the end of it all, a fish holding the world on its back."[2] A fish with the world on its back: such a conception of "geography" does not allow the villagers to draw lines of *connection* between Oblomovka and anyplace else. As a result, almost everything "outside" becomes simply "the world far away."

In Oblomovka distances are not measurable, and they are not traversable in any predictable way. Instead, the people of Oblomovka live in what Mikhail Bakhtin calls (in his description of Greek romance) "an *abstract* expanse of space."[3] This is a decidedly premodern conception of space, structured by what Franco Moretti has termed the "absolute distance" between "Home" and "the Wide World" outside.[4] It is also the antithesis of the rational, modern topography created by space-ordering systems like the coach network and railway grid, a series of intersecting lines that—by enabling people to plot courses and measure distances—allow for efficient movement from one node to another. Being able to engage in this kind of movement, Goncharov suggests, is a necessary precondition of participating in the modern economy. And this is why Oblomov's energetic and efficient alter-ego, the businessman Stolz, always knows exactly where he is going, how much time will be required to reach his destination, and the route he will take to get there. When Stolz first leaves the countryside (presumably by coach), his father tells him precisely how to travel to Petersburg, and he actually measures the distance in rubles (to travel from Verkhliovo to Moscow will cost forty rubles, he tells his son, and from there to Petersburg will be another seventy-five).[5] Stolz has learned to understand space in terms of modernity's "relative distance": in Moretti's words, this is "distance [that] has been brought down to earth: it can be measured, understood; it is no longer a function of Fate."[6] Bekasova and Schenk help us to understand how new technologies conditioned this re-visioning of geographic space.

While the relationship between mobility, modernity, and autonomy is at issue in Koenker's and Phillips's work as well, both of these essays go a long way toward complicating any simple equation of movement with freedom. Koenker examines two parallel developments in the Soviet period—state-sponsored tourism and "carceral travel" (the transportation of prisoners and various categories of deportees), both of which, she argues, "represented investments in the state's twin projects of nation-building and the creation of citizen-subjects." Phillips's topic is the disabled-rights movement in post-Soviet Russia and Ukraine, particularly the ways in which activists have "[framed their] arguments for equal rights in terms of the individual's right to independent movement."

Koenker argues that the Soviet Union's vast size made "human mobility . . . a prerequisite for acquiring knowledge of and thereby assimilating space." (This observation, one might add, holds for the Imperial period as well: at least as early as the 1830s, the state decided that genuine *narodnost'* required "knowledge of one's homeland" of "every educated patriot"—which was why the central bureaucracy began sending out data collectors to gather statistical knowledge about the far-flung empire.[7]) The Soviets celebrated their famously "unbounded" spaces, but as Koenker notes, they also liked these spaces to be "controlled through knowledge." Proletarian tourism was one of the practices they enlisted in their efforts. In 1926, *Komsomol'skaia pravda* described a proper Soviet tourist as "a tireless investigator," moving through space consciously and with purpose (meaning, implicitly, the state's purpose).

Thus "pleasure travel too had its own requirements," and "the 'freedom' to travel . . . remained subordinate to the state's interest in that travel"—a fact that Koenker uses to link tourism to forms of human mobility that were far more obviously dictated by authoritarian power (the relocation of kulaks as "special settlers," the shipping of prisoners to the gulag, and so on). Analyzing travel accounts from the 1930s and 1960s, Koenker concludes that the state was ultimately quite successful in encouraging Soviet people to use tourism as a way to imagine themselves as citizens participating actively in the life of the nation. While these tourists never passively accepted all attempts to orchestrate their experiences (through guidebooks, regulations, and so on), by and large they used pleasure travel the way it was officially intended—as a way to foster a bond with their country (its history, peoples, and institutions) while enjoying themselves as private individuals.

In this sense, Koenker's analysis anticipates questions that are raised in Phillips's work on disability activism in the post-Soviet period. Phillips notes that as early as 1990, advocates for the disabled began arguing (or simply making arguments that assumed) that spatial mobility should be treated as a basic human right—above all, it seems, because such mobility is seen as essential to participation in a globalized economy. Much as Soviet tourists were at times able to use the state's rhetoric of mobility for their own purposes, disabled people have adopted a language based in capitalist notions of individuality in order to stake their claim as modern subjects. And once again in such arguments, we see that mobility itself is marked as modern: in this case, it is assumed to be a requirement for becoming, as Phillips writes, "the kind of 'mobile, flexible, self-enterprising subject' that increasingly represents the idealized standard of what it means to be a citizen in a world of global capitalism."

In fact, this right-to-mobility discourse recalls Goncharov's Stolz, the model capitalist of *Oblomov*. Stolz stands for movement through space and for the incipient (in mid-nineteenth-century Russia) modern economy with which this movement is so strongly associated: he is "constantly on the move."[8] For Stolz, to work is to travel, thanks to the ways in which he is engaged in capitalism's "continuous dissolution of objects into money."[9] Always "trading with some company shipping goods abroad,"[10] Stolz keeps moving himself around because he wants to keep his wealth traveling through the necessary circuit, from commodities to money to more commodities to more money, and so on. Oblomov, of course, does the opposite: he never moves, and he puts nothing back into circulation—and it is this lack of mobility that marks his failure to become a modern (economic) subject. In Yuri Slezkine's terms, Oblomov and the Oblomovka villagers will never make it as the supremely mobile "service nomads" whose skills are demanded by modernity; they cannot function in an economic world where success depends crucially on the ability to "cross conceptual and communal borders," because this kind of traffic requires a kind of movement that they abhor.[11]

In effect, the activists Phillips describes are demanding the opportunity to become more like Stolz. Their arguments assume that a good citizen is "a person who is moving rapidly through space" (in part because he or she is "engaging with the material world primarily through consumption"). In the 1990s these activists made their case in part through demonstrations of extreme mobility—fantastic exploits of well-publicized (and commercially sponsored) ground-covering in which they performed such feats as traveling by wheelchair from Vladivostok to Petersburg. (And here we should note the gendered nature of this kind of heroic individual movement, a model that clearly draws on Soviet images of ultramasculine heroes—explorers and the like—capable of overcoming all spatial barriers.) Phillips describes the "wheelchair super-marathons" as events in which "globalizing processes—the flow of capital, people, and discourses—were brought down to earth," made visible for participants and especially, it was hoped, for spectators. Here as in *Oblomov,* movement itself is marked as modern and positive, as a "free flow" (of people, money, goods) that should not be impeded.

This was the kind of movement that Russian officials had foreseen—some with fear, some with enthusiasm—as early as the first half of the nineteenth century. Schenk quotes, for example, Nicholas I's finance minister, Georg von Kankrin, who warned that railroads would encourage a dangerous degree of "communicability" in the empire's population, thereby "making unstable people even more unstable." "Communicability" is a telling word in this context: it conveys both the dangerous risk of contagion and the enticing possibility of productive free *flow*—flow of goods and money, but also, unavoidably, of people and ideas. Schenk notes that early supporters of railroads did not argue that people needed to be able to move around, but rather that the state needed to be able transport goods and military equipment (though this latter category included, presumably, troops). But it soon became evident that new technologies of transportation necessarily implied not only geographic mobility for people but also a huge increase in virtually all forms of dissemination and exchange, particularly of information.

We might draw a parallel between officials' efforts to control the movement of people and their efforts to limit the circulation of texts: just as the state soon found that it had no choice but to relax the strict rules originally intended to regulate coach and rail travel (both of which initially required not only a passport but a letter from the police granting permission to travel every time one boarded a coach or train), over the course of the century officials concluded that prepublication censorship was impracticable as well. Both these attempts at control implied a desire to mark as forbidden all movement that was not explicitly permitted—a state of affairs that ended up being incompatible with modern economic conditions. Yet the risks of "communicability" were real, and Russians of various political persuasions were well aware of them. These risks are at the center, for example, of Dostoevsky's novel *Demons* (serialized in 1871–72), in which revolutionaries use the railways to travel around Russia disseminating violent propaganda. Dostoevsky likens their tracts to cholera, circulating contagions always in the air seeking new hosts—with trains as their chief vectors. Yet when Dostoevsky describes *Demons* itself as a "pamphlet," he is signaling his conviction that there is no escape from such circulation, no possibility of shutting it down: instead one must fight texts with texts, circulation with circulation.[12]

By the later decades of the century, the government had come to more or less the same conclusion: officials recognized that a modern economy demanded that people and things (and thus, inevitably, ideas) be able to move around. Kankrin's successor Sergei Witte declared in the 1890s that population mobility was essential for the "enhancement of exchange . . . and the intensification of the economic and social bonds between the various geographical regions of the country." When Witte argued for railroad-tariff reform by noting that migrant workers were "unproductively consuming time and energy" by traveling on foot, he was clearly aware of modernity's time-is-money equation—which in turn implied the equation covering-space-is-money. No wonder, then, that Witte identified mobility as "one of the most important prerequisites for the increase of the empire's economic wealth."

In light of such glowing assessments of mobility's benefits, it is perhaps easy for us to smile ironically at those who, like Kankrin, warned of the risks that attend "communicability." From our perspective these voices sound antimodern (or, at the very least, antimodernizing) and even antifreedom—and who does not want to be modern and free? But those urging caution when it came to geographic mobility were in no way wrong: they were in fact right about such movement's destabilizing and destructive power. In a series of traumas ranging from the erosion of local traditions and the death of indigenous languages to species extinction and increased possibilities for economic exploitation, large-scale mobility has played a decisive role. One thing these essays do is remind us that we need not idealize mobility by equating it (only) with freedom and opportunity, even as we recognize it as an inescapable fact of modern life.

Notes

1. I. A. Goncharov, *Sobranie sochinenii v 8 t.,* vol. 4 (Moscow: Gosudarstvennoe izdatel'stvo khudozhestvennoi literatury, 1953), 67.

2. Ibid., 108.

3. Mikhail Bakhtin, "Forms of Time and Chronotope in the Novel," in *The Dialogic Imagination: Four Essays by M. M. Bakhtin,* ed. Michael Holquist, trans. Caryl Emerson and Michael Holquist (Austin: University of Texas Press, 1981), 99.

4. Franco Moretti, *Atlas of the European Novel, 1800–1900* (London: Verso, 1998), 22. See also Bakhtin, "Forms of Time and Chronotope," 90–101.

5. Goncharov, *Sobranie sochinenii v 8 t.,* 165.

6. Moretti, *Atlas,* 23–24.

7. Qtd. in W. Bruce Lincoln, *In the Vanguard of Reform: Russia's Enlightened Bureaucrats 1825–1861* (DeKalb: Northern Illinois University Press, 1982), 117.

8. Goncharov, *Sobranie sochinenii v 8 t.,* 167.

9. Robert L. Heilbroner, *The Nature and Logic of Capitalism* (New York: W. W. Norton and Co., 1985), 56.

10. Goncharov, *Sobranie sochinenii v 8 t.,* 167.

11. Yuri Slezkine, *The Jewish Century* (Princeton, N.J.: Princeton University Press, 2004), 28.

12. F. M. Dostoevskii, *Polnoe sobranie sochinenii,* vol. 29, part 1 (Leningrad: Nauka, 1974), 112.

[blank page 198]

9

The Making of Passengers in the Russian Empire

Coach-Transport Companies, Guidebooks, and National Identity in Russia, 1820–1860

ALEXANDRA BEKASOVA

Created by several joint-stock and state-owned commercial coach companies established in Russia from the 1820s through the 1840s, public transportation greatly reduced the burdens of travel and led to the intensification of domestic mobility. Thanks to the construction of a network of broken-stone (macadam) roads and the organization of regular public-transportation services, travel in Russia became more comfortable and more popular during the middle decades of the nineteenth century, with the number of passengers increasing considerably. Russians previously had "traveled" in Europe, while at home they went largely on business. Moving from one place to another, they preferred to lie motionless in a coach and not even look around. Coach companies brought into existence new travel practices and new forms of interaction among people on the road. Along with timetables, passage tickets, cheap souvenirs, and hotel and restaurant price lists, guidebooks became new accoutrements of travel in Russia.

When and how did the passenger as a specific sociocultural phenomenon emerge in Russia? Arguing against the widespread opinion that passengers appeared as a result of the development of railroad and urban public transport, in this essay I claim that it was the coach-transportation network that first produced the mobile body and self of the passenger.

How did the means by which mobility was produced and consumed (the organizations, modes of governance, infrastructures, vehicles, and so on) shape senses of identity, expectations, and practices? How did various modes of transportation and travel influence the perception of space and time? Focusing on innovations in transportation technologies and in travel practices introduced by the coach companies, I will explore how the travel companies helped promote domestic travel. Through analysis of the travel guides designed to be used on the main road of the Russian Empire between St. Petersburg and Moscow, I explore the narrative strategies of the first Russian guidebooks and the ensemble of images of road infrastructure, territory, and people created in the guidebooks' narratives.

A study of the links among everyday travel practices, innovations in transportation technologies, travel literature, and the formation of national consciousness in Russia of the first half of the nineteenth century helps bridge a gap between mobility history and the history of the building and invention of nations. As Benedict Anderson has shown in his influential study, cultural changes in the perception of space and time were crucial to national-identity formation in many countries.[1] Christopher Ely and Guido Hausmann have historicized the Russian landscape as a cultural construction and described the emergence of new aesthetic norms of perception in the nineteenth century.[2] For a somewhat earlier period, John Randolph has shown how the traditional Russian postal network—the so-called *iam* system—provided a practical as well as symbolic frame for the early ethnographies of Russia.[3]

In recent years, intensive research has significantly increased our understanding of the role of travel and guidebooks in establishing national and cultural norms.[4] Russian studies too have benefited from the renewed interest in travel writing and travel cultures.[5] But a large body of travel literature has been only partially explored and has been analyzed primarily in the framework of literary studies.[6] Compared to the historiography of tourism in late Imperial and Soviet Russia, Russian everyday travel practices before the age of the railroad have received little scholarly attention so far. Focusing on the rather neglected issue of the building and function of the stagecoach transportation network from a user's perspective, I hope to show that the new modern age of railroad communications was shaped much more by the old one of coach travel in imperial Russia than historians have been ready to admit.[7]

The Russian Troika: Russian Postal Roads and the Traditional Mode of Travel

To understand the extent and importance of cultural changes induced by the activities of coach-transportation companies in Russia during the first half of the nineteenth century, it is essential to have a general idea about the customary mode of travel on Russian postal roads during the previous period. During the eighteenth and the early nineteenth centuries, road conditions in the Russian Empire remained very poor. Bad road conditions could be partly explained by the fact that the Russian monarchy, governing a huge territory with a vast network of navigable waterways, for a long time considered land roads to be of secondary importance. European travelers often complained that Russian roads were "undoubtedly ways to hell." They were much surprised by old-fashioned techniques—particularly, the use of wood for paving surfaces—employed in Russia for road building. Accustomed to careful forest management at home, they couldn't understand why Russians didn't use stones for paving road surfaces. Land roads were usually made of fascines, buried in sand or sometimes gravel and surfaced with logs. Made of wood, such roads were short-lived and required constant maintenance. Only short sections of roads—those close to the capitals and important trade centers—were paved with stones. The cost of a road's upkeep was carried by local authorities and local inhabitants, who lived in settlements along the road.[8]

The intensity of traffic on Russian roads depended heavily on seasons and weather. For about four months a year (November, December, March, and April), Russian roadways became virtually impassable, so people usually traveled in summer and winter. But summer travel was very uncomfortable: the wheeled vehicles then in use had no springs! Experienced travelers preferred to lie motionless in a coach, without even looking around, as did one of the characters in Vladimir Sologub's story "Tarantas." Not surprisingly, the most popular traveling season was winter. During the nineteenth century, numerous travelogues, fictional accounts, and artistic depictions made a swift sledge ride through a snow-covered road on a sunny winter day a recognizable symbol of the Russian national identity: the Russian troika.[9]

The reality was much less inspiring. To get from one place to another, a traveler needed an official "post-horse order" (*podorozhnaia gramota*). This document permitted the traveler to follow a set route through the system of Russian postal roads, and it allowed him or her to obtain—at road stations scattered along the way—a certain number of horses fixed according to his social rank.[10] The practice of changing horses at every station and riding them hard between the stations gave travelers the possibility of traveling rather fast. Alas, not every traveler had this chance. Speed was a privilege reserved for the monarch, the court messengers' service, top-level officials, and wealthy nobility. Travelers on official business received travel money, but those traveling for private needs had to pay their own expenses. Prices for long-distance journeys were high, and many private travelers preferred to use their own carriages and horses, piling them up with everything they needed during the trip (bedding, food, etc). This made a journey cheaper but considerably longer.[11]

But even using the postal road system, travelers often could not estimate how long it would take them to get from one place to another, because they spent much time waiting at postal stations for available horses and coachmen, who, following an age-old tradition, were casting for turns and quarrelling with each other before embarking on a journey. It is not surprising that many people considered this mode of moving hard work, or even a trial.

On Roads and Coaches: Construction of Highways, Rise of Mobility, and Commercial Coach Companies

Russian roads began to change for the better shortly after the Napoleonic Wars, when military necessity prompted the government to undertake the construction of a network of macadam highways. Starting in 1817 and continuing through the 1860s, the improvement of old roads and the construction of a vast network of new, up-to-date highways helped to create an elaborate coach-transportation network for the Russian Empire. Important managerial changes contributed greatly to the construction process. Road building was entrusted to the professionals—engineers, technicians, and skilled workers. By the end of the 1820s, the organizational structure of the Waterways and Roads Board (Upravlenie vodianymi i suhoputnymi putiami soobshcheniia), founded in 1809, had taken a definitive shape. Renamed the Communication and Public Buildings Board (Glavnoe upravlenie putei soobshcheniia i publichnykh zdanii) in 1833, it was managed by a director and an advisory council. The board included three main divisions, controlling, respectively, the management and construction of waterways, land roads, and commercial ports. It had its own permanent workforce of laborers, a special police unit, and the Corps of Waterways and Land Roads Engineers with an Institute of the Engineers of Means of Communication (Korpus i Institut Korpusa inzhenerov putei soobshcheniia) and a Military-Technical School (Voenno-stroitel'naia shkola), opened in 1820.

The first to be built was the St. Petersburg–Moscow highway (it was called the Moscow Road). The road connected two Russian capitals: the new one, St. Petersburg, founded by Peter the Great on the banks of the Neva River close to the Baltic Sea, and the ancient one, Moscow, situated in the central part of European Russia. It stretched for 778 kilometers and went through three large central provinces. Its construction took nearly seventeen years: begun in 1817, during the reign of Alexander I, the road was finished only in 1833 under Nicholas I. Contemporaries welcomed enthusiastically the opening of the first highway and were very proud that the road was "considered to be among the best macadam roads constructed in the most enlightened states of Europe" by professional engineers. The road's condition was praised by almost every traveler. "To be sure, I don't mind paying a toll for this highway, a virtually flat road, which is convenient for driving and nice-looking," noted one traveler.[12] During the following decades of intensive road construction, a network of highways with crushed-stone surfaces was produced that stretched for nearly ten thousand kilometers, mostly through the territories of central and western parts of the European Russia. Particular attention was paid to bridges, which were built using up-to-date technologies, as well as to the construction of accompanying road infrastructure (rest stations, inns, restaurants, and so forth) in accordance with a general plan. A militarized system of land-road maintenance proved to be effective, and road surfaces were kept in good condition. These newly constructed highways were turnpike roads, and travelers paid tolls for using them.[13]

Parallel to intensive road improvement, a number of joint-stock and state-owned coach companies emerged in Russia from the 1820s through the 1840s.[14] All of them were commercial enterprises that specialized in the transportation of goods and passengers. These companies received powerful backing from Russian emperors and the state postal authorities, who held a strong interest in their activities and accorded them various privileges. They introduced their services not only on the highways but also mastered new routes, using not only the newly built macadam roads but also side county tracks in the regions where their services were much in demand among merchants, low-ranking officials, military personnel, and tourists. All in all, they organized transportation on almost thirty different routes. By the beginning of the 1860s, just before the coach companies went broke and collapsed, being eclipsed by the railroad companies, a vast coach-transportation network had connected major administrative centers (St. Petersburg, Moscow, Warsaw), ports on the Baltic coast, industrializing regions, market towns, and resort areas, all of which were situated in European Russia.[15]

A noticeable increase in the number of transportation companies and the number of passengers they transported reflected the ever-growing demand for transport services by the Russian public during the middle decades of the nineteenth century. So far, I have no combined quantitative data on the exact number of users of transport companies' services at my disposal. Nevertheless, some figures extracted from the reports on activities of particular companies give insight into an impressive rise of transport-mobility flows on Russian roads from the 1820s to the 1850s. For instance, during the first ten years of its operations, a joint-stock company called the Original Stagecoach Company (Obshchestvo pervonachal'nogo zavedeniia dilizhansov), which was the first transport company and was founded in 1820, served nearly thirty-four thousand passengers.[16] By the end of the 1840s, the Department of Postal Coaches (Otdelenie pochtovykh karet i brik), which the state postal authorities organized some twenty years later in 1839, transported approximately the same number of passengers annually. During the twenty-three years of its operation from 1839 to 1863, the Department served almost 670,000 passengers with its horse-drawn vehicles of different types.[17]

The development of commercial stagecoach-transportation companies may be described in terms of three general stages. The first stage started from 1820 and lasted ten years. Only three privileged companies were established during this period. They were granted permission to use horses on postal stations free of charge. In addition, they were granted a monopoly right to provide transport services on the established routes during those ten years. Konstantin Bulgakov, the director of the St. Petersburg post office, together with his good friend Mikhail Vorontsov, one of the most popular Russian military commanders during the Napoleonic Wars and a staunch Anglophile, were the first to introduce the idea of stagecoach services to the Russian public. They invested great energy in launching a commercial enterprise, and their joint efforts soon resulted in bringing stagecoach travel into fashion. The shareholders of the first coach company, who belonged to military and bureaucratic elite or were well-off tradespeople and bankers, were also the first customers to "taste" regular transportation in stagecoaches. The experiment was successful and profitable. When the term of their monopoly expired, the founders of the companies extended their activities on a new basis.

The second stage lasted approximately ten years, starting in 1830. The abolition of the coaching monopoly resulted in the creation of new companies. Using European models for technological, managerial, and organizational innovation, they thrived on an emerging demand for transport services. In addition to transporting passengers, these companies also specialized in the carrying of heavy and bulky goods, including liquids and explosives, which were prohibited from being sent through the postal system. Faced with growing competition for customers from traditional carrier traders and among themselves, these companies were forced to reduce prices and speed up delivery time.

The third and final period began when postal authorities organized the Department of Postal Coaches in 1839. During the next twenty years the coach-transportation network enjoyed its heyday. Transportation and traffic regulations were generalized, and transport technologies became much more standardized.

The Making of the Passenger: Regular Stagecoach Transportation and the Emergence of New Travel Habits

The travel companies brought into existence new travel practices, new forms of interaction among people on the road, and new literary genres of travel guides and travelogues. Unacquainted passengers were often put together into a coach compartment, taking seats according to the tickets they had purchased. Obliged to follow coach rules, they sat squeezed together and expected indulgences from each other. Free of annoying travel troubles, which now were passed into the hands of coach conductors, passengers could enjoy themselves, talking, reading, and contemplating landscapes through coach windows.

Stagecoach companies introduced the system of ticketing, which had never before existed in Russia. In order to use coach-company services, the traveler had to buy a ticket in a traffic office, which gave him or her a right to take a particular seat. The seats inside the coach compartment were more expensive than those outside. The traveler could also buy the services of a coach entirely for him- or herself. Although ticket prices were rather high, travelers didn't complain, since it was still much cheaper to travel by coach as compared to the amount of money spent on traveling in the traditional manner. The ticket—a rather large piece of paper—contained information about the seat number, price, final destination, and the date of departure. The ticket was signed by the manager of a traffic office. A list of regulations and rules for passengers, printed in Russian and German, occupied nearly one half of the ticket. The first item listed documents required from travelers: a passport and an approval for departure from the police. At the beginning of coach-company operations, passengers were even required to provide the address where they planned to stay upon their arrival to their destination. As the number of passengers increased, controls became weaker, and some passengers managed to successfully avoid strict prescriptions.[18] Travel restrictions were noticeably lifted shortly after the first railroad line began to operate in 1851, as Frithjof Benjamin Schenk points out in chapter 10 of this volume.

There were also limitations on the weight and dimensions of the luggage, which passengers could take with them on a journey. Each passenger was allowed to take onboard luggage weighing twenty Russian pounds (around eight kilograms) free of charge, while for another thirty Russian pounds, he or she had to pay a high extra fee. Liquids, explosives, and all other items that could damage the passengers' luggage were strictly prohibited onboard, as were letters and packages. Each ticket included advice on time management and reminded passengers that stagecoaches departed regularly from a particular place and at an exact time.

"Equality was introduced into practice in Russia by regular coach transportation, and we hope that railroads will help to develop it further," remarked one Russian essayist, who had witnessed important sociocultural changes in Russia during the first half of the nineteenth century.[19] Indeed, contemporaries immediately perceived a close link between egalitarian sentiments among the Russian public and the emergence of public transportation, which became the subject of a wide discussion. In the influential monthly *Otechestvennye zapiski,* one Russian journalist greeted the opening of the first stagecoach-transportation line between St. Petersburg and Moscow with great enthusiasm. Noting that previously this convenient mode of travel had been an exclusive privilege of the very rich, he wrote: "We are very happy from the bottom of our hearts and are congratulating our compatriots with the founding of such a useful enterprise, since it demonstrates vividly the achievements of national education, the development of industry, and the government's efforts to ensure equal distribution of public benefits among inhabitants of all estates and classes."[20]

Advertising the new mode of travel and cultivating new travel habits, coach companies—in cooperation with postal authorities—worked out a number of regulations for passengers, coachmen, conductors, and station masters, which also addressed issues of "equality." These were published in a leaflet format, in special handbooks on travel and transportation, and in official newspapers, along with other information regarding the functioning of the stagecoach-transportation system. "People of all ranks, ages, and both sexes may travel in stagecoaches," stated one regulation.[21] To demonstrate the effectiveness and success of their activities, company officials stressed in their reports that among thousands of passengers traveling through the highways in stagecoaches were people of modest means, as well as senators, generals, and other high-ranking officials.[22]

The new mode of transportation found a market among women, who soon became active customers of transportation services. Using coaches themselves, ladies of high rank were influential in contributing to the favorable reception of regular coach transportation and to making public opinion about it. Governing bodies of the transport companies tried to do their best to meet their needs.[23] In his memoirs, Filipp Vigel describes a journey in a coach when he was accompanied by two ladies who felt obliged to keep polite conversation. The problem was that while one lady could speak only French, the other could speak only Russian. Being placed against the wall of the coach compartment by the stout girl servant, Vigel had no other option but to serve his female companions as an interpreter during the way from St. Petersburg to Moscow.[24]

Following Wolfgang Schivelbusch's ideas, I suggest that stagecoach travel, like that in a train compartment later, juxtaposed "passengers of different social and professional groups and genders into a kind of a living mosaic of all the fortunes, positions, characters, manners, customs."[25] Stagecoach transportation created a space for fraternal social relations. While traveling on equal terms together for three to four days, to the same destination, passengers got acquainted and became members of a specific travel community—the "traveling community of wise men," as one novelist named it in his novel *Stagecoach; or, An Observer of Native Customs*. A list of members of that community is revealing. Among the numerous characters traveling in the same stagecoach from St. Petersburg to Moscow are a helpful and devout Conductor; a retired Military Officer, who keeps a travel diary during the journey; a man from the Russian provincial town of Tver', whom his fellow-travelers name the Historian for his great erudition; a trade agent from Hamburg, who is going to see relatives in Moscow; an architect from Moscow, who is returning home from St. Petersburg; a factory owner from an old-believer family; a merchant from Liveland, one of the Russian Empire's western provinces; a lady, who serves as a governess for some well-to-do noble family in Tver'; and an old gentlemen from Livland with his young and pretty lady-companion. The author places much emphasis on different communicational situations in the stagecoach compartment, in inns, restaurants, and shops along the way, and describes them in great detail.[26]

Regulations determined rules of conduct and were intended to cultivate civility among the passengers and those who served them. Beatings and abusive language, common in the old days, were replaced by the system of fines. Coachmen were strictly forbidden from drawing lots to determine whose turn it was to drive, as they had long been accustomed. While coachmen dwindled and lost their prestige, coach conductors became more important, being responsible for time, serving passengers, and keeping order during a journey.[27]

Passengers were not permitted to disturb fellow travelers and were to expect kindnesses from each other. They were permitted to smoke in the coach only if all other travelers did not object. They were not allowed to take along dogs and other domestic animals. A particular item of the regulations concerned children. Adults could take one child not older than ten years of age into the coach free of charge. The child was to be seated between two adults and was to behave politely, not to disturb other passengers.[28] Although during the journey passengers had to follow the rules and couldn't affect the speed of the coach or change other organizational details that were in the hands of coach conductors, in some situations they could make decisions in conference. For example, passengers could discuss whether they wished the coach to stop for the night or to continue on the journey without a stop. Passengers could insist on removing fellow travelers who breached the public order and were asked to give the conductor a receipt, confirming their collective will.[29] One such episode was humorously depicted by Aleksander Kul'chitskii in his play *The Omnibus*. Passengers on a coach in this play make a drunken young man get off but have a lot of trouble thereafter, because the inebriated gentleman follows their coach and shouts insults.[30]

By establishing regular transportation and reducing journey times, coach-travel companies taught contemporaries to follow timetable requirements and to live according to schedule. The main difficulty the travel companies and postal authorities confronted was to explain what it meant "to do something immediately" and to train their personnel and customers to be on time. It was so unusual and even strange for everybody involved that a good deal of organizational and advertising effort was necessary to convince the public of the advantages of coach travel.[31] As Dmitrii Grigorovich explains in his memoirs, Prince Vladimir Odoevskii believed that the establishment of regular coach-transport services would be useful not only to capital-city dwellers; he also stressed the importance of this innovation for provincial cities, towns, and villages, believing that it would be extremely important for the entire Russian nation (*dlia vsego russkogo naroda*), since "coaches, which departed according to time, would train Russians to take time into account [*rasschityvat' vremia*], which they haven't heretofore done because of their carelessness."[32] Clocks on the walls of road stations, and watches in conductors' and passengers' pockets, became not only important cultural symbols but also effective instruments for establishing a new travel regime, which influenced the rhythm of everyday life in the capitals and in the provinces.

Coach companies' organizational innovations helped train rational consumers. Considering passengers' comfort and security to be their most important objectives, the governing bodies of the companies contributed much to the reconstruction of old station facilities and to the building of new ones. The stations included waiting rooms as well as inns, eating houses, and small shops where travelers could buy souvenirs. A central coach terminal in St. Petersburg, rebuilt and opened to the public in 1845, was equipped with gas lighting and water-supply systems. Limiting the weight of the luggage that passengers were allowed to bring on board and demanding high extra payments for excess weight, transportation companies discouraged customers from taking with them everything they might possibly need during the journey and compelled them to use more intensively the road's facilities. In *Moscow and Muscovites,* Mikhail Zagoskin portrays a passenger who had trouble miniaturizing his luggage to the required weight. He protested having to pay for the excess weight of his luggage, a price equal to the one he had paid for his ticket, but he was not prepared to leave some things, which he was accustomed to take with him.[33] Step by step, travelers got used to following the requirements and were compelled to use services and goods, which they were offered.

As in other countries in Europe and North America, the emergence of regular transportation spurred a heated public debate in Russia. Passengers appreciated very much a noticeable reduction in the burdens of travel, but they didn't want to become "simply packed parcels." One character in a novel, who rejects stagecoach services, exclaims: "In a stagecoach you are not traveling, you are being transported like freight."[34] Perhaps an aversion to the rationalization and commercialization of travel forced many Russian *littérateurs,* who themselves used the coach services intensively, to write much more frequently about the traditional mode of travel in a carriage-and-three than about journeys in the stagecoach, perpetuating the romantic image of "Russian troika."

"The Guidebook Kingdom":
The World through the Coach Window

Being transported in a stagecoach, passengers were not only trained to be rational consumers and civil travelers; they were also getting used to living according to a schedule. Moreover, passengers were taught how to discover the human and physical environments of their own country. Travel guidebooks instructed them in what to see and how to appreciate historical and natural sites. The new modes of travel gave rise to new literary genres of travel guides and travelogues. As travel in Russia became more comfortable, the demand for travel literature grew.

Many passengers took along books when they traveled. "In the stagecoach compartment, as in a prison cell, every book is very welcomed, especially when you are not inclined to communicate with your neighbors," the renowned Russian author Alexander Pushkin pointedly remarked, as he traveled from Moscow to St. Petersburg as soon as the highway was opened. Having no guidebook available, he took along Alexander Radishchev's scandalous *Journey from St. Petersburg to Moscow,* a semifictional work Catherine the Great had ordered burned four decades previously.[35] The Aksakov family, who traveled with Nikolai Gogol in a stagecoach from Moscow to St. Petersburg in 1839, watched through an inner window (that divided the stagecoach compartment into two separate parts) how their fellow passenger took out a book from his travel bag and got absorbed in it.[36] Traveling and writing have always been closely associated, but in this period not only writing but also reading became intimately linked with travel. As Ivan Dmitriev wrote in the preface to his 1839 *Guidebook from Moscow to St. Petersburg and Back*: "Every day, curiosity and the necessity for every Russian to visit Moscow and St. Petersburg become more and more evident, and many thousands of Russians and foreigners are traveling along the Moscow road. But perhaps not everyone knows that on the space of 674 versts[37] between the two capitals, there are places and things of interest that deserve careful study or attention. . . . The urgent need to have a pocket-sized guidebook that can replace a chaperone is obvious."[38]

Though the first guidebooks for the capital cities of St. Petersburg and Moscow were published in the second half of the eighteenth century, until the very beginning of the nineteenth century there were no guidebooks for travel in Russia. The postal service did develop several handbooks that contained information on the postal stations, distances, and prices on main routes, which were helpful in making up particular itineraries. But these contained no cultural or historical commentary.

The first pocket-sized guidebook intended for use by travelers en route from St. Petersburg to Moscow was written by Ivan Glushkov. He was born in the beginning of 1770s into a merchant family in the provincial city of Tver', made a successful career as a state official in St. Petersburg, became a nobleman, and after retirement returned to his native city, where he died in 1848. His guidebook was published in 1801 with a dedication to the Russian Empress Elizabeth, the wife of Alexander I. Having received an enthusiastic welcome from the reading public, it was reprinted a year later with a number of engravings and soon was translated into German.[39] Comparing Alexander Radishchev's *Journey from St. Petersburg to Moscow* to Glushkov's guidebook, the historian P. Lubomirov called the latter a "loyalist journey" (*blagonamerennoye puteshestviye*).[40]

A new type of Russian guidebook appeared in the 1830s, at the same time as John Murray and Karl Baedeker published their travel guides in Britain and Germany. While Murray and Baedeker made their guides for train travelers, Russian guides were intended for stagecoach travel. The first such guide was published in 1839 by Ivan Dmitriev. The guide was praised by contemporaries for its impressive comprehensiveness and was reissued eight years later, without any important changes. A second guide was published in 1841 by an anonymous author and was written in a breezy and ironic manner. It was rather thin compared to Dmitriev's guide.[41] Little is known about the authors of these two guidebooks. Like their predecessor Glushkov, they didn't publish anything else. Apparently Dmitriev and his anonymous colleague came from the urban intellectual milieu of St. Petersburg or Moscow; each possessed a skillful pen, was well-read in contemporary literature, and had a ready wit and courage to pioneer a new style of Russian guidebook. They addressed their books to people of the same intellectual milieu from which they themselves came and intended to acquaint educated inhabitants of the Russian metropolises with the rural and urban environment of the provinces of the Russian Empire.

These two guidebooks contained practical information on transportation services and the use of the road infrastructure. They actively advertised hotels and restaurants as well as shops and added comments on the kinds of specialty goods one could expect to find in towns along the way: where to get spice cakes in Tver', for example; or the famous Pozharsky beefsteaks and leather and morocco goods of Torzhok; or the round rolls and sleighbells of Valdai; or trout and pearls in Iazhelbitsy. Having been taken home, all those small souvenirs were meant to help travelers retain vivid recollections of local inhabitants, who were generally depicted in the guidebooks as industrious, talented, and hospitable.[42]

Another noticeable innovation was the inclusion of long historical accounts about the towns and villages situated along the route. Guidebooks sought to educate travelers not only about Russia's history but also its geography, means of communication, commerce, and natural resources.

The utilitarian view of the road surroundings that dominated the accounts made by eighteenth-century academicians (the first tradition of travel writing about the empire) remained influential and shaped the style of representation in the Russian guidebooks of the 1830–40s, informing key points in the descriptions of particular landscapes.[43] Thus, the guides described uncultivated natural terrain with thick forest and uninhabited natural spaces as unspectacular and unappealing. In contrast, they depicted densely populated territories with villages, settlements, and towns, where inhabitants cultivated land and were engaged in commerce, trade, and shipping operations, as attractive and picturesque. To highlight the impression of activity, the guides depicted local inhabitants and landscapes almost exclusively during the frost-free seasons. A constant summer reigned on the pages of the guidebooks: birds were chirping, butterflies fluttering, and flies buzzing; herdsmen were singing, as were happy peasants, seasonal workers, and coachmen.

The guides helped passengers define the collective self and the other, serving as a means of developing new national coherences and identities. While they described Russian peasants as friendly local inhabitants, the peoples living not far from St. Petersburg in Ingermanland were depicted as foreign. "Our" Russian villages were situated in picturesque surroundings and healthy climates, and their inhabitants were happy and rich. The others' poor settlements were situated "in Lapland kingdom, which was all a marshland, dirty and damp," and their inhabitants were "stupid, mistrustful, inclined to indulge in vices," requiring constant supervision. Using such a literary mode of describing the provinces of the Russian Empire and its inhabitants, the authors tried to define a symbolic boundary that divided so-called Inner Russia from the territory situated somewhere outside it.[44] The guidebooks also promoted a sense of "Russianness." Providing their readers with knowledge of various locales, the guides helped cultivate patriotic sentiments. Their authors considered the passengers' movement between two Russian capitals as a source of self-identity as well as national identity. The guidebooks encouraged would-be coach passengers to grasp what was specifically Russian in climates, landscapes, and their inhabitants' occupations, customs, and clothing. The travel guides also sought to instill in their readers a passion for their Fatherland. According to Pavel Svinin, the travelers would be successful in discovering an authentic image of their native Fatherland only if they were passionately fond of it. As he put it in one of his publications: "Only high-minded passion may inspire the talent for that. Why dismiss that a Russian can feel such passion?"[45]

The guidebooks sought to cultivate in their readers an aesthetic viewpoint. They preferred to present general views of picturesque settlements or monasteries against the background of bright verdure, as well as panoramic views of rivers with built-up environments along the banks. They made the Russian provinces appear familiar by basing descriptions of provincial cities and landscapes on images of Switzerland or Germany, which may have been familiar to readers from their foreign travel experiences. Prescribing particular scenarios of visual perception, the guidebooks were intended to help the reader-traveler become absorbed in the contemplation of native landscapes, to be inspired by their beauty, and to feel him- or herself an authentic Russian, "a descendant of great Slavs." Recommending that his readers climb a hill near the settlement of Bronnitsa, Dmitriev described the resulting view of the city of Novgorod:

> You are a Slav, a descendent of those great Slavs for whom the glory was a cradle and the victory a herald of their very existence. . . . Wouldn't you hurry (if only in your mind) to cast a glance at the cradle of this great, powerful, and glorious kingdom—Russia? Wouldn't you take a look at that ancient nest where the two-headed eagle had hatched, at that seed from which an enormous tree had sprung during [the past] ten centuries? Under the shade of this tree, which is still growing and spreading its roots and branches ever further, millions of many different nations have come. . . . And this cradle, this great seed is almost before you. . . . From here you see the first object of the Slavs' glory—Il'men' Lake . . . What a scene! Climb up the Bronnitsa hill, I beg you: of course, it is high and rather steep; but you are probably used to climbing up, now and then, to the third or the forth ring at a theater; wouldn't you then climb up a little higher to admire the wonderful panorama?[46]

The guides familiarized the Russian provincial environment not simply by providing information and establishing the common knowledge of particular territory, its environs, and inhabitants but by encouraging patriotic sentiments and by sustaining a powerful sense of belonging to that territory as one's native land. Moreover, together with other travel literature, the guidebooks promoted the idea that middle-class members could distinguish themselves from enlightened aristocrats, who, despite their perfect command of nearly all European languages, had lost their original national identity.[47]

Conclusions

My story of the building of a land-road network in the period between 1820 and the 1850s, the rise of stage coaching, and the concurrent creation of a travel culture differs from many other narratives, which have been written in the spirit of the popular maxim that Russia has always suffered from two main misfortunes: "fools and bad roads" (*duraki da dorogi*). As I have attempted to show, the intensive construction of macadamized roads resulted in the emergence of a more efficient land-road transportation network, providing movement for passengers and freight throughout the European part of the Russian Empire between 1820 and the 1850s. The regular transportation of travelers was put into practice by joint-stock and state-owned transportation companies. Interested in raising their profits, the coach companies opened transportation lines not only through the major highways but through many roads of secondary importance, contributing to the further expansion of the highway's network. The intensification of domestic mobility from around 1815 gave rise to the growing demand for regular transportation services, which were provided by commercial coach companies and contributed to the adaptation of new transportation technologies, which in turn shaped the formation of the new sociocultural role of the passenger. The introduction of regular coach services helped to establish new travel habits, spreading the sense of middle-class and national identity. Organizational innovations introduced by the coach companies did not merely facilitate domestic travel and increased mobility; they also promoted the establishment of a new travel regime. To become a passenger, one needed to acquire cultural skills that could bridge social divisions, to get used to living according to a schedule, to become a rational and economical consumer, and to fill the travel time with projects of self-improvement through discovering the human and physical environments of one's own country.

At the same time, my analysis of travel guides and travelogues, which recorded passengers' individual travel experiences, reveals that travelers were not only service customers but objects of governance and control. Like Soviet tourists later (see Diane P. Koenker's contribution to this volume), stagecoach travelers were asserting their own agency. They successfully evaded travel restrictions and chose freely between different modes of transportation and transport companies. Getting used to innovations, they may have enthusiastically welcomed challenges or strongly opposed them. Coming to coinhabit the new public spaces of Russian roads' infrastructure, they creatively learned to perceive the environment of their country.

Commercial travelers and vacationers formed a growing market for guidebooks. Though in contrast to Murray's and Baedeker's guides, Russian guides were published in lesser numbers and were intended for stagecoach passengers, the emergence of these guides also related to the expansion of consumption and national consciousness. The authors of the guides addressed their narratives to readers from lower-income groups and taught them to consume time and space. The travel guides offered middle-class city dwellers an escape from the confines of their urban environment and the opportunity to experience new vistas.

Typically, as others have shown, Imperial Russian artists and writers presented the Russian landscape as an uncultivated terrain with dense forests and vast open steppes only lightly speckled by human habitation. But the guidebook literature discussed here shows that there was an alternative image. The guidebooks presented Central Russian provinces as a densely populated territory, rich with natural resources, with picturesque landscapes and historical sites; with well-off, cheerful, healthy, and industrious inhabitants portrayed as the descendants of the ancient Slavs. The guides contributed to the rise of an emotional sense of a collective self and to the strengthening of new national ties that bound together geographical spaces, historical times, and people.

Notes

I am very grateful to Professor Nicolai Krementsov at the Institute for the History and Philosophy of Science and Technology, University of Toronto, and Dr. Julia Lajus, director of the Center for the Environmental and Technological History, European University at St. Petersburg, for encouragement, helpful comments, and suggestions. Earlier versions of this essay were presented at the 2008 Society for the History of Technology conference at Lisbon; the 2008 Annual Conference at European University at St. Petersburg; the Fisher Forum 2009, "Russia's Role in Human Mobility: Historical and Contemporary Perspectives" at the University of Illinois at Urbana-Champaign in 2009; Cultural Histories of Sociability, Spaces, and Mobility Conference at York in 2009; and the First World Congress on Environmental History at Copenhagen; and to the seminar at the Royal Institute of Technology in Stockholm in 2008. I would like to thank all those who kindly commented on part of all previous drafts.

1. Benedict Anderson, *Imagined Communities: Reflections on the Origin and Spread of Nationalism* (New York: Verso, 1991).

2. Christopher Ely, *This Meager Nature: Landscape and National Identity in Imperial Russia* (DeKalb: Northern Illinois University Press, 2002); Christopher Ely, "The Origins of Russian Scenery: Volga River Tourism and Russian Landscape Aesthetics," *Slavic Review* 62.4 (2003): 666–82; Guido Hausmann, *Mütterchen Wolga. Ein Fluss als Erinnerungsort vom 17. bis zum frühen 20. Jahrhundert* (Frankfurt a.M.: Campus Verlag, 2009).

3. John Randolph, "The Singing Coachman; or, the Road and Russia's Ethnographic Invention in Early Modern Times," *Journal of Early Modern History* 11 (2007): 32–61.

4. Rudy Koshar, *German Travel Cultures* (New York: Berg, 2000); Rudy Koshar, "What Ought to Be Seen: Tourists' Guidebooks and National Identities in Modern Germany and Europe," *Journal of Contemporary History* 33 (1998): 323–40; Jan Palmowski, "Travels with Baedeker: The Guidebook and the Middle Classes in Victorian and Edwardian Britain," in *Histories of Leisure,* ed. Rudy Koshar (New York: Berg, 2002), 105–30.

5. For instance, see Anne E. Gorsuch and Diane P. Koenker, eds., *Turizm: The Russian and East European Tourist under Capitalism and Socialism* (Ithaca, N.Y.: Cornell University Press, 2006); Louise McReynolds, *Russia at Play: Leisure Activities at the End of the Tsarist Era* (Ithaca, N.Y.: Cornell University Press, 2003).

6. For instance, see *Putevoditel' kak semioticheskii ob'ekt* (Tartu: Tartu University Press, 2008); Andreas Schönle, *Authenticity and Fiction in the Russian Literary Journey, 1790–1840* (Cambridge, Mass.: Harvard University Press, 2000); E. Ivashina, "O spetsifike zhanra puteshestviia v russkoi literature pervoi treti 19 veka," *Filologiia* 3 (1979): 3–16.

7. For useful observations on the state of transport and mobility history and the prospects for its further development, see Colin Divall and George Revill, "Cultures

of Transport: Representation, Practice, and Technology," *Journal of Transport History* 26.1 (2005): 99–111; Gijs Mom, "What Kind of Transport History Did We Get? Half a Century of JTH and the Future of the Field," *Journal of Transport History* 24.2 (2004): 121–38.

8. See Trancy Nichols Busch, "Connecting an Empire: Eighteenth-Century Russian Roads, from Peter to Catherine," *Journal of Transport History* 29.2 (2009): 240–58; A. S. Kudriavtsev, *Ocherki istorii dorozhnogo stroitel'stva v SSSR (dooktiabor'skii period)* (Moscow: Dorizdat, 1951), 78–132. On the history of Russian waterways and the development of water transportation, see E. G. Istomina, *Vodnye puti Rossii vo vtoroi polovine XVIII–nachale XIX v.* (Moscow: Nauka, 1982).

9. For instance, see L. I. Sazonova, "Literaturnaia rodoslovnaia gogolevskoi ptitsy-troiki," *Izvestiia Academii Nauk. Seriia literatury i iazyka* 59.2 (2000): 23–30.

10. L. I. Bazhitova, "Podorozhnye gramoty," *Pochtovaia sviaz'. Tekhnika i tekhnologii* 10 (2005): 15–19.

11. On the functioning of the Russian post-route system during the eighteenth century, see A. N. Vigilev, *Istoriia otechestvennoi pochty,* vol. 2 (Moscow: Svaiz, 1979).

12. *Neskol'ko sutok v doroge ot Peterburga k Simbirsku* (St. Petersburg: Tipografiia E. Pratsa, 1840), 48.

13. On road building in Russia during the nineteenth century, see Kudriavtsev, *Ocherki istorii dorozhnogo,* 135–89; A. A. Gelfer, *Ocherk razvitiia dorozhnogo i mostostroitel'nogo dela v Vedomstve putei soobshcheniia v piati tomakh,* vol. 1 (St. Petersburg: Upravlenie vnutrennimi vodnimi putiami i schosseinimi dorogami, 1911), 13–44.

14. The number of established transport-coach companies varied from only a few in the 1820s to around twenty in the 1840s. See *Materiialy po istorii sviazi v Rossii. XVIII–nachalo XX vv. Obzor dokumental'nikh materiialov,* ed. N. Mal'tseva (Leningrad: Leningradskaia tipografiia n 5 glafpolitgrafproma komiteta po pechati, 1966), 209–11. Joint-stock transport companies were among dozens of other companies established in Russia between the 1820s and the 1840s. On those corporate enterprises in general, see Thomas C. Owen, *The Corporation under Russian Law, 1800–1917: A Study in Tsarist Economic Policy* (Cambridge; N.Y.: Cambridge University Press, 1991); Leonid E. Shepelev, *Aktsionernye kompanii v Rossii* (Leningrad: Nauka, 1973).

15. Dmitry Anuchin, *Ob'iasnenie k karte soobshchenii evropeiskoi Rossii* (St. Petersburg: N.p., 1859), 15–41.

16. Konstantin Bazilevich, *Pochta v Rossii v XIX veke,* pt. 1 (Moscow: Sviaz,' 1927), 43.

17. "Otchet direktora pochtovogo departamenta N.I. Laube o deistviiakh pochtovikh ekipazhei za 23 goda," in *Materiialy po istorii sviazi v Rossii,* 217.

18. Dmitri Novikov, *Dilizhans ili nabludatel' otechestvennikh nravov* (Moscow: Tipografia N. Stepanova Pri Imperatorskom Teatre, 1829), 5.

19. *Zapiski Filippa Filipp'evicha Vigelia,* (Moscow: Tipografiia torgovogo doma S. Strugovshchikova, G. Pokhitonova, N. Vodova i Ko, 1892).

20. Pavel Svin'in, "Sovremennye Peterburgskie letopisi. Novoe uchrezhdenie v Rossii pochtovikh ekipazhei na obrazets izvestnykh dilizhansov," *Otechestvennye zapiski* 3 (1820): 118.

21. For instance, see *Pravila zavedeniia letnikh dilizhansov* (St. Petersburg: Tipografiia K. Kraiia, 1835), 5.

22. For instance, see "Vysochaishii doklad ot 18 iiunia ob otchete po uchrezhdeniiu pochtovykh karet i brikov i o predlozhenii uchredit' ikh ot Moskvy do Nizhnego Novgoroda," Dokumental'nye fondy, Tsentral'nyi muzei sviazi imeni A.S. Popova, f. Pochta, d. 382, l. 15.

23. On ladies as users of coach-transportation services, for instance, see "Iz pisem Aleksandra Iakovlevicha Bulgakova bratu Konstantinu Iakovlevichu Bulgakovu," *Russkii arkhiv* 12 (1900): 406–7.

24. *Zapiski Vigelia*, 73–74.

25. Wolfgang Schivelbusch, *The Railway Journey: The Industrialization of Time and Space in the Nineteenth Century* (New York: Berg, 1986).

26. Nokivov, *Dilizhans*.

27. On fines and managerial innovations, see Central State Historical Archives of St. Petersburg (TsGIA SPb), f. 1543 (Petrogradskii pochtamt), op. 3, d. 111, ll. 1–15. On coach conductors and post-station holders' duties and polite-behavior requirements, see *Instruktsiia nadziratelu pochtovoi kareti; Instruktsiia Glavnoachal'stvuiushego nad pohtovim departamentom stantsionnim smotriteliam i pochtkomisaram* (St. Petersburg: N.p., 1842).

28. On regulations for passengers, see *Ustav pervonachal'nogo zavedeniia dilizhansov,* 14 maiia 1831 goda (St. Petersburg: N.p., 1831), paragrafi 19–38.

29. *Pravila zavedeniia,* 16.

30. A. Ia. Kul'chitskii (Govorilin), *Omnibus,* in *Fiziologiia Peterburga,* vol. 2 (St. Petersburg: A. Ivanov, 1845), 95–140.

31. On the discussion the issue of "doing at once" in internal bureaucratic correspondence, see TsGIA SPb, f. 1543, op. 3, d. 111, ll. 55–62, 77, 80.

32. Dmitrii V. Grigorovich, *Literaturnye vospominaniia* (Moscow: Khudozhestvennaia literature, 1987), 101.

33. Mikhail Zagoskin, *Moskva i Moskvichi. Zapiski Bogdan Il'cha Bel'skogo* (Moscow: Tipografiia N. Stepanova, 1842–50), 58–59.

34. Ibid., 61.

35. Alexander Pushkin, "Puteshestvie iz Moskvy v Peterburg (Belovaia redaktsiia) (1834)," in *Polnoe sobranie sochinenii v 16 tomakh,* vol. 11 (Leningrad: Izdatelstvo An SSSR, 1949), 243–44.

36. Sergei Aksakov, "Istoriia moego znakomstva sGogolem, 1832–1843," in *Sobranie sochinenii,* vol. 3 (Moscow: Khudozhestvennaia literatura, 1986), 18–20.

37. An Imperial Russian unit of distance, approximately equal to a kilometer, or .621 miles.

38. Ivan Dmitriev, *Putevoditel' ot Moskvy do Sankt-Peterburga i obratno, soobshchaiushchii istoricheskie, statisticheskie i drugie svedeniia o zamechatel'nykh gorodakh, mestakh i predmetakh, nakhodiashchikhsia po doroge mezhdu obeimi stolitsami,* 2d ed. (Moscow: Tipografiia P. Stepanova, 1847)

39. Ivan Glushkov, *Ruchnoi dorozhnik dlia upotrebleniia na puti mezhdu imperatorskimi vserossiiskimi stolitsami, daiushchii o gorodakh, po onomu lezhashchikh izvestiia*

istoricheskie, geograficheskie i politicheskie, s opisaniem obyvatel'skikh obriadov, odezhd, narechii i vidov luchshikh mest, 2d ed. (St. Petersburg: Imperatorskaia tiporrafiia, 1802).

40. P. Lubomirov, "Blagonamerennoe 'Puteshestvie iz Peterburga v Moskvu' (Glushkov i Radishchev)," *Uchenye zapiski Saratovskogo universiteta* 3 (1926): 317–30.

41. *Sputnik ot Moskvy do Sankt-Peterburga, Sputnik ot Sankt-Peterburga do Moskvy* (Moscow: Tipografiia A. Semena, 1841).

42. Ibid., 47; Dmitriev, *Putevoditel'*, 30, 34–35, 44, 50, 135, 216–17.

43. On the Russian Academy's expeditions of the eighteenth century and their description of the territory of the Russian Empire through the lens of cameralism, see Alexandra Bekasova, "Izuchenie Rossiiskoi imperii ekspeditsiiami 1760–1780 godov: 'Vzgliad' estestvoispitatelei i formirovanie predstavlenii o gosudarstvennih bogatstvakh," *Istoriko-biologicheskie issledovaniia* 4 (2010): 13–34; David Moon, "Russian Academy of Sciences Expeditions to the Steppes in the Late Eighteenth Century," *Slavonic and East European Review* 88 (2010): 206.

44. Dmitriev, *Putevoditel'*, 567.

45. "Nachertanie, sdelannoe grafom Kapodistriia dlia zhivopisnogo puteshestviia po Rossii," *Moskovskii telegraf* 43 (1832): 142.

46. Dmitriev, *Putevoditel'*, 284–86.

47. In particular see *Dilizhans*, 82.

10

"This New Means of Transportation Will Make Unstable People Even More Unstable"

Railways and Geographical Mobility in Tsarist Russia

FRITHJOF BENJAMIN SCHENK

According to an old but still strong historical consensus, late tsarist Russia was a rather immobile and static country. Even after the abolition of serfdom in 1861, the argument goes, the peasants of European Russia were bound to their communes by various legal restrictions and economic obligations, people from the lower classes and national minorities like the Jews suffered from a restrictive passport regime, and the country's economic backwardness hindered the majority of the people from traveling freely and communicating with regions far away from their home area. Even so, recent scholarship on the history of peasant colonization, on processes of seasonal migration and the emergence of tourism in late tsarist Russia, is beginning to alter this stereotypical picture significantly. Nevertheless, a comprehensive history of geographical mobility in nineteenth-century Russia still waits to be written.[1]

Part of the problem is that, although we know a lot about formal constraints on movement, we know little about actual movement practices. Interestingly enough, even those scholars who have previously worked on the history of transport have contributed very little to our understanding of the changing modes of mobility at the dawn of the era of high modernity in the Russian Empire. Railway historians in Russia and the West have until recently studied their topic primarily from an economic and technical point of view, reflecting more on the impact of the steam engine on the process of industrialization than on migration and mobility. They have focused more on planners and builders of railroads than on the users of the new means of transportation.[2] From this scholarship we know a lot about engineers, workers, and employees who built and ran the iron network and very little about the passengers who populated the trains and railway stations of the empire.

In this essay I want to turn to this oft-neglected aspect of railway history and examine the impact of rail transport on the development of geographical mobility in nineteenth-century Russia. I will analyze political discourses and policies regulating passenger traffic in the second half of the nineteenth century and look at the dynamics of railway mobility since the 1870s as they are represented in the statistics of the Russian Ministry of Ways of Communication (MPS). One important goal of this essay is to bring railway history back into the larger picture of the social, political, and cultural developments in late tsarist Russia. In contrast to traditional works of Russian railway history, I argue that we have to shift our attention from the railroads as a means of transportation of wheat, coal, and iron ore to those people who populated trains and railway stations and used the steam engine for moving from one spot of the large country to the other. If we look at railroads from this perspective, it becomes obvious how many itineraries intersected at the sites of the Russian railway space and to what degree larger historical developments of nineteenth-century Russia intertwined with the construction and use of railroads by people from various social and ethnic groups. The construction of the railroads fueled and linked diverse historical processes that are often analyzed separately, from worker mobility from rural to urban areas, to peasant colonization of Siberia and Central Asia, to the beginnings of middle-class tourism, as well as the empire's territorial consolidation through the movement of troops and bureaucrats from the center to the peripheries. For this reason, a history of how people used transport may provide a window into how these processes interacted while people traveled in close quarters.

Of course, each of these developments deserves its own investigation, and none of them will be discussed in this essay in detail. The goal of this essay is rather modest. As a starting point for further research in this field, I want to take a closer look at the dynamics of passengers' movements in the railway age in tsarist Russia and thereby generate a first idea of how the construction of railroads contributed to geographical mobility.

★ ★ ★

In the 1840s, after a long period of hesitation, the Russian government finally decided to start the construction of railroads in the largest continental empire in the world. It perceived this technological innovation first and foremost as an opportunity to ease the transport of goods, and as a strategic device that would enable the quick mobilization of troops in peace and war. As a result, the first rail lines of national significance were not built with the aim of enhancing the mobility of the country's populace.[3] On the contrary, conservative advisers such as the minister of finance, Georg von Kankrin, and the minister of the interior, Lev Alekseevich Perovskii, warned Tsar Nicholas I that the construction of railroads in Russia might cause a dangerous rise in geographical mobility. Von Kankrin predicted that the construction of railroads would stimulate "communicability" (Communicabilität) among the empire's population and feared that the new means of transportation would make "unstable people even more unstable."[4] Conservative authors had warned in earlier years that passengers traveling the "iron horse" (*chugunka*) in large numbers might devastate the country like "hordes of Arabs and Bashkirs" had done previously.[5]

When the first Russian railroad of national importance, a trunk line connecting the imperial capitals of St. Petersburg and Moscow, was finally inaugurated on 1 November 1851, passengers buying a train ticket had to show an official document issued by the local police, stating that the authorities had no objections against the prospective traveler's journey. Exceptions were made only for civil servants traveling on duty, passengers on their way to summer houses, farmers transporting agricultural goods to the marketplace, servants accompanying their masters, and children traveling with their parents.[6] The cashiers of the railroad company were obliged to register the names of all passengers in a special book, documenting who was leaving the station and affirming that all necessary documents had been checked.[7] These regulations resembled the traditional rules for traveling by post in the Russian Empire and the obligation to apply for a post order (*podorozhnaia*) specifying one's itinerary and the number of horses one could demand at the post-horse stations.[8] Apparently, the tsarist authorities, when drafting the regulations for passenger traffic on Russia's first long-distance railroad, still dreamed of curtailing geographical mobility in the Russian Empire in the railway age as much as possible.

But it was merely a matter of time until the strict regulations of autumn 1851 had to be withdrawn again. Already on 13 December 1851, the Main Administration of Transportation and Public Buildings issued a decree abolishing the need to show police approval when purchasing a train ticket.[9] Instead of demanding that passengers apply for special permission to embark on a train, it was now sufficient to show any document proving the passenger's identity. The traffic of train passengers from the lower strata of the society (*prostogo naroda*) was regulated according to the regular passport legislation.[10] In 1857, just as Tsar Alexander II gave the go-ahead for the construction of a comprehensive railway network in European Russia, the obligation to show a passport when buying a ticket at a Russian railway station was abolished.[11] Even without knowing the exact reasons for this decision, one may speculate that the authorities soon understood the impracticability of the original rules. Perhaps the government was surprised by the great acceptance of the steam engine among the public.[12] According to Richard Haywood, the decision of 13 December 1851 illustrates that from this point on "the railway was seen [by the authorities] as an instrument in reducing internal travel restrictions for at least part of the population."[13]

Even though Russian railroads were not built primarily for the purpose of passenger traffic, various proponents had already predicted great success for the steam engine in the Russian Empire and its acceptance as a means of transport in all strata of society. Pavel Melnikov, one of the first Russian engineers of railway construction and later the empire's first minister of ways of communication, pointed in 1840 to the advantages of railroads for passenger transport. After his return from a study trip, during which he had analyzed the systems of transportation in England, Belgium, the German states, and France, Melnikov concluded that railroads stood out among forms of transportation due to their speed, comfort, safety, steadiness, and reliability. The young engineer emphasized that both the government and ordinary passengers from the "poorer classes" would benefit from the velocity of railroads.[14]

One year later, an interministerial committee evaluating the projected railroad from St. Petersburg to Moscow predicted that passenger traffic between the capitals would triple after the line's inauguration, from 270,000 to 810,000 persons a year. The committee assumed that 45 percent of all passengers of the Petersburg-Moscow railroad would be migratory laborers.[15] Earlier, advocates of the trunk line identified such workers, many of whom walked each spring to St. Petersburg, as a viable target for the new rail connection.[16] If the railroad could attract 85 percent of the seventy thousand workers wandering annually to the capital and back, the planners argued, the company would earn 360,000 silver rubles per year from this group alone. They assumed that workers would prefer to gain three weeks of working time—previously consumed by their long trips to the building sites and factories in St. Petersburg—and therefore would willingly pay three silver rubles for a one-way ticket in third class.[17]

Authorities later came to realize that migratory workers were actually reluctant to switch from the slow but cheap walking trail to the fast but expensive railroad. Still, this report of 1841 illustrates that some representatives of the Russian elite were beginning to see the notion of an increase of popular mobility in a utilitarian light, as a tool for accomplishing a useful purpose. The proponents of the railway line from Petersburg to Moscow referred to the large group of passengers-to-be from the working class in part because they had to justify in internal political debates the high expenditures of the ambitious technical project. Indeed, it seems that Melnikov and the other advocates of the trunk line were not primarily interested in alleviating travel conditions of the poor classes but in covering the expenses of the railroad by tapping the workers' own scarce financial resources.

After Nicholas I finally gave the go-ahead for the construction of the railway line in 1842, the argument that railroads might serve the interests of passengers (of any social class) almost completely disappeared from the debates over the building of new rail connections in the Russian Empire. From now on, the discussions about the construction of new railroads in Russia was dominated by two camps: one arguing for the building of a network serving the needs of the country's economy (i.e. primarily the needs of Russian agriculture), and the other demanding the construction of a system of strategic railway lines serving the interests of the military.[18] It is true that most of the railway companies operating in the empire offered passenger services to customers from all parts of society. But one has to keep in mind that none of the numerous rail connections in Russia was built primarily for this purpose and that the transport of travelers was in most cases a loss-making undertaking.

* * *

As a result, the interests of passengers were often neglected by planners and operators of new railway lines. Unsurprisingly, people traveling by rail in Russia frequently complained of poor passenger service. Travel accounts and complaints collected in the files of the archive of the MPS give ample evidence of the high degree of dissatisfaction among railway passengers traveling with private and state-run companies. In particular, passengers were dissatisfied with the large distances between train stations and the cities they claimed to serve, with the legendary slow motion of Russian trains, with expensive travel fares, with the rude manners of railroad officials, and with what they saw as the eternal state of disorder (*bezporiadok*) afflicting the whole system.

As the network of railways in Russia grew larger and the number of railway travelers increased in the 1860s and 1870s, the tsarist administration started to pay more attention to the question of the system's effectiveness in terms of passenger transportation. When in 1876 the government installed the so-called Baranov Commission, an interministerial committee assessing the Russian railway system from all perspectives, special attention was given to the issue of passenger mobility. In 1881 the commission published a comprehensive report on current travel conditions on the Russian railway system.[19] This document casts a damning light on the daily life in crowded train stations, on poor sanitary conditions in packed third-class carriages, on problems of passengers' alimentation at buffets and restaurants in railway stations, and a great number of other issues. Several of the problems that had been identified by a number of regional subcommittees were later addressed in the *General Regulation for the Russian Railroads* (*Obshchii ustav Rossiiskikh zheleznykh dorog*), adopted by the authorities in December 1885, and a special law regulating the rights and duties of passengers in railway stations and trains, issued in 1891.[20]

These uniform regulations did not even partially solve the problems mentioned in the report of the Baranov Commission, but they contributed significantly to the standardization of Russian railway space. By the end of the nineteenth century, no matter whether a traveler was using a train operated by a private or a state-run company or whether he or she embarked the carriage in Warsaw, Samara, or Baku, the schedule indicated a train's arrival and departure according to the St. Petersburg time—the bell was rung three times before the train's departure, and each passenger was charged the same price for a train journey. Large railway maps decorating the waiting rooms in Russian railway stations showed the tsarist empire as a homogeneous white space, uninterrupted by internal political, geographical, or cultural borders and bound together by a network of black lines stretching from the network's center in Moscow to the country's distant peripheries.

As in other countries, the proponents of the railroads in tsarist Russia imagined the new system as an instrument enabling the accelerated transport of goods and people across large geographical distances. Even though Russian trains ran much slower than their counterparts in Western Europe or in North America, from a historical perspective, railway traffic did contribute significantly to the reduction of travel time also in tsarist Russia. Whereas before the construction of railways, journeymen on Russia's poorly developed system of roads and waterways were able to traverse no more than 125 kilometers a day, in 1851 the train ride from St. Petersburg to Moscow (680 kilometers) took only twenty-two hours. Whereas a journey by sledge in the winter of 1856–57 from Moscow to Irkutsk took about thirty-three days, in 1912 the same distance of 5,080 versts could be traveled by express train in five days or by ordinary postal train in eight days.[21] In 1890, on some Russian railway lines, trains were already running quicker than forty versts per hour, waiting times at the stations included.[22]

In Russia, as in other countries, truly *rapid* rail transportation was still a privilege limited to passengers traveling in the first two classes—people from the wealthier parts of society. Tradesmen who could afford a train ticket in the first or second class reached their destination much more quickly than those in third class.[23] In 1881 a ticket for the night train from St. Petersburg to Moscow cost ten rubles in the slow postal train and thirty rubles in the luxurious express train.[24] Though traveling by train in Russia was—from an international perspective—relatively cheap, buying a train ticket in the tsarist realm was still an expensive undertaking.[25] Before the introduction of a differentiated system of travel fares in 1894, the price of a train ticket was generated based on a fixed rate per verst (approximately a kilometer). This system, which made long railway trips extremely expensive, excluded, for mere economic reasons, members of the poorer strata of society from the privilege of railway mobility.

⋆ ⋆ ⋆

Indeed, by the late 1870s planners and economists were increasingly alarmed by the fact that migratory laborers continued to make the long journey from their villages to their places of employment by foot instead of using the services of Russian railroads.[26] Members of the Baranov commission anxiously observed in 1881 that the "poor working class" in Russia, due to "specific economic conditions" of the country, depended on seasonal migration for work.[27] Yet since traveling by train was too expensive for people from these "dependent classes" (*nedostatochnye klassy*), workers' continued reliance on foot travel was causing significant damage to agriculture, and thus to the whole Russian economy.[28] The commission suggested abolishing the special tax on train tickets, the introduction of a special "fourth-class tariff," and reduced travel fares for trips longer than one thousand versts.[29] Nonetheless, the adoption of the General Regulation for the Russian Railroads in 1885 did nothing to meet the needs of migratory workers.

Finally, in 1894 the minister of finance Sergei Witte (famous for his expertise in railway affairs) suggested fundamentally changing the system of ticket prices for the Russian railroads.[30] In a memorandum to Alexander III drafted on 20 May 1894, Witte argued that Russia, "due to her vast geographical expanses," depended like no other country on the mobility of her population. Whereas thirteen years earlier the members of the Baranov Commission had presented their plans in terms of the needs of migratory workers, Witte elevated the status of the question by stressing the importance of seasonal migration for the national economy. The minister even identified mobility as "one of the most important prerequisites for an increase in the empire's economic wealth."[31] Passenger statistics revealed that in comparison to other European countries, in Russia relatively few people traveled by rail.[32] In particular, the "masses of the rural population," Witte pointed out, "annually had to travel large distances to their seasonal place of employment in agriculture and industry," but instead of traveling by train, they walked large distances by foot, "consuming unproductively time and energy."[33] With the aim to attract more passengers from the poorer parts of the society, Witte suggested the introduction of a new system of passenger fares differentiating between long- and short-distance train rides. A new system that made traveling by rail on long distances—trips longer than 160 versts—cheaper was introduced on 1 December 1894.[34] The effect of the new law was dramatic. Whereas in 1894 only 42.5 million third-class tickets had been sold, the number reached 93.5 million in 1903 and 163.1 million in 1912.[35]

Another instrument aimed at the alleviation of railway mobility of people from the poorer parts of society was the introduction of a "fourth class" on Russian railroads—the transport of passenger-workers in converted freight cars. Already in the 1870s some railway companies had offered this cheap travel option to their customers. But the number of passengers traveling in this primitive class only slightly exceeded the margin of one million per year.[36] After 1894 the statistical bureau of the MPS registered rising numbers of people using the so-called workers' fare.[37] Whereas in the beginning only about 1.8 million people chose this option, in 1903 already 7.8 million people traveled in fourth class. In 1912 about 44.2 million passenger-workers populated Russian trains and railway stations.[38] Additionally, in the 1890s an increasing number of peasant-colonists traveled by rail with a reduced ticket price to their new settlements in Siberia and Central Asia. In 1900 the number of this group topped one million for the first time. Between 1907 and 1909, the peak of Russia's colonization politics in the Asian periphery, more than three million settlers were transferred annually to their Eastern destination.[39]

The rising numbers of passengers in the lower classes illustrates that the increase of railway mobility in Russia since the 1890s was a phenomenon embracing in particular the economically weaker part of society. In comparison with the 208.9 million passengers traveling third or fourth class in 1912 or having bought reduced tickets for peasant colonists, the group of 22.4 million travelers in the first two classes even resembled a small minority.[40] Thus the experience of the quick transition of geographical space in the railway age was no longer an exclusive privilege of the empire's social and economic elite. The administration's attitude about mass mobility had also changed significantly. Whereas Georg von Kankrin had warned of the consequences of too much "communicability" in the 1840s, his successor Sergei Witte fifty years later stressed the urgent need for geographical mobility to enhance "the economic and moral bonds [*nravstvennye sviazi*] between the various geographical regions of the country."[41]

Even after 1894, a large number of migratory workers still hesitated to use the railroads and instead preferred walking large distances and saving travel fare.[42] It is also true that in international comparison, the degree of railway mobility in Russia at the end of the century was rather low. Moreover, Russian trains were traveling the country much more slowly than their counterparts in Western Europe or in the United States.[43] But in comparison with the patterns of mobility in Russia before the introduction of railroads, the new means of transportation provided large parts of society with new possibilities to travel large distances quickly within the boundaries of the vast empire.[44] Hereby the railroad contributed undoubtedly to an enlargement of the geographical radius of mobility of large parts of the society.

★ ★ ★

Russia entered the railway age in 1851, when the country's first rail connection of national importance was put into operation. But reliable statistical data on the development of passenger mobility in the empire are available only for the period after 1873, when the statistical department of the Ministry of Transport was founded. From that year on, the administrations of all railway companies were obliged to send annual reports to St. Petersburg, documenting the development of their transport services.[45] The charts in the ministry's statistical yearbooks give us a good overview of the increase of passenger mobility (in total numbers of train rides and of versts traveled) between 1873 and 1913.

The development of passenger traffic in the Russian Empire can be divided into two phases: a first period, from 1873 to 1894, and a second one from 1895 to 1913. During the first period, we can observe a moderate increase in the numbers of railway passengers and versts traveled. Whereas in 1877 approximately 32 million passengers populated Russian railway stations, seventeen years later, more than 53 million people were moved by Russian trains (an overall increase of 67.5 percent). After 1894 this development experienced a radical acceleration. During the next seventeen years (until 1911), the number of Russian railway passengers increased by 285.7 percent. In 1912, 231 million passengers traveled by rail in Russia.

The increase of railway mobility in tsarist Russia at the end of the nineteenth century corresponded to the growth of the empire's population and to the massive extension of the network of railroads in the Witte era. Moreover, it mirrors perfectly the process of rapid industrialization and urbanization the country was experiencing during this period. But apart from this general development, the effect of the reform of the system of passenger tariffs in 1894 is striking. Without the introduction of a system of differentiated travel fares (and the introduction of a special fare for suburban traffic one year later), the growth of passenger mobility in the middle of the 1890s would probably have been less significant. During the three years between 1895 and 1897, the increase of versts traveled on the Russian railways was larger than the accumulated growth during the previous twenty-two years.[46] Whereas in 1894 Russian passengers traveled only 4.4 billion versts on the railways in European Russia, in 1897 this figure had grown by 52 percent to 6.7 billion. In 1912 this number was 18.8 billion.[47]

Before 1894, neither periods of economic decline nor major political events like the war against the Ottoman Empire in the 1870s had a significant impact on the numbers of Russian railway passengers. After the reform of 1894, the curve depicting the development of passenger traffic in Russia reflected the major events of the empire's political and economic life. The numbers of versts Russian passengers traveled on the country's railways increased significantly, for example, during the economic boom of the second half of the 1890s and between 1909 and 1913, and decreased in 1904 and 1905, when the empire was traumatized by the war against Japan, the general strike of October 1905, and the turbulences of the Revolution of 1905–6.[48]

Russian railroads from the very beginning served primarily the needs of those passengers who were either not able or not willing to pay expensive first- or second-class fares. Travelers from abroad and from Russia who chose the comfortable but expensive way of traveling in tsarist Russia repeatedly reported almost empty compartments and wagons in the first class. In 1877 the number of passengers traveling third or fourth class (22.1 million) was more than five times higher than the number of tickets sold to first- and second-class travelers (4 million). In 1912 the gap between the respective numbers had widened further. Whereas in this year, 22.4 million passengers populated compartments in the luxurious carriages of the first or the second class, the number of travelers in the third and second class was more than nine times higher (207.3 million—*pereselentsy* not included).

Unfortunately, we don't know anything about either the social origin of the railway's customers in the various classes nor about the ratio of male and female passengers. Since the railroad was a "democratic" means of transportation, a farmer who came into money in theory was entitled to buy a first-class ticket and to share a compartment with a nobleman. But we may assume that people from the lower strata of society, like workers, peasants, and small merchants—if they could afford buying a train ticket at all—in general used the third or fourth class. Likewise, the first class apparently remained an almost exclusive social space populated by noblemen, high-ranking officials, rich merchants, and foreigners. The chance of encounters between people of different social background in Russian railway space was higher in second-class carriages, but, unfortunately, we don't know to what extent the railroads in tsarist Russia really became a scene of "socialization."

It is likewise almost impossible to assess to what extent Russian railways enhanced the geographical mobility of women. Russian railway companies offered their services to passengers of both sexes. Russian railway stations and trains, like those in other European countries, were even furnished with specially designated waiting rooms and compartments for women. But we don't have any reliable sources indicating how many women made use of them and whether women benefited to a similar degree as men from the increase of geographical mobility in Russia in the railway age.

Most Russian railway passengers used the train for rather short trips. In 1913 about 92 percent of all railway journeys in European Russia were shorter than 250 versts, and 46 percent of all passengers took the train for a trip which was even shorter than twenty-five versts.[49] Apparently, railway journeys by passengers populating the cheaper classes—*pereselentsy* not included—tended to be shorter than those using the first or the second class. Whereas the average traveling distance of a first-class passenger in 1912 was approximately 219.8 versts, Russian voyagers in the third class roughly made eighty versts each trip.[50] From 1912 about 70.5 percent of the 231.4 million railway passengers in Russia traveled third-class, the majority using the train for journeys within a smaller regional context. The decline of average traveling distances per passenger from 142.23 versts in 1906 to 103.96 versts in 1912 can be interpreted as a further indicator of the increase of numbers of passengers from the lower strata of the society and as a reflection of the process of "democratization" of Russian railway customers.[51]

The increase and decrease of railway mobility in Russia was closely connected to the annual rhythms of economic life in the empire. Since Russia remained until the end of the *ancien régime* primarily an agricultural country, life on Russian railroads became rather dim in winter. Railway mobility reached its lowest point in February, when the numbers of sold railway tickets equalled only 69.7 percent of the annual average. In May, with the beginning of the working season in agriculture and on the building sites in the urban centers, one could observe a significant increase of passengers populating stations and railway cars (130 percent of the annual average). A second wave came in August, when workers were needed in large numbers on the fields for the harvest in the southern and central regions (123 percent of the annual average).[52]

* * *

Whereas in early years of the railway age in tsarist Russia, the carriages of the "iron horse" were populated primarily by representatives of the wealthier classes, at the end of the century passengers from the lower strata of society formed the overwhelming majority of the railway's customers. This fact may be interpreted as an indicator of the great success of the new means of transportation among the Russian population and of the significant increase of geographical mobility in late tsarist Russia in general. Even though the railroads were a "democratic" means of transportation, offering their services to noblemen and workers and peasants alike, the spatial spheres of the respective classes remained to a high degree segregated in Russia's railway space. In theory, an aristocrat from St. Petersburg on his way to his estate in the countryside could get in touch with a peasant colonist, moving from the western *gubernia* to Siberia when the itineraries of both men intersected on the platform of a provincial railway station.

Yet even though Russian writers were repeatedly inspired by the idea that representatives of different social classes could meet and get in contact in a train compartment—think, for example of the opening scene of Dostoevskii's *The Idiot*—it is an open question to what extent the Russian railroads in late tsarist Russia really contributed to this kind of "fraternization" that transcended social barriers. The analysis of the patterns of railway mobility in Russia in the second half of the nineteenth century given in this essay points in a different direction. It suggests that the spaces of mobility of the upper and the lower classes remained separate even at the beginning of the twentieth century. Whereas the average passengers of the first class used the new means of transportation for long and rather expensive journeys, travelers populating the third and fourth class could afford the services of the *chugunka* only for comparatively short distance journeys. To what extent the itineraries of people from different social classes really criss-crossed at the sites of Russia's railway space needs further investigation.

Moreover, it is worthwhile to ask whether the new possibilities to personally experience the vast territory of the Russian Empire and its cultural and geographical diversity altered the railway passengers' perception of Russia as a polyethnic and multicultural imperial space and changed the mental maps of the country's population. But this must be the topic of a separate essay.

Notes

1. See, for example, Willard Sunderland, *Taming the Wild Field: Colonization and Empire on the Russian Steppe* (Ithaca, N.Y.: Cornell University Press, 2004); Nicholas B. Breyfogle, Abby Schrader, and Willard Sunderland, eds., *Peopling the Russian Periphery: Borderland Colonization in Eurasian History,* (London: Routledge, 2008); Barbara A. Anderson, *Internal Migration during Modernization in Late Nineteenth-Century Russia* (Princeton, N.J.: Princeton University Press, 1980); Louise McReynolds, *Russia at Play: Leisure Activities at the End of the Tsarist Era* (Ithaca, N.Y.: Cornell University Press, 2002); Anne E. Gorsuch and Diane P. Koenker, eds., *Turizm: The Russian and East European Tourist under Capitalism and Socialism* (Ithaca, N.Y.: Cornell University Press, 2006).

2. See, for example, Vladimir M. Verkhovskoi, *Istoricheskii ocherk razvitiia zheleznykh dorog v Rossii s ikh osnovaniia po 1897 g. vkliuchitel'no,* vols. 1–2 (St. Petersburg: Tipografiia Ministerstva Putei Soobshcheniia, 1898–99); John Norton Westwood, *A History of Russian Railways* (London: Allen and Unwin, 1964); Aida M. Solov'eva, *Zheleznodorozhnyi transport Rossii vo vtoroi polovine XIX v.* (Moscow: Nauka, 1975); Gennadii M. Fadeev, et al., eds., *Istoriia zheleznodorozhnogo transporta Rossii, vol. 1 (1836–1917),* (St. Petersburg: Ivan Fedorov, 1994).

3. Here we disregard the "toy-train" line built between Tsarskoe Selo, Pavlovsk, and Petersburg in 1837. See Franz Anton von Gerstner, *Über die Vortheile der Anlage einer Eisenbahn von St. Petersburg nach Zarskoe-Selo und Pawlowsk, deren Ausführung durch eine Aktiengesellschaft mit Allerhöchstem Privilegium Seiner Kaiserlichen Majestät statt findet* (St. Petersburg: Carl Kray, 1836), 29, 38, 42–43.

4. *Aus den Reisetagebüchern des Graf Georg Kankrin ehemaligen Kaiserlich Russischen Finanz-Ministers, aus den Jahren 1840–1845: Mit einer Lebensskizze Kankrin's nebst zwei Beilagen,* pt. 1, ed. Alexander Graf Keyserling (Brunswick: Leibrock, 1865), 23.

5. "Chugunnye dorogi," *Biblioteka dlia chteniia* 8 (1835), sec. 3, 106–7, qtd. in Richard M. Haywood, *The Beginnings of Railway Development in Russia in the Reign of Nicholas I, 1835–1842* (Durham, N.C.: Duke University Press, 1969), 177.

6. "Prikaz S. Peterburgskogo Ober-Politseimeistera po S. Peterburgskoi Politsii (17 October 1851), Nr. 227," *Severnaia Pchela* 234 (20 October 1851): 935.

7. "Polozhenie o dvizhenie po S. Peterburgsko-Moskovskoi zheleznoi doroge," § 39, *Severnaia Pchela* 247 (5 November 1851): 985–87.

8. Passengers traveling on the first Russian railroad from St. Petersburg to Tsarskoe Selo or Pavlovsk likewise had to show their personal documents at the station to a "commissar" of the private company before boarding a train. Nicholas I had demanded that such controls be introduced. The procedure was supported logistically by the military governor-general of St. Petersburg. Haywood, *Beginnings of Railway Development*, 99–100, 135.

9. Departament zheleznykh dorog, ed., *Sbornik svedenii o zheleznykh dorogakh v Rossii. 1867, otdel III: Vysochaishiia poveleniia, ukazy pravitel'stvuiushchago senata i minister-skiia postanovleniia*, (St. Petersburg: N.p., 1867), 99; *Polnoe Sobranie Zakonov Rossiiskoi Imperii* (hereafter PSZRI), 2d ser., vol. 26, pt. 2, no. 25821 (13 December 1851): 166; *Severnaia pchela*, 21 December 1851, 1138.

10. "Ustav o pasportakh," *Svod Zakonov Rossiiskoi Imperii*, vol. 14 (St. Petersburg: N.p., 1857), §§ 98–122.

11. *PSZRI*, 2d ser., vol. 32, no. 32545; Valentina Grigor'evna Chernukha, *Pasport v Rossii. 1719–1917* (St. Petersburg: Liki Rossii, 2007), 113, 120. The construction of railroads led to a liberalization of passport laws in other European countries as well. After 1889, personal documents lost their importance even in international travel in Western and Central Europe. See Andreas Fahrmeir, "Passport and the Status of Aliens," in *The Mechanics of Internationalism: Culture, Society, and Politics from the 1840s to the First World War*, ed. Martin H. Geyer and Johannes Paulmann (Oxford: Oxford University Press, 2001), 103–6. On the German case, see John Torpey, *The Invention of the Passport: Surveillance, Citizenship, and the State* (Cambridge: Cambridge University Press, 2000), 77–78.

12. On the number of passengers on the St. Petersburg–Moscow railroad in 1851, see Richard M. Haywood, *Russia Enters the Railway Age, 1845–1855* (New York: Columbia University Press 1998), 443.

13. Ibid., 451.

14. Pavel Petrovich Mel'nikov, "Ob otnositel'nykh vygodakh razlichnykh sistem vnutrennykh soobshchenii," *Zhurnal putei soobshcheniia* 3 (1840): 207–27, esp. 221–23.

15. In England only 17 percent of all passengers traveled third class in 1845. Haywood, *Russia Enters the Railway Age*, 445. In 1852, 59 percent of the 249,099 passengers of the Petersburg-Moscow railroad traveled third class. Another 374,422 persons (apparently soldiers) were transported in freight cars (508).

16. Haywood, *Beginnings of Railway Development*, 217.

17. "Vsepoddanneishee donesenie o proekte ustroeniia zheleznoi dorogi mezhdu S. Peterburgom i Moskvoi 1841 goda," in *P. P. Mel'nikov. Inzhener, uchenyi, gosudarstvennyi deiatel'*, ed. Mikhail I. Voronin and M. M. Voronina (St. Petersburg: Gumanistika, 2003), 152–76. The planners assumed that sixty thousand migratory laborers would annually buy return tickets to St. Petersburg (six silver rubles each) in third-class carriages. In fact, a return ticket from Petersburg to Moscow in the third class cost seven rubles in 1851. Haywood, *Russia Enters the Railway Age*, 445.

18. See, for example, Alfred Rieber, "The Debate over the Southern Line: Economic

Integration or National Security," *Synopsis: A Collection of Essays in Honour of Zenon E. Kohut,* ed. Serhii Plokhy and Frank Sysyn (Toronto: Canadian Institute of Ukrainian Studies Press, 2005), 371–97.

19. Vysochaishe uchrezhdennaia Kommisiia dlia issledovaniia zheleznodorozhnago dela v Rossii, ed., *Doklad o passazhirskom dvizhenii,* (St. Petersburg: Vysochaishe uchrezhdennaia komis. Dlia issledovaniia zh.-d. dela v Rossii, 1881).

20. *Obshchii ustav Rossiiskikh zheleznykh dorog i polozhenie o sovete po zheleznodorozhnym delam* (St. Petersburg: N.p., 1886); "Rasporiazhenie, ob'iavlennoe Pravitel'stvuiushchemu Senatu Ministrom Putei Soobshcheniia (St. 211) o pravilakh pol'zovaniia passazhirskimi pomeshcheniiami zheleznodorozhnykh stantsii i pravilakh dlia passazhirov v poezdakh zheleznykh dorog (8.1.1891)," *Zheleznodorozhnoe delo* 10.11 (1891): 135–36.

21. On the speed of travel before the construction of railways, see Roland Cvetkovski, *Modernisierung durch Beschleunigung: Raum und Mobilität im Zarenreich* (Frankfurt: Campus Verlag, 2006), 77, 179. On Siberia, see Harmon Tupper, *To the Great Ocean: Siberia and the Trans-Siberian Railway* (Boston: Little Brown, 1965), 13, 47. On the Petersburg-Moscow railway in 1851, see Haywood, *Russia Enters the Railway Age,* 443; on the schedule of the Siberian railway in 1912, see Karl Baedeker *Russland, nebst Teheran, Port Arthur, Peking: Handbuch für Reisende,* 7th ed. (Leipzig: Baedeker, 1912), 503.

22. But in fact only three Russian companies offered such quick services of passenger transportation: Nikolai-Railroad, St. Petersburg–Warsaw Railroad, and South-Western Railroads. More than 70 percent of all passenger-versts were generated at the end of the 1880s by trains running slower than 30 versts per hour. See Praktik, "Skorost' perevozki passazhirov pervykh trekh klassov po russkim zheleznym dorogam," *Zheleznodorozhnoe delo* 9.37–38 (1890): 337–38.

23. Cvetkovski, *Modernisierung,* 289. Since 1857, passenger tariffs were regulated by law: every passenger had to pay three kopeks per verst in the first class, two and a half kopeks in the second class, and one and a quarter kopeks in the third. See "Ukaz i polozhenie ob osnovykh usloviiakh dlia sooruzheniia pervoi seti zheleznykh dorog (28.1.1857)," 179; *Doklad o passazhirskom dvizhenii,* 181. Since 1879, railway passengers had to pay additionally a kind of mobility tax—an *osobyi sbor* of 15 percent of the price of a third-class train ticket and 20 percent of the price of a second- and first-class ticket. *Doklad o passazhirskom dvizhenii,* 182. Children, soldiers and convicts were charged reduced fares.

24. *Doklad o passazhirskom dvizhenii,* 190. A Russian industrial worker in 1880 earned an average of sixteen rubles and fifty-six kopeks per month; a worker in agriculture in 1903 made twenty-five kopeks a day. See Boris Mironov, *Sotsial'naia istoriia Rossii perioda imperii (XVIII–nachalo XX v.),* vol. 2 (St. Petersburg: Dmitrii Bulanin, 2000), 389; N. V. Shachovskii, *Zemledel'cheskii otkhod krest'ian* (St. Petersburg: Vysochaishe uchrezhdennoe Osoboe Soveshchanie o nuzhdakh sel'skokhoziaistvennoi promyshlennosti, 1903), 112.

25. According to an investigation of the Baranov Commission, Russian passenger tariffs were low in comparison to other European countries. Only in Norway was traveling by rail cheaper (per verst) than in Russia. *Doklad o passazhirskom dvizhenii,* 217.

26. *Zapiska ob otkhozhikh (zemledel'cheskikh i nezemledel'cheskikh) promyslakh i o peredvizhenii rabochikh partii po zheleznym dorogam* (St. Petersburg: N.p., 1879); Cvetkovski, *Modernisierung*, 290.

27. *Doklad o passazhirskom dvizhenii*, 219.

28. Ibid., 221; *Doklad o peredvizhenii rabochikh partii po zheleznym dorogam* (St. Petersburg: Vysochaishe uchrezhdennaia Kommisiia dlia issledovaniia zheleznodorozhnago dela v Rossii, 1881), 5, 9, 12, 65.

29. *Doklad o passazhirskom dvizhenii*, 226.

30. On the reform of passenger tariffs of 1884, see Liudvig I. Perl', *Po voprosu o reforme passazhirskikh tarifov* (St. Petersburg: Tipografiia br. Shumakher, 1892); Sergei Iu. Witte, "Vsepoddanneishaia dokladnaia zapiska ministra finansov po departamentu zheleznodorozhnykh del o reforme passazhirskogo tarifa (20.5.1894)," in *Sobranie sochinenii i dokumental'nykh materialov v piati tomakh*, vol. 1: *Puti soobshcheniia i ėkonomicheskoe razvitie Rossii*, book 2, part 2 (Moscow: Nauka, 2006), 209–13; Sergei Iu. Witte, "Vsepoddanneishaia dokladnaia zapiska ministra finansov po departamentu zheleznodorozhnykh del o reforme passazhirskogo tarifa (18.11.1894)," in *Sobranie sochinenii i dokumental'nykh materialov v piati tomakh*, vol. 1: *Puti soobshcheniia i ėkonomicheskoe razvitie Rossii*, book 2, part 2 (Moscow: Nauka, 2006), 216–18; "Ponizhenie passazhirskikh tarifov na russkikh zheleznykh dorogakh," *Zheleznodorozhnoe delo* 13.12 (1894): 126.

31. Witte, "Vsepoddanneishaia dokladnaia zapiska (20.5.1894)," 209.

32. Witte argued that in Russia during the last three years, an average of 33.7 million passengers traveled by rail, among which 30.9 million (91.5 percent) bought third-class tickets. In contrast, the railway systems of Great Britain moved 817, Germany 315, France 208, and Belgium 57 million passengers. Whereas the transport of goods on Russian railways increased between 1873 and 1891 by 210 percent, the traffic of third-class passengers increased during the same period only by 129 percent. The statistical yearbooks of the Russian Ministry of Transport give slightly higher numbers for the indicated years than Witte in his file: 37.3 million third-class passengers in 1891; 38.8 million in 1892; 39.6 million in 1893. See *Statisticheskii sbornik Ministerstva Putei Soobshcheniia*, vol. 46 (1897), chart VII. Maybe Witte referred in this document to passenger numbers of railroads earned and operated by the state.

33. Witte, "Vsepoddanneishaia dokladnaia zapiska (18.11.1894)," 216.

34. A third-class ticket cost one and a quarter kopeks for the first 160 versts. Passengers traveling further had to pay 0.9 kopeks per verst for the remaining distance (until three hundred versts). A third-class ticket for a journey longer than 1,500 versts cost 0.4 kopeks per verst. Passengers traveling second or first class had to multiply the respective fare by 1.5 or 2.5.

35. *Statisticheskii sbornik Ministerstva Putei Soobshcheniia*, vol. 46 (1897), chart VII; 81 (1905), chart VII; 131 (1916), vols. 2–3, chart VII. On the consequences of the reform of 1894, see N. A., "Po povodu reformy passazhirskago tarifa i vyzvannoi eiu stat'i g-na M. Filonenko," *Zheleznodorozhnoe delo* 14.11 (1895): 85–87; "Pervye priznaki vliianiia ponizhennago passazhirskago tarifa na russkikh zheleznykh dorogakh," *Zheleznodorozhnoe delo* 14.21–22 (1895): 206.

36. Fourth-class wagons in 1873 were operated by the Warsaw-Vienna railway, the Warsaw-Bromberg railway, the Lodzinskaia railway, the Kursko-Khar'kovo-Azovskaia railway, and the Moskovsko-Brestskaia railway. That year, 1.07 million passengers bought a fourth-class ticket in Russia. See *Statisticheskii sbornik Ministerstva Putei Soobshcheniia*, vol. 1 (1877), chart IV.

37. Passengers using the "worker's tariff" had to pay three quarters of a kopek per vert for the first 920 versts. Longer trips were even cheaper. In contrast to the travel fares of the first three classes, the workers' tariff could be used only by groups. See K. I. Gutsevich, *Perevozka rabochikh po zheleznym dorogam. Spravka i perechnia voprosov po delu ob uporiadochenii zemledel'cheskago otkhoda krest'ian* (St. Petersburg: N.p., 1903), 1. Passengers were moved also in other countries in primitive freight cars. On the German case, see Ralf Roth, *Das Jahrhundert der Eisenbahn: Die Herrschaft über Raum und Zeit 1800–1914* (Ostfildern: Thorbecke, 2005), 137–38.

38. *Statisticheskii sbornik Ministerstva Putei Soobchsheniia*, vol. 46 (1897), chart VII, 81 (1905), chart VII, 131 (1915), vols. 2–3, chart VII.

39. *Statisticheskii sbornik Ministerstva Putei Soobchsheniia*, vol. 81 (1905), chart VII, 113 (1912), vols. 1–2, chart VII. This movement reached its peak in 1907, when 3.56 million settlers were transported by rail to Russia's Asian peripheries.

40. *Statisticheskii sbornik Ministerstva Putei Soobchsheniia*, vol. 131 (1916), vols. 2–3, chart VII. Also in other European countries the railways were particularly used by third- and fourth-class passengers. See Roth, *Jahrhundert der Eisenbahn*, 138–39 and 243.

41. Witte, "Vsepoddanneishaia dokladnaia zapiska (20.5.1894)," 209.

42. This problem remained a burning issue in debates among railway planners and economists. In 1903 a special commission was founded to discuss possible solutions: Vysochaishe uchrezhdennoe Osoboe Soveshchanie o nuzhdakh sel'skokhoziaistvennoi promyshlennosti. See Nikolai V. Ponomarev, *O peredvizhenii sel'skokhoziaistvennykh rabochikh, napravliaiushchikhsia v novorossiiskie gubernii* (St. Petersburg: N.p., 1895); Nikolai V. Ponomarev, *O peredvizhenii sel'skokhoziaistvennykh rabochikh, napravliaiushchikhsia v iugovostochnyia mestnosti Rossii* (St. Petersburg: N.p., 1896); I. Karyshev, "Ideal'nyi tarif dlia russkikh zheleznykh dorog," *Zheleznodorozhnoe delo* 15.3–4 and 5–6 (1896): 19–23, 33–36; "Dal'neishiia zhelatel'nyia reformy passazhirskago tarifa," *Zheleznodorozhnoe delo* 15.30–31 (1896): 250; Shachovskii, *Zemledel'cheskii otkhod krest'ian*; Gutsevich, *Perevozka rabochikh*; "Zhurnal Vysochaishe uchrezhdennago Osobennago Soveshchaniia o nuzhdakh sel'skokhoziaistvennoi promyshlennosti. Nr. 17. Zasedaniia XXXV, XXXVI i XXXVII. 1, 8, i 22 noiabria 1903 goda. Po delu ob uporiadochenii zemledel'cheskago otkhoda krest'ian," in *Rossiia. Gosudarstvennyi Sovet, Vremennye organizatsii, Materialy,* vol. 41 (Russian National Library, St. Petersburg).

43. Praktik, "Skorost' perevozki passazhirov pervykh trekh klassov."

44. Whereas in 1894 every inhabitant of the Russian Empire made an average of 0.38 train journeys a year, in 1913 this number had almost quadrupled (1.35). In comparison with respective numbers from Germany (24.2), France (12.8), or the United States (10.2), this number was still rather small. Evgenii Vladimirovich Michal'tsev, *Ėvoliutsiia passazhirskikh perevozok na zheleznykh dorogakh v dovoennoe vremia* (Moscow: NKPS Transpechat', 1926), 9–10.

45. See "Tsirkuliar tekhnicheskogo-inspektorskago komiteta zheleznykh dorog, Nr. 4461 (19.9.1873)," *Sbornik ministerskikh postanovlenii i obshchikh pravitel'stvennykh rasporiazhenii Ministerstva Putei Soobshcheniia po zheleznym dorogam,* vol. 1 (St. Petersburg: N.p., 1874), 206.

46. Michal'tsev, *Evoliutsiia,* 42.

47. Ibid., 16.

48. Passenger-versts (in billions) per year traveled on the railways in European Russia: 4.4 (1894), 5.6 (1895), 6.3 (1896), 6.7 (1897), 7.6 (1898), 8.3 (1899), 9.1 (1900), 9.6 (1901), 10.0 (1902), 10.8 (1903), 10.6 (1904), 9.7 (1905), 11.0 (1906), 13.0 (1907), 13.7 (1908), 14.6 (1909), 16.1 (1910), 17.3 (1911), 18.8 (1912), 20.9 (1913). See ibid., 16. Between 1904 and 1906, however, the numbers of soldiers transported by rail within Russia reached a climax. Whereas in 1903, 4.8 million recruits were moved by train within the empire, in 1904 this number more than doubled (9.7 million), and in 1906, when the huge army in Mandshuria was demobilized, almost twelve million soldiers were transferred by rail from one region to another. *Statisticheskii sbornik Ministerstva Putei Soobshcheniia,* vol. 81 (1905), 89 (1907), 113 (1912).

49. Michal'tsev, *Évoliutsiia,* 33, 44.

50. *Statisticheskii sbornik Ministerstva Putei Soobchsheniia,* vol. 131, vols. 2–3 (1916), chart VII. The average travel distance of peasant colonists was 734.05 versts in 1912. An average railway journey on the Russian network was 103.96 versts long. These numbers reflect railway journeys in the European and Asiatic part of the Russian Empire. For 1897, the statistical yearbooks give a similar picture: first class: 213.5 versts; third class: 89.7 versts; *pereselentsy*: 455.9 versts; average travel distance: 115.27 versts. *Statisticheskii sbornik Ministerstva Putei Soobshcheniia,* vol. 57 (1899), chart VII.

51. *Statisticheskii sbornik Ministerstva Putei Soobchsheniia,* vol. 89 (1907), 113 (1912), 131 (1916); Michal'tsev, *Évoliutsiia,* 43.

52. Michal'tsev, *Évoliutsiia,* 43.

11

Pleasure Travel in the
Passport State

DIANE P. KOENKER

In the history of the Soviet Union, the Great Turn of 1928–32 produced consequences for the history of Russian mobility as well as for so much else. The planned and unplanned labor recruitment for the First Five-Year Plan impelled hundreds of thousands of Soviet citizens to change their places of work and residence for work opportunities on myriad new construction and industrial projects. Hundreds of thousands of agricultural families—under the mad plan of dekulakization—were forced to leave their homes and settle in new work destinations under utterly inhospitable conditions. Even the relatively privileged graduates of higher educational institutions became subject to state placement in August 1928, and in 1932, by the end of this period of upheaval (and perhaps because of it), the state enacted its "infamous" passport decrees, requiring all urban residents to register for passports and denying the opportunity to hold a passport (and therefore to move freely) to the majority of the country's population.[1]

Yet this very moment of upheaval and legal restriction on movement also saw the launching of the proletarian tourism movement, first with the creation under Komsomol auspices of the Society of Proletarian Tourists in 1928, and then its consolidation as the voluntary Society for Proletarian Tourism and Excursions in 1930. The association explicitly promoted mobility; it encouraged Soviet citizens to move freely, voluntarily, and independently throughout the "vast expanse" of the Soviet land, to encounter and learn about its rich human and natural diversity: tourism would strengthen decision-making skills and citizenship, it would improve physical well-being, and it would produce a truly autonomous and self-activating Soviet subject. Thousands of other Soviet citizens traveled annually to take vacation cures in the health spas of the Black Sea, Crimea, and Caucasus mountains, their journeys also promoted by state policy.

Indeed, this "right to rest" became inscribed in the 1936 Constitution as one of the exemplary provisions of the socialist state, at the same time, of course, that thousands of Soviet citizens lost all of their rights and found themselves on nightmare journeys in sealed boxcars to destinations for which no guidebooks had been written: isolation prisons in Moscow, Vladimir, and Tomsk, and the work camps of the Gulag.

This essay explores the paradox of the coexistence of pleasure travel and punishment trains in a passport state. I will suggest that both types of mobility—forced and free—represented investments in the state's twin projects of nation building and the creation of citizen-subjects. The state forcibly relocated hundreds of thousands of its citizens in the name of economic development, while at the same time touting some of these forced labor migrations as projects for individual rehabilitation. Some Soviet citizens willingly accepted the challenge to transform themselves into new Soviet individuals, but others required the heavy hand of the state to impress upon them the new responsibilities and identities they must bear. The state's right and ability to relocate these individual bodies was one of the mechanisms of the transformation. At the same time, the state promoted pleasure travel using many of the same arguments about nation building and the creation of the autonomous loyal citizen. In this vein, Soviet pleasure travel was only one more element of the mobilization state.

But is that how individuals themselves experienced this travel, as state-directed and unfree? I will explore some parallel tracks of pleasure and carceral travel, as recounted by a sample of travelers from the 1920s to the 1960s, with an eye toward the question: Did the two forms of travel mutually constitute one another? Is "free" travel in a carceral regime qualitatively different from pleasure travel in a "liberal" regime? While the evidence to be presented here cannot definitively answer this last question, I would like to raise it as a problem for future research and contemplation. My primary concern will be to explore the way moving through the Soviet space models citizenship, models the nation, and models the relationship of the individual to the state. Looking at two key periods in the history of pleasure and punitive travel, the 1930s and the 1960s, I will argue that pleasure travel, although authorized and subvented by the state for the purposes of nation building, subject creation, and discipline, escaped from those strictures and became one means (if not the primary means) of Soviet citizens asserting their own agency and entitlement to what they considered the good life.

Space: Knowledge and Control

The sheer size of the Soviet Union often found expression in contemporary texts and discourse in terms of "unbounded" (*neob"iatnyi*) space and "expanse" (*prostranstvo*). In Emma Widdis's analysis, Soviet modernization produced knowledge about the once "ungraspable" expanse of the native land. Imperial or capitalist forces might conquer and possess such space, but in a socialist geography, unbounded space became an object of discovery and appropriation, not dominance. The success of the socialist state demanded a spatial revolution that would minimize distances and create an integrated social body.[2] In this context, human mobility became a prerequisite for acquiring knowledge of and thereby assimilating space: in popular culture and film, the scout (*razvedchik*) emerged as a major figure in the 1920s, the ordinary hero whose curiosity, zest for learning, and love of travel impelled him or her to explore the native land in useful journeys of discovery.[3]

The official ideology of the proletarian tourist movement in the late 1920s also emphasized the knowledge-producing and utilitarian functions of leisure travel: the proletarian tourist would acquire specimens of little-known flora and fauna for academic research collections; he or she would seek to discover new deposits of useful minerals and natural resources.[4] In this way, the unbounded space remained vast but controlled through knowledge. The literature of Soviet tourism adopted the language of the "unbounded": the space of the native land would become the arena in which to engage in the knowledge-producing activities that transformed space and created citizens. "Today the tourist is a sportsman, tomorrow a tireless investigator, a cultural worker along the borders of our huge [*gromadnaia*] country"; "the unbounded territory of the Soviet Union holds in its many parts extraordinary interest for any tourist or investigator."[5]

Pursuant to this knowledge-building effort, the state aimed to control and tame space in the form of the regulatory passport. In 1922, the new Soviet state abolished the remnants of the tsarist passport system and officially permitted "unhindered freedom of movement throughout the whole territory of the RSFSR."[6] Yet soon after, officials reinstated the requirement that travelers must register their presence in a new location within forty-eight hours of arrival.[7] The notorious passport law of 27 December 1932, suggests Widdis, brought an end to the shared project of exploration.[8] But even tourism advocates had already expressed deep concerns about the unregulated wanderings of so-called vagrants (*brodiagi*), whose rambles across the unbounded space of the Soviet Union lacked the purpose and conscious search for knowledge of the true proletarian tourist.[9] The "freedom" to travel, whether for pleasure or state purpose, remained subordinate to the state's interest in that travel.

Even the tourist itinerary itself, the *marshrut,* became subject to passportization in the 1930s. Unbounded space became marked in terms of "objects" (destinations and sights to see), routes (river and road), obstacles, time checks and estimated costs, and opportunities for social-political work.[10] The new "scout" was the tourist who blazed a trail for others to follow—a trail that was always laden with political and social meaning.[11] In leisure as well as in work, the Soviet citizen owed responsibility to the collective: the group, the enterprise, and the state. The state and its representatives aspired to regulate the mobility of all of its subjects.

Mobility and the Soviet State in the First Five-Year Plan

The movement of workers into Five-Year-Plan construction and industrial sites has long been a staple of the heroic narrative of Soviet economic development. The great construction projects—the Dnepr River Hydroelectric Dam (Dneprstroi), the Turkestan-Siberian railroad (Turksib), the Magnitogorsk industrial combine—have attracted attention from generations of scholars. Young people signed up for these projects as a way to establish a career, earn money, or develop a proletarian pedigree that would allow them to pursue higher education.[12] Industrial recruiters fanned across the country in 1930 and 1931 to hire labor for their projects. Potential recruits responded to these representatives, to letters from friends, and to the thrill of change. "The rumor that the biggest plant in the world [i.e. Magnitogorsk] would be built at Magnitnaia mountain excited everyone, old and young. It was said that huge numbers of people were going there. We, my cousin and I, decided to go, too."[13] In the heroic narrative, it was the genius of the plan and its agents (Organized Recruitment, or Orgnabor) that populated the shock construction sites. Individuals chose freely to travel to work, but at the same time they were compliant atoms of mobility in the state's overall plan.

Underlying this free movement of heroic workers, of course, were the considerable "push" factors of collectivization and dekulakization. Although the size of the industrial labor force doubled in the period of the First Five-Year Plan, urban unemployment, organized recruitment, and free will failed to generate the numbers of work hands required by industry. The concurrent campaign against the kulak in the countryside partially solved the problem of labor shortage: millions were forced to leave their villages after being dispossessed by the antikulak brigades; millions more acted on their own to seek safer jobs in industry. The great expansion of the Soviet labor force of the First Five-Year Plan was fueled by peasants traveling "freely" to cities and construction sites to escape the inevitability of coercive removal.

Many of these dispossessed peasant families were not even given the choice to leave voluntarily. As Lynne Viola and others recount, up to two million peasants were forcibly sent into internal exile in 1930 and 1931; named "special settlers," they were forced to populate work sites in the most inhospitable regions of the Soviet periphery.[14] Modeled perhaps on military transportation plans, another instance in which the state directed the movement of its citizens, the relocation of the special settlers created the model for the carceral journeys so achingly described by later victims of the 1930s purges. Double-tiered bunks, barred windows, bolted doors, armed guards, a bucket for a latrine, bread, and a pail of watery soup grudgingly provided at the occasional stopping point—all these would constitute the bitter memories of generations of punishment journeys, of travelers whose movements were completely and utterly directed by the state for its purported needs.[15]

As Lynne Viola emphasizes, these journeys and these exiles remained a closely guarded secret of the Soviet regime until after its demise.[16] By contrast, official travel opportunities for Soviet shock workers and for enthusiastic members of the new Society for Proletarian Tourism received the lavish attention of journalists, filmmakers, trade-union officials, and Komsomol activists. These accounts celebrated movement for pleasure, knowledge, and self-actualization; they emphasized that leisure travel should become a fitting reward for dedication to the goals of the state. They emphasized the liberation that travel endowed upon the individual; if these travelers were cognizant of the special settlers and prisoner transports moving in a parallel and secret world, they did not reveal this knowledge, and it is a rare source that lets us interrogate this silence.

The account of a group of three young women workers from Moscow's Semenovskaia manufacture could not be more distant from the experiences of the special settlers. In summer 1928, they undertook a journey by rail, foot, and rowboat through the lakes and rivers of Karelia, a voyage of self-discovery, empowerment, and service. For many travelers, the train journey itself was a memorable social event, filled with food, song, and conversation.[17] These young women were no exception. On the train from Moscow, passengers quickly became acquainted with one another, out came the teapots and the zakuski, and they arrived enthusiastically in Leningrad for a day of sightseeing. Continuing their journey northward, they encountered the "real" Karelia, a strange otherly place where many people spoke Finnish and where the sun did not set. The tourists organized industrial tours for themselves; they observed the "abnormal" relations between patriarchal Finnish husbands and their submissive wives, they partied with Karelian youth, and they pursued their primary mission of bringing "culture" to the Karelian peasants. Their report dwelled on the breathtaking beauty of the region, its lakes, and its waterfalls, and on the useful knowledge they could bring to its residents, but they also self-consciously marveled at the possibility of the journey itself.[18] Their published account was meant to inspire and encourage others.

With even greater publicity in the autumn of 1930, 257 shock workers from around the Soviet Union embarked on a journey aboard the newly commissioned passenger ship *Abkhazia,* sailing on its maiden voyage from its shipyard in Leningrad to its destination on the Black Sea. As with the young women of

Moscow, this was no mere pleasure voyage: "This was not a trip for holiday and amusement, to which capitalist Europe has become accustomed. No, these 257 Soviet shock workers, having observed the residents of Hamburg, Naples, and Constantinople, carefully recorded everything they saw in their notebooks. They traveled to Europe in order to broaden their horizons, to learn about the achievements of bourgeois technology and culture so that they could better serve the cause of socialist construction."[19] In Hamburg, the tourists marveled at the exemplary organization of the German shipyards and their cleanliness.[20] The days on shore represented the purposeful part of the voyage: to see the West, to observe the crisis of capitalism, to bring back lessons and experiences. But travel was also about the journey, and the voyage itself was an important element of these shock workers' leisure time and an attraction in and of itself. At sea during the days, the passengers could visit the engine room or hear lectures about the countries they were sailing by. Radio broadcasts kept them abreast of news back home; evenings were filled with games, talent shows, singing, and dancing. The travelers returned home different from how they had departed, and this, after all, was the point of touring, with its potential for expanding worldviews and improving the self. Standing up to German police with verses of "Stenka Razin," seeing firsthand the images of capitalist inequality and exploitation, and ultimately coping with the strangeness of their physical displacement generated confidence in themselves and in the system that had allowed them to travel.

Another traveler from the early 1930s earned his celebrity only in the years of the post-Stalin thaw, when a journalist published the tale of Gleb Travin, who had traveled by bicycle forty thousand kilometers around the perimeter of the Soviet Union between 1928 and 1931. From his Kamchatka home, Travin crossed through Central Asia, the Caucasus, and Crimea, reaching Leningrad by the end of his first year on the road. Over the next two years he traversed the northern coast of the Soviet Union, at times catching rides with polar explorers, losing several toes to gangrene after being trapped on an ice floe in the White Sea, and encountering shamans and bandits further to the east. The "stern, untracked" North was the perfect place for this journey of self-discovery, as it was often celebrated in tourist accounts that did receive publicity.[21] Travin left no diary, and his sister destroyed the letters that he sent from along his route; we do not know whether he encountered special settlers and labor-camp prisoners along with the native peoples and local fauna. He traveled to test his own mettle against the elements as well as to make a personal encounter with the Soviet Union in all its diversity. "Every day I took an examination. If I passed, I would remain alive. To fail—meant death."[22] He eschewed publicity, and only in the 1950s did he consent to tell his story: "I was a romantic! They should have put me on the Turksib or the White Sea Canal."[23] In this statement, directly counterposing his solo travel with official mobility projects (one of them—the

White Sea Canal—punitive), Travin acknowledges the superiority of the state's official transformatory labor projects and suggests that he felt himself to be a less worthy Soviet man by choosing to blaze his own trail rather than to throw in with the collective. But at the same time, his motives reflected those of the more celebrated Soviet tourists of the early 1930s: a thirst for knowledge, a ready willingness to lend his help to those he encountered on his journey, and the desire to test his ability to survive the unknown. This too was a model of Soviet mobility.

Mobility and the State in the Time of Terror

The expansion of coercive and pleasure travel continued on their parallel tracks through the 1930s. Punitive and touristic mobility became more routinized and regulated, stiffening the rigor with which the regime dealt with its internal enemies and rewarding favored leisure travelers with better amenities and "Stalinist care" for their recreation and recuperation.

Eugenia Ginzburg's memoir captures the experience of many caught up in the vise of the great purges, beginning in 1935. Her first trip from Kazan' to Moscow as a prisoner placed her in an "ordinary third-class coach divided into compartments, each seating four." But the windows were painted over so there could be no contact between the prisoners and the outside world; guards patrolled the doors of each compartment. "Only when we went to the lavatory did we occasionally catch sight, through the half-open door of the platform at the end of the carriage, of some well-remembered landmark on the familiar Kazan-Moscow route."[24] Later, after two years of solitary confinement, she boarded prison car number seven for the long, slow journey to the Kolyma goldfields. The seventy-six women in the car, labeled "Special Equipment," were permitted to speak only while the train was in motion, not at stops or stations. Their food ration consisted of salted soup and herring tails, and they had to beg the guards for plain water to drink or with which to wash.[25] Vladimir Petrov made a similar journey from Leningrad in 1935, in a prison car with two tiers of plank beds on either side, no light, and no air. At stops, the guards would throw their food rations of bread and herring directly onto the dirty floor of the car. And at every stop, "innumerable guards appeared from nowhere and formed a close line all around the train. This was done not so much from fear of prisoners' escaping as to prevent any contact between them and the signalmen, greasers, couplers, and other railway personnel who might happen to be near." The sealed trains carrying the country's pariahs could not be allowed to mix with the paths of the free and the favored. Carceral mobility was also excruciatingly slow, if routinized. Ginzburg recalled that her train moved "at the pace of a slow-motion film, or the kind of sledges in which the Decembrist wives drove to rejoin their menfolk"; Petrov's car reached Vladivostok only after "forty-seven days of traveling in a closed freight car, in stifling air, in dirt, without once washing my face.... Forty-seven days of lying on a crammed plank bed extending from one end of the car to the other, of eating food that wouldn't have satisfied dogs."[26]

Anna Larina, the wife of the high-value prisoner Nikolai Bukharin, received better treatment, at least in her first journey under guard. Like Ginzburg, she also traveled in a third-class carriage, but this was an ordinary passenger carriage, and the other travelers were not to know that she had been forbidden to mix with them. Later, she too transferred to the more efficient Stolypin-style prison car. "I stopped in horror at the entrance to a narrow walkway down one side of the car. To the side was a series of three-tiered compartments, called coupes, behind a sturdy wire grid running from floor to ceiling; the outside windows along the walkway were fitted with gratings. In other words, the prisoners were caged like animals at the zoo." The damp corridor, the horrific stench of the open toilet, the smelly salt fish and boiled black wheat for rations: "[T]hese created the special atmosphere of the Stolypin cars, which transformed yesterday's people into today's creatures only resembling human beings."[27]

Notably, Larina digressed from describing her first journey under guard to remember a trip in the parallel world of leisure, a voluntary journey to Siberia with her husband during a vacation in August 1935. In her memoir, she employs the familiar rhetoric of tourist wonder that could be found in any issue of the 1930s tourist journal *On Land and on Sea*. The Altai's "picturesque landscape lives in my memory today," she wrote in the 1990s. "The unharnessed Katun River hurled its emerald waters headlong against the barriers of moss-covered rocks piled up in the river Biya, there to merge with it and form the mighty Ob. The precipitous cliffs bordering the banks of the Katun stood like trusty watchmen, directing its flow down the course conceived by nature." Later, this trip would be used in the indictment against Bukharin: whereas for an ordinary tourist, such travel was meant to bring the peoples of the nation together and to allow all to develop pride in the natural and social diversity of the country, Bukharin's purpose in the Altai was allegedly to foment peasant revolt and effect the separation of Siberia from the USSR.[28] Normal tourist travel built the nation; punishment travel resulted when criminals attempted to destroy the nation.

Soviet citizens freely traveling for pleasure increased in numbers in the later 1930s, even while the Stolypin passenger traffic to the east also expanded. Domestic tourists on package trips organized by the Society for Proletarian Tourism and Excursions and later the Central Council for Trade Unions numbered eighty-four thousand in 1936, up from twenty-four thousand in 1930 and seventy thousand in 1934. (Additional travelers journeyed to vacation destinations at "all-union" sanatoria and spas, some forty-seven thousand in 1934.)[29] Pleasure travel had its own rules and requirements. Guidebooks and guides offered instruction in what to see and how to see it, as well as the state's preferred way of interpreting what was seen. Individual travelers were encouraged to blaze their own trails across the Union, but they too received detailed instructions on how to march, how often to stop, how to take pictures, and how to write up their travels to share with others.[30]

The health-spa vacation gained new popularity in the mid-1930s as the regime poured hundreds of thousands of rubles into developing Sochi and other coastal spas as exemplary pleasure palaces for the deserving Soviet people. In practice, obtaining a scarce *putevka* (travel voucher) to one of these palaces was easier for the rich and famous than for the average shock worker in a factory, but the local press diligently publicized the awards to the lucky few, and the lucky few dutifully recorded their thanks in published letters home. Sochi is "not life, but paradise," wrote the shock worker Polina Kolevevskaia to her factory mates at Moscow's Hammer and Sickle plant in May 1936; "We are surrounded with great attention and care. The meals are splendid. You go to eat, and find yourself in an actual restaurant, you can order any dish you want. In the afternoon we rest, and in the evenings we go for boat rides."[31] In the old days, wrote another, workers and servants were not even permitted to walk in the parks of the Caucasus mountain spas, but now he was vacationing with "workers, collective farmers, red army men, white-collar workers—all toilers of our multinational USSR," for which he thanked the Communist Party and Stalin, too.[32]

The memoir of the American Mary Leder, who returned with her Russian-born parents in the 1930s to help build socialism, is one of the few to acknowledge the irony of pleasure travel amidst the pain of the Terror. For her, leisure travel served explicitly as an escape, a reward, a chance to breathe, a break from her university-student life. "The moment I boarded the train for the two-day journey to Novorossiisk, the nearest railroad station to Gelendzhik, I left my cares behind me. . . . It was a month full of fun, including an innocuous summer romance, and I enjoyed every minute. In September, I returned to the university and to the Stromynka dormitory.

"Back at school, arrests were rampant."[33]

Passports, arrests, vouchers, and guidebooks: all emanated from the government, and all served as methods for the state to direct its subjects whither it willed. Prisoners and special settlers traveled under guard to the destinations set by the state; tourists were exhorted rather than compelled to travel the pathways of civil-war partisans, to admire the edifices of new socialist construction projects, or purposefully to bring culture to the Soviet masses. But in its leisure-travel policy, the state also encouraged tourists and travelers to use this mobility to develop their own self-actualizing personalities. "Tourism is a path to knowledge,"[34] wrote tourism advocates in the Komsomol newspaper in 1926. Encountering the unknown, to "see what has never been seen before," taught the tourist self-reliance: "You overcome obstacles, and sometimes danger—which strengthens the body and steels the will."[35] Planning one's own itinerary allowed the tourist to be an actor, a "skilled traveler," not a passive participant over well-trodden routes.[36] Developing tourist skills, the Soviet tourist would learn to plan but also to develop the resources and resiliency to change the plan, to adapt to changing circumstances.[37] "Self-organization and self-activism are the basis of tourism," instructed the Komsomol in 1927. And Soviet tourists in the 1930s responded to the opportunities to become the architects of their own itineraries and the masters of their traveling destinies. Their accounts conveyed pride in accomplishing difficult journeys: "We felt ourselves to be real Columbuses," discovering "if only for ourselves, the never-before-seen 'America' of the Soviet north."[38] In the face of doubts about their abilities to navigate the rigors of mountain hiking, a group of young Moscow women reported their success: "Let them laugh, let them not believe. We accomplished our task."[39] Like Gleb Travin, "Every day I took an examination. If I passed, I would remain alive."

How can we relate these celebrations of autonomy and free mobility to the brutal facts of the Stolypin railway cars and the Gulag? Were these free travelers of the 1930s simply unaware of the dark realities of carceral travel? Did they take pride in their accomplishments and their personal growth in spite of the parallel world of punishment and fear, or was their sense of accomplishment and triumph more poignant because they realized their good fortune in remaining on the radiant side of the Soviet project? While I can only pose these questions, not answer them, I suggest that when we look ahead to leisure mobility in the 1960s, we will find that Soviet citizens expressed pride and self-confidence in their ability to travel freely around their country; this learned mobility constituted one of the achievements of the twin projects of nation building and the creation of citizens, a promise of the 1930s that became fulfilled in time.

The Passport State Relents: Travel in the 1960s

The Patriotic War and its aftermath generated a tremendous volume of state-mandated as well as spontaneous mobility, but the end of the war brought a return to strict state practices of control and incarceration. The death of Stalin, however, ushered in a new era of expanding free mobility. The passport law was amended in 1953 to relax some restrictions on access to mobility (although rural residents would not gain the right to a passport until 1974); in 1956, workers regained the right to change jobs if they wished.[40] Meanwhile, the dismantling of the Gulag produced its own halting and fearful amnesty of former prisoners, whose return to normal life remained a matter of great anxiety among officials and the population alike.[41] For many other released prisoners, mobility remained restricted: in the mid-1950s, by one account, half of the returnees were prevented from returning to their homes because of passport restrictions.[42] Nonetheless, these limited freedoms could provoke great joy. Significantly, Eugenia Ginzburg expressed the emotion of liberation in terms that directly linked carceral and pleasure mobility. Recalling her walk to freedom on the Kolyma highway, she wrote:

> When I search my memory for moments of real, unthinking happiness, I can recall only two. It happened once in Sochi. For no particular reason—simply that I was twenty-two and waltzing on the veranda of the sanatorium with a professor of dialectical materialism, who was some twenty-five years older than I, and with whom the entire class had fallen in love. The second time I managed to grab the Firebird by the tail was the day I have just described, February 15, 1947, on the Elgen-Taskan highway in a blizzard.[43]

Her linkage with the carefree holiday in Sochi conveys the powerful meaning of freely won pleasure that Soviet vacations and tourism experiences had engendered.

The state also sponsored work-related mobility as it promoted new five-year plans of economic development. In 1954, the campaign to transform the "Virgin Lands" of the Kazakh steppe drew three hundred thousand young men and women from all over the Soviet Union to lend their hands and enthusiasm to agricultural expansion.[44] Work sites beckoned young people—and families—to pack up their households and travel to new employment opportunities all over the Soviet Union, as illustrated in a 1957 poster, "A New Place for the Whole Family," sponsored by the Administration for Population Resettlement and Organized Recruitment of Labor (Orgnabor). The illustration depicts a family of five—mother, father, two children, and a granny—traveling in a brightly lit railroad compartment, poring over a map of the Siberian part of the Russian Federation. The poster models a new era of mobility by evoking family, coziness, anticipation, technology (an airplane above), socialist construction (a framed-out house on the shore), patriotism, and unbounded expanse (the painted landscape, the airplane, the map), packaged in the comfortable confines of the railway coupe.

Leisure travel also returned to the official agenda of the Soviet state as early as April 1945, when the Central Council of Trade Unions directed its tourism organizations to prepare their facilities for the coming season.[45] The reconstruction of the vacation industry also received new attention and investment from 1946 onward, and by 1948, tourist excursions were drawing thousands of grateful travelers (particularly school teachers eager to "educate our pupils about our great land, its many peoples, its expanse, and wealth") to Leningrad, Crimea, the north Caucasus, Estonia, and elsewhere.[46] Travel abroad—mainly to friendly socialist countries to the west—began to take place as early as 1955, and in 1963, over fifty thousand Soviet tourists traveled to countries in the so-cialist bloc. In 1970, according to another estimate, 838,000 Soviet citizens took a foreign trip.[47] Tourism planners now targeted families as well as individual tourists, evidently sharing the costs of their publicity campaign with Orgnabor. The identical image in the 1957 poster described above appeared the same year in another poster with the exhortation: "Take the whole family on vacation." The message is similar but also different: now one can visit and experience the unbounded space, the nation, and technology, with family and in coziness—and then return home!

Even while leisure travel expanded, however, the state continued to transport some of its citizens on involuntary journeys in conditions that differed little from those of the 1930s. Andrei Amalrik's 1965 journey to Siberian exile almost exactly replicated the travels recounted by Larina, Ginzburg, and others. Sur-rounded by guards with dogs, he and his fellow prisoners climbed into their "Stolypin" car behind one of Moscow's main stations, like the others juxtapos-ing the "ordinary" mode of railway transport with the carceral reality within. "It was like an ordinary railroad coach, except that there were cages instead of compartments, and a corridor down one side for the armed guards. Each cage had seven bunks: three on each side and an extra one that could be pulled down in the middle. . . . There are no windows in these cars except a barred one in the door."[48] And yet only a few months later, when summoned to Moscow to see his gravely ill father, Amalrik traveled like an ordinary third-class traveler, catching the Trans-Siberian express. "I had tea morning and evening, and one meal in the restaurant car. My return journey to Moscow was thus consider-ably more comfortable than the one from Moscow to Tomsk."[49] The developed socialist state now provided carceral travel with a human face.

Meanwhile, train travel devoted specifically to leisure began to develop on the initiative of the Moscow trade-union tourist administration in 1960. No longer just the means to reach a vacation or tourism destination, these tourist trains served as transportation and as a "tourist base," offering a mobile version of the minimal, often tent-based leisure accommodations of Soviet tourism in the early postwar years. Train number 187 made four twenty-day excursions from Moscow to the Caucasus shore of the Black Sea in 1960, carrying a total of 1,648 tourists. The majority (which would become a rule for subsequent trips) were women; most were under the age of thirty-five; and while most of the travelers claimed Moscow as their home, the four train journeys also included three hundred travelers from other countries.[50] Along the way, the passengers stopped to demonstrate their international friendship with local populations, and the general intermingling of the group on the train led to the nickname "Friendship Train," a label that stuck to subsequent railway tours, whether to the Black Sea, the Baltic Coast, or Ukraine.[51]

And what did this new generation of Soviet tourists seek to achieve? Like their predecessors from the 1930s, they wanted to participate in the construction of their nation and to envision themselves as its citizens. They wished to encounter the rich and varied regions and peoples of their native land and, within the packaged time frame of the twenty-day tour, to expand their horizons. "We learned about the culture, talent, and genius of those peoples with whom we visited"; "We will not only remember the blue sea and the white walls of the health spas but also the dances and songs of adults and children of talented Dagestanis, Georgians, Adzhari, and Abkhazi."[52] They sought to visit and familiarize themselves with monuments of Russian culture: "We especially liked the excursions to the Lermontov places."[53] Opera, concerts, and museums of writers and painters also figured on the itineraries. Tourists wanted to test their physical mettle on mountain hikes and to bask in the sun along the Black Sea coast.[54] Friendship and camaraderie also numbered among the valued experiences of the railway tourists (and others): the "tourist campfire" had become a treasured memory of Soviet tourists since the 1930s. At the campfire for the train passengers at one Black Sea tourist base, the tourists sang and danced, together and in friendly competitions. Soviet tourists and vacationers customarily enjoyed their holiday away from home to engage in harmless sexual fun.[55]

The official reports from these trips indicate that the state's tourism officials sought to contain and to control these behaviors and generally to dictate the norms of leisure mobility. Even pleasure travel in the 1950s and 1960s remained embedded in the state's nation-building project. The scripts of tour guides were carefully reviewed for factual accuracy and political correctness.[56] Guidebooks instructed tourists about the most important sights, even suggesting where to photograph.[57] Rules for the tourist train stipulated that no one could leave the train without permission from the director, and when they left, to travel always in groups accompanied by appointed group leaders. Tourists who violated these rules would be sent home immediately without a right to a refund.[58]

The tourists' own comments, however, reveal a counternarrative that emphasized an entitlement to comfort, autonomy, adventure, and respect. They asked for more amenities aboard the train, such as better toilets, showers, mending kits, irons, transformers for shavers, and electricity during long station stops.[59] They wanted more hikes, more sports, more physical activity, and more time at the beach.[60] They preferred to choose their own group leaders rather than to accept one assigned by the tourist administration.[61] They liked arranging their own excursions in places where the train stopped a few days: they used the free time to climb to waterfalls or visit museums on their own; the men on one trip went their separate way to taste the local wine.[62] They complained when excursions were canceled due to poor planning and about bad food (not enough fresh fruits and vegetables).[63] And they altered the rules: when two female tourists were expelled from the train for returning drunk from an excursion, the other tourists appealed for leniency, and the two ended up with only a reprimand. In their reports to the center, the trip directors included the lists of the tourists' own wishes and desires.[64] The regime still wished to regulate, but it also listened to the concerns of its subjects.

By the end of the 1960s, not only the possibility of pleasure travel but the sense of entitlement to it spread to other regions and to other social strata. Vasilii Shukshin conveyed this sense in his 1972 film and short story, "Pechki-lavochki." A Russian tractor driver, Ivan, from the Altai receives a voucher to a health resort in Crimea, "to the sea, the first time in his life." He wants to share this opportunity with his whole family, but in the end, the children stay behind, and only he and his loving but timid wife Niurka embark on the long train journey to Moscow. The journey itself is the focus of the film: friendships are formed, thieves are uncovered, and they wonder at their new mobility. "They go and go and go, sleep, read, play cards, dominoes, tell each other the stories of their lives."[65] The tractor driver and his wife are befriended by their compartment-mate, a linguistics professor from Moscow. Enchanted by their pure Russian speech and their innocent simplicity, he offers them hospitality in Moscow before they catch their next train to the south. A final challenge awaits them at journey's end, because there is only one voucher, and the sanatorium director will not accept Niurka. But Ivan, emboldened and empowered by his newfound mobility, convinces the director to accommodate them both.[66]

Conclusion: Mobility and Citizenship

The right to rest (including the right to travel freely in order to rest) constituted only one of the vaunted benefits of the 1936 Soviet Constitution, and yet the right to travel became one of the enduring memories of the late Soviet experience. Among the informants in Donald Raleigh's oral histories of the Soviet class of 1967, memories of travel abroad and around the country appear in every account, along with regret that new borders have bounded the once unbounded space.[67] The state permitted this travel to happen, just as it directed the controlled mobility of work-assigned or imprisoned subjects. The state regulated movement, for pleasure and punishment, but it also actively promoted mobility, and in this process it created the autonomous citizen-subject, the paradox with which I began this essay. The accounts of generations of Soviet tourist travelers from the 1930s to the 1960s reiterated the liberating and state-building values of travel: tourists became better acquainted with their native land (including by comparison with others); they made new friendships and cemented family relations; they recovered their physical and mental health. They had a good time. And they learned self-reliance, to live apart from the state's direct tutelage. This was the state's reward to its citizens (as long as they remained loyal to the state), and with the development of the Soviet economy, access to leisure travel became increasingly normal and increasingly independent of state control.

In June 2008, the *New York Times* reported on the transformational effect of pleasure travel, citing the Russian writer Viktor Yerofeyev:

> "Through all this travel, we are seeing a change in mentality at home," Mr. Yerofeyev said. "People are now seeking pleasure, whether it is in the night clubs of Moscow or in restaurants. Travel is a continuation of that pleasure. Just to have pleasant lives, not to suffer, to feel positive. Their life compass changes, from 'I don't care about anything' to 'I would like to have a better life.' Travel is a part of this."[68]

In this realm, the interests of state and citizen coincided: productivity led to knowledge, pleasure, and freely chosen mobility. But in travel, citizens also began to break free of the state, to take charge of their individual itineraries, to claim their own autonomy; yet they remained, in the end, and perhaps precisely because of this better life, loyal to the state that had enabled their voyages of self-discovery.

Notes

1. Lynne Viola, *The Unknown Gulag: The Lost World of Stalin's Special Settlements* (Oxford: Oxford University Press, 2007); Mervyn Matthews, *The Passport Society: Controlling Movement in Russia and the USSR* (Boulder, Colo.: Westview Press, 1993), 21, 27.

2. Emma Widdis, *Visions of a New Land: Soviet Film from the Revolution to the Second World War* (New Haven, Conn.: Yale University Press, 2003), 97, 2–3.

3. Ibid., 103.

4. *Turist-aktivist* 2–3 (1933): 29.

5. *Komsomol'skaia pravda* (hereafter *KP*), 16 December 1926, 3; *Vsemirnyi turist* 1 (1929): 28; editorial in *Trud*, 24 May 1941.

6. Matthews, *Passport Society*, 19.

7. Ibid., 20.

8. Widdis, *Visions*, 144; Gijs Kessler, "The Passport System and State Control over Population Flows in the Soviet Union, 1932–1940," *Cahiers du Monde russe* 42.2–3–4 (April–December 2001), 477–504.

9. *Na sushe i na more* (hereafter *NSNM*) 10 (October 1929): 15; *NSNM* 4 (February 1930): 1; V. Antonov-Saratovskii, "Doloi brodiazhnichestvo!" *NSNM* 7 (April 1930): 1–2; *Vecherniaia Moskva*, 24 April 1930; *NSNM* 4 (April 1936): 31; *NSNM* 4 (April 1936): 31.

10. *NSNM* 4 (April 1937): 22; *NSNM* 10 (October 1937): 31. *Puteshestviia po SSSR* (Moscow: Fizkul'tura i turizm, 1938) is a collection of the passportized routes.

11. *NSNM* 10 (October 1937): 23.

12. Anne D. Rassweiler, *The Generation of Power: The History of Dneprostroi* (Oxford: Oxford University Press, 1988), 93–97, 136–37; Matthew J. Payne, *Stalin's Railroad:*

Turksib and the Building of Socialism (Pittsburgh: University of Pittsburgh Press, 2001), chap. 3; Stephen Kotkin, *Magnetic Mountain: Stalinism as a Civilization* (Berkeley: University of California Press, 1995).

13. Memoir of N. P. Sapozhnikov, qtd. in Sheila Fitzpatrick, "The Great Departure: Rural-Urban Migration in the Soviet Union," in *Social Dimensions of Soviet Industrialization,* ed. William G. Rosenberg and Lewis H. Siegelbaum (Bloomington: Indiana University Press, 1993), 26.

14. Viola, *Unknown Gulag,* 2; Andy Bruno, "Modernizing the Environment: A History of Economic Transformation and the Natural World in a Northwest Russian Region in the Twentieth Century" (Ph.D. dissertation, University of Illinois at Urbana-Champaign, 2011), chap. 2.

15. Viola, *Unknown Gulag,* 38–39, 41.

16. *Ibid.,* 2.

17. *NSNM* 9 (May 1930): 14; Zara Witkin, *An American Engineer in Stalin's Russia: The Memoirs of Zara Witkin, 1932–1934* (Berkeley: University of California Press, 1991), 214–15.

18. *Proletarskii turizm. (Iz opyta raboty Baumanskogo otdeleniia obshchestva proletarskogo turizma). Materialy k X Baumanskoi raikonferentsii VLKSM* (Moscow: Baumanskii dom VLKSM, 1929), 70–75.

19. *Korabl' udarnikov: Sbornik ocherkov uchastnikov pervoi zagranichnoi ekskursii rabochikh udarnikov na teplokhode "Abkhaziia"* (Leningrad: Gosudarstvennoe izdatel'stvo khudozhestvennoi literatury, 1931), 8.

20. Ibid., 51, 46–47.

21. *NSNM* 1 (January 1929): 14.

22. Gleb Travin, "Bez skidki na vremia," *Vokrug sveta* 11 (November 1975): 60.

23. A. Kharitonovskii, *Chelovek s zheleznym olenem: Povest' o zabytom podvige* (Petropavlovsk-Kamchatskii: Kamchatskaia Pravda, 1960), 212.

24. Eugenia Ginzburg, *Journey into the Whirlwind,* trans. Paul Stevenson and Max Hayward (New York: Harcourt Brace and World, 1967), 139.

25. Ibid., 274–301.

26. Vladimir Petrov, *Escape from the Future: The Incredible Adventures of a Young Russian* (Bloomington: Indiana University Press, 1973), 99, 280, 107.

27. Anna Larina, *This I Cannot Forget: The Memoirs of Nikolai Bukharin's Widow,* trans. Gary Kern (New York: W. W. Norton, 1993), 76, 164.

28. Ibid., 79, 84.

29. Gosudarstvennyi arkhiv Rossiiskoi Federatsii (hereafter GARF), f. 9520 (Tsentral'nyi sovet po turizmu i ekskursiiam), op. 1, d. 8, l. 56; Tsentral'nyi gosudarstvennyi arkhiv Sankt-Peterburga, f. 4410 (Leningradskii oblastnoi sovet vsesoiuznogo obshchestva proletarskogo turizma i ekskursii), op. 1, d. 398, l. 8 (OPTE presidium meeting 8 August 1932); GARF, f. 9493 (Tsentral'noe upravlenie kurortami, sanatoriami i domami otdykha), op. 1, d. 30, l. 190b., 21.

30. O. A. Arkhangel'skaia, *Rabota iacheiki OPTE po samodeiatel'nomu turizmu* (Moscow: TsS OPTE, 1935); O. Arkhangel'skaia. *Kak organizovat' turistskoe puteshestvie* (Moscow: Profizdat, 1947).

31. *Martenovka,* 30 May 1936.

32. *Martenovka,* 4 July 1938.

33. Mary M. Leder, *My Life in Stalinist Russia: An American Woman Looks Back,* ed. Laurie Bernstein (Bloomington: Indiana University Press, 2001), 121.

34. *KP,* 16 December 1926; *Fizkul'tura i sport* 18 (5 May 1928): 3.

35. *KP,* 16 December 1926; 15 June 1927.

36. G. Bergman, *Otdykh letom* (Moscow-Leningrad: Molodaia gvardiia, 1927), 56–57; G. Bergman, *Pervaia kniga turista* (Moscow-Leningrad: Molodaia gvardiia, 1927), 16.

37. Bergman, *Pervaia kniga,* 17; *KP,* 15 June 1927.

38. *NSNM* 1 (January 1929): 13–14.

39. *Proletarskii turizm,* 47.

40. Matthews, *Passport Society,* 31–34.

41. Miriam Dobson, *Khrushchev's Cold Summer: Gulag Returnees, Crime, and the Fate of Reform after Stalin* (Ithaca, N.Y.: Cornell University Press, 2009).

42. Ibid., 110.

43. Eugenia Ginzburg, *Within the Whirlwind,* trans. Ian Boland, intro. Heinrich Böll (New York: Harcourt Brace Jovanovich, 1981), 183.

44. William Taubman, *Khrushchev: The Man and His Era* (New York: W. W. Norton, 2003), 263; Michaela Pohl, "The 'Planet of 100 Languages': Ethnic Relations and Soviet Identity in the Virgin Lands," in *Peopling the Russian Periphery: Borderland Colonization in Eurasian History,* ed. Nicholas Breyfogle, Abby Schrader, and Willard Sunderland (London: Routledge, 2007), 467–518.

45. GARF, f. 9520, op. 1, d. 24 (reports of trade-union tourist authorities on plans for reopening tourist bases and camps, 1945), ll. 43–44; see also Anne E. Gorsuch, "'There's No Place Like Home': Soviet Tourism in Late Stalinism," *Slavic Review* 62.4 (Winter 2003): 760–85.

46. GARF, f. 9520, op. 1, d. 80 (reports on tourist work for regions K-E, 1948), l. 186.

47. *Trud,* 4 September 1955; Anne E. Gorsuch, "Time Travelers: Soviet Tourists to Eastern Europe," in *Turizm: The Russian and East European Tourist under Capitalism and Socialism,* ed. Anne E. Gorusch and Diane P. Koenker (Ithaca, N.Y.: Cornell University Press, 2006), 206; John Bushnell, "The 'New Soviet Man' Turns Pessimist," in *The Soviet Union since Stalin,* ed. Stephen F. Cohern, Alexander Rabinowitch, and Robert Sharlet (Bloomington: Indiana University Press, 1980), 192.

48. Andrei Amalrik, *Involuntary Journey to Siberia,* trans. Manya Harari and Max Hayward (New York: Harcourt Brace Jovanovich, 1970), 125.

49. Ibid., 193.

50. Tsentral'nyi arkhiv goroda Moskvy (hereafter TsAGM), f. 28 (Moskovskii gorodskoi sovet po turizmu i ekskursiiam Tsentral'nogo soveta po turizmu i ekskursiiam), op. 1, d. 9, ll. 1–3.

51. TsAGM, f. 28, op. 1, d. 10 (Report on tourist trains 1960), l.2; f. 28, op. 1, d. 17 (Report on Tourist Train Druzhba no. 226, 1961).

52. GARF, f. 9520, op. 1, d. 386 (comment books for Train Druzhba 1961), l. 9.

53. GARF, 9520, op. 1, d. 386.

54. TsAGM, f. 28, op. 1, d. 12, ll. 3, 5, 7.

55. See Diane P. Koenker, "Whose Right to Rest? Contesting the Family Vacation in the Postwar Soviet Union," *Comparative Studies in Society and History* 51.2 (2009): 415–17; and Anna Rotkirch, "Traveling Maidens and Men with Parallel Lives: Journeys as Private Space during Late Socialism," in *Beyond the Limits: The Concept of Space in Russian History and Culture*, ed. Jeremy Smith (Helsinki: Finnish Historical Society, 1999), 131–49.

56. Gosudarstvennyi arkhiv goroda Sochi, f. 242 (Ekskursionnoe biuro Upravleniia kul'tury ispolkoma Sochinskogo gorodskogo soveta), op. 1, d. 202; f. 242, op. 1, d. 65.

57. M. I. Khibarov, *Kislovodsk—vsesoiuznaia zdravnitsa, 2d ed.* (Moscow: Medgiz, 1960); B. Miasoedov, *V turistskom pokhode* (Moscow: Profizdat, 1958); *Sputnik turista* (Moscow: Fizkul'tura i sport, 1959).

58. TsAGM, f. 28, op. 1, d. 9, l. 12.

59. GARF, f. 9520, op. 1, d. 386, ll. 27, 94–940b; TsAGM, f. 28, op. 1, d 10, l. 10; TsAGM, f. 28, op. 1, d. 9, l. 5.

60. TsAGM, f. 28, op. 1, d. 12 l. 7; TsAGM, f. 28, op. 1, d. 17, ll. 3–5.

61. GARF, f. 9520, op. 1, d. 386, l. 530b.

62. TsAGM, f. 28, op. 1, d. 31, l. 73; TsAGM, f. 28, op. 1, d. 17, l. 3.

63. TsAGM, f. 28, op. 1, d. 17, l. 6.

64. TsAGM, f. 28, op. 1, d. 17, l. 3.

65. V. M. Shukshin, "Pechki-lavochki," in V. M. Shukshin, *Kinopovesti*, 2d ed. (Moscow: Iskusstvo, 1988), 271.

66. Ibid., 288.

67. Donald J. Raleigh, trans. and ed., *Russia's Sputnik Generation: Soviet Baby Boomers Talk about their Lives* (Bloomington: Indiana University Press, 2006).

68. Clifford J. Levy, "Free and Flush: Russians Eager to Roam Abroad," *New York Times*, 15 June 2008, 1.

12

Citizenship and Human Mobility

Disability and the "Etatization" of Soviet and Post-Soviet Space

SARAH D. PHILLIPS

In 2005 I interviewed Tanya, a middle-aged woman from a small town in eastern Ukraine who uses a wheelchair after a spinal-cord injury.[1] Tanya told me how she recently had traveled from her home to Kiev with hopes of a hearing with members of Parliament. Tanya wanted to lodge a complaint about the slow pace of improvements in accessibility in her town. She was disgusted (but not surprised) to find that the Parliament building (Verkhovna Rada) had outdated, dangerously steep steel rails serving as wheelchair ramps, ironic in light of Parliament's recent passage of extensive accessibility legislation. When she learned that the space for civic hearings where citizens could make complaints was located on the second floor with no elevator access, Tanya complained to a vice minister she encountered in the hallway:

> I asked him, "Am I not a citizen? Am I a citizen of your country? Then why can't I access that space? I want to. Have me carried up there! I want a civic hearing." They bounced me all around the city, like a ball. They sent me to the Cabinet of Ministers, which then sent me to the President's Administration. Then I was sent back to the Parliament, where I tried to catch different committees. Finally I returned to the President's Administration and gave them my letter. My hands were raw by then, and my backpack was torn. I didn't get in anywhere, and all the time they were there on the second floor. Why? Aren't I a citizen?

Tanya's insistent questioning of officialdom makes equal demands on scholars. How should we understand and conceptualize the relationship between mobility and citizenship in the postsocialist world?

In this essay, I use an ethnographic perspective to explore this issue, focusing on post-Soviet Ukraine and Russia in particular. I argue that in the postsocialist milieu, mobility and citizenship (which I take to mean a collective bargain of statehood and a meaningful belonging) come together at the intersection of three primary interrelated forces or phenomena: globalization, neoliberalization, and the state's withdrawal from particular social spaces.[2] To get at these intersections, the various ways they come together, and the effects for everyday people's lives, I take the case of a population with major stakes in how human mobility and citizenship are linked: the mobility disabled—people who have trouble getting around, many of whom are wheelchair users. Mobility here is defined as the possibility to move freely through space both physically and, increasingly, virtually.

Since 2002, I have spent a total of eight months in Ukraine studying the disability-rights movement, and I traveled to Moscow for several weeks in 2006 for comparative research. In total I have conducted nearly ninety taped personal interviews with activists, policy makers, and others with ties to this movement. The research centers primarily on people with spinal injuries and others with mobility disabilities.[3] I undertook participant observation with leaders and members of twenty-six disability-related nongovernmental organizations (NGOs) in various towns and cities in Ukraine, and I have been following the work of some of these groups for the past six years. I combine this present-day inquiry with an historical perspective on disability in the former Soviet Union to track changes over time.[4]

Early on in my research I identified an "action" narrative as a key component of disability-rights discourse in Ukraine. For example, one major transnational initiative that has taken root is a system of "active rehabilitation" for persons with spinal injuries. Also, in their everyday speech, my informants frequently talked about the importance of living an "active" lifestyle. An important aspect of the "action" narrative is the privileging of not only a sense of "taking the bull by the horns," being a "self-starter," and keeping busy, but also the stress placed on motion and mobility. This apparent contradiction—that people whose movement is restricted triply by physical disability, social stigma, and an oppressive built environment would narrate themselves in such dynamic, motion-and-action focused terms—made me want to investigate further how claims for citizenship are changing for people with mobility disabilities. Without discounting the ongoing importance of biological citizenship, or claims for "a form of social welfare based on medical, scientific, and legal criteria that both acknowledge biological injury and compensate for it,"[5] I want to explore the ways in which people with disabilities are looking to become the kind of "mobile, flexible, self-enterprising subject" that increasingly represents the idealized standard of what it means to be a citizen in a world of global capitalism.[6]

I have found that, in complex ways, the material, the symbolic, and the spatial come together in my informants' strategies to operationalize what I call "mobile citizenship" in contexts of rapid political, economic, and personal transformations. As members of a marked category ("invalids") whose status as full citizens is not a given, people with disabilities are compelled to jockey for citizenship using strategies that are often contradictory, messy, selective, and situational. Still, mobile citizenship is difficult to operationalize in the absence of a willing state and in the face of negative public opinion and ignorance. For this reason, although the individual self, personal initiative, and independence (all hallmarks of neoliberalization) are critical components of citizenship claims among my informants, they also find themselves in a constant conversation with the state. These conversations take multiple dimensions, including the symbolic and discursive (models and meanings of disability, the respective roles of the individual and society) to the material (calculations of social worth and economic "compensation," the politics of the spatial environment). These conversations are informed simultaneously by the spatial politics of the state gone by (which effectively excluded people with disabilities from public space) and by the changing significance of spatial arrangements and new possibilities for physical and virtual mobility in today's postsocialist market and information economies.

In what follows, I draw on ethnographic material to tease out manifestations of citizenship as mobility politics at the crossroads of the socialist past, where states controlled populations by limiting people's movements through space, and the uneven effects of globalization and neoliberalization in the postsocialist, globalizing present, where physical mobility and rapid movement through space have become increasingly important criteria for citizenship.[7] Although the experiences of the mobility disabled bring these politics into especially vivid relief, I argue that the common experience of state socialism, with its particular regulations of bodies in space, makes spatial mediations of citizenship a vital part of present-day citizenship negotiations throughout the postsocialist sphere.

Disability and (Im)Mobility under Socialism

The socialist state's spatial politics in many ways boils down to what I am calling the "etatization" of space. This idea takes inspiration from Katherine Verdery's masterful exploration of the etatization of time in Romania under Ceausescu.[8] Verdery examines how the organization of socialist political economies, which effected economies of shortage, produced seizures of citizens' time to increase the manufacturing of goods within the system of scarcity. She considers specific examples of state seizures of time, such as the state-produced fuel shortage in the mid-1980s, which wreaked havoc on public and private transportation, forcing people to walk long distances, wait for hours in bus and train queues, and so on. The "immobilization of bodies in food lines" is probably the most familiar example of the socialist state's seizure of time, an imposition that served to enhance state power by forcing accumulation, destroying people's capacity for alternative uses of time, and choking off possibilities for lower-level initiative and planning.[9]

As she details how the Romanian state seized time from the purposes that people wanted to pursue, Verdery convincingly argues for a focus on the body as the vehicle through which various devices (rituals, calendars, curfews, workday schedules) were used by the state to appropriate and organize people's time. The etatization of time, I argue, is also about the state's etatization of space. The socialist state, for political reasons, sought to organize time *and* space in particular ways to constrain movement and immobilize bodies. The appropriation of citizens' time and the spatial regulation of bodies were very much related and intertwined; temporal uncertainty and ritualized waiting meant that "bodies were transfixed, suspended in a void that obviated all projects and plans but the most flexible and spontaneous."[10]

The planned immobilization of certain populations, such as those with physical (and mental) disabilities, is a striking example of the etatization of space. Under state socialism, through a politics of exclusion and social distancing, persons with physical and mental impairments were stigmatized, hidden from public, and thus made seemingly invisible.[11] The spatial isolation and forced immobility of people with disabilities was a coordinated strategy to exclude people with disabilities from public space. The existence of individuals with physical impairments challenged the ideal of the fit, uniform, and capable body of the New Soviet Man, thus threatening to disrupt the hegemonic "body cultures" of socialist states.[12] The visibly disabled, who disturbed the trope of a healthy nation, did not even rank in the official bodily hierarchy and thus were excluded from the endless demonstrations and parades to celebrate socialism. Spaces were carved out where people with disabilities could survive separately from the general population, so as not to "spoil the view for others," as one of my informants quipped.

Although some efforts were made to facilitate the social integration of a few privileged categories of "invalids"—the war-wounded and those disabled on the job, persons whose social contributions were indisputable—overall, rehabilitation of individuals with serious disabilities was lackluster or nonexistent.[13] People with disabilities were offered instead "compensation" for their physical limitations in the form of modest pensions and a few other entitlements. The spatial politics of disability policy were quite clear-cut: people with disabilities were either housed in large concentrations at some distance from urban centers, or they were dispersed in isolation, confined to "their own four walls" at home. A network of *internaty* (residential institutions) for people with disabilities and the elderly stretched across the vast territory of the USSR (numbering 1,500 in 1979), and *internaty* were, and continue to be, common in other socialist states, especially Bulgaria and Romania.[14] There was intense pressure from state and medical authorities, and from the public, for parents of children with disabilities to place them in *internaty,* total institutions where the lives of residents were highly regulated and their activities surveilled.[15]

Just as the socialist state preferred to house people with disabilities en masse and otherwise socially isolate them, so too were state programs for medical treatment and rehabilitation, education, and job training and work organized according to a strategic spatial logic. For example, persons with physical impairments throughout the Soviet Union were offered "health trips" to specialized sanatoria like the Burdenko sanatorium in Saki (in the Crimea, Ukraine), known as the "invalids' capital" and "an island for wheelchair users."

Education of persons with disabilities was similarly arranged—usually school-age residents of *internaty* and special residential schools were offered a basic, and always onsite, education. Inclusive education for disabled children in regular schools was rare, and those who lived in private residences usually received at-home instruction. In the Soviet Union it was uncommon for persons with serious disabilities to undertake university studies, and those who did usually completed correspondence courses.

Although administrators paid lip-service to the vocational rehabilitation of people with disabilities in the socialist workers' state, in reality work opportunities for this population were constricted, often limited to menial piecework at home or to segregated work collectives called "artels." Promoted as an "oasis" to protect people with disabilities (particularly the vision- or hearing-impaired) from cruelty and prejudice, the artel functioned as a sort of closed mini-city with its own infrastructure, enterprises, and culture.[16]

This politics of exclusion and imposed immobility was directly related to the state's definition of citizenship for the population deemed "invalids." Residents of *internaty* were officially referred to as *gosopekaemye,* or "wards of the state," terminology that underscored their status as state subjects. Through the compensatory policies of the socialist ideology, persons with disabilities were guaranteed a minimum of social protection in an elaborate (yet usually inadequate) system of benefits, including disability pensions and entitlements such as reduced utility expenses and rent, free or discounted public transportation, and the free provision of technical equipment. For "invalids," to be a citizen was to maintain basic rights in exchange for complacency, immobility, and invisibility.

Marafon

Although a few Soviet-era dissidents did initiate short-lived protests of this discrimination, there were no possibilities to launch serious challenges to the state's exclusionary practices until Gorbachev's glasnost of the mid- to late 1980s.[17] In the early 1990s, two major disability-advocacy initiatives, so-called supermarathons of wheelchair users, took place. It is telling that these events, the first disability-rights campaigns in the former Soviet Union to garner international attention, were so centrally focused on mobility. In fact, it could be said that the super-marathons were a performance of *extreme* mobility by wheelchair users, who endured months "on the road" as "they overcame pain . . . they overcame sickness . . . they overcame exhaustion," as one of the organizers put it.[18]

The two super-marathons, which were similar in form and shared the same overarching ideas, shed light on the importance of mobility issues as a crucial "hook" for citizenship claims for people with disabilities during the postsocialist transformation. Analysis of the super-marathons also reveals how globalization has contributed to claims for disability rights, as activists leverage the international against the national and local and incorporate transnational disability-advocacy narratives in their own advocacy efforts. Further, the narratives of super-marathon participants and analysis of media coverage of the events points to the effects of neoliberalism and individualization in the post-Soviet market economies and societies.[19]

On 12 May 1991, around a dozen wheelchair-using athletes set off from Moscow's Pushkin Square on a grueling trip of 1,400 kilometers. Over the course of several months, they traveled in their wheelchairs from Moscow to Kiev, and from Kiev to Kryvyi Rih, in the south of (then) Soviet Ukraine. The super-marathon participants were accompanied by an array of people and automobiles—local law enforcement (GAI); fellow athletes (cyclists and runners); and buses carrying spare wheelchairs and parts, comfort items, trainers, medical personnel, and so on. Local media outlets covered the super-marathon extensively, and according to one participant, Oleksandr Sukhan from Mukachevo, Ukraine, the group attracted crowds of onlookers who came out to "see for themselves that it was possible, to verify that we were doing it ourselves."[20]

The second super-marathon in 1992 included only three participants: the Ukrainian Sukhan, and the Russians Yuri Shepavalov and Evgenii Klichkov from Magadan and Novokuznetz, respectively. These men all had taken part in the 1991 Moscow–Krivyi Rih super-marathon, which for them was really training for this, the ultimate wheelchair super-marathon: Vladivostok to St. Petersburg, a distance of some eleven thousand kilometers. A personal representative of the secretary general of the United Nations pronounced the official start of the super-marathon with the words, "Good luck, good speed, and good health."[21] Eight months later, the men arrived safely in St. Petersburg to considerable fanfare.

There is much to be said about the super-marathons, but I will limit my discussion to intersections of globalization, mobility politics, and neoliberalization as three key components of mobile citizenship. The importance of these components becomes apparent when we examine the organization of the super-marathons themselves, the public reaction to the events as reflected in media coverage and participants' narratives, and the participants' own personal interpretations of the super-marathons and their significance for them as individuals and as members of a stigmatized social group. It is difficult to disentangle these aspects, but for the sake of argument I will take them in turn.

GLOBALIZATION

One of the most striking characteristics of the super-marathons, which took place just as the newly independent states of the Soviet Union were introducing free-market economic policies, was the very visible presence of corporate sponsors. The main initiative for the super-marathons came from the Moscow club called Prikliuchenie (Adventure).[22] However, the events were financed in part by global companies such as McDonald's, Coca-Cola, and Mitsubishi, as well as German and Dutch medical firms, all of which highlights the region's (then) nascent participation in the global capitalist economy. One of the most visible sponsors was the German wheelchair manufacturing company Meyra, which provided a variety of specialized wheelchairs for the super-marathon participants.[23] At the same time, the presence of other sponsors reflects the continued active presence of state enterprises and ministries. For example, the state steel company Krivorozhstal' provided sponsorship for the 1991 super-marathon. Curiously, the major financial sponsor of the 1992 super-marathon was the Russian Ministry of Defense, which provided large buses equipped with showers, medical equipment, beds, and other amenities.[24] In a demonstration of the intermingling of Soviet state bureaucracy and global capitalism, the Meyra logo (in Russian) was prominently displayed on these vehicles.

Naturally, some organizational aspects of the super-marathons also reflect the changing political situation within the former Soviet Union. The first super-marathon began on 12 May 1991, and Ukraine declared independence in August 1991. During the 1992 super-marathon, Oleksandr Sukhan (from Western Ukraine) was considered by the international community to be a representative of Russia (and the Russian organization Prikliuchenie initiated the event), but he identified strongly with newly independent Ukraine. Sukhan told interviewers that when asked for his autograph, he always identified himself as being "from Ukraine, Zakarpattia, or Mukachevo."[25] He lamented the fact that no

Ukrainian disability-advocacy NGOs took part in the organization of the 1992 super-marathon.[26] Further, in one interview Sukhan stated that, in addition to the overall goals of the 1992 super-marathon to "inspire other invalids" and draw attention to the problems of vulnerable populations, another, more personal goal of his was "to inspire people to make the new independent Ukraine successful. To show the non-disabled that if we invalids can do this, you can also use your strength to the fullest."[27]

This political tension was also present when the three 1992 super-marathon participants (Sukhan and the Russians Shepavalov and Klichkov) were invited to join a Russian delegation to the United Nations in New York. On the one hand, Sukhan reported that he was proud to be a member of the first Russian delegation to participate in the work of the U.N., and he appreciated the huge round of applause his group received.[28] At the same time, however, he was dissatisfied that no Ukrainian U.N. representatives approached him personally, "even though Barbara Bush did."[29] In interviews Sukhan tried to smooth over this tension by stating that, in any case, he "was very glad to see that the U.N. was paying attention to the problems of invalids in Ukraine, and in the CIS."[30]

Sukhan, and presumably others connected with the super-marathons and their aftermath, seized upon opportunities to travel abroad, where they witnessed living conditions for the disabled that were much better than those they had experienced back home. This information, and the cachet that went with having traveled internationally, could be leveraged against the national and local to argue for reforms. In addition to his trip to the United Nations in New York, where he found that "disabled people have cars and live very well, because they work,"[31] Sukhan also took advantage of an invitation from the Mitsubishi Company to travel to Japan, where he participated in another super-marathon, along with Shapavalov and Klichkov. In one interview Sukhan explained how, in Japan, employers are obligated to offer available positions to disabled workers. He contrasted this with the situation in Ukraine, where "invalids are only given work that is very low-paid."[32] Sukhan frequently referred to such stories of contrast when speaking with the press, stressing them as positive examples for the (new) Ukrainian state to follow. For example, he expressed his hope that the disabled in Ukraine would be able "to live an independent life, which they've been doing for a long time in the West."[33] Sukhan also said, "I'm hopeful that in Ukraine, like in other developed countries, the disabled will be put on an equal footing with the nondisabled."[34]

In this way, the super-marathon and subsequent opportunities for international travel and making transnational connections allowed the activist and athlete Oleksandr Sukhan (and other disabled persons) to leverage the international to articulate claims to the state and local administration in post-Soviet Ukraine. Globalizing processes—the flow of capital, people, and discourses—

were brought down to earth. Sukhan frequently pointed out the irony of the fact that, until the national and international press seized upon the story of the super-marathon, he was relatively anonymous in his own village, town, and *oblast* (region). And, he said, even though he is now somewhat of a local celebrity, the local administration continues to ignore him. Sukhan expressed a desire to found an advocacy group for the disabled in his community but criticized the local government for failing to provide support. In all of these ways, through the super-marathon globalizing forces—whether movement of global capital, accelerated travel and mobility, or transnational empowerment discourses—intersected to produce change at the national and local levels.

MOBILITY

There are many reasons why a super-marathon, with the emphasis on covering extreme distances, facing daunting barriers, and performing amazing feats of physical exertion, became the venue through which the mobility disabled asserted empowerment claims during the early 1990s. As the Soviet Union collapsed and hopes were high for reforms in social services, medicine, human-rights policy, and many other areas, the super-marathon was a way to garner national and international attention for the plight of the disabled and to assert the physical presence of the mobility disabled in a context where they had been forcibly immobilized and made all but invisible. Media footage of the super-marathons dwells on the often-impassable conditions participants confronted— washed-out roads and obstacles such as fallen trees and gargantuan potholes. Sukhan reported that in some areas locals would follow the super-marathoners to verify that "we were really doing it all ourselves," since they were traveling through spots where cars could not even go.[35]

It may seem a trivial point, but in nearly every example of video coverage of the super-marathons I viewed, the earthy music of Vladimir Vysotsky, the Russian actor and bard, accompanied footage of participants struggling to navigate their wheelchairs through mud and over and around barriers. The combination of images and songs seems to connect the super-marathoners with a time gone by, positioning them as valiantly struggling to "catch up" with the society (and political economy) that has left them behind.

When asked why he thought the super-marathons were organized, Sukhan answered thus: "We thought that in order to really get people's attention, we had to do something really over the top, something that people wouldn't believe was possible. We wanted to get people's attention, to say, 'Here we are, we live among you.'"[36] Setting in motion a politics of recognition was central here.[37] Interestingly, Sukhan identified a further goal as "working to pressure the government to help invalids support themselves." This is reflective of the neoliberal shift that has occurred in postsocialist states such as Ukraine: as

Sukhan summarized, "The disabled don't just want benefits; they want to work. They want to live a normal life."

NEOLIBERALIZATION

It is this idea—that paid employment, self-sufficiency, and personal independence should be at the center of "normal life" for every citizen, even those labeled "invalids" and previously deemed incapable of earning a living and presumed to be dependent on the state and other citizens—that marks the shift toward neoliberal thinking in postsocialist states. Although providing paid employment to people with disabilities was an important component of Soviet disability policy (at least on paper), the state took an uneven, piecemeal approach, and unskilled work in segregated collectives was the norm.[38] Beginning in the early 1990s, often fueled by narratives of "independent living" and self-sufficiency stressed by transnational advocacy groups working in Eastern Europe, local disability-rights groups and people with disabilities began calling for increased access to education and paid labor. As one activist put it, "The Soviet state gave us a label ["invalid"], a pension, and a license to do nothing." In 2002 I conducted a survey of disability-advocacy NGOs' members and was surprised that, when asked, "What does independent living mean to you?" the majority of respondents answered "economic independence" rather than "unassisted living" or "caring for myself." These are critical assertions in a context where most people with disabilities in Ukraine (85.5 percent) are unemployed, rely on a very small monthly disability pension (usually less than $150), and thus are extremely marginalized economically.[39]

Related to this shift to privileging self-sufficiency and individualization is that the *independent* movement of bodies through space is often a key component of contemporary citizenship claims for the mobility disabled. As Vasyl,' a disability-rights activist and entrepreneur from Lviv told me, "Even when I'm going up a hill, I tell people, 'Don't help me.' As soon as someone starts to push me, I feel like an invalid. As long as I'm doing it myself, I'm a normal person." This is a common position among the wheelchair users I know, who often frame arguments for equal rights in terms of the individual's right to independent movement. Such formulations mirror other neoliberal processes of individualization, privatization, and personification that now characterize life in formerly socialist spaces.[40]

Mobile Citizenship

I have described certain aspects of the 1991 and 1992 super-marathons in some detail as a short case study of how mobility has become a crucial hook for citizenship in contexts of socialist collapse, globalization, and neoliberalization. What of the present-day situation? Today, in postsocialist countries such as Ukraine, in contexts of new market economies and the global capitalism of which the former socialist states of Eastern Europe are increasingly a part, the importance of mobility for citizenship has only sharpened. In many ways, the promoted idea of a good citizen is a person who is moving rapidly through space, and one who is engaging with the material world primarily through consumption.[41] Yet even if the importance of movement is increasingly amplified, opportunities for increased mobility are not offered to all citizens equally. While some segments of the population are speeding up, people with disabilities (and other marginalized persons) face a range of material and spatial impediments to enacting mobile citizenship. In this way, neoliberalism can be said to have contradictory consequences for human mobility.

Indeed, these uneven consequences are in evidence in many areas of life. The Soviet-era methods of police control have not been fully dismantled, and a whole range of new controls on mobility has emerged. These include privatization of public spaces, entrance fees, gated communities, private security, the prohibitive expense of travel for many, a host of new national borders within an until-recently unified Soviet Union, as well as increasingly restrictive international-migration regimes. Also, many citizens of Ukraine and Russia now find their freedom of movement curtailed not by their own states but by many of the countries they wish to visit, especially the states of the European Union, which require entry visas. Indeed, the much discussed phenomenon of sex trafficking of Ukrainian and Russian women and children, as well as the less discussed trafficking of male laborers from Ukraine, are usually facilitated by the international migration regime when, for example, victims' passports are seized by their employers.

The realm of public transport is another important example. As ever-increasing numbers of people are buying cars, the streets of cities such as Kiev and Moscow are clogged by massive traffic jams, which in turn slow modes of public transportation like buses and trolleybuses to a snail's pace. As an alternative, state and private companies now run minivans (*marshrutki*) to provide faster travel. But the *marshrutki* are at best a piecemeal response to the growing division between those who own cars—which are clogging the roads—and those who must make do with a deteriorating system of public transportation. In Kiev, on the whole the mobility disabled are denied service in these *marshrutki* and are instead offered passage in fifteen specialized, wheelchair accessible vans with "TRANSPORT FOR INVALIDS" emblazoned along the sides. They must request pickup and dropoff twenty-four to forty-eight hours in advance and be prepared to adjust their schedules according to the whims of drivers. Therefore, even the rather broken system of minibus taxis is unavailable to the mobility disabled.

Train travel involves similar paradoxes. In recent years the state-run railway has begun to offer "fast trains" without stops to select cities, extending to most travelers more rapid and comfortable transit. These new trains, however, were not designed with accessibility in mind. Even less accessible are the more common "regular" (i.e. Soviet-era) trains, whose corridors are not even wide enough to accommodate a standard-size wheelchair. In fact, in a system transporting over five hundred million passengers a year,[42] only four train cars are "adapted" for the mobility disabled, and these only partially—wheelchair users are offered a single accessible private sleeping cabin at one end of the train car with its own toilet. And even as another heavily utilized form of rapid transit—the metro (subway)—is being expanded in large cities, almost nothing is being done to offer the mobility disabled access to this accelerated mode of transportation. The metro accounts for 34 percent of Kiev's transport load and carries 1.7 million passengers a day (Kiev's population is 2.6 million). Most of the metro's stations are located underground and are accessible only by the metro's 119 escalators. Only two stations—both built within the last couple of years—feature elevators for passenger use.[43] Clearly, this rapid-transit system was not designed to serve all citizens; it was not built to accommodate those whose physical impairments, it is assumed, necessarily make them immobile.

Thus, the spatial arrangements they encounter day in and day out are preventing wheelchair users and others with disabilities from enacting the kind of "mobile citizenship" characterized by rapid movement that is increasingly valued (but rather unattainable) in the postsocialist world. In other words, consumer citizenship and rapid movement through space may be the ideal in global capitalism, but many citizens' ability to access it is quite circumscribed. In response, people with mobility disabilities are taking up a new citizenship agenda that addresses the etatization of space, and their citizenship negotiations often are mediated in decidedly spatial terms. One result of wheelchair users' continuous conversation with the state as they bump up against disabling spatial environments is the development of ways to literally "push through" inaccessible spaces to access the newly promoted form of mobile, consumer citizenship. One such strategy is a program of "active rehabilitation" introduced by the Swedish advocacy group Rekryteringsgruppen for Active Rehabilitation (R.G.), whose representatives began visiting Ukraine, Belarus, and Poland in the 1990s.[44]

In the R.G. program, methods for active rehabilitation are introduced to small groups of wheelchair users during an intense seven-to-ten-day camp where they are exposed to a strict philosophy of individual independence and receive training in wheelchair sports and overcoming architectural barriers and how to independently carry out activities of daily living. Informants who had attended an active rehabilitation camp—which today are organized rather infrequently in Ukraine by local NGOs and coalitions such as the National Assembly of Disabled of Ukraine—said that their lives had been transformed. The camps, they said, give wheelchair users the self-confidence and skills necessary to "venture out in public" and "actively participate in society" in spite of the disabling built environment.[45]

Related to this emphasis on mobility, independence, and self-sufficiency, I have noticed that my informants increasingly make reference to a hand-controlled car as a necessary entitlement for the mobility disabled. In Ukraine, the state guarantees persons with serious mobility disabilities (so-called Group 1 invalids) a car. However, several obstacles often prevent the fulfillment of this promise. For example, the car is not fully subsidized, so recipients must still pay around one thousand dollars. Whereas previously these cars were fitted with hand controls at the state's expense, today recipients are responsible for making these modifications themselves. Most importantly, the wait for receiving one's car is currently fifteen to twenty years. People with disabilities may import cars from abroad without paying customs taxes, but only late-model cars in good condition are allowed, a luxury that few can afford.

The assertions of Tanya, a woman I interviewed in eastern Ukraine in 2005, were typical for how she connected car ownership with self-sufficiency. For Tanya, a car means mobility and initiative; it is a literal and figurative vehicle for personal independence. In staking her claim, she employs the powerful tropes of the new market economy—she emphasizes that a car would enable her to secure and hold a job and thus become economically independent. She sees that others have fewer constraints on their mobility: they can access various forms of accelerated transportation, and they may take advantage of the expansion of shopping arenas, including Western-style malls and supermarkets, and sprawling open-air bazaars. All these opportunities are limited for Tanya and others with mobility disabilities, who are dealing with the "postpresence" of the socialist state and its particular arrangements of space, even as the state is withdrawing from many areas of life.[46]

One such area is the market sphere. In state socialism, access to consumer goods was seen as a *right*; states subsidized prices and controlled the distribution of goods. Today, states have retreated from this paternalist presence to, in some cases, a complete abandonment of any responsibility toward providing basic goods and services. Consumption is a key component of citizenship claims in the postsocialist world, where markets are shutting some groups of persons (i.e. the poor) out of access to basic goods. Many of my informants emphasized how lack of accessible spaces and buildings (in addition to a lack of economic capital) limits their opportunities to engage in the consumer practices now deemed "normal" for post-Soviet citizens.[47]

In calling for greater accessibility, the mobility disabled increasingly position themselves as potential consumers and users of services whose patronage could benefit businesses and the economy in general. They often articulate practices of competitive consumerism to connect with the mainstream concerns of the new market economy and stake citizenship claims.[48] During the fall of 2006 I carried out research in the eastern Ukrainian city of Kharkiv, where I attended a week-long camp for wheelchair users. The camp was designed to facilitate social interaction between wheelchair users and help them improve their skills of wheelchair use and daily living. The culmination of the camp was a trip to a supermarket, a relatively new fixture in large Ukrainian cities. Some of the participants were nervous, and so were the store's staff: as we entered the front door, a worker announced over the loudspeaker, "Dear shoppers, please be careful—a group of invalids is entering the store."

Since the turnstiles through which customers were expected to pass were too narrow to accommodate wheelchairs, my friends ended up using a passage intended for delivering shopping carts in and out of the store. We were glad to see that the supermarket had an accessible restroom, but upon inspection we discovered it was being used as a broom closet. These arrangements of space precluded Kharkiv's wheelchair users from fully participating in consumer citizenship, and they clearly were marginalized consumers in this environment. The retreat of the state from any position of responsibility toward consumer needs ends up shutting out those who have specific needs not defined directly by raw market capitalism.

Of course, people with mobility disabilities are not the only ones unable to fully enjoy the accelerated movement and new cultures of consumption associated with the postsocialist transition. Although many seek to steer themselves toward the "fast lane" of mobile citizenship as consumers moving rapidly through space, it is difficult to attain this ideal form of being a citizen. In many instances the major constraints are economic and related to structures of power that produce and perpetuate inequalities. We might juxtapose, for instance, the greater freedom of mobility for bourgeois travel after the fall of socialism alongside the "forced mobility" of shuttle traders struggling to make a living through cross-border trade.[49] Striking too is the fact that even in an era of globalization and "opening up," most "regular" citizens can no longer afford the kind of domestic and cross-border travel they enjoyed during the Soviet era.[50] Ironically, although states like Ukraine have done away with the *propiska* system, its replacement, *registratsiia* (registration at one's place of permanent residence), functions similarly to facilitate surveillance and regulation of people's movements. Although their situation is especially vivid, people with disabilities are not alone in their struggles to enact a kind of mobile citizenship in the postsocialist milieu. We might consider, for example, the spatial politics of land privatization and changing property rights, debates over immigration to and emigration from the region, and matters of housing and the rearrangement of spaces of living.[51]

For people with disabilities—and I suspect this is true to various degrees for a majority of postsocialist citizens—mobile citizenship is predicated not only on moving through space ever faster and more freely and engaging in competitive consumerism but also on continuing one's ongoing conversation with the state. As people navigate shifting state formations that result in "patchy and variegated spaces of differential regulation" in the modern state, there is a sense that too much and too little state presence in their lives is equally unacceptable.[52] The pursuit of mobile citizenship is likely to require ever more deepening engagements with the state, especially for people with disabilities, whose lives have been shaped so directly by the socialist and postsocialist state's politics of space, (im)mobility, and social services. This is vividly illustrated in this article's opening vignette—Tanya's thwarted quest to access the halls of power to lodge a civic complaint. A wheelchair user who wanted to protest the slow progress of accessibility improvements for the disabled in her small town, Tanya was given "the runaround" by lawmakers in the capital. The very problem she wanted to protest—lack of accessibility for disabled citizens—prevented her from confronting the powerful bureaucrats "one floor above." Ultimately, one important way the mobility disabled can make themselves citizens is by occupying and utilizing spaces in ways that challenge the status quo, much like those ever-mobile wheelchair-using super-marathoners from the early 1990s.

Coda: Virtual Mobility and Citizenship

An intriguing development, and one I hope to research further, is the creative way that the mobility disabled are tapping into computer and Internet technology to enact mobile citizenship. Via the Internet, for example, people whose physical movement is impeded by stigma and inaccessible built environments (i.e. they are disabled by the environments in which they live) are able to virtually rove the globe to access information, engage in social networking, become salaried employees, and so on. These possibilities were brought to my attention by several informants, especially a young man named Sasha who was described to me by a friend as "living in a virtual reality." Sasha is a former wheelchair athlete who, after several injuries (caused by falling from his wheelchair trying to navigate barriers such as stairs and curbs) is unable to race and leaves his apartment less and less frequently. However, he participates in several virtual worlds through the Internet, works for several local firms doing computer programming and other Web-based jobs (he designs Internet sites), and does much of his socializing via online chats. More research needs to be done to assess how widespread this virtual mobility is among the disabled, but my sense is that it is becoming more common.

Is such virtual mobility a beneficial alternative to physical mobility—a strategy for empowerment? Or does being plugged into the world of the Internet mean that people then check out of the "real world," becoming even more socially isolated and excluded from active citizenship? And what factors determine one's access to a computer and Internet connection and possibilities to acquire knowledge about their use? My informants often refer to the "parallel world" of the disabled to describe how people with disabilities have been excluded from full citizenship. Is information technology empowering persons to break out of this parallel world, or will the virtual reality draw them even further into it?

Notes

1. Except for Oleksandr Sukhan, I have assigned all informants (such as "Tanya") pseudonyms, to protect their privacy.

2. Stephen P. Dunn and Ethel Dunn, "Everyday Life of People with Disabilities in the USSR," in *People with Disabilities in the Soviet Union: Past and Present, Theory and Practice,* ed. William O. McCagg and Lewis Siegelbaum (Pittsburgh: University of Pittsburgh Press, 1989), 199–234.

3. There are an estimated thirty-two thousand people with spinal and spinal-cord injuries in Ukraine. The Russian journalist and activist Lev Indolev estimates that there are between 250,000 and 300,000 wheelchair users in Russia. See *Zhit' v koliaske* (Moscow: Soprichastnost',' 2001), 9.

4. See Sarah D. Phillips, "'There Are No Invalids in the USSR!': A Missing Soviet Chapter in the New Disability History," *Disability Studies Quarterly* 29.3 (2009); accessed 1 October 2011, http://www.dsq-sds.org/article/view/936/1111.

5. Adriana Petryna, *Life Exposed: Biological Citizens after Chernobyl* (Princeton, N.J.: Princeton University Press, 2002), 6; Matthew Kohrmann, *Bodies of Difference: Experiences of Disability and Institutional Advocacy in the Making of Modern China* (Berkeley: University of California Press, 2005).

6. Aihwa Ong, "Mutations in Citizenship," *Theory, Culture, and Society* 23.2–3 (2006): 499–531.

7. David Harvey, *The Condition of Postmodernity: An Enquiry into the Origins of Cultural Change* (Oxford: Blackwell, 1989).

8. Katherine Verdery, *What Was Socialism, and What Comes Next?* (Princeton, N.J.: Princeton University Press, 1996).

9. Ibid., 46.

10. Ibid., 49.

11. Dunn and Dunn, "Everyday Life."

12. Susan Brownell, *Training the Body for China: Sports in the Moral Order of the People's Republic* (Chicago: University of Chicago Press, 1995).

13. For discussions of "invalids" of the Second World War and uneven state policy, see Beate Fieseler, "'Nishchie pobediteli': Invalidy Velikoi Otechestvennoi voiny v Sovetskom

Soiuze," *Neprikosnovennyi zapas* 40–41.2–3 (2005); accessed 5 November 2011, http://magazines.russ.ru/nz/2005/2/fi33.html; Beate Fieseler, "The Bitter Legacy of the 'Great Patriotic War': Red Army Disabled Soldiers under Late Stalinism," in *Late Stalinist Russia: Society between Reconstruction and Reinvention,* ed. Julianne Furst (London: Routledge, 2006), 46–61; Lev Gudkov, "The Fetters of Victory: How War Provides Russia with Its Identity," *Neprikosnovennyi zapas* 40–41.2–3 (2005); accessed 5 November 2011, http://magazines.russ.ru/nz/2005/2/gu5.html; Anna Krylova, "'Healers of Wounded Souls': The Crisis of Private Life in Soviet Literature," *Journal of Modern History* 73 (2001): 307–31; Ol'ga Shek, "Sotsial'noe iskliuchenie invalidov v SSSR," in *Nuzhda i poriadok: Istoriia sotsial'noi raboty v Rossii, XX v.,* ed. Pavel Romanov and Elena Iarskaia-Smirnova (Saratov: Center for Social Policy and Gender Studies, 2005), 375–96; Ol'ga Shilova, "Razvitie gosudarstvennoi seti statsionarnykh uchrezhdenii po obsluzhivaniiu invalidov i pozhilykh grazhdan v Samarskom krae," in *Nuzhda i poriadok: Istoriia sotsial'noi raboty v Rossii, XX v.,* ed. Pavel Romanov and Elena Iarskaia-Smirnova (Saratov: Center for Social Policy and Gender Studies, 2005), 102–27; Ekaterina Tchueva, "'Mir posle voiny': Zhaloby kak instrument regulirovaniia otnoshenii mezhdu gosudarstvom i invalidami Velikoi Otechestvennoi Voiny," in *Sovetskaia sotsial'naia politika: Stseny i deistvuiushchie litsa, 1940–1985,* ed. Elena Iarskaia-Smirnova and Pavel Romanov (Moscow: Variant, 2008), 96–120.

14. For estimates of the number of *internaty,* see Bernice Madison, "Programs for People with Disabilities in the USSR," in *People with Disabilities in the Soviet Union: Past and Present, Theory and Practice,* ed. William O. McCagg and Lewis Siegelbaum (Pittsburgh: University of Pittsburgh Press, 1989), 180.

15. Valerii Fefelov, *V SSSR Invalidov net!* (London: Overseas Publications Interchange, 1986), 37–41; Ruben David Gonzalez-Galego, *Beloe na chernom* (St. Petersburg: Limbus Press, 2004).

16. Lev Indolev, *Kak eto bylo: Ocherki istorii invalidnogo dvizheniia v Rossii i sozdaniia VOI* (Moscow: VOI, 1998), 22–26. Of course, artels and other collectives offered some advantages, especially when organized and controlled by the disabled themselves. For consideration of deaf culture and deaf work collectives in Russia and the Soviet Union, see Susan Burch, "Transcending Revolutions: The Tsars, the Soviets, and Deaf Culture," *Journal of Social History* 34.2 (2000): 393–401.

17. For analysis of Soviet-era disability protests and profiles of key dissidents, see Valerii Fefelov, *V SSSR invalidov net!* (London: Overseas Publications Interchange Ltd., 1986); Lev Indolev, *Kak eto bylo: Ocherki istorii invalidnogo dvizheniia v Rossii i sozdaniia VOI* (Moscow: VOI, 1998); Phillips, "'There Are No Invalids in the USSR!'"; Paul D. Raymond, "Disability as Dissidence: The Action Group to Defend the Rights of People with Disabilities in the USSR," in *People with Disabilities in the Soviet Union: Past and Present, Theory and Practice,* ed. William O. McCagg and Lewis Siegelbaum (Pittsburgh: University of Pittsburgh Press, 1989), 235–52; Anne White, *Democratization in Russia under Gorbachev, 1985–91: The Birth of a Voluntary Sector* (New York: St. Martin's Press, 1999).

18. Dmitrii Shparo and Irina Grigorieva, *Repetitsiia s anshlagom: Super-marafon Moskva-Kiev-Krivyi Rog* (Moscow: Klub "Prikliuchenie," 1992).

19. Elizabeth Dunn, *Privatizing Poland: Baby Food, Big Business, and the Remaking of Labor* (Ithaca, N.Y.: Cornell University Press, 2004); Sarah D. Phillips, *Women's Social Activism in the New Ukraine* (Bloomington: Indiana University Press, 2008); Michele Rivkin-Fish, *Women's Health in Post-Soviet Russia: The Politics of Intervention* (Bloomington: Indiana University Press, 2005). In 2002 I interviewed an athlete and activist who participated in both super-marathons, Oleksandr Sukhan from Mukachevo Oblast, Ukraine. The ethnographic data presented below are gleaned from this interview and from several videotaped interviews conducted with Sukhan by representatives of the Ukrainian press.

20. From the Ukrainian television series *Skhodzhennia* (Ascent), written and produced by Volodymyr Maryntsivs'kii, Zakarpats'ke teleradiomovne ob'ednannia (hereafter *Skhodzhennia* 1993).

21. From the video *Marafon* (Marathon), produced by Klub Prikliuchenie (Adventure Club), Studiia ANIS, 1992 (hereafter *Marafon*).

22. The club was organized by the explorer Dmitrii Shparo in 1989 and is considered a "nonprofit rehabilitative fund." Adventure Club specializes in organizing adventure trips all over the world. See the club's website at http://www.shparo.ru/index.htm (accessed 18 March 2011).

23. Ironically, according to interviews with many people who became wheelchair users during the Soviet period, the only wheelchairs available to them were poorly made Soviet chairs or rather outdated ones made by Meyra, unwieldy clunky wheelchairs (such as the KIS model) that no one liked. That the much-maligned Meyra company was a major sponsor of these events seems somewhat paradoxical.

24. *Marafon.*

25. *Skhodzhennia* 1993.

26. Ibid.

27. Ibid.

28. Ibid.

29. From unidentified Ukrainian media footage, in possession of the author.

30. From unidentified Ukrainian media footage, in possession of the author.

31. *Skhodzhennia* 1993.

32. From the Ukrainian television series *Skhodzhennia* (Ascent), written and produced by Volodymyr Maryntsivs'kii, Zakarpats'ka studiia telebachennia, 1992 (hereinafter *Skhodzhennia* 1992).

33. From unidentified Ukrainian media footage, in possession of the author.

34. *Skhodzhennia* 1992.

35. *Skhodzhennia* 1993.

36. Ibid.

37. On the politics of recognition, see Nancy Fraser, *Justice Interruptus: Critical Reflections on the "Postsocialist" Condition* (New York: Routledge, 1997).

38. See Phillips, "'There Are No Invalids in the USSR!'" for further details on Soviet labor-related disability policy.

39. Derzhavna Dopovid, *Pro stanovyshche v Ukrayini ta osnovy derzhavnoi polityky shchodo vyrishennia problem hromodian z osoblyvymy potrebamy* (Kiev: Sotsinform,

2002). At the beginning of 2008, the average monthly pension for a Group 1 or "total invalid" (the category to which most spinally injured persons and other wheelchair users are assigned) was 740 UAH ($148).

40. Phillips, *Women's Social Activism*; Rivkin-Fish, *Women's Health*.

41. Dunn, *Privatizing Poland*, 76; Harvey, *Condition of Postmodernity*.

42. From the official website of the Ukrainian Railway (Ukrzaliznytsia), accessed 4 April 2008: http://www.uz.gov.ua/?m=all.structure.today&lng=uk.

43. See the official website of the Kiev metro, accessed 2 April 2008: http://www.metro.kiev.ua/ua.

44. See RG's website, accessed 18 March 2011: http://www.rekryteringsgruppen.se/.

45. For more on active rehabilitation in Ukraine, see Sarah D. Phillips, *Disability and Mobile Citizenship in Postsocialist Ukraine* (Bloomington: Indiana University Press, 2011).

46. Elizabeth Dunn, "Postsocialist Spores: Disease, Bodies, and the State in the Republic of Georgia," *American Ethnologist* 35.2 (2008): 254.

47. Adele Marie Barker, ed., *Consuming Russia: Popular Culture, Sex, and Society since Gorbachev* (Durham, N.C.: Duke University Press, 1999); Melissa Caldwell, "The Taste of Nationalism: Food Politics in Postsocialist Moscow," *Ethnos* 67.3 (2002): 295–319; Jennifer Patico, "To Be Happy in a Mercedes: Tropes of Value and Ambivalent Visions of Marketization," *American Ethnologist* 32.3 (2005): 479–96.

48. George Lipsitz, "Learning from New Orleans: The Social Warrant of Hostile Privatism and Competitive Consumer Citizenship," *Cultural Anthropology* 21.3 (2006): 451–68.

49. Jennifer Dickinson, "Gender, Work, and Economic Restructuring in a Transcarpathia (Ukraine) Village," *Nationalities Papers* 33.3 (2005): 387–401.

50. Kristen Ghodsee, *The Red Riviera: Gender, Tourism, and Postsocialism on the Black Sea* (Durham, N.C.: Duke University Press, 2005).

51. On rights, see Jessica Allina-Pisano, *The Post-Soviet Potemkin Village: Politics and Property Rights in the Black Earth* (Cambridge: Cambridge University Press, 2008); on immigration, see Olena Braichevska et al., *Nontraditional Immigrants in Kyiv* (Washington, D.C.: Woodrow Wilson International Center for Scholars, 1994); on housing, see Caroline Humphrey, *The Unmaking of Soviet Life: Everday Economies after Socialism* (Ithaca, N.Y.: Cornell University Press, 2002).

52. Dunn, "Postsocialist Spores," 255.

[blank page 272]

Contributors

EUGENE M. AVRUTIN is an assistant professor of modern European Jewish history and Tobor Family Scholar in the Program of Jewish Culture and Society at the University of Illinois at Urbana-Champaign.

ALEXANDRA BEKASOVA is a researcher at the S. I. Vavilov Institute for the History of Science and Technology, Russian Academy of Sciences (St. Petersburg branch).

FAITH HILLIS is an assistant professor of history at the University of Chicago.

GIJS KESSLER is head of the Eastern Europe and Russia Desk of the International Institute of Social History in Amsterdam.

DIANE P. KOENKER is a professor of history at the University of Illinois at Urbana-Champaign.

CHIA YIN HSU is an assistant professor of history at Portland State University.

EILEEN KANE is an assistant professor of history at Connecticut College.

ANNE LOUNSBERY is an associate professor of Russian and Slavic Studies at New York University.

MATTHEW LIGHT is an assistant professor of criminology at the University of Toronto.

SARAH D. PHILLIPS is an associate professor of anthropology at Indiana University.

JOHN RANDOLPH is an associate professor of history at the University of Illinois at Urbana-Champaign

ANATOLYI REMNEV is a professor of history at Omsk State University, Russian Federation.

JEFF SAHADEO is an associate professor in the Institute of European, Russian, and Eurasian Studies and the Department of Political Science at Carleton University.

FRITHJOF BENJAMIN SCHENK is a professor of East European history at the University of Basel.

CHARLES STEINWEDEL is an associate professor of history at Northeastern Illinois University.

WILLARD SUNDERLAND is an associate professor of history at the University of Cincinnati.

ELENA TYURYUKANOVA is the director of the Center for Migration Studies in Moscow.

Index

STUDIES OF WORLD MIGRATIONS

The Immigrant Threat: The Integration of Old and New Migrants
    in Western Europe since 1850   *Leo Lucassen*
Citizenship and Those Who Leave: The Politics of Emigration
    and Expatriation   *Edited by Nancy L. Green and François Weil*
Migration, Class, and Transnational Identities: Croatians in
    Australia and America   *Val Colic-Peisker*
The Yankee Yorkshireman: Migration Lived and Imagined   *Mary H. Blewett*
Africans in Europe: The Culture of Exile and Emigration from
    Equatorial Guinea to Spain   *Michael Ugarte*
Hong Kong Movers and Stayers: Narratives of Family Migration
    Janet W. Salaff, Siulun Wong, and Arent Greve
Russia in Motion: Cultures of Human Mobility since 1850
    Edited by John Randolph and Eugene M. Avrutin

The University of Illinois Press
is a founding member of the
Association of American University Presses.

Composed in 10.5/13 Adobe Minion Pro
with Scala Sans display
by Jim Proefrock
at the University of Illinois Press
Manufactured by Sheridan Books, Inc.

University of Illinois Press
1325 South Oak Street
Champaign, IL 61820-6903
www.press.uillinois.edu